second edition

The Management of Retail Buying

John W. Wingate

Professor Emeritus of Marketing
The City College of the City University of New York

Joseph S. Friedlander

Consultant on Distribution
Formerly Adjunct Professor of Marketing at the Bernard M. Baruch College
City University of New York

PRENTICE-HALL, INC., Englewood Cliffs, New Jersey 07632

Library of Congress Cataloging in Publication Data

WINGATE, JOHN WILLIAMS, (date)
The management of retail buying.

Includes bibliographical references and index.
1. Purchasing. 2. Retail trade. I. Friedlander, Joseph S., joint author. II. Title.
HF5437.W53 1977 658.8'7 78-5445
ISBN 0-13-548859-1

Printed in the United States of America

10 9 8 7 6 5 4 3 2 1

PRENTICE-HALL INTERNATIONAL, INC., *London*
PRENTICE-HALL OF AUSTRALIA PTY. LIMITED, *Sydney*
PRENTICE-HALL OF CANADA, LTD., *Toronto*
PRENTICE-HALL OF INDIA PRIVATE LIMITED, *New Delhi*
PRENTICE-HALL OF JAPAN, INC., *Tokyo*
PRENTICE-HALL OF SOUTHEAST ASIA PTE. LTD., *Singapore*
WHITEHALL BOOKS LIMITED. *Wellington, New Zealand*

Contents

Preface

Although the first edition of this book was published 15 years ago, it has continued to enjoy a steady demand both in the colleges and among practitioners who wish to sharpen their skills. Its treatment in depth of a central activity in retailing, the one that has major appeal to young people, has supported its place in the literature.

With the fast changes in the retail field, however, a revision has long been called for. Yet, as the authors focused on the task, they were surprised to find how much of the information and the emphasis is as pertinent today as it was before. The formalized statements of observed practice continue to be true.

Yet there have been significant developments that call for a revision, especially in connection with changes in consumers and their demands, with central buying arrangements, with spread of electronic data processing, and with foreign buying. Although the latter subject was allotted only a few pages in the former edition, it is now given an entire chapter. The five chapters in Part II on "What to Buy" have been completely reorganized, and in all other chapters there has been an updating of facts and emphasis. Fortunately, many current experts in the field have been ready to help and to supplement the experience of the authors.

Today there is a great interest among students in fashion buying and merchandising. Although this text treats all kinds of merchandise, fashion goods are given a great deal of attention, especially from the vantage point of planning and control. The enduring knowledge about how to buy fashions is here, without the rapidly changing facts of current fashions and the artists that create them.

The evolution of this work deserves brief mention. The first thorough attempt to organize and present the facts about buying for resale was made in 1925 by Dean Norris A. Brisco and John W. Wingate when they completed *Retail Buying*. Since then, the book underwent several revisions. With the assumption of joint authorship by Joseph S. Friedlander, the material was organized and published under the present title, *The Management of Retail Buying*, in order to place more emphasis on the management functions of buying. The present major revision brings this material up-to-date.

Management techniques applicable to retail buying and merchandising are explored. The new analytical approaches to assortment planning and quantitative merchandising, especially by means of the computer, are presented along with an introduction to the application of the mathematics of probability. An attempt has been made to take the reader on step-by-step tours through the minds of practicing buyers as they work out their analytical approaches.

As in the previous edition, the book has not attempted to explore in depth some of the subjects closely integrated with the buying function. Subjects like merchandise control, pricing, and merchandise arithmetic are covered more fully in companion books also published by Prentice-Hall.

The aim of this book is to communicate with two groups of readers: professional buyers and college students. In the first group, the material presented is essential for the new assistant buyer and the trainee who is soon to be given the responsibility of merchandise selection. Many stores have organized training programs directed toward the buying function. The book provides a logical way to explore the subject in depth, both in group sessions and in individual study by practitioners.

For college use, both at the senior and community college levels, the material is suited to courses of varying length. If the school is on the semester basis, the text may be covered in two semesters provided that the students are expected to study some of the reference material and to analyze the issues suggested by the discussion questions at the end of each chapter. Many of these are well suited for class debate. The material can be covered in one semester, with Chapters 4 and 5 in one week, and about one week devoted to each of the other 13 chapters. If the school is on the quarter or term plan, there is plenty of material for two quarters, although the subject can be quickly surveyed in one.

The authors wish to express their deep appreciation to the following practitioners who have provided material and/or made suggestions in regard to the current revision, some reading and criticizing entire chapters. Much of the new information has been obtained from oral and written communication with these authorities rather than from secondary sources.

Howard P. Abrahams, TV Retail Advisors, New York City.
Ernest L. Arms, National News Director, Sears, Roebuck, Chicago.
Howard Biederman, Vice President, Allied Stores International, New York City.
Vincent Brennan, Executive Vice President, Bloomingdale's, New York.
Frank Burnside, President, Fowler, Dick & Walker, Wilkes-Barre, Pa.
Patrick Cash, Manager, Merchandising Division, National Retail Merchants Association, New York City.
Beatrice Cohen, Administrator, Traffic Group, National Retail Merchants Association, New York City.
Harry E. Cohen, Stern Associates, New York City, and formerly Adjunct Professor of Marketing and Supervisor of Evening Session Marketing, Baruch College, New York City.
Dorothy Cook, Merchandising Division, National Retail Merchants Association, New York City.
Howard Eilenberg, Senior Vice President for Research, Frederick Atkins, Inc., New York City.
Nathan Epstein, Vice President, Lerner Shops, New York City.
Henry Goldsmith, Merchandise Manager of Women's Accessories, J. C. Penney Co., New York City.
Murray Krieger, Associate Professor, Bronx Community College, New York City.
Jack Leh, Leh & Co., Allentown, Penna.
Felix Lilienthal, Jr., President, Felix Lilienthal & Co. Inc., New York City.
William F. Luddy, Publisher, Retail News Bureau, New York City.
Robert McGreevey, President, McGreevey, Werring & Howell, New York City.
Barbara J. Patterson, Corporate Training Director, Brandeis, Omaha, Nebraska.
Daniel C. Schwartz, Bureau of Competition, Federal Trade Commission, Washington, D.C.
Joseph Siegel, Vice President and Store Manager, Bloomingdale's, Hackensack, New Jersey.
Jack Vivian, Vice President, Fowler, Dick & Walker, Wilkes-Barre, Pa.
Lawrence W. Ward, President, Men's Wear Division, Palm Beach Company, New York and Cincinnati.

In addition, we would like to thank our reviewers, Professor Dorothy Rogers of New Hampshire College and Professor William W. Hanks of Youngstown State University, for their constructive comments.

JOHN W. WINGATE
JOSEPH S. FRIEDLANDER

part I

Organizing for Buying

chapter 1

The Buying Function

Buying is a business of choosing; *retail buying*[1] focuses on choosing products to satisfy the subsequent demands of ultimate consumers. But the complete performance of this job far transcends the process of selecting one product over another. Involved is a tightly integrated complex of decisions and skilled performances, ranging over the tasks of procurement, negotiation, transportation, store-keeping, inventory management, pricing, and promotion. At the end of Chapter 3 is an appendix that outlines the skilled activities involved in the buying-selling cycle.

Nevertheless, at the heart of the buying function is the idea of serving the ultimate consumer and all the implications that flow from that idea. All main line thinking must be directed toward satisfying the consumer, and all conflicting interests must somehow be reconciled with the perceived needs and wants of the consumer.

BUYING FOR RETAIL

Some economic thinkers have come to the conclusion that the consumer has little freedom of choice, that the dominant manufacturers and the mass retailers control what is produced and, through high pressure selling, manipulate the consumer to buy what they find profitable to sell.

[1]Mechanically, the function may be viewed as the purchase of consumer goods in relatively large "wholesale" quantities for subsequent resale in smaller quantities to the ultimate consumer.

Practicing retailers do not accept this theory because they have suffered heavy loss through failure to act on the consumer's changing wants. Most retailers have come to accept the so-called "marketing concept." Its central requirement is that both production and purchases for resale must be adjusted to the needs and wants of consumers in contrast to the still common concept of manipulating customers to buy what the producers and distributors are best equipped to provide.

From this requirement flows the inference that consumers must be studied as individuals and as mobile members of shifting groups. Moreover, because no retailer can serve all consumers, each retailer must determine the groups to focus upon—the groups whose patronage he or she will seek, the consumers he or she will try to convert to *customers*.

The phrase "subsequent resale" implies *anticipation* of consumers' convenience and requirements. The inference here is that some kind of reservoir or stock must be prepared *in advance* of demand. This preparation involves (1) making decisions about what, when, and how much to stock, and (2) the supervision of purchases between the time of procurement and the time of resale.

Where, when, and how to effect the purchase of consumer goods—that is, the purchase of items that translate the plans into reality—is itself a challenging task in the huge complex of today's procurement markets. Nor is the task finished with the placement of an order. Vendors must be prodded to expedite shipments. Goods must be received, checked, priced, stored, and moved to the final selling location. And goods in stock must be constantly checked as a basis for new planning.

THE BUYER'S JOB

A survey of the duties of 89 buyers in 27 department stores with branches concludes: "The requirements made upon him (the buyer) for a successful job performance are diverse, yet specialized; they are increasingly technical while at the same time demanding great qualities of creativity, intuition, and sensitivity."[2]

It is logical to define the retail store buyer as the specialist who performs the function of buying for resale to ultimate consumers. But the total buying is commonly shared with others—merchandise managers and committees—and is seldom limited to the performance of the buying function as defined. Buyers usually have responsibilities for the pricing and the selling of what they have bought and the training of sales personnel. Accord-

[2]John Wallis Johnston, *The Department Store Buyer, A View From Inside the Parent-Branch Complexes*, Bureau of Business Research, University of Texas at Austin, 1969.

ingly, although this book covers the buying function, the qualifications for the job, and the analysis of what, how much, when, where, and how to buy, the final chapter is devoted to the reponsibilities for pricing and sales promotion that are often assigned to buyers.

Emergence of Scientific Procedures in Buying

There are quiet backwaters of activity where consumers are concerned chiefly with the conveniences of time and location in the purchase of staple goods, such as commercial grades of bread and milk or cigarettes. Buying for this kind of retail can be a simple adjunct to the performance of a host of other tasks involved in "the running of a store." Adding to the simplicity of the buying task is the fact that deliveries are extremely regular and that replenishment of the inventory follows swiftly on its depletion.

Even in this simple situation, the possibility of error in inherent. Stocks can run short, and products can decay or become stale. However, a very low level of competence in inventory management is required to reduce these risks to insignificance. Introduce an element of irregularity into the delivery pattern and complications ensue. Add a touch of competition and the penalty for being out of stock is increased. The customer can now go elsewhere to satisfy a thwarted want, and there is the constant danger that going elsewhere may become a habit.

When department stores, the first of our large-scale retailing institutions, were being formed in the last half of the nineteenth century, buying for them was by no means simple. These stores assumed the complicated task of providing broad assortments of new and exclusive merchandise at low prices in addition to stocking the readily replaceable staples. Nevertheless, great progress was achieved under the aegis of specialized buyers who performed their function with acumen and imagination but with an intuitive skill that could be acquired only through apprenticeship.

As competition grew, as new retailing forms such as mail-order houses and chains entered the large-scale field, as burgeoning productive facilities put greater demands on marketing agencies, as customer tastes became more differentiated and demands more exacting, the complexities of buying for retail increased. Shortened fashion cycles further complicated the task of meeting customer demand. And a proliferation of new materials increased the need for technical understanding. Analytical approaches and formalized controls began to appear. Analysis of situation and function began to result in an organized body of literature. Learning no longer had to be by hit-or-miss apprenticeship alone.

But a sort of idolatry was still reserved for those merchants who built or helped to build great institutions by "shirt-sleeve" methods, who seemed able to "fly by the seat of their pants"—and fly so skillfully! Even today we see great retail enterprises fashioned by intuitive merchants. Notably, however, their success occurs in the "new forms" of retailing, like the "discount" chains of the 1950s, where conditions simulate the era of earlier department store and specialty chain growth. As the number of big retailing institutions increased, the demand for these "talented primitives" rapidly outran the supply. Those with lesser gifts, who nevertheless could have performed adequately with more "scientific" approaches, often paid disastrous prices for refusing to learn or use these approaches, for trying to emulate those whose special talents they did not have in the required degree. This form of idolatry still persists, albeit with a shrinking congregation.

Today, however, is the day of the "professional" buyer. Although buying for retail still compounds both art and science, its more complex phases can no longer be adequately performed by artistry alone. Special gifts are valuable assets. But the knowledge and skills required demand systematic study. Available for the purpose is a considerable body of literature and training faculties and programs in several colleges and in some of the larger retail institutions.

Because buying is an aspect of social science, its laws cannot always be expressed in absolute and exact terms. But there are generalized theories and principles for decision and action that may serve as valuable guidelines and lodestars. The galaxy of individual situations forms patterns that can be analyzed, mapped, and studied. Thinking approaches and techniques are transferable from one situation to another, once one has learned to recognize their kindred nature.

Techniques

Intellectualized approaches and sophisticated techniques become increasingly important to the buyer who must function under the complexities imposed by a great industrial economy. In such an economy, production is almost compulsive. The resulting product cannot flow gently through the sort of static distributive mechanisms envisaged by older economic theory. Production must be vigorously pumped through to potential consumers, and a maw must be developed at the consumption level. New desires must be foreseen and encouraged. Production cannot wait for goods to wear out. Long before that time, inspired obsolesence must create the desire for replacement. In short, marketing agencies and functionaires have the triple task of indicating what should be produced, of pumping the production through to the ultimate consumer, and, indeed, of helping to get the production consumed.

For the retailer, the requirements of highly differentiated products coupled with swift obsolescence are at once boon and bane, They provide the opportunity for increased sales while providing serious problems of inventory management. It becomes increasingly hard to predict demand: to provide the proper balance of product variants in an inventory that is always subject to practical limitations of time, space, and money. At the same time the penalty for errors of prediction becomes more serious, because whatever becomes obsolete to the customer *ipso facto* becomes obsolete in the merchant's stock.[3]

The Buying-Selling Cycle

Because buying is dependent on customer demand, and because customer demand is best determined from actual customer response to goods made available by the buyer, it is clear that buying cannot function independently of selling and that the buyer cannot escape involvement in the selling process. In fact, buying–selling is really a single cycle of activity, having three distinct phases:

1. Estimating customers' requirements.
2. Procuring the required goods and making them available when and where wanted.
3. Motivating customers to buy the goods made available to them.

Although the three phases would seem to have a beginning and an end, they actually form a circular, continuing pattern. Measurements of customer acceptance or rejection, in the third phase, yield important clues for anticipating later customer demand, and the cycle begins again.

The first two phases of the cycle comprise the job of anticipating customer demand. It is more than a guessing game and even more than a careful analysis and projection of future requirements. *Demand has not been "anticipated" until requirements are translated into specific assortments of merchandise—an inventory from which customers may select.* The inventory must be managed. Its composition must be planned, organized, and coordinated, and its content bought and priced. To be effective in serving demand and generating a profit, the work must be carefully controlled as it progresses.

The cycle is finally completed when someone selects the specific items with features of greatest appeal to the customers, so that they may be duly "notified"—and, incidentally, be persuaded to buy. Buying for retail includes this reponsibility for recommending or deciding what will be promoted, where, when, and to what extent, and for disseminating information about the selling virtues of the goods to all concerned with promoting their

[3]Chapter 5 includes a discussion of product variants and their relationship to productivity. Computer-generated information is an aid in such analysis.

sale. Sometimes buyers and their superiors become even more deeply involved in the selling function. This is a controversial matter investigated in Chapter 15.

Merchandising

Merchandising has been defined in various ways. Broadly, it includes the entire buying–selling cycle explained above. More narrowly, it may be limited to the management of the cycle, and still more narrowly to the management of the first two phases: estimation of customer requirements, and procurement, which comprises the function of anticipating demand. In fact, merchandising has been defined as "the planning and supervision involved in marketing the particular merchandise or service at the places, times, and prices, and in the quantities which will best serve the marketing objectives of the business."[4] This definition was intended to include coordination and control and to exclude advertising and selling but may not have succeeded.

As used generally in retailing, the function of merchandising is equated with the work of the functionaries, the buyers and merchandise managers in the merchandise division of a store. The degree to which they are responsible for the selling phase varies greatly, so this description does not wholly define what the activity entails.

Regardless of the exact definition, it must be noted that both the buyer and the merchandise manager *merchandise.* The merchandise manager manages the function of anticipating customer demand in many lines, each with its buyer. The buyer manages these functions in a narrow line and also, in varying degrees, actually performs the work involved.

In some firms, however, the responsibility for final selection rests with a committee. As a matter of fact, later discussion shows that there is considerable variation among retailers in the degree of the buyer's authority over final selection of specific merchandise. On the other hand, the reader will also become aware that the duties of a buyer often extend far into the management of the selling function. In that case the title of the functionary is *sometimes* changed to that of "Department Manager."

The Buyer's Legal Standing

Although the buyer for a retail store may be an owner (a principal), making contracts with vendors in his or her own name, he or she is usually both an agent and an employee. The buyer is a special agent, representing his or her principal (the store) in so far as he or she is authorized to make buying contracts, with certain limitations, that are binding on the principal.

The buyer is usually also an employee of the store, working under the

[4]Committee on Definitions, *Marketing Definitions, A Glossary of Marketing Terms,* American Marketing Association, Chicago, 1960.

direction of superiors. This is particularly true of stock-keeping and selling and promotional activities and in the making of merchandise plans and controlling inventories.

THE MANAGEMENT OF THE BUYING FUNCTION

Management itself must be distinguished from work managed. Estimating customer demand, selecting goods in the market, and arranging purchase and delivery are specific elements in the buyer's work. But other duties have to be brought into play if the work is to be performed purposefully and economically. These managerial functions that provide direction are classified in various ways but for our purposes may be stated as *planning, organizing, coordinating, achieving,* and *controlling.*[5] We discuss *achieving* first because it has to do with getting the work done as distinguished from doing it.

Getting the Work Done

Wherever a work force is involved, the task of supervising and motivating the force to get the work done is what we mean by *achieving.* As we move up the rungs of an organization ladder, we find executives engaged less in doing work and more and more in getting others to do the work. But the retail buyer, although recognized as a major executive, is somewhat of an exception to this generalization.

The buyer must perform much of the specialized work of selection and negotiation, which cannot be readily delegated to subordinates.[6] Also, the buyer frequently participates in doing some of the less specialized work for purposes of instruction or to lend a hand when the work load is heavy. Otherwise, routine reordering and selection of specific items for staple stocks may be delegated to assistants or even qualified salespeople. In this way, the buyer is better able to concentrate on the task of winnowing the market offerings of more intricate, new, or short-lived merchandise while training a subordinate in the special skills required for performing this task.

In fact, much of the "motivational" part of a buyer's managerial function consists of training, coaching, counseling, and directing subordinates. In addition, the buyer as manager is expected to appraise the work of those subordinates, using praise and censure as means for their development;

[5]For a study of management applied to marketing, see Kenneth R. Davis, *Marketing Management,* 3rd ed. (New York: The Ronald Press Co., 1972).

[6]It is estimated that the chain store grocery buyer receives 1000 calls a year from manufacturers' and brokers' representatives. ("The Salesman and the Buyer," *Progressive Grocer,* Nov. 1973.)

recommending promotion and/or approving hiring, transfer, or discharge; and acting as advocate for proper compensation of subordinates.

The development of branch systems has made an important change in the buyer's job, as is presented in Chapter 2. Buyers for multistore firms must develop the ability to instruct and motivate store personnel who are not under the buyer's supervision and who must be reached largely by means of impersonal methods of communication.

Duties of the Merchandise Manager

This executive, the direct superior of the buyer, is much less involved in doing buying work and can devote much more attention to the functions of planning, control, and motivation. The motivational aspects of the job are like those just described for buyers: training, coaching, counseling, and directing; appraising and developing; and acting as participant or prime mover in hiring, promoting, transferring, discharging, and compensating. The difference is that in this case the buyers are the subordinates and the merchandise manager is the supervisor.

New buyers must be trained in established techniques and procedures and experienced buyers trained in new techniques and procedures. Following are some examples of applied supervision.

In degree, as required by each buyer, the merchandise manager *aids* in merchandise selection, keeps buyers in touch with style trends, and makes trips to the wholesale markets to attend season openings and trade shows to contact major sources of supply and to investigate new resources. The manager *counsels* on orders to be placed after checking them against open-to-buy plans; *helps* to develop private brands, exclusive agency agreements, and group buying activities; and generally *aids*, as required, in purchasing negotiations and in pricing and repricing decisions.

The merchandise manager *prods* buyers to prepare staple stock lists, clear out slow-selling merchandise, and follow up best-sellers, and checks that buyers make use of unit-control and open-to-buy reports—*training*[7] them in analysis and interpretation. The merchandise manager *aids* buyers, if they are responsible for selling, by addressing groups of salespeople, and also *helps* buyers to prepare for their periodic meetings with the sales force.

The nature and amount of supervision provided by the merchandise manager depend on the strength and weakness of each buyer. Probably most buyers tend to be weak in the planning and stock-keeping functions. Al-

[7]The verbs used in describing the management function are a clue to its basic nature. Notice how often verbs like *help, guide, counsel, train, direct, review,* and *authorize* appear in the discussion. They emphasize that *management is a set of techniques for getting work done most effectively* as opposed to actual doing of specific work.

though likely to be good selectors and good promoters, they often fail to manipulate sales volume, stock investment, markup, and expenses in a coordinated effort that will yield optimum profit. They have to be trained, counseled, and coached to make formal plans to guide themselves and to pay attention to stocks on hand. Buyers tend to defer markdowns in the hope that goods may one day sell at the original price. If not restrained, they tend to buy too much, virtually duplicating numbers in stock in their zeal to have everything that is new. Market rumors often upset a buyer's judgment, leading to over-buying or under-buying. Closeness to the firing line sometimes prompts hasty action unless cautioned by someone with a broader perspective.

Two viewpoints are generally better than one. An aggressive buyer of the promoter type and a conservative merchandise manager of the control type make a complementary team. This has been found true even in small stores, where frequently one partner is the buyer and the other the administrator.

Organization

The specific ways stores have organized the buying function are discussed in the next chapter,[8] but it should be observed at this point that organization, as a function of management, is to a considerable degree a matter of delegation of responsibility.[9] It is important to observe that although a buyer may delegate responsibility[9] to a subordinate or a merchandise manager may delegate responsibility to a buyer, neither can delegate accountability. Those to whom the buyer has delegated the simpler tasks of selection are accountable to the buyer for their performance. But the buyer is accountable to the merchandise manager for *every* item appearing in the department's stock. In turn, merchandise managers are accountable for the assortments in all their departments, regardless of the fact that they have delegated the responsibility for assortment composition to the individual buyers.

"Passing the buck" is a maneuver that's doomed to failure in the field of merchandise management. The problem of matching accountability with split responsibility is at the root of much controversy about how to organize for the performance of the buying–selling cycle in retailing.

To "*organize*," managers must first identify all the work in their area of responsibility, make groupings of related work, and place an executive in charge of each group. These executives, in turn, become managers. They

[8]The reader may find it helpful, at this point, to refer to the chart of organization on p. 34, in Chapter 2.

[9]Some scholars insist that "responsibility" cannot be delegated. They equate the term with the way in which we have used its synonym "accountability." For a full discussion, see Harold Koontz and Cyril O'Donnell, *Principles of Management*, 5th ed. (New York: McGraw-Hill Book Co., 1972), chap. 4.

must be given enough authority to exercise their responsibilities.

Good merchandise managers, for example, give their buyers responsibility and the authority to exercise it. They are careful not to usurp the authority delegated to the buyer taking over the job and not to relegate the buyer to a position of assistant. At the end of each season, the merchandise manager should be able to hold the buyer strictly accountable for results. This is impossible if the merchandise manager has dictated the particular merchandise to be bought and has reduced the buyer to merely carrying out orders. Although, it is psychologically sound for the merchandise manager to give the buyer wide freedom of action, it must be borne in mind that the store management holds merchandise managers responsible for profits in their departments. They cannot evade this accountability by delegating complete responsibility to their buyers.

The way they delegate responsibility and authority to buyers and the ways in which the latter accept are matters of delicate personal relationships. The timid buyer is too conscious of accountability—too often running to the superior for guidance or decision or falling short of adequate performance. In the end, timid buyers leave themselves accountable for another's decisions and may "hang" for someone else's mistakes. The too aggressive buyers tend to usurp authority not delegated to them and may thus commit costly errors that their superiors would have been unwilling to risk. Besides, it is an unhappy fact of organization life that overly aggressive executives may pose an uncomfortable threat to their superiors' job security.

Company policies and attitudes, the personal qualifications of individual buyers, and the character of the merchandiser all play a part in the resolution of these relationships. But buyers should always try to understand very clearly the extent and depth of their responsibilities and accompanying authority even though the two cannot be completely equated.

Line Organization

In this process of delegation, a distinction must be made between line and staff functions. The word *line* has a connotation of purposefulness: *the direct chain of responsibilities leading to the achievement of the main objective*—profitable sales. The twin line functions aimed at the objective of profitable sales are buying and selling.[10] All other functions, such as providing premises, personnel, financing, and other facilities, are considered ancillary to the main job. This is analogous to the military view that the main line of command runs from the top, right through to the smallest combat unit. All other services, such as supply, general planning, and intelligence, are considered as supporting services to the main work of actual combat.

The term *line* as used in the language of management organization is

[10]Some consider selling as the one main line function and buying as auxiliary to selling.

rooted in this concept but is used to denote the chain of command itself. An executive "in line" receives responsibilities and authority from the direct superior. *Authority implies, among other things, the right to direct or command performance* from those to whom the superior has, in turn, delegated responsibilities. Thus the general merchandise manager, who is accountable for the complete buying performance in all departments, delegates a large share of the work to divisional merchandise managers. Each supervises a group of departments and the buyers who procure the merchandise for them. Each buyer, in turn, delegates work to assistants, heads of stock, control clericals and, frequently, to the floor selling staff. However reciprocal the working relationship among all these people, certain facts remain paramount: Each executive in line may direct or command action by those he or she supervises or may enforce decisions upon them. Each person along the line is accountable directly to his or her supervisor for the performance of assigned work.

Staff Organization

In an ideal relationship, each member of the line may give information and advice to a superior and participate in the formulation of policy and objectives. But some managers are predominantly engaged in just such functions. They are without power to enforce their ideas, decisions, or will. Their sole duty is to service the line managers. These are the "staff" members of the organization. A fashion coordinator assists a general merchandise manager in carrying out a store's policies and objectives regarding its chosen fashion image. The director of comparison shopping reports on the competitive comparability of a store's merchandise from the angles of price and quality and may recommend action. These staff specialists may give valuable information to divisional merchandisers and to buyers, may suggest, counsel, and offer critiques, but usually cannot command. This is understandable: In spite of all the special skills and knowledge possessed by the specialist, *decision is the prerogative of responsibility,* and responsibility rests with the line managers.

But the lack of power to command must not be confused with lack of power per se. It is a foolish line manager who will not make use of the knowledge and service offered by capable staff. Also, there is the alternative that the superior to whom both report will heed the advice of staff and pass it down the line in the form of directive, if need be. In practical relationships, it usually becomes clear that able staff "speaks with the mouth of management."

It should also be noted that a staff bureau with a roster of personnel is itself organized in line for the performance of its own work. A good example of this is the controller's division in a large business. In the work of helping the general manager with responsibilities of financial control and preservation of the assets, and in the service function of maintaining records and controls for all other divisions, controllership is a staff function. But in the management of a large force of people organized to do the work, the controller is a line executive. Similarly, under the merchandise manager there may be staff bureaus with their line organizations, such as comparison, fashion, testing, and research.

Coordination

This management function includes the work of balancing, timing, matching, and integrating work and the activities of workers. For example, a buyer may match the design and color of sweaters or other "tops" with skirts or pants or other "bottoms" to induce ensemble purchasing or to conform to a "mix or match" fashion decree; in fact, such pairings are known in the trade as "coordinates."

Coordination on a broader scale is an important part of the work of the merchandise manager, whose very position is the outgrowth of large-scale operation involving the buying and selling of distinct lines of goods that should be coordinated so that the store may present an integrated personality to its patrons. Following are some of the specific ways by which departments are coordinated.

First, uniform observance of store policies is insisted upon. Price lines, for example, need to be coordinated so that the typical customer may find goods within his or her means in all departments. Uniform standards should govern the breadth of assortments. It would not do for some departments to carry wide varieties to suit a wide range of customers while others "creamed" temporary profit advantage by concentrating on narrower assortments of key items, or for some departments to reap temporary sales advantage by promoting low price lines in a store that strives for the patronage of higher-income consumers. A similar uniformity should govern standards of quality, position in fashion leadership, and relative concentration on branded, unbranded, or private-brand goods.

Second, in stores and departments where it is important, the actual styling with respect to materials, color, and design should be coordinated so that customers may mix and match sets and ensembles so that sales promotion departments may tell unified stories.

Third, the merchandise manager seeks coordination by cooperating with other divisions of the store organization in implementing policies like those that govern service, personnel administration, expense control, publicity, advertising, and display.

Planning and Control

Although planning and control are distinct management functions that usually represent the first and last stages of a management cycle, they are actually directly related. New planning grows directly out of the control exercised over the operation of former plans. As results are evaluated, new plans are made.

Planning involves the activities of (1) forecasting, (2) setting objectives, (3) formulating policies, (4) setting standards for both merchandise and operations, (5) formulating procedures, programs, and schedules, and (6) summing all estimates into budgets.

Controlling involves measuring performance against standards, projecting the effect of deviation, and taking corrective action, either in adjusting the work or the objectives. This involves reviewing and authorizing the performance of many jobs to be sure they conform to standards, or to permit calculated deviations.

Although buyers do participate in planning and control, this kind of management work is more likely to be an important duty of the merchandise manager or the sole function of staff specialists. This has been more true of chains than of department stores, because the former have had to contend with the complexities of multistore operation. As department stores began to expand by opening branches, they too found the need for more sophisticated techniques of planning and control and the consequent need for developing staff specialists in this kind of work.

Qualified merchandise managers exercise planning and control responsibilities in the following ways:

1. They participate actively in making long-range merchandise plans covering sales, stocks, purchases, initial margins, stock levels, advertising, and selling costs.
2. They then control the operation by checking the results daily, weekly, monthly, and seasonally against the plan.
3. They control the purchases by means of some kind of open-to-buy plan to show how much more the buyer may order for delivery within a period without exceeding the purchase allotment.
4. Most large stores require all merchandise orders for appreciable amounts of merchandise to carry the merchandise manager's countersignature in order to insure a sound relationship between the amount invested in stock and the actual sales. Limits vary with the size of store and the management's confidence in its buying staff.
5. Whereas the making of model stock and unit buying plans is primarily a planning activity delegated to the buyer, the merchandise manager exercises control by approving them before they are acted upon.
6. Returning of goods to vendors is also controlled by the merchandise manager, who authorizes returns in order to maintain a uniform policy and to avoid unfair returns.
7. The merchandise manager controls markups and markdowns by comparing actual figures with plans.
8. Price changes generally have to be approved. By reviewing requisitions for changes in price, the merchandise manager ascertains that the merchandise that needs such attention *is* being repriced and that the repricing privilege is

not being abused. The merchandise manager also keeps informed as to the causes of markdowns so that he or she can give informed counsel in regard to future preventive measures.

9. To the extent that buyers are responsible for the selling function, the merchandise manager helps to plan their major sales activities, cooperating with the store manager and expense controller in the planning of selling expenses and the number of salespeople needed each week and even each hour of the day. The merchandise manager supervises the planning of advertising expense, in cooperation with the advertising manager, and works out with the buyers major departmental promotions and specific advertising schedules for each month.
10. Many stores prepare departmental sales plans for 1 week to 6 months or more. When these are formally made, they indicate chief sales events for each month, types of goods and price lines to be promoted, advertising media to be used (including newspapers and linage), cost of each promotion, and anticipated sales results. Such plans must be approved by both the merchandise manager and the publicity manager.

As a basis for intelligent control, merchandise managers regularly review reports that may have a bearing on their departments. These may include departmental profit-and-loss statements, reports on each merchandise classification, unit control reports, reports from fashion comparison or testing bureaus, financial reports, surveys of business conditions and consumer demand, and analyses of the conditions of supply, demand, and price in the commodity markets.

PERSONAL QUALIFICATIONS FOR BUYERS

Many of the personal qualifications needed for success in buying and merchandising are common to all managerial or professional occupations. The special skills and powers required depend on the particular duties assigned to a given buying job, the kind of merchandise involved, the nature of the firm, the character of its organization, plans for the individual, and personal aims for the future.

Following are some of the qualities, aptitudes, cultivated skills, and developed abilities and powers especially pertinent to the buying function.

Decision Making

Probably no business executive of any kind makes as many decisions as does the retail-store buyer. Every inspection of a new item, every negotiation of terms, every setting of a price, every promotion plan, every markdown and markup, every reorder, and every return to the vendor or adjustment requires a decision. Many of these are made on the basis of policy, established procedure, or habit. Most decisions are not as "earth-shaking" as those of top management and political leaders, but they are more frequent and often must be made in the face of uncertainty as to the results. Accordingly, the buyer must have the mental quality that enjoys making decisions readily and quickly and must not be overly swayed by personal preference. The many persons who find it hard to do so are not cut out for buying. One of the favorable aspects of such decision making is that the feedback usually occurs in a relatively short time. Thus the buyer knows quickly when a mistake has been made and can learn by the experience. To make decisions and choices is often difficult and frustrating, but the mature buyer is not afraid to make mistakes—to make some is better than inaction. The knowledge that error is inherent in a given percentage of decisions may cause hesitancy in "swinging at the ball." Successful buyers learn to overcome this hesitancy, to develop faith in their perspicacity and to back it with resoltuion.

Drive

Commonly, successful buyers exhibit a zest for conflict, a resiliency toward rebuffs and an ability to thrive under tension. They tend to be aggressive and dominant. They couple initiative with perseverance to generate an enduring drive and exhibit the stamina to maintain it. The stamina is partly physical but, more importantly, is a nervous endurance that impels to action long after initial zeal or enthusiasm has faded and the strains of tension have taken their toll.

Self-mastery is a prime virtue for several reasons. Much of the work is done outside of the reach of direct supervision. Much of it is complicated, and appraisal of its effectiveness must wait for some future date, thus creating temptation to postpone unpleasant corrective actions in the hope that the need will somehow go away. It doesn't, and the buyer who postpones is always plagued by self-created emergencies.

Manager and Specialist

Chain or resident buyers may specialize in the core buying function for one of a narrow group of product lines. They concentrate on accumulating knowledge about the goods and their procurement market, on developing aesthetic discrimination and other powers of value judgment. In other words, they concentrate on cultivating skills for doing their own reserved work, with managerial capacities being decidedly secondary. When buyers are charged with managing a selling department, the management powers have to be much more highly developed. This would appear to hold true in the event of promotion to merchandise manager but is not necessarily true, however, because some firms are so organized that the merchandise manager is a super-buyer, a buying specialist in several related departments. Even so, it would be necessary to develop capacities in at least two of the management functions: those of organization and coordination.

Artist and Craftsman

With the growth of large-scale retailing with multiunit operations and private branding, it is not enough for the buyer to be a good selector in the market. Central buyers and buyers catering to a sophisticated clientele have often had to develop a knowledge of materials and technology to the point that they assist in creating product versions on a craft level and even draw up specifications to direct the vendor's production processing.

Those who can create completely, produce a line with distinctive characteristics that give their goods a recognizable style or quality. Those who alter can, at least, distinguish their merchandise from the commonplace—take it out of the competitive ruck. Sometimes the end purpose is to strip goods of certain costly features that are low in significance and observability, thus achieving a low price or better markup advantage.

Gifts of inventiveness and ingenuity serve best in the "cut, make, and trim" trades of clothing, accessories, textile home furnishings, and even in furniture. These skills serve less where manufacturing economy depends on expensive dies, tooling operations, or highly fixed procedures for turning out masses of identical items. Thus the buyer of dresses or coats must be more creative (in the senses described) than the buyer of rickrack and seam binding; the buyer of draperies, more so than the buyer of housewares.

Some buyers with a great deal of artistic or inventive skill have attempted to take over the designing process but with not wholly satisfactory results. The buyer who presumes him- or herself a designer is likely to neglect his or her selective function. Some such have quit retailing to join a manufacturer's marketing staff. Others have been paid for their designs by the manufacturer and have thus created a conflict of interest.

Art and Science

Art and science are everywhere interlocked in buying, but not always of equal importance. Planning and control work is highly intellectualized, depending on abilities to classify and interpret data, draw inferences, and establish verifiable principles and courses for action. Implied are logical ordering, reasoning, or disciplined thinking. Not that the planner cannot use imagination, creativity, instinct, and intuition—but they must be based on the first list of abilities.

Sometimes the artistic buyer is deficient in scientific powers, in which case planning and control may be placed in the hands of another, as a complementary function. The buyer who has more aptitude for science than for art may do best in administering staple departments, such as drugs, groceries, and housewares, where orderly management of inventory is an important challenge.

Intuition

Even though an increasing quantity of up-to-date data is available to buyers from both the consumer and the procurement market, and even though they may be equipped with sophisticated statistical tools for forecasting, buyers must often depend on an intuitive sense of what will or will not sell. How this is acquired is yet to be determined. Some believe that the mind organizes all the information received from the five senses, evaluates it subconsciously, and comes up with better judgments of future events than a laborious, analytical study may provide. Others, especially the parapsychologists, who investigate psychic phenomena, have collected evidence that some sensitive people can accurately forecast future events, at least sometimes. A recent study of major business executives[11] reports that those who have been most successful profit-wise do better on a standard test for precognition (with a randomly selected number sequence) than those who have not been so successful in their business results; also, top-notch performers report that they frequently make judgments that fly in the face of the advice of their more analytical assistants. Although no such study has been made of buyers, outstanding buyers of fashion merchandise may be endowed with this "sixth" sense, because they are able to pick styles destined to become runners better than can the majority. They seem to have the ability to generate hunches and to follow them resolutely.

Flexibility and Curiosity

Retailing is a business of constant tactical maneuvering. Besides the usual social, political, and economic changes that challenge business strategy, retailing must cope with volatile demand factors, changing clientele, shifting market situations, and changing competitive structure and practice. The buyer must make frequent adjustments of viewpoint and arrive at quick judgments. Replenishment of inventories represents a multitude of decisions, big and small, with seemingly never enough time and data for a judicious decision.

[11]Douglas Dean, John Mihalasky, Shiela Ostrander, and Lynn Schroeder, *Executive ESP* (Englewood Cliffs, N.J.: Prentice-Hall, Inc., 1974).

Procedure and practice should never go long unchallenged, because a certain proportion of error is inherent in the situation. The buyer must be quick to observe and recognize error and to adjust strategy.

Perception and Verbalizing

Buying demands keen observation and at least a short-time memory for detail. Hundreds of items may be inspected before tens are chosen from versions that may represent slight but sometimes significant variations. A few people have photographic memories; others make a mistake in imitating their techniques. Memory should be frequently sifted and valuable observations written down.

Perception of detail must feed back to sensitivity about the details that interest customers. This is needed, not only for selection, but for expert communication, translating the salient selling features of the merchandise to those who are charged with selling it or promoting its sale. Whether by bulletins or catalogs to stores, face-to-face discussion with a sales force, information to display, sign-writing, or advertising specialists, all kinds of buyers are involved in verbalizing the stories their purchases have to tell—in explaining why they were bought and what will make them sell.

When buyers were responsible for only one store and handled both the buying and selling, their communications were oral and on a continuous basis. The buyers of today are likely to purchase for many outlets and to visit the selling units infrequently. Thus they must depend largely on written communications and must acquire the knack of preparing merchandise and promotion information in a form that is not only readily grasped by the selling staff but motivates them positively. Such buyers must also succeed in eliciting personal communications from the various sales managers that go well beyond the statistical reports submitted. Lack of adequate communications in multiunit retail organizations is reported to be a major stumbling block to a smooth operation.

Trading Acumen

Much purchasing today is governed by law or by industry practice involving standard goods. To that extent, trading may not be the demanding factor it once was. But where pricing alternatives exist, buyers must be shrewd in appraising the price needed to pay in order to get precisely the quality and service they want. This presupposes a knowledge about goods, markets, and people. Buyers cannot judge the price asked by a given vendor for a given shirt without knowing the going market price of that precise quality and style of shirt and without knowing this vendor's likelihood of delivering what is promised. Nor can they judge the base price without weighing all the terms and conditions surrounding it.

Trading demands a quality often described as "nerve," because, in many instances, vendors' pricing policies are not as uniform as they pretend. An offer far below the asking price may be met with a certain kind of personal abuse. Those buyers whose skin is thick enough accept this abuse as part of the ritual and go on from there. But trading is not brute force or rapier thrusts alone. It also demands of a buyer certain gentler forms of persuasiveness—of the kind that must be cultivated in dealing with co-workers and in helping to motivate customers.

Today, buyers are subjected to demanding government constraints that set merchandise standards and restrict selling claims. Buyers have had to adjust themselves to these regulations without limiting their effectiveness as buyers. They must be fair and within the law. But these requirements should never be translated into softness or complacency. Buyers must know the positive aspects governing their rights and prerogatives as well as the negative aspects that limit their bargaining. And they must be sharply aware not only of the claims they make for the goods they sell but of possible faults that can cause damage to purchasers. Retailers now have a specific liability in these matters and are charged with the responsibility for quickly reporting such dangerous defects.

Education and Training

More and more, the important buying jobs are being filled by college graduates. This does not imply that academic preparation alone can produce ready-to-work buyers or even assistants. But the intellectual skills and disciplined training acquired in college enable graduates to learn better and faster on the job—and subsequently to make wider application and more creative use of what they have learned. They are better able to study the customers and economic factors that are so vital to their work. They are better able to understand and to cope with the functional and societal complex of big institutions. And, lastly, well-educated people are better equipped to participate in community life at the level expected of executives by the organizations for which they work. If the collegiate preparation includes an in-depth study of marketing and retail merchandising, the graduate can enter into the complex world of buying with a knowledge of objectives, organization, and techniques that it would take many years to master on the job.[12]

Nevertheless, most of the specific training takes place in the retail environment. Experience in selling directly to the customer and in sales floor

[12] A study made in 1961 by Karen R. Gillespie, Professor Emeritus of business education, New York University, of 144 senior executives in large retail stores revealed that the four college subjects deemed most important for a retailing career were merchandise mathematics, business English, human relations, and management.

management is of major importance. In the independent store, this experience may be gained as an assistant buyer who is assigned to the selling floor for most of the time.

Many large stores with branches have executive training programs that are geared toward the buying position. Work assignments are provided on the selling floor and behind the scenes in such places as the warehouse or stockroom, the fashion bureau, the unit control office, the statistics department, the receiving and marking department, and the merchandise manager's office.[13] These experiences are supplemented by a course in the fundamentals of the job.

Although the order of advancement varies after the formal training program, a common plan is to make the trainee an assistant to a buyer in the central office of the branch-store system. Next he or she becomes a department manager in one of the company's branches, perhaps a year later is returned to the buying office as an associate, and before long assumes the position of buyer of one of the smaller departments. The entire process usually takes from 3 to 5 years. Thus young men and women can aim at becoming full-fledged buyers while still in their twenties.

Some trainees are diverted to the department manager position, because they may be better suited to supervising salespeople and dealing with customers than to selecting merchandise.

Although most buyer positions can be filled as indicated, when a new department is being introduced or where special market experience is required to make a merchandise department a success, management looks outside for talent. This may be secured from other stores or from manufacturers in the consumer goods field.

In some chain-store organizations, less emphasis is placed on store experience, and most of the training takes place in the central buying office and in the market. In one large general merchandise chain, the college graduate is started on a buyer training program that includes some store visits. He or she is then appointed as an assistant buyer and can normally achieve a buyership in one of the smaller departments within 6 years. Promotions are made to larger departments, not necessarily in the same division, and eventually to a merchandise manager's position. During the first few years of employment, personnel reviews are held a number of times a year and less frequently as the person progresses. Within a year or less, a judgment is made as to whether the young person has the potential to become a full-fledged buyer. It is usually the practice not to retain a person who, although a good assistant, is not deemed to have the qualities needed in a professional buyer, responsible often for millions of dollars worth of purchases each year.

[13]Branch department managers are sometimes taken on visits to the wholesale markets but not during the mass buying season.

Opportunities for Women

In 1965, an opinion survey of 2000 business executives[14] indicated that there were more executive opportunities in retailing for women than in other industries and that in retailing women had almost the same opportunities as men. With the present emphasis on women's rights, the opportunity for women is even better today.

Changes in the Qualifications of Buyers

There are still those who decry the virtues of intellectual approaches, logical ordering, aesthetic emotion, empathy, persuasive leadership, and cooperation within complex organizations. They claim that delegation is approaching abdication, that there is too much managing and not enough doing, that the powerful, individualistic prime mover of yesterday is fading into the societal background and becoming the "organization man." They consider the new buyer to be a timid taster in selection and a "nice Nelly" in trading. All in all, they view the new breed not as products of a maturing society but as harbingers of decay.

Nietzsche, over 100 years ago, described a set of qualities that resemble those of our old-time buyer and lauded them as characteristic of a Dionysian society—one that he equated with youth, virility, and upsurge. The qualities that we have ascribed to the new breed he called Apollonian and equated with age and decay. He may have been entirely right about youth and age—but wrong in ascribing decay to Apollonian characteristics. There are broader, more fundamental, and irresistible forces of nature that produce inevitable decay. In any event, the successful buyer today seems to be well endowed with many of the qualities we have described. But none is endowed with all. Most important to remember is that there are different kinds of buying specialization calling for different combinations of the personal qualities we have listed. Matching the job with the person still remains an important objective for candidate and employer alike.

EVALUATING AND MOTIVATING THE BUYER

Although the ultimate success of a buyer depends on the personal qualifications discussed previously, management judges on objective results rather than personal qualifications per se. The measures commonly used are discussed in the following paragraphs.

[14]G. W. Bowman, N. B. Worthy, and S. A. Greyser, "Are Women Executives People?" *Harvard Business Review* (July–Aug. 1965). The winter 1977 issue of the *Journal of Retailing* (New York University) contains an up-dated study on women in retailing.

Sales Results

These may be measured (1) in dollars, (2) in units of merchandise or in number of sales transactions, and (3) in sales per square foot of selling space.

Increase rather than actual volume is commonly the major consideration here. The buyer is expected to achieve planned sales goals that are based on a reasonable appraisal of both outside and inside conditions and of trends already established. Public and private reports of sales results for different types of stores and the major merchandise lines in various districts are found useful in evaluating the actual results in a given department. Government agencies and trade associations provide much of this comparative data.

Inventory Results

These are revealed by:

1. Stockturn,[15]
2. Proportion of old stock carried over to the new season or year, and
3. Merchandise shortage and its percentage to sales.

Management commonly sets stockturn goals for each department and (in some kinds of stores) goals as to what percentage of ending inventory should be less than 6 months old, less than 1 year old, etc. Trade associations, particularly the National Retail Merchants Association in the case of department and specialty stores, provide standards of comparison.

Margin Results

There are four levels of analysis:

1. Initial markup (aggregate original retail prices less aggregate invoice costs),
2. Gross margin realized (final selling price less cost of goods sold, commonly reflecting cash discounts and alteration costs).
3. Controllable margin realized (gross margin less direct department expenses), and
4. Operating profit realized (gross margin less all expenses chargeable to the selling department).

Which of the four margin criteria is used depends on the degree to which management holds the buyer responsible for price changes and expenses. If advertising and selling payrolls are largely controlled by others, the buyer's

[15]Stockturn is defined as "sales for a period divided by the average amount of inventory during the period." The period most commonly referred to is 1 year. But stockturn is sometimes computed for half-yearly periods or by months. See Chapter 7 for a discussion.

responsibility does not go beyond the gross margin level. If the buyer exercises considerable control over direct expenses, particularly the sales force, advertising, and display, he or she is judged at the controllable margin level.

Buyers can properly be evaluated on the operating profit level only when the store sets up an expense plan whereby every item of store expense is broken down into a unit service cost, with the buyer purchasing from management units of service that have price tags attached to each. Thus management would set a unit cost for auditing every sales check, for heating and lighting a cubic foot of space, for receiving a unit of incoming merchandise, for training each new employee, and for providing personnel administration for each worker. Buyers would "buy" from the store at predetermined rates the specific services they demand. From this point of view, buyers become responsible for all expenses attributable to their departmental operation.

Regardless of the level of control, the margin is generally judged on a percentage-to-sales basis. Although the dollar margin is more important, the dollars are the result of achieving sales at a *ratio* of margin. Thus a buyer may be given a sales goal of $500,000 at a margin of 30 percent. This is a dollar margin goal of $150,000, but were the buyer to achieve it by obtaining sales of $600,000 with the same assortment at a margin of 25 percent, the results would not be equally satisfactory. The buyer has broken away from the intent of management to operate at a higher margin and has in all probability increased expenses considerably to move a 29 percent[16] greater physical volume of goods with no increase in dollar margins.

In recent years it has become common practice to check buyers' performances by using a figure known as "Gross Margin per Dollar of Cost Inventory." This is the return on the merchandise investment measured by dividing the gross margin realized by the average inventory at cost.[17]

Check of Current Operations

Buyers should be evaluated not only on results expressed in figures but also on their buying, pricing, and control activities as observed by actual inspection. One merchandise manager makes such checks as the following example indicates: First, he checked the hosiery buyer's outstanding order file to determine if orders indicate style, size, and color assortments in the popular price ranges. He checked the order dates and the shipping dates; where the latter dates had been reached, he looked for evidence of follow-up.

[16]Let $1.00 equal planned retail and 70¢ planned average cost (at 30 percent margin). At a margin of 25 percent, the average retail is 70¢ divided by 75 percent (complement of margin realized) or 93.3¢. This is a margin of 23.3¢. Because each sale was expected to contribute an average of 30¢ and actually contributes only 23.3¢, the resultant increased volume needed is 30 divided by 23.3 or $1.29. This is an increase of 29 percent.

[17]This index is discussed in some detail in chapter 7.

Second, he visited the buyer's department in one of the branches. He asked the salesperson for the best selling style in the best selling size and the best selling color. He then asked for three pairs in that style, size, and color. Only two were in stock, evidence of inadequate stock control.

Third, he asked to see a sample of every brand carried in nylon hosiery. He found 11 in stock but many not selling well. (This led to reducing the brands to four).

Fourth, he checked competition. The store's lowest price was $1.15, but small neighborhood shops were doing a good business at 85¢.

The purpose, of course, was not simply to evaluate the buyer but to improve his operation. Progressive managers now consider this purpose, development of their people, as an important if not the prime purpose of appraisal and evaluation.

Exchange of Merchandising Data

Another device to evaluate the buyer and to motivate better performance is to organize or join a figure exchange group of stores of similar size and merchandising policies. Monthly or seasonally, the group exchanges data for each selling department on such profit factors as increase or decrease in both dollar sales and transactions, stockturn, and percentages of markup, markdowns, gross margin, advertising expenditures, and selling costs. The like departments in the stores are rated on each factor. Techniques of the buyers who report the best ratios are carefully studied by the other buyers concerned and by their merchandise managers.

Ratio of Buyer's Salary to Sales Results

In a department store a buyer's salary typically averages 1½ to 2 percent of departmental sales but larger than this in the very small stores and smaller in the very large ones. The adequacy of any particular ratio depends on the trend in the other factors under review, the risks that the buyer has assumed growing out of the obsolescence factor, and other less tangible measures of success. These include programs that the buyer has introduced that hold promise for the future, good will that he or she has developed for him- or herself in the market, and his or her success in overcoming special problems that may have plagued the department, such as merchandise shortage, poor employee morale, unbalanced inventories, unsatisfactory merchandise resources, and pedestrian promotional methods.

Outcome of the Buyer's Evaluation

At a seasonal or annual review of the buyer's accomplishments, management decides what rewards to confer or penalties to exact. Favorable performance normally leads to a year-end bonus, often of substantial size, and perhaps to an increase in base salary. Where special planning and supervisory skills are evidenced, the buyer may be offered a merchandise manager's job or the position of assistant merchandise manager.

Unsatisfactory performance may be judged to be the result of unfavorable outside conditions over which the buyer had no control, so he or she may not be subject to penalty or censure, but is not likely to receive a cash bonus that is really a sharing of satisfactory profits with the people who made them possible.

Where the buyer seems to be to blame for unsatisfactory results, more careful supervision and training by the merchandise manager would seem to be the first move. If unsuccessful, a transfer to another department may be tried. A buyer may not have the qualifications to buy fashion merchandise successfully but may be very successful in a staple goods line.

Where such measures do not work out, the buyer is normally given an opportunity to resign and to secure a new job before leaving the present one. Nor is the new potential employer ill-advised to hire someone who has not been successful somewhere else. A person has to fit into a particular organization and get along well with superiors there as well as with established co-workers and subordinates. Very often, an unsuccessful buyer making a new connection enters a human society that offers a new challenge and security that makes for great success in the new buying job.

DISCUSSION QUESTIONS

1. Is it sound thinking to equate *merchandising* with the work of a *merchandise manager?*
2. Koontz and O'Donnell in their text *Principles of Management*[18] (McGraw-Hill Book Co., Inc.) classified the functions of management as *planning, organizing, staffing, directing,* and *controlling.* Although they don't regard *coordination* as an additional function, they call it the "essence of management." How does this classification compare with the one in the text?
3. Why is a buyer able to delegate less work than most managers?
4. Which is the greater problem: (a) for buyers to usurp authority not delegated to them, or (b) for buyers to avoid accepting authority that has been delegated to them?
5. Is it a sound practice for the line manager of a store organization—the general manager—to allow staff bureaus, such as comparison and testing, to issue orders in his or her name?
6. Is the merchandise manager ever justified in doing the work of actual buying rather than simply managing the work?

[18]The current edition of this book is *Management Systems: A Contemporary Analysis,* 6th ed. (New York: McGraw-Hill Book Co., Inc., 1976).

7. Should a young college graduate who becomes a full-fledged buyer at the age of 25 be paid about as much as a buyer in the same organization who has had 20 years of experience on the job?
8. A merchandise manager in a chain feels that a large seasonal commitment should be made to a new product, that such a purchase will result in much needed volume and additional profit. But the buyer is dead set against it, and the merchandise manager is not able to convince her. What action, if any, should the merchandise manager take?
9. A young woman has recently been appointed buyer of a sportswear department. She has "inherited" a competent male assistant buyer who shows that he resents her authority over him. How may she win his cooperation and loyalty?
10. In selecting candidates for a buyer-oriented training program, is there any justification for the retail employer to give preference to a college graduate with a specialization in marketing, including retailing, but with little practical experience as compared with a high school graduate who has had considerable retailing experience and has similar personal qualifications?
11. Production managers and government authorities, both concerned with increasing business output per man hour of labor, are challenging the marketing concept discussed in this chapter. Since this concept calls for quick adjustment of output to changing customer demand and to wide variations in consumer tastes, it tends to proliferation of product with higher production and marketing costs. Concentration on a relatively few basic products would reduce production and marketing costs and tend to reduce inflation. Should the marketing concept give way to a policy of strict limitation of variety in order to reduce costs and prices?

chapter 2

Organization and Control of Buying: Single and Multi-unit Stores

DEPARTMENTALIZING THE INDIVIDUAL STORE

In the small independent store, as previously stated, buying is just one of the functions performed by the store merchant. As the store grows in size and variety of merchandise carried, the assortment may be split into "departments" with separate buyers and/or separate accounting for sales, purchases, inventories, profit margins, and even expenses. Thus a specialty store may establish separate departments for such lines as coats and suits, dresses, separates and coordinates, and accessories.

As the store becomes still larger, it may set up a "budget" department for lower-priced garments. It may split "junior" sizes out of the regular coat and dress departments. (See Fig. 2–1.) Sometimes separate sections are established to appeal to special interests and age groups among the clientele. Skiing supplies, patio furnishings, and teen-age apparel are examples of such specialized groupings. These sections may not necessarily achieve full departmental status, with separate buyers and accounting records. As specialized "shops," they may be presentation devices under the supervision of floor managers or assistant buyers and with separate statistics only for purposes of inventory management and not for profit analysis. Sportswear had just such modest beginnings and grew into a major department. Teen-age shops have progressed similarly.

FIGURE 2–1 Expansion of a Basic Department

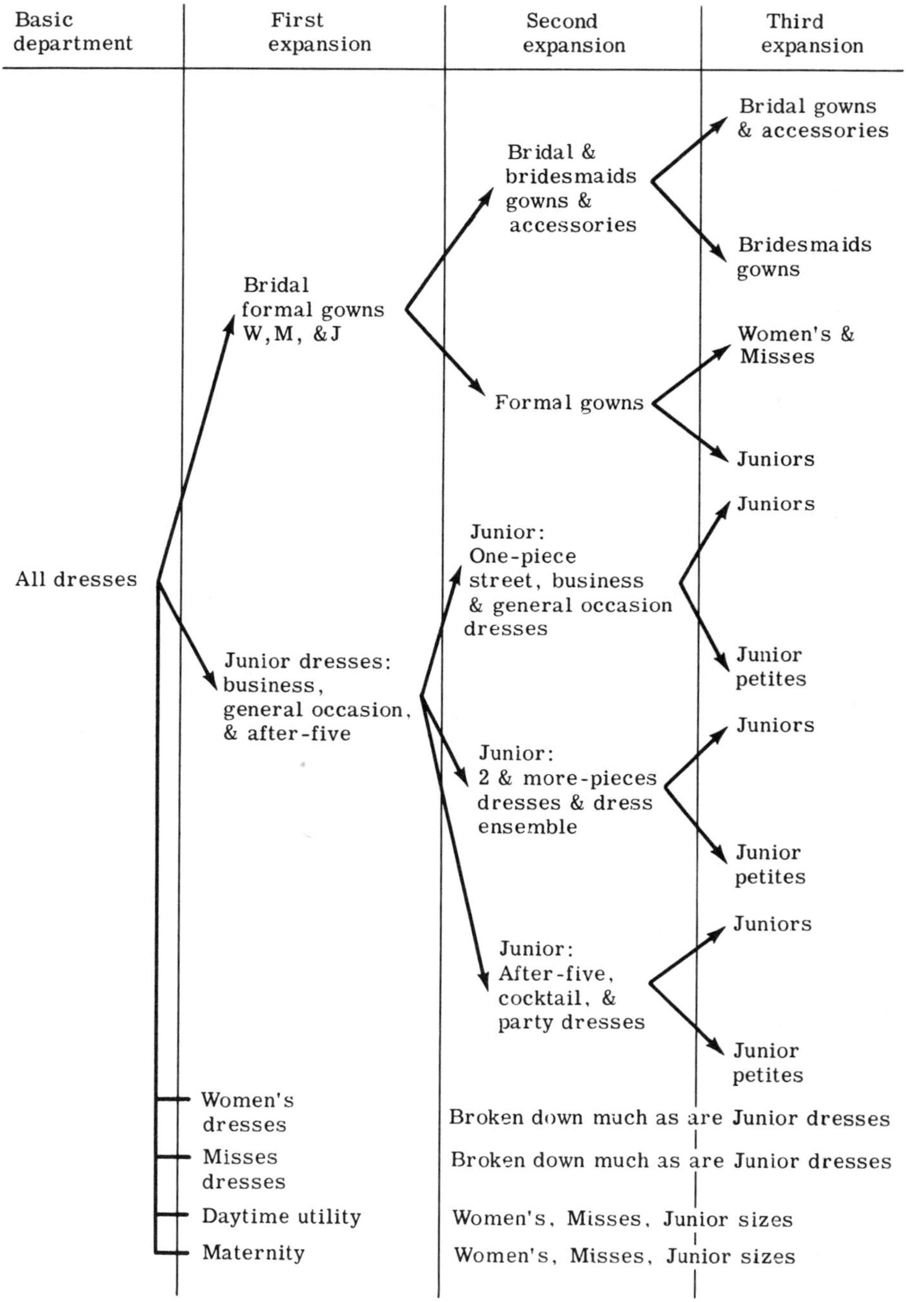

Note: A further expansion may be included that segregates long and short gowns, and woven and knit, and pants suit dresses.

Organizing Divisions and Departments

In establishing merchandise departments for purposes of promotion and control, a large multiline store first organizes its merchandise into broad divisions on similarity of end use. It then sets up in each division a number of departments with a buyer in charge of each. Table 2–1 shows the divisions that have been standardized for department stores. It is interesting to note the differences in the volume profile of the small store compared with the

TABLE 2–1
Merchandising Divisions of Department Stores 1975[a]
Median Data

	Sales volume % of total			*Sales $50 million & over*
Divisions	*$½–$1 million*[b]	*$1–$5 million*	*$50–$100 million*	*Largest department in each division*
Adult female outer apparel	35.1	21.5	19.3	Separates and coordinates
Adult female accessories & intimate apparel	17.0	14.5	13.2	Lingerie/Sleepwear/Robes
Adult male apparel	31.5	9.4	14.1	Men's clothing
Infants'/Boys'/ Girls' clothing & accessories	14.4	7.9	9.3	Boys' clothing
Personal needs & small wares	(*c*)	7.1	7.1	Cosmetics/Toiletries/ Drugs
Hobby/Recreation/ Transportation	(*c*)	2.0	4.1	Audio-visual appliances
Home furnishings: furniture & decorative accessories	3.1	6.0	7.6	Furniture & bedding
Appliances & utilitarian equipment	(*c*)	5.6	3.6	Housewares
Domestics/Draperies/ Piece goods	(*c*)	9.4	7.3	Linens & domestics
Total upstairs	(*d*)	(*d*)	84.9	
Budget departments (downstairs)	(*c*)	6.9	8.0	Women's outer apparel
Leased departments	(*c*)	5.3	1.3	Fine jewelry & watches
Cost departments	(*c*)	(*c*)	0.4	Restaurant
Totals	(*d*)	(*d*)	(*d*)	

[a]MOR Report 1976, Financial Executives Division, NRMA, New York.

[b]Includes specialty stores.

[c]Negligible.

[d]Totals do not add up to 100% because they are medians not arithmetic averages.

large one. The degree of departmental specialization within each division varies with size and product lines carried.

Large food stores, including all supermarkets, have also departmentalized. See Table 2–2. Health and beauty aids and other general merchandise, especially cosmetics, patent medicines, staple clothing, housewares, and basic stationery products, have been added to the traditional lines. The present trend is to increase the proportion of nonfood lines, because of the high margins above cost that they provide. Profits approximately only 1 percent of sales in the industry, and a higher overall margin is deemed essential.

In departmentalized stores, each department may have a separate buyer, but in some stores a number of departments are assigned to a single buyer. Although there is danger of energies being spread sparcely over a number of departments, some stores have found that it is better to have one good buyer supervise a number of departments than to rely on a number of lower-priced buyers, each devoting attention to a single department. With an assistant in each department, an able buyer can be more productive with an enlarged field of activities.

Some stores separate the department management function from that of buying. Buyers are then able to spread their specialized work over more departments. On the other hand, there are those who imitate the mitosis of living cells by routinely dividing into complete new cells. These stores split departments as soon as they show promise of being able to support the salaries of two buyers, each of whom is then expected to bring sales up to the level of the original department.

TABLE 2–2
Departments in Food Stores 1974[a]

Departments	*% of store sales*	*% Margin*
Grocery[b]	38.6	15.9
Meats	23.3	20.6
Frozen foods	6.4	20.5
Produce	7.4	33.5
Bakery	4.7	69.3
Snack bar/Deli	4.3	49.0
HABA/General merchandise[c]	4.9	30.4
Dairy	9.5	18.9
Ice Cream	0.9	25.0
Total	100.0	23.6

[a]From the 42nd Annual Report of the Grocery Industry, *Progressive Grocer*, New York, 1975.

[b]Includes approximately 40 classifications of which the largest are cigarettes/tobacco, paper goods, soft drinks, coffee/tea/cocoa, soaps/detergents, and cereals.

[c]Health & beauty aids, clothing, etc.

Merchandise Managers

As the number of departments and buyers increases, it becomes impossible for a single merchandise manager to coordinate and supervise all of them. Divisional merchandise managers then come into being. Logically, there would be one for each grouping of related merchandise as suggested by the table. But sometimes physical location seems to be the determinant in grouping departments; all the departments on a single floor may be supervised by one divisional merchandise manager. This does not always clash with the more logical device of grouping by closely related merchandise categories, because the departments on a single floor (except for many street floors) are likely to be fairly homogeneous.

There is no absolute standard for the number of divisions or of divisional managers needed to organize the merchandising management of a retail business, whether it is an independent or a chain. One of the limiting factors is the number of people reporting to a given manager. A store with 84 departments may have only 54 buyers. Six divisional men would average 14 departments each but would have to supervise an average of only nine buyers. How many departments each could handle effectively depends on the capabilities of both merchandiser and buyers, the extent of their responsibilities, and the philosophy of store and merchandiser with respect to the autonomy of buyers. Sears Roebuck and Co., the country's largest chain, is basically organized into 55 merchandise buying departments headed by 46 national merchandise managers, who have approximately 500 buyers reporting to them. This is an average of 11 line subordinates reporting to each manager (besides other staff personnel). Some consider it a good rule of thumb to assign not more than 12 buyers to a merchandise manager.

Organization Profile

The organization for management becomes more elaborate as the cellular structure of the business becomes more complicated. In a firm that uses only two to four divisional merchandise managers, they can report directly to an owner, president, and/or general manager. Above that number, a position of general merchandise manager may be created, to whom will report all divisional managers and staff officers that service buying. Figure 2–2 shows the merchandise organization for a large store, but there are many variations.[1]

[1]The line of responsibility shown in Figure 2–2 is usually the line of promotion. Therefore, merchandisers are typically recruited from the ranks of successful buyers. However, buyers are sometimes successful because of their highly developed intuitive or artistic talents, most evident in that vital function of merchandise selection. They may lack the administrative qualities of a successful merchandise manager. In many departments, these buyers should be able to earn high rewards for the exercise of their special talents. To promote such a buyer may result in a popular phrase: "made a bad merchandiser out of a good buyer."

FIGURE 2–2 Chart of merchandising organization

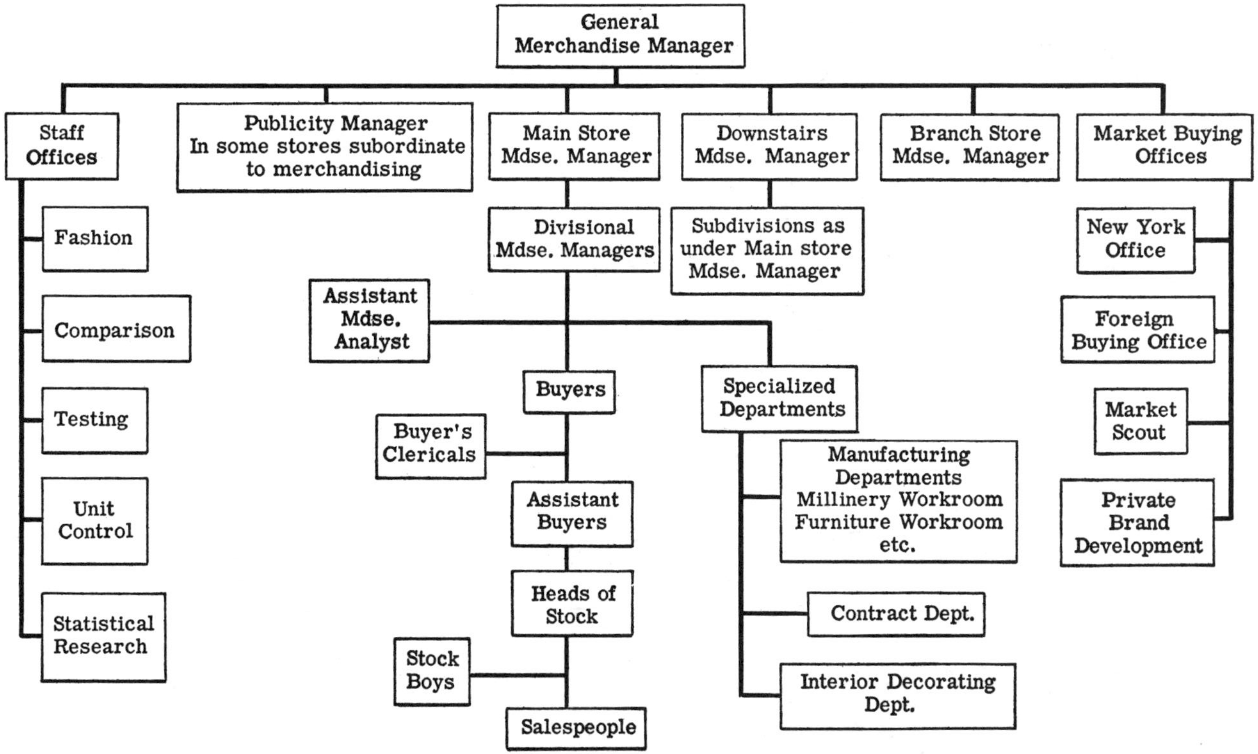

There are many variants of this plan. The group headed "specialized departments" is commonly found in the operating division. Salespeople, too, are sometimes assigned to the operating division rather than to the merchandise division and occasionally are under the sales promotion division. Occasionally, sales promotion and merchandising are unified under one manager just below the general management level. In such a case, divisional merchandise managers may report to two or three intermediaries (sometimes called "administrators") who in turn report to the merchandising and sales promotion manager. Buyers may act as subdivision managers for a group of closely related departments, and their immediate subordinates, with greater responsibilities than those of assistant buyers, may be called "associate buyers."[2]

Merchandise managers frequently have assistants, and a distinction should be made between an assistant manager and an assistant *to* a manager. The latter may be a young person in advanced training who looks forward to a buyership, or a specialist in some technique such as planning and control or fashion coordination. In any event, the "assistant to" works in a staff capacity. An assistant manager is generally a line executive who has been given specific operating responsibilities and commensurate authority. This assistant, also, may specialize in fashion coordination or planning and control but with authority to direct decision. He or she may have graduated from the ranks of buying and be in training for further promotion to the job of merchandise manager.

Supportive Staffs

Some buying functions are assisted or supported by merchandise management staffs. Comparison shoppers, for example, may serve as close and methodical observers of competition, reporting on new items, good sellers, in-store promotions, and the pricing of merchandise. A fashion director may be a powerful influence in the purchase and promotion of new fashions, in home furnishings, apparel, or wherever they may prevail. The fashion expert may also be charged with coordination of styling among departments. This is done not only to promote sales of related merchandise but to ensure that the firm presents a unified fashion image that reflects a predetermined set of fashion policies.

The work of the specialized fashion staff may be classified under four headings:

1. *Fashion forecasts:*
   a. Prepare and revise fashion forecasts for each season based on all available sources of information. When accepted, these become the basis for the pur-

[2]In one of the country's largest retail chains handling general merchandise, there are about 200 buyers in the organization and about 300 assistants.

chase of fashion-right merchandise, for ensemble, selling, for advertising and window display emphasis, and for the training of salespeople.

b. Keep merchandise managers, buyers, and publicity people informed on new developments in the world of fashion—what is coming in and what is going out.

c. Check on the execution of the forecasts accepted by the merchandising staff.

2. *Merchandise selection and control:*

   a. By inventory check, suggest to the buyers the types of merchandise in each line that are likely to prove best-sellers if given promotional emphasis and those that have no fashion appeal and are ready for removal.

   b. Accompany buyers to market and express opinion on the desirability of styles observed and occasionally assist manufacturers in styling certain items in their lines.

   c. Prevail upon store buyers of related items to purchase harmonious styles that will help provide an ensemble for the customer.

3. *Sales promotion:*

   a. Assist the merchandise manager in securing the cooperation of all departments—in the case of a buying office, the cooperation of all *stores*—in promoting a uniform fashion program.

   b. Suggest goods and the key fashion ideas for advertising and special promotion, giving copywriters fashion information and talking points, and, sometimes, writing fashion copy. Sketches for reproduction may also be provided in the case of a group of stores.

   c. Approve proposed advertising and display materials from the standpoint of fashion rightness.

   d. Direct fashion shows for customers and demonstration selling in departments where more effective selling will result.

4. *Training:*

   a. Assist the training department in preparing fashion instruction, including fashion bulletins and posters.

   b. Prepare fashion coordination charts.

   c. Direct fashion shows for employees, and present fashion information to groups of salespeople.

A supportive staff may also be set up to keep unit control records. While the analysis of sales and stock may be undertaken by each buyer perhaps with a "unit-control clerical," or the work may be centralized in a unit-control office. Centralization has the advantage of making use of the skills of a systems expert, of facilitating ready interdepartmental comparisons, and of preparing and using standardized forms and procedures throughout many departments. Clericals can also be transferred from one department to another, depending on the work load. The use of the computer for unit analysis is making supervision a must.

Rather than having all unit-control records kept in a central place, somewhat inaccessible for direct reference by buyers, a workable plan, if a computer is not in use, is to keep the controls in departmental or divisional offices but to provide centralized supervision. Under this arrangement, the unit-control manager (1) installs appropriate systems, (2) trains and assigns the clerical staff to the offices where they are to maintain the day-by-day records of sales, purchases, orders, and inventory counts, (3) independently of the buyers, analyzes the records and recapitulations issued to make sure that the buyers are acting on the information made available to them. More on the subject of unit control is developed in the general discussions of inventory management in chapters 7 and 8. A few store groups maintain testing bureaus, discussed in Chapter 10.

CENTRALIZED BUYING AND MERCHANDISING IN THE MULTI-UNIT OPERATION

A major trend in modern merchandising has been for two or more stores to unite to centralize their buying activities. Central buyers replace or supplement buyers for individual stores. The stores may be under a single ownership (chains or branches), or, as independents, they may be associated as cooperatives or under the aegis of a wholesaler, a resident buying office, or even of a corporate chain. There are varying degrees of centralization and many different ways of organizing to do the work. Certain characteristics distinguish the buying–selling work of these multi-unit merchandisers from those of the comparable job in a single store:

1. *Central buyers must rely heavily on reports.* This involves long lines of communication that can be maintained satisfactorily only by the prompt and meticulous cooperation of each store and department in the system. As the number of outlets served increases and spreads further from headquarters, it becomes impossible to depend on personal observation and less possible even to supplement reports with personal observation on the selling floors. Reports on sales, stocks, and purchases must flow steadily to the central buyers.
2. *Lines of supply become longer and more complex.* Although purchasing power is consolidated, the quantities must somehow be split into the specific requirements for each store and distributed thereto.
3. *Demand patterns of individual outlets are not completely uniform.* Although it is true that consumer demand displays surprising concentration on certain selection factors, there are variations by area and by communities within an area. Stores of the same chain will sell larger sizes in one part of a city and smaller sizes in another, usually because of ethnic groupings. The same groupings can produce variable demands in color and design. Timing of seasonal goods varies from one area of the country to another, although this apparent disadvantage can be put to good use by establishing lag factors and using them for prediction of demand.
4. *The buying organization's involvement in the selling function changes.* Certainly, floor selling cannot be supervised by the buyers for numerous and

far-flung outlets. But their duty to report to the stores the selling features of the goods they have bought remains constant; so, ideally, does their responsibility for deciding what will be promoted, when, and to what extent.

5. *Planning and control functions are more vital to multi-outlet retailers.* Not only are techniques likely to be more sophisticated than those of single-store operations, but the functions are more apt to be performed by staff specialists. Buyers concentrate on specialized attention to the procurement function.

These differences require that work, facilities, and people be organized differently than in independent single stores.

Central Buying Versus Chain Operation

Central buying is not to be confused with chain operation per se; it is merely the way most chains organize their buying. Nor do all chains engage in central buying, some permitting each store to do its own buying. But most multistore operators, who have expanded by opening their own outlets rather than by acquiring existing stores, depend very generally on central buying. These include (1) grocery, drug, and variety chains, where the goods provided all stores are very similar; (2) merchandise chains such as Sears, Kmart, and Penney, where the assortment mix can be adjusted to the store size; (3) specialty store chains, where close response to market changes is essential; and (4) department-store branch systems, where the units are located mostly in the suburbs and secondary shopping districts of the city in which the parent store is located. Chains consisting of both once independent stores and independent stores cooperating through a resident buying office usually apply central buying techniques in only a limited way. The size of the individual stores makes it quite feasible for each to maintain its own buying staff. A chain like Allied Stores is an example. Composed largely of stores that were once independent,[3] the chain "inherited" the buying staffs in each store. Each store or branch system still has its own complement of buyers and merchandise managers, and these are grouped into approximately 17 divisions. But, through centralized steering committees, agreement is reached as to the vendors to patronize. A centralized private brand program accounts for approximately 10% of the chain's volume, and all stores are expected to carry the private brands developed, but the depth of the assortment is decided by each store.

Over the years, the central office has increased its "say" as to the items to be stocked so that it is no longer the limited service or resident buying operation it once was. This development has resulted in a great increase in market clout.

[3]Allied, started in 1929 with the acquisition of 18 stores in 14 states, has grown by further acquisitions and new installations into over 160 stores in 28 states, operating under various names. Most of the stores are grouped into 24 branch systems.

For every merchandise line, the central steering committee consists of a divisional merchandise manager, six or seven buyers selected from the major stores, and the market representative for that line. This committee acts as a bridge between the stores and headquarters. With the backing of the chief executive, it obtains the cooperation of the stores in following centrally developed policies, performance goals, and suggested merchandise resources.

Kinds of Central Buying

Centralized buying tends to take one of five typical forms; (1) central merchandising, (2) warehousing and requisitioning, (3) price agreement and listing, (4) opening stock distribution, and (5) automatic open-to-buy.

The choice of method depends on both the nature of the merchandise and the philosophy of management as to the degree of freedom to be delegated to the store managers. Those who are convinced that each store should control its own intake of merchandise and its own inventories lean toward the price agreement (listing) plan and toward central warehousing. Those who are convinced that the market and procurement expertise are of primary importance tend toward central merchandising. The adherents to the opening stock distribution and automatic open-to-buy divide the purchasing responsibility between the central buying staff and the store management. In practice, the same organization may use all five methods, depending on such factors as:

1. The nature of the goods, whether they are staples or fashions.
2. The ability of manufacturers to carry stocks for delivery as needed.
3. The relative costs of direct handling as compared with routing through a central warehouse or distribution point.
4. The number of store units to be served; for example, a branch operation with a few stores might depend on a requisition system to the parent store for fashion goods, whereas a chain with many units might depend on central merchandising.
5. The size of the store units: The smaller the units, the greater the dependence on a warehouse.
6. The composition of aggregate sales volume: If it is the result of small sales of a large variety of goods, full-scale warehousing operations may be desirable.

The Central Merchandising Plan

This is the most completely centralized buying operation for multi-unit retailing. It is most commonly—but not exclusively—used for so-called "fashion goods." This kind of merchandise has too short a selling life to a permit more than temporary warehousing. Nor should the ordering procedure be delayed by the need to notify stores of market-scouting finds and then to wait for their individual decisions before an order can be accumulated. Yet the buyer finds it advantageous to place orders large enough to constitute "cutting lots" or "factory runs."

Speediest action comes from permitting the central buying authority to make commitments on a basis of its own plans and its own judgment. The central buyer can thus keep a flow of new styles moving into the stores for customer inspection and for reorder as soon as customer preferences are determined. The central office thus assumes responsibility for composition of each store's inventory, for procurement, pricing, and indeed for the general management of the inventory.

Central Organization

The headquarters merchandising organization has a number of subdivisions. At the top is a merchandising manager, with a number of planning assistants who lay out budgets on a basis of the past performances of the chain as a whole and of current trends. Next there are the buyers who select merchandise in the quantities prescribed by the merchandise manager's office. Third is the distribution division, which is responsible for keeping each unit properly stocked. It often operates a distribution point[4] at which shipments from manufacturers are received, inspected, price ticketed, sorted out or distributed to each store according to its need, and shipped. The distribution point differs from the usual warehouse in that goods are not stored for an indefinite period until requisitioned by store units. Instead, most of the incoming flow is distributed to stores and sent out within 48 hours.

Here is an example of the attempt to separate the management functions of buying. The buyer participates in planning, but most of it is the responsibility of a specialized merchandising staff. The buyer's personal accountability in merchandise planning is typically confined to determining the actual items to be selected and the quantities to be ordered—subject to the limitations and controls of prepared category plans.

If the chain is very large, it may be necessary to have an even more elaborate merchandising organization, similar to the one given in Figure 2–3. Under the general merchandise manager are various merchandise divisions, such as dresses, coats, and accessories. Each division has its merchandise planner and divisional buyer.[5] The merchandise planner analyzes past

[4]See the discussion of the pros and cons of a distribution point near the end of this chapter.

[5]Or, as in Figure 2–3, the planner may be over the buyer, in which case the planner acts in a capacity equivalent to that of divisional merchandise manager. In some instances, the jobs of the planner and of the paper distributor are performed by the same person. Note that in all of these schemes the wording of titles presents semantic difficulties.

FIGURE 2–3 Organization for central merchandising

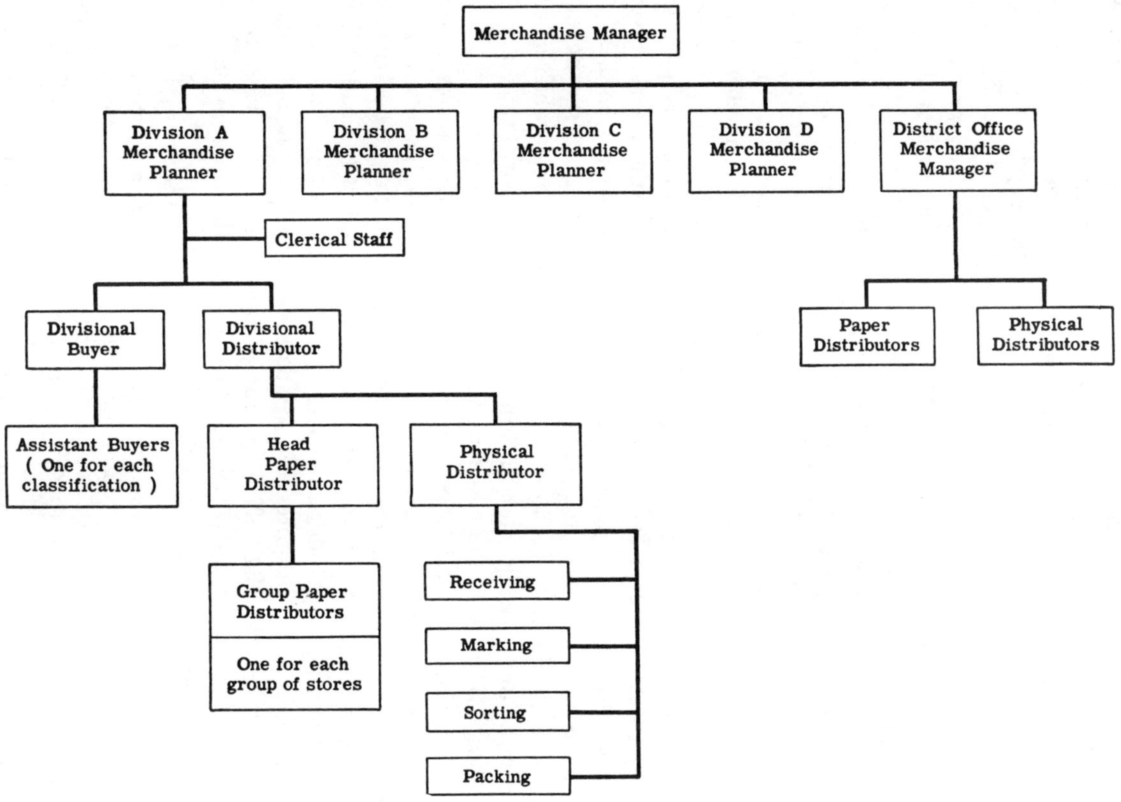

performance in the division and plans purchases by classification, price, fabric, color, and size for the organization as a whole. The divisonal distributor is in charge of distributing incoming goods. Subordinates are "paper" distributors, who plan how many of the incoming styles should be sent to each district and each store within a district, and "physical" distributors, who actually handle the goods. They receive and mark the goods, sort them by store according to the plans of the "paper" distributors, and pack them for shipment.

The "paper" distributors guide is a weekly sales and inventory report submitted by each store. See Figure 2–4. The form illustrated is prepared manually but may be compiled by a computer.

As with the single store, there are many variants of the organization plan for central merchandising. The unqualified term "distributor" usually refers to the functionaries who gather data from individual stores and plan shipments of merchandise to maintain planned inventory levels. In some cases, they take an active part in making complete plans for merchandising individual stores. The sum of these "built-up" plans is then reconciled with the "top–down" category plans previously mentioned. Summary planning and application of higher-level judgment factors may be the reserved work of a "head distributor," a "merchandise planner," or a "department head." Some chains prefer to have the distributors report directly to the buyers. The so-called "physical" distributors are usually warehousemen who report to the warehouse manager, who, in turn, is as likely to report to the store operations division as to the merchandising division.

Whatever the variations in plan, the buyer is typically responsibile for procurement and pricing and for sales information and has a strong voice in determining what, when, and how much to promote. The buyer is also responsible for quality inspection of merchandise if it is handled through a warehouse or distribution point at or near headquarters. For merchandise drop-shipped to the stores from vendors, the buyer may be able to do some inspection at the place of manufacture, but most inspection has to be done at the stores. The buyer is also responsibile for authorizing invoices and protecting the department against wrong charges.[6]

[6]In some mail-order houses, the central buying function has been even further differentiated. Not only are quantitative plans for buying and store distribution put into the hands of a merchandise planner, and allotments to stores in the hands of a distributor, but the reordering of styles is in the hands of a "rebuyer." This specialist carefully follows the sales of every new style introduced by the buyer and decides which styles warrant reorder and the size and color assortments most desirable in the light of initial acceptance and trends. Working under budgetary limits set by the merchandise manager, this executive has considerable freedom of action and is *not* an assistant to the buyer. The rebuyer relieves the buyer of reordering responsibility so that the buyer may concentrate on new item and resource development, including negotiation of terms of purchase.

FIGURE 2–4 Weekly sales and inventory report

CENTRAL BUYING DIVISION

WEEKLY SALES & INVENTORY REPORT

Store *JONES DEP'T STORE*

City *MIDVILLE, ALA.* Dept. No. *D3*

SECTION I ... MERCHANDISE ON HAND

INSTRUCTIONS:
1. Take stock count of business Saturday or early Monday morning.
2. Fill in sections I and II accurately and complete.
3. Enter sales by size and price from your copy of the Daily Sales Report.
4. List all orders not received in Section II.
5. Enter your comments for CBD guidance in space provided at bottom.

STORE NO.

Inventory for week ending: *10/12/74*

	MISSES 8 to 20		JUNIORS 5 to 15		JUNIOR PETITES 3 to 13		WOMEN $12\frac{1}{2}$ to $26\frac{1}{2}$		TOTAL SALES	TOTAL STOCK
	SALES	STOCK	SALES	STOCK	SALES	STOCK	SALES	STOCK		
12.00–1400 (COST 6.75 7.75)										
15.00–16.00–17.00 (COST 8.75)										
18.00–20.00 (COST 9.75 16.75)										
21.00–24.00 (COST 11.75 12.75)	2	12	1	5	1	8			4	25
25.00–28.00 (COST 13.75 14.75)	7	20	5	18	2	17	4	20	18	75
29.00–3200 (COST 15.75 16.75)	2	8	6	22	4	25	3	8	15	63
33.00 & UP (COST 17.75 & UP)	3	15	4	25	2	13			9	53
TOTAL	14	55	16	70	9	63	7	28	46	216
MARKDOWNS (All Prices)	4	15	2	9	4	10	1	4	11	38

STORE COMMENTS: *Could use more misses, particularly at $25-/28-*
Joe Jones

All other stock-keeping work is performed by warehouse personnel or in the stores. Together with the sales promotion division, the stores do all the work of selling. Stores have limited merchandising functions but do have liberal communication with merchandisers, buyers, and distributors for purposes of imparting information about customer demand and advice about how to meet it.

Advantages of Central Merchandising

The chief advantages of the central merchandising plan for fashion goods, compared to store buying are:

1. It provides a steady flow of merchandise from markets to stores, because buyers can spend more time in the markets and because central warehouses make the frequent small shipments needed to keep the store's stocks filled and balanced.
2. Because of the "safety in numbers," forecasts of demand for all units become more reliable than the forecasts for each unit separately. Although individual units may contribute estimates in the built-up phase of forecasting, the final, smoothed-out aggregate is likely to have a more accurate composite of future requirements by classification, price line, color, size, materials, style variations, etc. Then, by the frequent small shipments noted in (1), the central warehouse can keep the individual selling units supplied as their needs materialize.

   There is no hint of perfection in any method of forecasting, procurement, and distribution. But experience indicates that because of the workings of probability, the central buying method can do it *better*. And, because of the same workings of probability, the aggregate operation requires lower safety factors in stock levels to protect the inventory against errors of estimate. (See Chapters 7 and 8 for more on this subject.)
3. Centralized data allows more accurate forecasting and control of style movements than individual stores can possibly accomplish. The central buyer maintains a record of each style that shows—when necessary within 24 hours—the sales of that style in every unit of the chain. The small number of sales in any one store could not give a basis for quick and accurate judgement of the "destiny" of the style with the result that many potentially sucessful numbers are never reordered. The rapid assembling of style information at one central point, however, promptly reveals how acceptance of the new style compares with normal. Newer applications of "sampling theory" coupled with point of sale (P.O.S.) hookups to computers are speeding the work needed for this purpose in the central office.

   The central style record also provides a better basis for markdowns than do the records of a single store. When the sales of a style in many stores are assembled, it is easy to see when its rate of sale is falling off. A decline in any one store might be due to chance factors or to the fact that the size and color assortment has been depleted. The overall movement of the style, however, usually provides a signal for markdowns well before the style is out of fashion.

4. Central buying provides a high-grade specialist in merchandise selection. This leads to:
   (a) *More salable styles.* Not only are styles chosen more wisely, but central buyers can have orders processed at once because of their large size. Small buyers have to wait until the manufacturers can accumulate enough orders to manufacture economically. Thus central buyers may get new styles as much as 3 weeks ahead of independent buyers and also are less likely to suffer from cancellation of numbers for which manufacturers did not get enough orders from other buyers. Central buyers can also buy the "cream" of each line without having to buy a manufacturer's entire line, which small buyers are often forced to do in order to get desirable styles.
   (b) *Higher standards of quality* through the use of specification and testing techniques. Central buyers sometimes specify the raw materials to be used in manufacture, the methods and standards of construction, and the measurements, as well as the style features. Thus they are not limited to choosing from what the market affords: They create their own merchandise.
   (c) *Confined merchandise.* The volume that central buyers can handle often makes it possible for them to prevail upon manufactures to make up certain styles for them only.
   (d) *Lower prices.* Volume buying may lead to lower prices as well as to confined merchandise. Because clothing production, however, requires a great deal of manual labor, price savings, as an outgrowth of quantity, are not proportionately as great as they are in the case of goods produced largely by machine.
5. It provides quality control. Central buyers may inspect and test goods before shipment to stores, either in a manufacturer's shipping department or at distribution points maintained by the central buying organization. Faults are promptly detected and merchandise returned immediately rather than being shuttled back and forth across the country. Thus stores receive only the merchandise in good condition. This both increases sales volume and cuts down on customer complaints.
6. The central merchandising plan may reduce expenses, because each store does not need its own complement of buyers who have to make many trips to market.
7. Central merchandising leads to better stock control. All stores in the group enjoy careful merchandise planning. No store can shirk the problem of maintaining adequate assortments. Uniform systems are used by all stores. The expert central organization can plan and install control systems, now generally computer operated, that will give swiftly and accurately the information necessary for proper stock-keeping and proper buying. An individual store may introduce a good system but may not make effective use of the information revealed, and the cost of computer operation in each store may be expensive. Because central buying organizations must depend on uniform systems and records, data leading to complete stocks in all stores are continually used. The detailed records often make it possible to reduce markdowns by the transfer device. Instead of trying to force the sale of broken lots by heavy markdowns, headquarters can have the lots assembled in one store and thus provide better

assortment of the aging styles that may then sell with little markdown. Ordinarily, however, bad styles are bad everywhere, and *transferring is not an unmitigated blessing.*

8. Concentration of buying leads to specialization in selling.
   (a) Because the store organization is not concerned with buying, it can concentrate its attention exclusively on selling. Department managers with leadership and promotional abilities are much easier to find if they do not also have to be good selectors and good traders.
   (b) Advertising copy and art work can be provided by experts at headquarters who work closely with the buyers. Thus each store can achieve a standard of advertising normally available only to the very large store.
   (c) Display plans, layouts, and fixtures for both windows and interiors can be developed at headquarters by specialists, whose sample displays are photographed so that individual store managers can copy them. In some cases, itinerant display artists actually set up the planned displays in the various units. Fixtures are designed to suit the exact merchandise they are to house and are set up in the stores according to a standard plan.

Meeting the Disadvantages of Central Merchandising

In spite of its many advantages, central merchandising does have disadvantages, which may be overcome:

1. It is hard for central distributors to adjust their shipments to local conditions. For them a store too often is just a number on a page. Frequently, distributors have neither visited the stores nor studied the business situation in each city in which a store is located. Their world tends to be one of figures rather than of merchandise and customers.
   This mass merchandising is not as serious as it sounds, however. Except for climatic variations, demand in all parts of the country today is remarkably uniform, no doubt because of the mass-market periodicals, radios, television, movies, and the large amount of travel. There are nevertheless some undeniable differences among the clienteles of different stores: Some of the regional, ethnic, and other differences develop owing to demographic changes since the individual stores were opened or bought. A greater degree of selective judgement, however, may be obtained by one or more of the following devices:
   (a) Occasional visits of buyers or distributors to the stores.
   (b) Visits of store managers to headquarters to discuss with all distributors the special requirements of their trading areas.
   (c) Maintenance of a store history book in which an up-to-date chronicle of each store is kept, with significant facts about the community the store serves. This should be required reading for each distributor.
   (d) Classification of stores by type, with each type's merchandising requirements distinct. One successful chain-store operator reported that his organization treats each new store as a "baby." Every buyer, distributor, and merchandise manager makes an effort to learn the new store's particular needs and to merchandise it separately from all other stores. As soon as it becomes apparent that the new store has the characteristics of a group of stores already

formed, it then is made a part of that group and receives the same assortments as those allotted to the other stores in the group. Care must be taken, however, to watch for changes in the community that point to the need for regrouping.

(e) Analysis of styles to determine the geographic progression of demand. For example, one central buying organization reports that new styles are accepted first in the South and on the California coast, next in the East, then in the Midwest, and finally in New England. Once the time interval in this progression is determined, it is possible for central distributors to know when to send a style to a specific store.

2. Because there is a sharing of responsibility between store managers and buyers, the dual system of merchandising may lead to a lack of cooperation, accompanied by difficulty in fixing responsibility when styles do not sell. The lack of cooperation may result from an apathetic attitude on the part of store managers or from prejudice against goods selected by someone not on the spot. It may also be the fault of the central office, where distributors may be overworked or where executive attitudes may tend toward the dictatorial. When such friction leads to poor results, it is difficult for top management to know who really is to blame. Cooperation is imperative in central buying because of the division of functions. However, because this ideal cannot be achieved in the real world, central management must be content with knowing more about *what* is right at the sacrifice of some precision in determining *who* is right.

   This problem may be partially solved by fixing a clear-cut division of responsibility at the outset.[7] Each person in the organization, in both store and office, should know his or her exact responsibilities and over whom he or she has authority. Store managers must not be thwarted buyers, and buyers and distributors must not regard themselves as selling experts.

   Another solution is to give department managers bonuses on profit from operations even though they have no control over selection.

3. With central merchandising, it is difficult to maintain an informed and enthusiastic selling organization. Store managers and salespeople may be critical of merchandise sent to them by distributors who, they may feel, are too distant to comprehend their local needs. Psychologically, nothing can wholly replace store buyers who visit wholesale markets, come home with their own selections, gather the selling forces, arouse enthusiasm for their selections, ask for sales cooperation in backing up their judgments, and supplement it all by personal supervision.

   Central buyers frequently do send bulletins to the salespeople, explaining the new merchandise more fully than the typical store buyer does. Weekly or even daily fashion reports or forecasts and specific information on particular styles should be sent to each store to be presented by store and department managers to the sales force. But the printed word, even if orally relayed in the store, is hardly as effective as direct presentation. Perhaps a television showing may be devised, whereby store personnel are able to see and hear the central buyers presenting their new merchandise when it arrives in the stores.

[7]In practice, this turns out to be a solution blessed as much by hope as by reality. But it remains the "best solution in town."

These advantages and disadvantages are of some concern to chains. As will be seen, they also use other methods of central buying that are more advantageous for particular lines and situations. But the pros and cons are of special importance to independents who have to make decisions about when and how to use central buying. It should be noted that some of the advantages and disadvantages of central merchandising, from the independent's point of view, are common to the whole concept of central buying.

In spite of the fact that there is a strong case for the central merchandising of fashion goods, independent department stores associated by means of a resident buying office have been successful only with budget dresses where styling factors are less subtle and changes in demand are less unpredictable than in higher-priced garments or in separates and coordinates.

Generally, store buyers have resisted any diminution of their authority and both they and their superiors have supported the concept that buyers who are on the selling floor for a considerable portion of their working hours can be better selectors of the goods their customers want.

The Warehouse and Requisition Plan

This is a central buying procedure wherein store managers have little control over the composition of their assortments but do exercise control over depth by assuming responsibility for requisitioning fill-ins from a warehouse stock. The method is commonly used for staple goods or lines that require the stocking of wide varieties of goods in steady demand. Grocery and drug chains provide good examples of this plan. They find it economical to buy in large quantities and to store the goods in a central warehouse (or in area warehouses). Stores are provided with checklists and are required to compare their stock against these lists at stated intervals. Store manager's are responsible for ordering enough of each item to carry them safely through the next checking period and subsequent delivery time. If the store is large enough, the work may be assigned to stock or salespeople or to department managers.

The completed checklist then becomes a requisition and is sent to the warehouse. The central buyer treats the warehouse as one big store (or as a single "benevolent wholesaler") and is responsible for maintaining a safe level of inventory to fill promptly the incoming requisitions. Reports of selling activity by the warehouse are the data for anticipating future sales.

The warehousing plan is also used for some imported goods when the needs of each store cannot be determined in advance and for lots in short supply that would not be available from a manufacturer under the listing system described below.

Figure 2–5 illustrates the kind of form used to carry out and report on this cycle of activities. Some forms require that the store list its stock as well as its

FIGURE 2–5 Warehouse requisition form. A store manager enters on the stub at the extreme right the amount of each item to be reordered and sends the stub to the warehouse weekly. A similar form may be used for the Price Agreement Plan

DEPT. MEDICINE STAMFORD WAREHOUSE | STORE NO. | STORE NO. | STORE NO. | STORE NO.

PAGE NO. 6 USE ONLY DURING PERIOD SHOWN 12/18–01/21

DESCRIPTION PACK	COST	RETAIL	RATING	F. TRADE	FED TAX	STORE RECORD 5	4	3	2	1	ORDER 4 CODE	QTY	ORDER 3 CODE	QTY	ORDER 2 CODE	QTY	ORDER 1 CODE	QTY
PABLUM MIX CEREAL	.38	16 OZ .43	3								04289		04289		04289		04289	
S.M.A. LIQ	.18	12 OZ .27	1	X							04296		04296		04296		04296	
S.M.A. POWDER	.80	1 LB 1.03	3	X							04298		04298		04298		04298	
SIMILAC LIQUID	.20	13 OZ .27	1								04299		04299		04299		04299	
SIMILAC LIQUID W/IRON	.20	13OZ .27	1								04301		04301		04301		04301	
SIMILAC POWD 16OZ	.77	.99	1	X							04300		04300		04300		04300	
SIMILAC POWDER W/IRON	.77	16OZ .99	1								04302		04302		04302		04302	
SOBEE LIQ 15 1/2OZ	.37	.49*	1	X							04291		04291		[illegible]		04291	
J&J BABY OIL 2OZ	.20	.37*	2	X							04341		04341		04341		04341	
J&J BABY OIL	.33	5 OZ .59*	1	X							04342		04342		04342		04342	

NOTE: * IN RETAIL COLUMN INDICATES CHANGE IN RETAIL PRICE X = FAIR TRADE ITEM
F IN COST COLUMN INDICATES FREE GOODS INCLUDED IN COST B = FEDERAL EXCISE TAX ITEM
WHERE EVER POSSIBLE ORDER IN MULTIPLE PACKS AS INDICATED–COST AND RETAIL PRICE ARE CURRENT AT PUBLICATION SUBJECT TO CHANGE

FORM 228 - 8-59 REV 1

order quantities. The information can then be used for analyzing the judgment factors used and in helping to improve them, either for safer service levels or for better stockturn in the stores. The store manager may order what appears on the checklist but may be permitted to omit some items if the items are not advertised specials. Some chains on the warehouse requisition plan do permit store managers to order certain other merchandise. Buyers may set up an arrangement with a local wholesaler to service stores on low-value items that are not economical to warehouse or that supply demands peculiar to a local area.

The Price Agreement Plan (Listing System)

Under this plan, the central buyers provide the store managers with lists of approved resources and of the particular items carried by each so that the store may order directly from the resources. The plan is used by limited-price variety chains and by the general-merchandise chains, such as J. C. Penney, for much of their staple and semistaple requirements. For a great deal of the merchandise of this type, it is unnecessary to assume the cost of warehousing, because many vendors are willing to provide completed goods in their inventories ready for prompt shipment when called for by the stores. Goods may be shipped directly to the stores ordering them or to the chain's distribution point to be consolidated with all other purchases destined for each store. These stores are large enough to be administered by store managers who can control their own inventories, at least for the relatively staple goods they carry.

Buying Arrangements

Central buyers make the buying arrangements. They select the resources and the specific items their stores may stock, many made according to their own specifications for private branding. They negotiate the cost prices and terms of sale, free-on-board (F.O.B.) points, and freight allowances; and they determine transportation routes and methods of shipment. Central buyers may have to place firm orders for the quantities they are reasonably sure their stores will order during the season. They often provide vendors with listings that simply describe the goods with agreed price and shipping instructions, with no specifications of quantities. The volume of many manufacturers is so large that they are willing to commit themselves to certain prices and terms on a basis of estimated potential, with no agreement as to the quantity that will be ordered from the stores during the season.

Vendors who are asked to make up goods according to the specifications of the central office for private branding, whether staple or promotional goods, are loathe to proceed unless the central buyer places a firm order before the stores have had a chance to react to the listing. The central buyer is then forced to gamble to an extent. The order should be large enough to meet the needs of the stores and yet not so large as to present a serious risk of markdowns. To avoid over-buying, the central buyer attempts to prevail on the vendor to provide a substantial "back-up" stock, for which no firm commitment is made, often equal to the original order. This is not always possible. If commitments are not backed up by store orders, the central buyer may have to reprice to make the goods more attractive. He or she is thus accountable for the profit margins generated by his or her purchases. Obviously, the listing pages sent to the stores must be persuasive. The buyer must present the selling virtues of his or her selections so that stores may be induced to use and promote the items and have ammunition for cogent promotion.

Large chains are increasingly careful that all goods listed, or centrally purchased, adhere to quality standards and specifications set and that reorders are filled (shipped) promptly as agreed. Delinquents are dropped from the preferred list. In the case of private brands, the same product is often made up for the chain by a number of different manufacturers in different parts of the country. Should there be a breakdown at one location, a vendor at another location can give prompt attention to an order from any of the stores.

The smaller stores in some chains that rely on the listing system do not buy enough to warrant direct ordering from manufacturers. To take care of this, a warehouse may be set up to service them. The warehouse functions just like a large store, ordering goods from manufacturers by means of the standard listings. In turn, it fills requisitions from smaller stores. These are allowed to buy direct, however, when their orders equal the minimum quantities agreed upon for direct order.

The price agreement system may be used for special promotional purchases as well as for staple stock. If the central office finds an unusual opportunity in the market that presents excellent promotional opportunities, it suggests that the store order the goods and even recommends a model assortment adjusted to store size. Although the store manager does not have to follow the distribution suggested, it serves as a guide in placing an order.

The Responsibilities of Central Buyers and Store Managers

The central buyer provides the store managers with a packet of loose-leaf sheets on which the approved styles and lot numbers are listed with all the information for ordering and selling each item: vendor name and address, point of shipment if different, method of shipment, F.O.B. point, description of the item often accompanied by an illustration, cost price in buying units, retail price in selling units, and markup percentage. Guidance on how to display the item may also be provided. These comprise the entire market from which the stores may select their requirements.[8]

Central buyers are responsible for keeping the store lists up to date. They add new items and resources and cancel old ones, where desirable. Although they set original retail prices, they usually leave the store managers free to take markdowns at their own discretion, except for company-required markdowns caused usually by a wholesale price break. In rare instances, central buyers may negotiate to transfer certain items from one store to another.

Central buyers give the store managers considerable guidance as to which items to select from the listing sheets. This is based largely on the size of the store and the relative importance of staple as contrasted with fashion stocks. The offer of promotional goods to the stores needs to be accompanied by a leaflet explaining the nature of the promotional opportunity and suggesting desirable assortments for large and small units and retail prices. The leaflet may contain a sketch of an ideal display counter for the merchandise and present detailed instructions as to the measurements of the fixture to be used and its best location.

Central buyers sometimes require copies of all orders by the stores directed to vendors to be forwarded to the central office so that shipments may be expedited, an order rerouted to another resource if the vendor listed is not now in a position to ship, or when a superior substitute is available elsewhere. But some large chains feel that they do not require the receipt or order copies, that the gains do not offset the expense. They get their knowledge of store response from the listed vendors, who inform them of the orders they receive from each store. Thus central buyers can appraise store response and evaluate the acceptance of the listed items. There is sometimes a tendency for store managers to attempt to buy from vendors not listed or to buy items not listed from vendors who have other products listed. Local resources may be able to make quicker delivery, or the store manager may simply have a preference for another source. Permission to make exceptions is not freely given, because the centrally available goods are nearly always a better value and because future relationships with the vendor do not materialize if store managers fail to cooperate.

For many goods that meet the demands of a mass market similar to what is carried by the national general-merchandise chains, this listing plan proves satisfactory. It develops a feeling of responsibility on the part of store managers and reduces the expenses of central warehousing and of maintaining detailed records of each store at headquarters—a necessity under the central merchandising plan.

[8]The lists may include new items that are not subject to order by the stores but are distributed by the central buyer under an opening stock or automatic open-to-buy discussed later in this chapter.

Objections to the listing plan are that (1) the vendor may not provide enough merchandise to fill promptly orders that flow in from the stores, (2) the store managers are often slow to react to new and promotional offerings listed, leading to lost opportunities and disappointment when they finally get around to the ordering, and (3) store managers may lack the expertise to maintain balanced stocks.

Opening Stock Distribution Plan

Chains that depend primarily on the listing system of central buying for staple and semistaple goods find it necessary to supplement the system with a plan that gives the central buyer greater authority for making store commitments for fashion and semifashion goods. This may be the automatic open-to-buy plan, discussed in the following subsection, or a combination of this and a plan that permits the central buyer to control the initial shipment of all new items that flow to the stores. In a major chain, this plan functions as follows:

1. Two or four times a year, in advance of each selling season, the central buyer of each department, with the approval of the merchandise manager, selects the style or lot numbers that he or she believes should be represented in the stores. The styles are arranged according to their probable sales importance. This list includes both continuing numbers (those already carried in store stocks) and new numbers that are now being made available by the chain's vendors.
2. Next the like-selling classifications, or departments, in the stores are grouped into volume categories—such as (a) $5000 of sales during the coming 6-month season, (b) $10,000 of sales and so on up perhaps to $100,000—and for each size category, an opening stock is planned in dollars and as a percentage of total expected season requirements. Thus, for the (b) category, with season sales of $10,000, the opening stock may be set at 30%, or $3000.
3. The styles listed as in (1) are assigned to each store-size category. The smaller categories are assigned only a few of the top style or lot numbers, and the larger the category, the greater the number of styles provided for. For each category, opening stocks in both units and dollars are set for each of the styles provided for in that category in order to provide adequate depth. The totals in each category are checked and adjusted against a dollar opening stock figure planned in (2) for the entire category.

It is the responsibility of the department managers in each store to control the opening stock set for each basic and reorder style by means of direct orders to the vendors for fill-ins. But the opening stocks set for the new and fashion styles are the responsibility of the central buyers. They consolidate the opening stock requirements of each new item for all the stores and have the vendors specify upon shipment what portion is destined for each store.

The goods are shipped to the central distribution point for forwarding. The vendors are informed of the total quantities that are likely to be demanded by the stores before the season is over in order to provide back-up stock as the reorders flow in directly from the stores. As indicated earlier, firm commitments for the seasons requirements are made when necessary.

Thus the stores are provided opening stocks for each new item each season, and the stores' department managers take over from there. Any new items that the buyer believes should be added after the opening distributions have been made are handled by the automatic open-to-buy plan.

Automatic Open-to-Buy

A plan that may be used in conjunction with the opening stock distribution plan is based on dollar appropriations (open-to-buy figures) that each department in each store assigns to the central buyer for a 3-month, 6-month, or 1-year period.

For example, a store department's manager may estimate 6-months purchase requirements of $50,000 and decide to allow 10% of this to the central buyer for new items to be received during the season. When the buyer orders goods against this open-to-buy, he or she depends on both market offerings and new styles he or she has helped to develop. The ordering is usually completed well in advance of the end of the season so that the store has perhaps 45 days left in the season in which to dispose of the last shipment or to find some other way to fill gaps in the stock that may occur.

This plan may be used only for new style numbers that become available after opening stock distributions are made, or in some organizations it may be the method of determining the dollar value of all new buying, which is at the discretion of the central buyer.

The delegation of a considerable portion of the open-to-buy to the central buyer without keeping him or her informed of each store's stock condition at all times (an expensive process) is likely to lead to an unbalanced stock assortment. Even though the buyer feeds in only new styles, the proper balance of sales by classification, price line, color, and type may not be maintained, because it is very difficult to coordinate the buying of two people far apart with overlapping responsibilities. If the plan is used for all new-item buying, the buyer needs a copy of each store's department buying plan and an up-to-date inventory assortment report. If used only for new items bought between purchases made by means of opening stock distributions, it is not likely to distort assortments seriously.

Branch-Store Organization for Buying

When department stores and large specialty stores began to set up branches, they attempted to treat them simply as offshoots of the main store and held buyers responsible for the total merchandising of their departments even though segments were in different geographic locations. They were expected to visit each branch once or twice a week, carrying out their continuing responsibilities with an assistant in each branch. In fact, the practice still prevails as stores of less than giant size open correspondingly small branches that cannot support a complete operating organization of their own.

But other solutions became necessary as the number of branches multiplied, as their size began to rival—and in some cases even to exceed—the size of the so-called "flagship" stores, and as their locations spread toward and beyond the peripheries of the original trading area. This last factor, together with the shifting character of demographic and psychographic population factors, chipped away at the need for homogeneity in the merchandise assortment and even in the total image among the member stores of a branch-store system. Previously diverse demands were handled by the visiting central buyers and their on-site assistants. Then the increasingly large branches could afford high-salaried organizations of their own—organizations that were given more and more autonomy in merchandising and promoting their stores.[9]

The growing, widely dispersed branches of the modern branch-store system can afford the best of several worlds of organization for buying: from highly centralized to virtually autonomously operated units, from the warehouse and requisition system to the price agreement system, and from straight chain-store distribution to selective cooperative efforts (with the consent of the governed) like those in use by resident buying offices and the voluntary cooperatives of grocery and hardware retailing. Furthermore, a single store may be merchandised by more than one method, suited to the differing requirements of different lines of merchandise.

Examples of Branch-Store Organization of the Buying Function

1. One large parent store with branches in three western states is completely centrally merchandised. The central buyer receives weekly sales and inventory reports from each branch for each stock-keeping unit (SKU) and assumes the responsibility for all reorders as well as all orders for new goods. Basic stocks appearing on approved lists of vendors may be reordered by clericals rather than by the buyers themselves. Branch managers are not notified when multistore orders are placed. Nearly everything, including bulk goods, is received at the distribution center near the parent store and distributed from

[9]*Stores*, the magazine of the National Retail Merchants Association, publishes annually a listing of "Typical Branch Store Sales." The August 1973 issue included estimates of 1972 sales for 99 selected branches. Of these, 57 were in the $10- to $20-million range and 10 were over $20 million. No wonder, then, that many of these stores were headed by a corporate vice president, managing a typical department store organization. It is interesting, too, that of the remaining stores in the list, nearly all were in the $5- to $10-million range.

there. The only goods sent by vendors directly to the branches are those procured from local resources, such as candy and foods. But the orders for these are also placed by the central buyers.

2. A major branch system in the East, renowned for exclusive merchandise, gives the department managers in the branches somewhat more control over reorders. Unit sales reports are sent in daily from the branches to headquarters either by means of price ticket stubs or electronically from point of sale recorders. The latter will become the general procedure. Book inventories are centrally calculated automatically for each SKU so that the central buyers have up-to-date data for reordering purposes. However, most of the reordering is done by the various branch department managers who send copies of their orders to the central office. Thus the central buyer has information to check on what the department managers are doing.

   The purchase of new merchandise is the central buyer's responsibility. He or she has a copy of the merchandise plan for each store that indicates how much merchandise in dollars (and in many cases, in units) is to be received each month in each department or classification. The buyer determines the timing of orders required to get the amount of goods specified into the stores in each month. For example, one store's planned purchases in one classification may be $50,000 for March. The buyer starts ordering this merchandise in November, alloting perhaps 10% of March requirements for November ordering, 40% for December, 30% for January, 15% for February, and 5% for March itself (late March requirements). The records available to the buyer indicate how much has already been ordered (both new and reorder merchandiser), and he or she keeps ordering within the open-to-order available.

   New merchandise shipments are made by the vendors to a consolidator who acts as a central distribution point rather than directly to the branches in order to keep down transportation costs, but each branch's requirements are segregated by the vendors so that daily forwarding to the branches is facilitated.

   Merchandise checking and ticketing is generally done in the branches, but hanger goods (mostly ready-to-wear) are shipped to the consolidator, who also marks and tickets the merchandise.

   Staple merchandise subject to periodic reorder such as cosmetics, stationery, lamp shades, housewares, and china are handled by means of the listing system already described. Thus the control of the store inventories in these lines is the responsibility of the department managers.

   Some merchandise, especially furniture, china, glassware, and housewares, is warehoused by the central buyers. Each store carries a minimum floor stock and has a record of what is available in the warehouse. Deliveries to customers are generally made from the warehouse, not from the branches.

Question of the Distribution Point (Where Goods Are Checked and Marked)

Under any one of the central buying plans, whether used by a chain or a branch system, goods may be shipped by the vendor either to the stores directly or to a central distribution point maintained by the group. This differs from the warehouse in that goods are not normally held there awaiting orders from the store. Rather, they may be checked for quantity and quality, price marked, sorted by store, and then shipped to each store. The chief advantages of maintaining such a distribution point are:

1. The inspection of goods before shipment to the stores facilitates the prompt detection of faulty goods and failure to follow specifications.
2. The price marking of the goods can be better controlled and performed at less expense than in the stores.
3. Decision as to how much of each purchase to distribute to each store can be based on the current inventory requirements in each store at the time of shipment rather than on estimated requirements at the time the order was placed, weeks or even months before.
4. A steady flow of merchandise to each store can be provided. A part of a shipment can be retained at the distribution point until sales information from the stores determines just where additional supply is needed, at once.

Nevertheless, many central offices have not set up distribution points. They may be more expensive than having the vendors ship direct. Store managements can be trained to mark goods properly, or the vendor may be prevailed upon to attach tickets. Inspections can be made on the vendors' premises just before shipment, and it is possible to give the vendor distributions when the goods are ready for shipment rather than when ordered. And vendors may agree to carry back-up stocks ready for quick shipment to the stores as needed.

DISCUSSION QUESTIONS

1. Criticize the organization chart of the merchandising division shown in Figure 2–2. What changes would you suggest?
2. Which would be more efficient: (a) to set up divisional unit control bureaus, attached to each divisional merchandise manager's office, (b) to set up a central unit control bureau, or (c) to provide separate unit control clericals attached to each buyer's office?
3. Would it be more productive to send out regular salespeople on scheduled comparison shopping trips than to set up a distinct comparison bureau with a staff of shoppers?
4. Which of the advantages for central merchandising given in the text are of major importance in improving a store's merchandise offerings?
5. Are the disadvantages of central merchandising serious enough to prevent its spread?
6. Which of the central buying plans gives the greatest freedom to store and department managers?
7. How can a central buyer make intelligent estimates of the seasonal sales

of new and continuing items in a store falling into a particular sales volume classification?

8. Is the automatic open-to-buy plan likely to lead to unbalanced stocks if the central buyer orders new items that the store managers reorder?
9. Which of the five central buying plans would you recommend (a) for a chain of similar stores, and (b) for a department-store branch system, in the case of each of the following lines: (i) handbags, (ii) women's suits, (iii) men's suits, (iv) housewares, (v) drugs, (vi) underwear, (vii) hosiery, (viii) notions, (ix) bed sheets, (x) women's shoes?
10. If quick response to customer demand is the cornerstone of successful retailing, how can central buyers, removed from direct customer contact, make better merchandise selections than can store department managers, or can't they?
11. What is likely to become the usual organization of the buying function in branch-store systems?

chapter 3

Resident Buying and Other Associated Buying Activities

THE RESIDENT BUYING FUNCTION

Resident buyers[1] act as assistants and advisers to store buyers as distinct from central buyers. In essence, the resident buying office functions as a staff bureau located not on the premises but in some major wholesale market. Although many offices engage in wholesaling and central buying activities for certain categories of merchandise, buying for stores is usually done only by specific authority of the store buyers. It will be seen, however, that resident buyers, by tangible and intangible means, enable their clients to pool purchasing power and know-how so that they obtain procurement and promotion advantages beyond their capacity as individuals.

Reasons for Development

The resident buying office is an outgrowth of the need of all stores, large and small, to be represented in the market centers of the country. Typically, resident buyers serve independent department and specialty stores, mostly in the $1 to $10 million category, many located in the hundreds of smaller trading areas of the nation. However, a number of independent, smaller and middle-size specialty shops are depending instead on one of the market reporting services such as the Retail News Bureau or the Retail Reporting

[1]They are also known as "purchasing agents" in the hardware field and as "commissionaires" in foreign buying operations.

Bureau (both with headquarters in New York City) for information about new items and emerging new resources in the major markets of the country. See Chapter 6 for an example of the information provided to store subscribers. The apparel shops try to avoid direct conflict with the big distributors and try to carry styles that are clearly different. Some shops arrange with a former store buyer, now residing in the market city, to select specials on the market for individual customers. A telephone call to this person is sufficient to describe the particular merchandise sought by the store buyer. Many wholesalers also use resident buying offices in spite of the fact that they offer overlapping services to retailers.

Resident buyers are important to the independent merchants they serve for six basic reasons:

1. The increasing importance of fashion in consumer goods as a whole and the rapidity of fashion change have made it imperative to maintain representatives in major markets. Decentralization of markets has caused the growth of resident offices in cities like Los Angeles, Atlanta, Chicago, Dallas, and Miami, although concentration is still prevalent in New York City.
2. Through maintenance of vendor contact in these markets, and through exertion of centralized power on vendors, resident buyers have been able to generate a steadier flow of goods into their member stores.
3. Merchandise costs are reduced in many instances by making it possible for the individual store to buy smaller quantities directly from manufacturers, rather than through wholesalers, by means of group purchases and by providing a more thorough shopping of the market for lowest prices.
4. Another way in which market representation reduces costs is by reducing the time and travel costs that accrue from more frequent and more extended market trips by store buyers.
5. Perhaps more important than the cost savings is the opportunity the resident office provides to engage in specification buying, private branding, and obtaining exclusive merchandise—beyond the capacities of many clients operating as unassociated individuals.
6. The resident buying office brings stores together for research projects, promotional activities, exchange of information (particularly performance data), and general pooling of know-how. Formerly, each store regarded its methods of operation and statistical results as its own private affair, but most have now come to realize that "he who gives, gets."

TYPES OF RESIDENT BUYING OFFICES

Resident buying offices may be classified as follows:

1. Independent offices.
   (a) Salaried (or paid or fee) offices.
   (b) Merchandise brokers.[2]

[2]Technically, these are not resident buying offices, as the text explains.

2. Store-owned offices.
   (a) Private offices (individual-store offices).
   (b) Associated (cooperative) offices.
   (c) Syndicate offices.

The independent resident buying office actively seeks stores as paying clients. The store-owned office is entirely owned by the store or stores it represents and works for them alone.[3]

Salaried Offices

The salaried offices receive their remuneration directly from the stores they represent and not from the manufacturers from whom they buy or to whom they bring store orders. They usually enter into annual contracts with stores to provide service in exchange for a stipulated annual fee or "salary." The fees of a salaried buying office vary with sales volume of the stores and service required and are subject to negotiation. They approximate 3/10 of 1% of store sales with a minimum of about $200 a month. A $2-million store would pay about $500 a month or $6000 a year, and a $20-million store would pay relatively less percentage-wise—about $4500 a month. If some of the store's departments, such as appliances, require no market assistance, the fee may be adjusted to the volume of the departments serviced. Although the cost is relatively high for a small store, many of these stores specialize in apparel where market representation is almost essential. Besides, the amount of work required to service a store does not decrease proportionately with reduction in size. The savings on one deal a month in which the small store participates may more than offset the fee.

Although American stores are nearly always charged a fee by the American buying offices, foreign stores represented are charged a commission on their net cost purchases. This is similar to the practice of the foreign commissionaire that charges American stores a commission, not a fee.

[3]In 1974 there were over 230 resident buying offices of the fee (salaried) type in New York City, only a few (3 or 4) associated offices, and a few private offices. There were about 85 merchandise brokers and over 70 chain-store offices, including a few of the syndicate type.

Compared with 1961, the number of fee buyers has increased from 196, but the number of merchandise brokers has declined from 150. Chain-store offices have also declined in number from 200, probably owing to consolidations.

The fee office with the largest number of stores is probably the Independent Retailers Syndicate, with approximately 350 stores. The Mutual Buying Syndicate enjoys one of the largest volume of sales. The largest merchandise broker is the Apparel Alliance with approximately 374 stores. But the largest volume is done by certain fee and associated buying offices that represent very large stores. The Associated Merchandising Corporation may handle the largest volume.

Data compiled from *1975 Sheldon's Retail and Phelon's Resident Buyers* and *1961 Phelon's Resident Buyers,* Union Square, New York City.

Merchandise Brokers[4]

The merchandise brokers, once called "commission buying offices," receive their remuneration from manufacturers in the form of a percentage of the store orders they bring to each. Because they are representatives of a group of manufacturers, mostly in the fashion apparel trades, they are not really resident buyers, but they do function in many ways like a resident buyer. For the small specialty shop, unable or unwilling to pay a set fee to a resident buyer, they act as a satisfactory substitute. Many of their customers have sales of $1 million and less. Service contracts are not made with the stores because the stores are not principals. These brokers differ from the typical seller's broker in that they represent many manufacturers in the same field, who are often in direct competition with one another. The brokers function as a cooperative selling device for a group of competing manufacturers. Because they extend the market to small outlying customers whom the manufacturers cannot readily contact with their own salespeople, many manufacturers find it worthwhile to pay them commissions. Although not standard, these are usually 3 to 5 percent of the net price paid by the store. The broker may introduce the store buyer to a manufacturer who has what he or she believes to be the best merchandise for the buyer's requirements, or the broker may be given authority by the out-of-town buyer to make a selection of resource and styles.

From the merchant's point of view, there is a question of conflict of interest, because brokers are not their employees and not even their agents.

As indicated in footnote 3, merchandise brokers in the apparel field are decreasing in number and are much less important than they were some years ago. They are the victims of mergers and consolidations of both retailers and manufacturers that can provide close market contacts without the use of intermediaries.

Private Offices

There is the least conflict of interest where a store or a group of stores owns its buying office, but because of the investment involved and the limited opportunity to exchange information among a group of noncompeting stores, not many have been formed. Some private offices represent one "out-of-town" store, most likely a high-class specialty store. These are clearly staff bureaus physically located in the market, not in the store. Some stores maintain private offices on the premises of an independent or associated

[4]As the term *merchandise brokers* is used here, it does not include the majority of brokers in the field of marketing who bring buyers and sellers together, collecting a commission on consummated transactions from either the buyer or the seller.

office. Thus they have access to all the services of the larger office and yet maintain in the market a representative who is on their own payroll and is responsible directly to them.

Associated Offices

These are owned and managed jointly by a group of independent stores. They are often called *cooperative offices.* The various expenses of these offices are distributed to the store owners in accordance with their size and with the amount of service they require. This type of office is relatively more expensive than the salaried office, and it is difficult to organize, difficult to join, and difficult to leave. In general, it stresses exchange of merchandise information among the member stores. There is a high degree of homogeneity among the member stores leading to mutual trust and willingness to exchange confidential data and to assist one another in all phases of merchandising, publicity, store management, and control. There are only a few associated offices in New York. The chief ones are the Associated Merchandising Corporation and its affiliate, the Retail Research Association, with 41 large department store members 11 of which are abroad; Frederick Atkins, Inc., with 48 department stores, and the Specialty Stores Association, with 19 women's apparel stores. Although they are few in number, the total sales volume of the stores in these groups is very large, with most of the stores operating branches.

Syndicate Offices

Although most chains have central buyers rather than resident buyers, some ownership groups of stores, as already noted, maintain buyers in the stores and resident buyers in the market. The buying office of such an organization functions in much the same manner as an associated buying office. It is in a more dominant position, however, being able to dictate to the stores controlled, whereas the associated office has to cater to the stores that control it jointly. The syndicate office can insist that the stores be merchandised in conformance with fixed policies and that its rules be carried out. The associated office may suggest standards and procedures but cannot force a store in the group to adopt them.

SERVICES OF RESIDENT BUYING OFFICES

The services performed by a resident buying office are of three broad types: buying, promotion, and research. The first includes assistance to the store buyers in obtaining merchandise, the second, aids in selling the merchandise, and the third, the conduct of interstore and market investigations.

Buying Service

The buying service may be subdivided into: (1) giving buying assistance to individual stores, both when the buyers are at home and when in the market; (2) reporting market information; (3) cooperative (group) buying of staples and fashions; (4) wholesaling, largely of staples; and (5) central buying, largely of popularly priced dresses.

Individual Assistance to Buyers at Home

When the buyers are in the stores, the resident buying office performs the following functions:

1. Answers requests for information on such matters as
   (a) The supply condition of the market.
   (b) Prices and styles available.
   (c) Location of new resources.
2. Places orders upon request.
   (a) *Open orders.* The store buyer specifies the type, price, and quantity of goods desired and leaves the selection of the resource and specific styles to the resident buyer's judgment.
   (b) *Special orders.* A store's customer may want a particular item that the store does not stock and may ask the resident buyer to obtain it.
   (c) *Reorders.* These are orders sent to vendors via the resident buying office so that any changes in prices or terms may be noted on the order, and to make it possible for the resident buyer to suggest a better resource.
   (d) *Sample orders.* Sometimes resident buyers are given authority to order vendors to send samples of new merchandise to the stores. Although this practice has advantages, there is some danger that too many samples will be sent and that they may not fit into the store's stock.
   (e) *Distribution.* In order to make it possible for stores to take advantage of special market offerings, for which quick commitments are necessary, some of the store buyers assign a portion of their open-to-buy allotments to their resident representatives, or they indicate the quantity that may be ordered for the store's account without prior approval. In making the distribution of a special offering, the resident buyer allots the styles to those stores that are most likely to sell them profitably.
3. Keeps on the lookout for merchandise a buyer may find of interest, such as new products and new styles; or the resident buyer may take an option on a job lot and wire or phone the buyer to ask whether he or she wants to go through with the deal; or the buyer may help develop lots for special sales.
4. Follows up and checks on deliveries. Some offices receive a copy of each

store's order for ready-to-wear and prod the vendor just before shipping date. In other offices, orders are followed up only on request.

5. Handles adjustments and complaints. Buyers who wish to return or exchange merchandise, cancel orders, or obtain allowances for vendor's failures to carry out contractual obligations find it wise to deal through their resident buyers rather than to depend on correspondence.
6. Maintains foreign connections. Some of the leading offices have foreign branches, and others have permanent arrangements with commissionaires to give service to all member stores. Chapter 15 discusses this matter in detail.

Assistance to Buyers in the Market

When the store buyers are going to market or are in the market, the resident buying office is equipped to perform the following services:

1. Prepare for the buyer's visit.
   (a) Locate merchandise in advance, based on receipt of a copy of the buying plan, and obtain the most favorable terms and service.
   (b) Survey particular lines in advance, on request.
   (c) Publish buyer's arrivals in advance in newspapers in the market city and arrange appointments with sales personnel at the office or vendors' showrooms.
2. Provide office space, service, and sample rooms (where the buyers can look at merchandise brought to the office by sales representatives) and reception rooms where they can meet those who do not bring samples.
3. Maintain seasonal displays of samples. A few offices maintain sample assortments of certain goods, such as foreign merchandise, where it is difficult to get to vendors' showrooms, and also of articles that are to be featured in a Christmas or other seasonal catalog that is centrally prepared for all stores that want to participate in the promotion.
4. Accompany buyers to market on request.
5. Occasionally act in the capacity of a merchandise manager. When a store buyer is in the market while the merchant or all the store's divisional merchandise managers are at home, the merchant may give the merchandising head of the office the authority to countersign the buyer's orders.
6. Provide personal service for buyers. The office helps buyers to find suitable hotel accommodations and helps them to make reservations.
7. Occasionally guarantee or vouch for the credit standing of stores they represent. The fact that a store is a member of a well-known office is likely to lead to a willingness on the part of the vendor to grant it favorable credit terms.

Concessions in Price and Service

A major buying service rendered by many offices, when buyers are either at home or in the market, is obtaining lower prices and/or better services for their accounts than the store buyers could obtain directly. Many of these deals are the result of group, central, and wholesaling activities, but membership in an office often brings concessions. This is sometimes called *intangible group buying,* a practice hedged by legal limitations.

When a number of stores are associated in a buying organization, they may obtain buying power in the market, even though they buy independently. Offices may arrange with certain vendors to (1) grant special prices on all orders coming from their members, (2) make quick deliveries by producing goods in anticipation of orders or by agreeing to ship merchandise to member stores first whenever a new style is produced and to honor reorders especially during times of high demand, (3) confine certain styles for sale only to members of the buying office, (4) produce exclusive merchandise according to the specifications drawn up by the store buyers themselves, and (5) assist the stores in promoting the merchandise to customers by such means as advertising allowances.

In the past, resident buying offices doubtlessly have obtained substantial price concessions for their clients, but under the Robinson-Patman Act of 1936, the concessions legally obtainable by stores, when they order through a buying office, are limited to demonstrable savings in costs to the seller growing out of quantities sold or special method of sale.

Reporting Market Information

In addition to the assistance a buying office renders each store separately, it undertakes the important function of keeping all its stores informed of market developments through periodic and special reports. Reports may be classified as follows:

1. Beginning-of-the-season fashion forecasts that report style, color, and fabric trends of the new season.
2. New-and-special-item bulletins that report new market offerings that are of unusual interest (see Figure 3–1).
3. Off-price bulletins that report manufacturers' close-outs and job lots.
4. Reorder bulletins that report fast-sellers reordered in various member stores.
5. Store shopping surveys that report what is selling in leading department stores.
6. Market and economic trend surveys that report major economic developments in specific markets of significance to member stores.
7. Promotion bulletins that list items for special seasonal sales.
8. Special booklets on special subjects, such as beach wear, bridal wear, or back-to-school clothes.
9. Catalogs of outstanding market offerings. The market catalogs deserve special mention, because they provide a market of selected resources that can supply most of a store's needs in staple lines. For example, the resident buyer of housewares in one large office prepared a mimeographed catalog covering over 1200 resources and listing major items and prices available from each.
10. Fashion shows.

FIGURE 3–1 A market report

the market place

ATT: MDSE. MGR., BUYER;
BUDGET JR. SPORTSWEAR

JEAN-O-GRAMS

by It's a Way of Life

Today's fastest growing fad is the Press-on Initial or Names that go on every Sportswear item.

Now...Initials on Jeans - Prewashed Indigo Denim with an attached package of 32 alphabet initials to iron-on the big back pockets or wherever strikes your fancy.

The above sketched counter card or rack sign is included in every shipment for your promotional aid, plus an extra emergency packet of initials.

BULL. NO.: 5008Y (See reverse side)

FELIX LILIENTHAL & CO., INC.

- 2 -

JEAN-O-GRAMS

#3001 Prewashed Indigo Denim - 2 back pockets - 24" leg....Initial Bag attached.

COLORS:	Indigo Blue
SIZES:	5-15
COST:	$7.00 each
PACKED:	2-2-3-2-2-1 to dz.
MIN.:	2 dozen

RESOURCE:	It's A Way Of Life
TERMS:	Net 10 EOM
DELIV:	A/R - 8/25
FOB:	New York
MDSE. MGR.:	Roseanne Berkowitz
BUYER:	Annette Rubinstein
BULL. NO.:	5008Y
DATE:	7/13/76

Fashion Shows For Store Buyers

A novel form of reporting service, occasionally employed, is a fashion show conducted at a time when most of the store buyers of the clothing lines involved are likely to be in the market. The office may rent a ballroom of a hotel for such a presentation to their store buyers. The show may be supplemented by talks and panel discussions on market conditions and on the merchandising of the lines presented. Shows are not limited to dresses and coats. They may feature millinery, shoes, or undergarments. Showings of home-furnishings lines are also held.

Group Buying

Almost from the beginnings of resident buying, shortly after World War I, it was apparent that the services of the office need not be limited to assisting individual store buyers in their market contacts. They could be brought together to buy as a group. Of course, this was nothing more than the extension of the buying club, where a group of merchants in a community, such as grocers or druggists, agreed to buy together certain articles that all carried in order to procure better prices and service.

Through their buying offices, department and specialty stores have elaborated on this idea by arranging for store or department buyers to meet for the purpose of selecting items largely in the staple and semifashion categories—that all are willing to order and often to sell under a common brand name. The purpose is not only to get lower prices but also to ensure high standards of quality, to obtain exclusive features, to obtain goods more quickly, and to facilitate reordering programs. At times, personal meetings are dispensed with, and the buyers are sent samples or illustrations of the styles proposed by the resident buyer; the store buyer then communicates the decision by mail, phone, or wire.

If it is inconvenient for all the member buyers to meet, they sometimes appoint a committee from their own number to buy for the group certain previously agreed upon types of merchandise. The committee is authorized to decide on individual styles, and, possibly, price. Committee buying is less cumbersome than the more usual type of meeting but is feasible only when buyers have full confidence in the committee's judgment.

Goods most commonly bought in this way are of the semistaple variety, such as men's white shirts; boys' furnishings; women's and children's underwear; blankets; draperies; housewares; and home furnishings. Often a price line known to be suitable to all the stores in the group is chosen in advance, and selections are limited to goods falling in that price range.

The group buying plan, along with private branding, has been used in connection with fashion apparel in the medium price ranges and for imports. After a resident buyer's trip abroad, store buyers meet to inspect the new styles and to determine which styles each store is prepared to order and how much. A consolidated order is then placed with delivery months ahead.

A separate corporation, affiliated with a resident buying office, has often been established to take title to a private brand name that may be applied to the purchases of the group and to give the group wholesaler status. The corporation also develops joint promotional and advertising plans for the group purchases at relatively low cost to the cooperating stores.

Advantages of Group Buying

The advantages to the store of group buying may be summarized:

1. Better selection of items, leading to greater sales volume, fewer markdowns, and larger profits.
   (a) Group judgment leads to obtaining more salable items than buyers could purchase individually.
   (b) Often items may be "created" by the resident buyer or by the buyers of the group. Specifications may be given to the manufacturer, covering not only the design, but materials and workmanship as well.
2. Better assortments. Manufacturers who deal directly with individual store buyers may insist on the right to ship certain standard color and size assortments that may not best meet the needs of the store. In the case of a group purchase, the stores involved have greater control over the assortments they are buying.
3. Styles selected may be "confined" to members of the group, leading to a reputation for exclusiveness and to less price competition. This can be done only if the order is large enough to make it worthwhile for the manufacturer to agree not to sell the style to competitors of any store in the group.
4. Quick availability.
   (a) In the case of fashion merchandise, the large-store group order can be put into production at once, with the result that stores will get the merchandise soon after order. Were orders placed individually, the manufacturer would wait until enough orders had accumulated to cut and make the garments, and the manufacturer might not even fill some orders at all, if he or she could not accumulate enough to make economical production possible.
   (b) In the case of staples or semifashion goods selected for private branding, the vendor may agree to carry a stock ready for immediate shipment to the stores as needed.
5. Lower cost, particularly in the case of staples bought in quantity but not necessarily for fashion goods, where much hand labor is involved.
6. Saving of department managers' time in the market. The steering committee does the leg work, and the assembled buyers can look over a great deal of merchandise in a short time.
7. Better promotion, growing out of seasonal planning, a brand name, central preparation of advertisements, and use of national magazine advertising. The manufacturer, too, many enter into a cooperative advertising arrangement or

propose mailing pieces to the stores to distribute to their customers. Group buying is also a major method of stimulating buyers to promote outstanding merchandise intensively.

8. Sometimes a higher average sale for the store. If group power is directed toward developing significant and observable selling features in items at or above best selling price lines, it may support up-trading plans.
9. Exchange of information. The meetings get the buyers and their merchandise managers acquainted so that they can exchange information on many common problems.

Some advantages are the result of pooled know-how, others of pooled purchasing power. These advantages parallel those of central buying in multiunit organizations.

Problems of Group Buying

Attempts to organize independent stores into groups that take united action is difficult and fraught with problems that have caused much discussion and concern in the trade. Much of the difficulty centers on the fact that individual buyers remain accountable for their total operation while being pressured into delegation of responsibilities outside of their complete control. Some of the problems may be itemized as follows:

1. The cost and effort involved in forming a group, assembling samples, holding extensive meetings and trying to get agreement in an atmosphere where every buyer thinks of his or her situation as unique. Equal attention to similar national brands available might be more productive.
2. The ever present possibility that the majority decision may not be suitable for some members of the group, yet they may be forced to "go along," partly because of national promotion plans.
3. The further possibility that the great promotional emphasis placed on the group purchases will cut in on the sale of high-priced merchandise bought individually.
4. The lack of mobility on a falling market. At such times, special but limited buying opportunities develop, often for distress merchandise. The group purchase, which is usually for goods still to be manufactured, is then not a bargain, and the buyer committed to the group feels that advantageous price opportunities elsewhere are being passed up.
5. Disturbance of the time-honored personal relationship between manufacturers' salespeople and individual buyers, the buyers learning to buy more objectively and becoming less dependent on pet resources. But such disturbance is probably a good thing.

Wholesaling by Resident Buying Office Subsidiaries

Although some group buying is conducted through special wholesale subsidiaries—partly because of the Federal Trade Commission's challenges of the legality of concessions to a buying group—the practice of wholesaling by resident buyers is limited to a few only. These open their wholesale divisions to all store buyers, not simply members of the resident office. One large associated office limits its wholesale offerings to special items of broad appeal that can be made available at very low prices rather than to complete assortments. Examples are towels, classic dresses, mens' short outer coats, certain kitchen appliances, pieces of glassware, and even bicycles.

Central Buying

A number of buying offices and other groups of independents have found the group buying method too cumbersome for fast-moving fashion goods, especially popular-priced dresses,[5] and have emulated the chains. They have prevailed upon member stores to turn over to a central "unit-control department" the merchandising of a certain price range, in dresses in particular. The store buyer becomes simply a department manager so far as this segment of the stock is concerned and is able to devote more time to promotion and to the purchase of other lines.

Equally importance is the development of private brands already discussed. Here, the member stores control their own stocks but reorder through the office's private-brand department. Goods are shipped from manufacturer directly to the stores.

Promotion Service of Buying Offices

Many resident buying offices have elaborate promotion departments to aid their stores in planning and executing promotional events. The central department draws up suggested advertising calendars some months ahead; it has illustrations prepared and copy written. Formerly, advertising mats were also prepared and made available to the stores. Today, many newspapers are printed by the offset method so that the office can prepare illustrations, that can be reproduced by the newspaper after the store's logo is inserted. Seasonal window and interior displays are also suggested. Consultations are held with each store's advertising and display managers. Special attention is given to the planning of semiannual promotions for centrally bought goods.

Mailing pieces for stores to distribute to their customers are also prepared. A number of offices issue excellent seasonal catalogs, especially for Christmas and "back-to-school" items. These are purchased by the stores for mail-

[5]Although the central buying of dresses by independents has been reasonably successful, it has not been easy to apply the concept to other fashion lines. There is a consistency of customer demand by classification, size, and price range in the case of dresses, but it is much more difficult in the case of separates and coordinates (tops and bottoms) that are today more important than dresses for women and suits for men.

ing to their customers with their own names imprinted on the catalogs purchased. The items included are selected by a committee of the buyers of key member stores that wish to participate and of the resident buying office. The vendors whose goods are chosen pay for the cost of preparing the catalog, and the stores buy the featured merchandise from them directly. This is really a price agreement system, as explained in the preceding chapter.

When a buying office has worked out an arrangement with a manufacturer to sell certain styles exclusively to member stores, it may arrange to have these styles advertised in national magazines, with the stores listed in the ads. Only a portion of the stores using the buying office may be involved in these promotions: those that agree to stock a minimum quantity of the advertised goods. The manufacturer usually pays for these ads, because it is beneficial to let the customer-reader know what store in his or her shopping area carries the advertised styles. Similar group advertising is also undertaken for private brands.

Research Service of Buying Offices

In addition to performing buying and promotional services, many resident buyers engage in research activities for their stores. It is the associated and syndicate resident buying offices that do most of this. The stores they represent are so nearly homogeneous and so closely related as to make their problems and their standards of performance very similar. The most common types of research are: (1) exchange of operating statistics and development of standards, (2) study of methods of procedure in different departments and of systems operating throughout the store, (3) consultant services on merchandising and operating problems, (4) space productivity studies, and (5) recruiting of executive personnel.

Improving Service to the Stores

A common complaint made by store buyers is that resident buyers are so close to the manufacturers that they tend to become representatives for the manufacturers rather than agents for the stores. Resident buyers sometimes do develop preferred resources and are more interested in obtaining business for the manufacturers than in analyzing the peculiar problems of their own stores. The plan of submitting bulletin information to a screening committee minimizes this danger. Of course, merchandise brokers are actually sellers, but even they must be careful to avoid any semblance of pressing their customers to buy a certain line, unless admittedly it is an outstanding one.

Again, resident buyers often wait for store buyers to express a demand for merchandise before they start looking for it. But leading offices insist that their resident buyers make out tentative buying plans based on seasonal changes and that they line up resources and merchandise for a new season even before store buyers request the merchandise. Thus, when the buyers do come to market, they find their needs anticipated in that the resident buyers are prepared to suggest the best resources and the best merchandise assortment for the new season.

The store buyers, too, must cooperate if they are to obtain the best service from the office. First, they should send copies of their buying plans to the resident buyer before they come to the market so that advance spade work may be done. Second, they must provide resident buyers with full information as to the assortment they want whenever they send in open orders. Yet, many store buyers merely wire, "Send me 100 good dresses to sell at $14.95." This is certainly not adequate information to ensure an intelligent buying job. It is sometimes desirable to provide the resident buyer with an inventory record showing the current assortment on hand. Third, the buyers must discard the notion that the demands of their customers are entirely different from those of anyone else. They must recognize that much is to be gained by going along with the group in methods of cooperative and central buying. It is only by mutual trust and cooperation that the store can obtain maximum results from its buying group. Fourth, individual store buyers must overcome the jealousy with which they guard their privileges and prerogatives if they are to make effective use of a resident buying office. The office may then be regarded as a valuable assistant and a place to concentrate purchasing power.

One of the oldest buying offices,[6] established in 1907, has succeeded in weathering the many changes that have taken place by going beyond the original service of the office to individual store buyers by introducing many of the services of the large chain-store groups. These include the development of private brands (mostly in apparel, accessories, and domestic classifications), both wholesaling and importing programs, centralized planning of merchandising, operating and promotion strategies, and even the centralized purchasing of supplies and fixtures. To cater to the varying needs of its members, it holds regional meetings.

CENTRALIZED BUYING BY COOPERATIVE AND ASSOCIATED INDEPENDENTS

For stores handling general merchandise, particularly with fashion characteristics, the resident buying office is the major device for interstore cooperation, but many stores find other types of affiliation desirable. When it is neither possible nor economic for each store handling such lines as foods and drugs to buy directly from the producer, advantages are gained by

[6]Felix Lilienthal & Co., Inc., New York, N.Y.

setting up a wholesale subsidiary cooperatively or by associating oneself with a wholesale distributor. These assume certain wholesaling functions such as scouting, assembling, storing, and delivering in economic size lots. Besides eliminating the wholesaler's profit[7] from the cost of goods, the theory is that the functions will be more effectively performed if they are directed *entirely* toward the benefit of the stores (the benevolent wholesaler concept).

Centralized buying by independents has taken four forms: (1) the buying club, (2) the joint retailer-owned wholesale establishment, (3) the voluntary chain, and (4) the central buying plan for some fashions and imports conducted by some resident buyers and discussed above.

The Buying Club

The buying club is simply a working agreement among a group of independents, often in the same town, to buy together stocks that all carry, splitting the shipment among themselves when received. The motivation is to secure a price advantage.

The Joint Retailer-Owned Wholesale Establishment

This is an extension of the buying club. The warehouse may be established by the retailers taking the initiative or it may be organized and controlled by promoters who sell stock ownership to retailers. It was first developed in the food and drug fields. It is now important also for general merchandise, with resident buyers setting up wholesaling subsidiaries with stock ownership transferred to store members.

This device is especially useful in purchasing staples that all the stores carry, but in limited quantities in each store, and for the development of private brands, which may be either warehoused or drop-shipped to the stores.

The service charge to the member stores is considerably less than the markup of an unaffiliated service wholesaler. This is because (1) selling costs are eliminated, (2) only items in active demand in all stores are stocked, and (3) some of the costs may be absorbed by resident buying operations for which a separate fee is charged. The unaffiliated wholesaler has to keep up selling pressure to assure repeat orders and has to carry broader stocks to satisfy the demands of diverse customers.

It should be noted that although an association of stores may set up a wholesaling firm for the use of its members, such formation of a subsidiary company may not legally entitle them to wholesalers' functional discounts. Accordingly, such subsidiaries have sought patronage from nonmember

[7]Note carefully that it is the wholesaler's final profit that is claimed to be eliminated, not the costs of performing the wholesaler's functions.

firms in order to achieve wholesaler status. Merchants who make arrangements with them are not really delegating part of their buying work; they are merely selecting a specific vendor. It might be well to keep this distinction in mind with respect to all such special buying arrangements.

The Voluntary Chain

An even more prevalent form of centralized buying is for a wholesaler, distributor, corporate chain, or even a manufacturer to sponsor a buying group of stores. This relieves the stores of financial investment and liability with respect to the centralized venture.

When wholesalers undertake this function, they may be called "contract" wholesalers in that they enter into buying and servicing contracts with each of a group of independent stores. They undertake to give the contracting retailers special values and assistance in merchandising and promotion. In return, the stores agree to make use of the wholesalers' facilities, voluntarily concentrate much of their buying with them, and frequently pay a fee. There is usually no contract to buy from the wholesalers, however, because that might be ruled to be in restraint of trade.[8] When contract wholesaling was started, the emphasis was all on providing the stores with lower-priced merchandise than the unaffiliated wholesalers could give them. The tendency today is for these wholesalers not only to sell at low markups but also to provide an advisory service. One Midwestern wholesaler of foods provides staples at a very low markup (frequently 2 percent and some items at cost except for the purchase discount) and provides four distinct services, each at a charge to the store of a fraction of 1 percent of the store's sales. These services are merchandising, accounting and record keeping, joint advertising, and supervision. If a store subscribes to all of the services, it pays 2 percent of its sales. Each separately costs approximately .5 percent. The contract wholesaler usually insists that member stores follow suggestions about store front, signs, and merchandising policies and will not hesitate to drop a store that gives only half-hearted cooperation.

The setting up of a retailer-owned warehouse or a voluntary chain represents a limited departure from the way independents commonly organize their buying function. What actually happens is a more thorough identification of interest between retailers and their primary sources of supply. In return for continuity and concentration of purchases with them, retailers assume some of the aspects of the benevolent wholesalers. In fact, retailers'

[8]In 1952, the FTC ordered the Gamble-Skogmo stores to stop negotiating exclusive-dealing contracts with independent stores whereby the stores are required to handle only Gamble-Skogmo products. This practice, together with attendant coercion to force retailers to comply, was ruled to be a violation of the Clayton Act. This continues to be the legal interpretation.

services move beyond the range of the buying function into helping with the entire function of store administration.

Franchising

A variation of the voluntary chain that has expanded rapidly in recent years is for a manufacturer or distributor to contract with independent retailers to act as selling agents, operating under a common name owned by the franchisor. Types of stores commonly franchised are gas stations, fast-food restaurants, certain automotive supplies such as mufflers and shock absorbers, and drug stores such as Rexall. These dealers buy their major merchandise requirements from the franchisor and abide by the merchandising and service policies.[9]

Some corporate chains, among them drug chains, enter into franchise arrangments with independents in localities where they are not ready to set up their own stores. These independents have the privilege of buying from the warehoused stocks and of enjoying the services provided the owned stores. These may be eventually absorbed into the chain.

Leasing

There are other ways by which independent retailers relinquish some or almost all the responsibilities for buying to outside agencies. The *leased department* has long been a common element in departmentalized stores. This involves an arrangement whereby the store "rents" space and furnishes facilities in return for a percentage of the sales volume of the lessee. Sometimes leasing is done with a line of goods somewhat foreign to the experience of the store owner. Often the arrangment has been made for certain specialty lines that merchants have found hard to merchandise profitably: millinery, women's shoes, and fine jewelry being common examples. A number of large discount operations are comprised entirely of leased departments.

Food markets that expand into nonfood lines use rack jobbers (cf. Chapter 9). They are assigned a designated space, which they merchandise with very little control by the markets themselves. Except for technical difference with respect to ownership of the inventory and the profit arrangement with the merchant, the operation is quite analogous to leasing.

Vendor Control

In some categories, transfer of buying authority to an outside agency takes the form of a working relationship between the store-buyer and the manufac-

[9]An excellent reference guide for the person interested in making contact with major franchising organizations is the *Franchise Opportunities Handbook* (U.S. Department of Commerce, March 1975) Superintendent of Documents, Washington, D.C.

turer's or wholesale distributor's selling personnel. In arrangements of this sort, the buyer exercises his or her function chiefly by selecting the lines or brands to be carried and the selling space each will have. The buyer watches over the store's sales and profit returns from that space but delegates all stock-keeping functions to the "detail people" or "missionary people" of the manufacturers. They visit the store regularly, fill in the floor fixture from reserve stocks, set up displays, count the inventory, and write up reorders. The practice is common to grocery products, greeting cards, brassières and other branded, standardized products. In some lines, like hosiery and underwear, manufacturers exercise control over store stocks by inserting punch cards in the stock boxes or attaching stub tickets to the goods. As the merchandise is sold, these cards or tickets are returned to the vendor, who uses them as a basis for reorders.

Retailers often encourage these practices simply because it transfers the costs of a tedious job to vendors. The latter accept the responsibility because they believe it to be the best way of assuring adequate stocks of their products in anticipation of customer demand. A rationale often advanced is that manufacturers can perform these services for their specialties more efficiently than is possible in the multiproduct complex of retailing. There is much debate about whether some of these functions are being justifiably delegated by retailers to others, or simply donated or abdicated, or usurped by those who eventually perform them. Regardless of the merits in the case, the fact remains that there is much scrambled functioning in the distributive channels.

Division of Responsibility of Essential Functions

This chapter has dealt with various ways by which retailers organize for the job of market coverage. None has demonstrated a clear, substantial cost advantage over the others—except where inefficient individual operation is replaced or bolstered. Different methods do not *eliminate* the tasks enumerated (Chapter 1) under the buying–selling function or those connected with wholesaling. The net is merely *shifting of the burden*. The cost of performance remains, whether absorbed by individual store, central headquarters, buying office, wholesaler, or manufacturer—and must somehow be passed on in the pricing of goods. It may be that efficient administration within the method is as important as the method itself.

DISCUSSION QUESTIONS

1. Do all independent stores, regardless of merchandise line, require some form of association with others in order to improve their buying?

2. Do merchandise brokers' conflicts of interest mean that retailers cannot depend on them for excellent service and broad market contacts?
3. What are the advantages to an independent of joining a good salaried office rather than an associated office?
4. Should a store look to a buying office primarily to obtain price concessions in the wholesale market or to purchase more saleable merchandise than could otherwise be located?
5. Is group buying likely to be replaced by central buying?
6. Is central buying for a group of independents likely to become the major activity of resident offices?
7. Does resident buying offer an excellent career for the merchandise-minded college graduate?
8. Why is resident buying not the appropriate method for independent convenience goods stores to use in improving their market contacts?
9. Because the Clayton Act prohibits the sale of merchandise on condition that the buyer will not deal in competing products, are voluntary chain and manufacturer's franchise arrangements seriously restricted?
10. What difficulties are likely to be encountered by independents after they have entered into franchise arrangements?
11. Does central buying offer a golden opportunity for independents to strengthen their assortments and their values, or will the loss of individuality more than offset the gain?
12. With retail trade increasingly concentrated in the hands of mammoth retail institutions that draw up specifications for much of the goods they handle and that qualify for rock-bottom prices, can able small merchants look forward to growing and profitable operations of their own?
13. Whenever the store buyer turns over to a resident buyer, a wholesaler, or a manufacturer the performance of certain marketing functions, is he or she reducing the cost of distribution or simply redistributing the cost? Discuss the conditions under which the answer would vary.
14. Some years ago, a New York resident office introduced the following plan to spot best sellers in the women's apparel field: On special forms provided, each store reported its fast-selling items and those that were providing unexpected sales volume, giving description, resource, cost, retail price, quantity sold, and quantity reordered. Approximately 400 to 500 items were reported each week. These were screened by the sales promotion department of the buying office, and those of general significance and probable continuing importance were referred to the merchandising division for further study. About 30 percent of the reported

items survived the two screenings. These were recommended to the stores for special promotion. Each store had its own promotion committee that had a special budget for these items and decided which of the recommended items to promote. Once an item was approved, it became a store-wide rather than a departmental promotion. These items were advertised separately from the store's regular advertising; their sales were closely watched; and they were removed from the group once the sales began to slip. What difficulties probably arose in operating this plan? It is no longer in operation.

15. Study the checklist in the Technical Appendix to Part I, at the end of this chapter. Which of the many activities presented are responsibilities jointly shared by the buyer and his or her superior, the merchandise manager? By the buyer and his or her assistant? By the buyer and the departmental branch managers?

Technical Appendix for Part I

AN OUTLINE OF THE DETAILED ACTIVITIES INVOLVED IN BUYING-SELLING CYCLE

For purposes of detailed analysis, the three phases of the buying–selling cycle may be expanded to describe the work of the functionary or functionaries involved. Five activities may be segregated: (1) buying, (2) stock-keeping, (3) pricing, (4) selling, and (5) planning and control.

The outline that follows may be for some stores a job analysis of the buyer's responsibility. For most, it will represent an analysis of the work of a number of people engaged in the functioning of the buying–selling cycle.

1. **Buying** is only briefly detailed here because the topic is greatly expanded in the following chapters. The work of buying includes:

(a) Deciding specifically what to buy and how much of it.
(b) Deciding when to buy and when to bring it into stock.
(c) Deciding where to buy, what to pay, how to pay, and how to ship.
(d) Doing or getting done the actual work of selection, negotiation, and placement of the order.
(e) Following up vendors to insure the timing of deliveries.
(f) Training assistants in the above activities.

There are no hard and fast rules defining the scope of the tasks involved in any specific buying function or in the concentration of time and effort devoted to particular tasks.[10]

2. **Stock-keeping** involves many activities of handling, checking, and protecting goods between receipt and sale. The term is also used to describe certain activities of ordering and of expediting sales in order to maintain planned inventory assortments. The work of stock-keeping has been classified into three groups of activity: (a) receiving, assembling, and distributing; (b) protection; and (c) inventory control.

(a) Receiving, assembling, and distributing includes:

(1) Checking for quantity received and for general condition and obvious conformance to purchase order,[11] viz., color, size, style number, etc. Except for small stores, this work is done by receiving department personnel who usually report to "operations" managers.

[10]A survey of 89 buyers in 27 department stores with branches reveals the following estimates of how they distribute their working time in percentage terms:

	1 or 2 branches (%)	*3–5 branches (%)*	*6 or more branches (%)*
Buying, including shipping competition	32.0	34.2	38.4
Pricing	2.3	1.6	1.3
Stock-keeping, including receiving and marking	6.2	9.0	6.7
Selling: supervision, promotion, customer service, and personal selling	27.1	19.8	13.0
Planning, including analysis of records	15.9	16.1	15.4
Other activities involving the above functions:			
Training assistants and sales personnel	6.1	6.9	6.3
Visits to branches	9.0	11.4	13.3
Miscellaneous	1.4	1.0	2.6
Totals	100.0	100.0	100.0

Compiled from data in Table 9 of J. W. Johnston's "The Department Store Buyers," University of Texas at Austin, 1969.

[11]This kind of checking may be done "blind," i.e., listing the goods against later comparison with an invoice. The invoice itself is checked against the purchase order—usually by the controller's division.

(2) Checking of less obvious elements of material and workmanship or conformance to a sample or to specifications is nearly always the buyer's responsibility.
(3) Marking or ticketing. This is done by receiving-room personnel in large stores and chain headquarters, or by store personnel in the individual units of a chain.
(4) Furnishing information for marking. It is the buyer's duty to indicate price, classification, and identifying code numbers.
(5) Determining where to store the incoming goods: in warehouse, reserve, or forward stock. In stores large enough to have this choice, the buyer decides. Within stores of a chain, the entire management of the routing and storage function is the responsibility of store management.
(6) Moving and storing the goods. Where stores have forward stockrooms, the function of handling these rooms and filling the selling fixtures is one of the responsibilities of the selling department's manager who may or may not be the buyer. Major storage and bulk movement of goods is a specialized materials-handling function and therefore a responsibility of the operations division.
(7) Distributing the goods. This function is peculiar to multiunit operations. Instructions about which stores are to receive what goods are contained in "distribution orders," which emanate from the merchandising division. Physical distribution—storage, order-picking, assembly, and shipping—is the work of the operating division through its warehouse or distribution center.
(8) Notifying about arrival of goods. It is the buyer's duty to inform all who are concerned about the scheduled arrival of goods so that they may schedule their work.
(9) Checking and authorizing invoices for payment.[12] It is the responsibility of the buyer to determine that the invoice represents precisely the agreements made with the vendor and that it records precisely the buyer's retail pricing and other marking instructions. In central buying operations where the buyer may be not wholly responsible for pricing, this part of an invoice inspection function may become chiefly a review for information rather than for authorization.
(10) Authorizing returns to vendors and transfers is the responsibility of the buyer or manager who is accountable for merchandise received in a department. Transfer among stores in a chain may be expressly or tacitly approved by the buyer. The directive work is done by distributors who, although not necessarily reporting to the buyer, are in the merchandising division. The physical work of transfers and returns follows procedures previously outlined.

(b) Protection includes:
(1) Safeguards against theft.
(2) Packaging, cleaning, folding, and other handling devices to protect against breakage, soilage, and spoilage.

[12]Quantities, prices, terms, etc., are doubly checked in the controller's office, where the invoices are compared with the purchase order.

(3) Repairing or reconditioning goods.

(4) Physical inventories for purposes of accounting audit and subsequent analysis to determine causes of loss and means of prevention.

Protection is the responsibility of the manager in whose charge the goods may be at any point. The buyer (as distinguished from a department manager) is responsible for proper packaging and for reconditioning and repair that may be done by the manufacturer. Supervision of routine floor work in this area is a duty of the manager in charge of the floor. Where large workrooms are maintained, they are typically supervised by the operations division, although the departmental buyer may assist in the purchase of materials and supplies.

(c) Inventory control refers to specific work performed in maintaining the planned unit composition of the inventory. In general, it refers to the operation of all unit controls[13] whether they be perpetual inventory records or periodic physical counts. Major planning and control functions are discussed later. Maintaining the planned unit composition of the merchandise assortment is predominantly a control function and, as later developments show, is subject to problems created by split responsibilities. The specific tasks (with some planning functions included for convenience) include:

(1) Checking the unit composition of the assortment as a whole. This involves the establishment and maintenance of *unit control* systems whereby information about unit stocks and movement may be collected, organized, coordinated, interpreted, and reported as a basis for further buying and selling action. Decisions must be made about grouping items for control and about how detailed the information should be. Definite programs and schedules must be made and followed.

(2) Special checking of staple stocks and "never-out" lists involves scheduled periodic counts of stock (or examination of the data in a "perpetual inventory" record) and determining sales between checking periods as a basis for determining required fill-ins and additions to or subtractions from the list itself.

(3) Special checking on fast-selling items; that is, determining a basis for so classifying them, installing and maintaining a system for speedily detecting and following them, and taking action to intensify their ordering and promotion programs.

(4) Special checking on slow-selling items; that is, following the procedures for fast-sellers, but with the opposite purpose of taking action to eliminate slow sellers.

(5) Distribution is a stock-keeping function peculiar to centrally merchandised multiunit operations. Its primary function is to maintain the unit composition of inventory assortments in the individual stores by checking their stocks and ordering appropriate replenishments from the total provision made by the central buyer. The function also involves the correction of inventories by transfer from one store to another.

[13]See Chapter 7. Also see John W. Wingate, Elmer O. Schaller, and F. Leonard Miller, *Retail Merchandise Management* (Englewood Cliffs, N.J.: Prentice-Hall, Inc., 1972), part IV.

3. **Pricing** is highly integrated with the activities of buying but also integrates tightly with selling to yield the final profit objective. To the extent that price influences demand, there is always an optimum dollar profit to be gotten from some particular combination of price and rate of sale. Pricing involves:

(a) Setting markup and margin goals.
(b) Setting price lines and zones.
(c) Pricing individual items.
(d) Repricing, to move slow-selling goods or to anticipate changing replacement costs.

Here too, the buyer must closely observe company plans and controls as well as competitive practive. Most buyers have either the authority to price or the obligation to suggest prices. One of the requirements in selecting merchandise for resale is to have the probable selling price in mind.

4. **Selling**[14] is the twin main-line function along with buying. It may take the forms of presentation of the merchandise to prospective customers through salespeople, "self-selling" fixtures, signs, display, catalogs, and promotion in advertising media. Buyers are responsibile for informing all concerned about the selling features of the merchandise they have bought. They also have a voice—ranging from recommendation to decision—in deciding what shall be promoted, when, and to what extent. The extent to which a buyer may become involved in selling activities determines which of the following functions he or she may be charged with:

(a) Management of the work and personnel required to operate a selling force, including some actual selling (especially in closing difficult sales) and arranging for special orders.
(b) Deciding or helping to decide what to promote and when to promote it.
(c) Requesting appropriate media and space for advertising, although decision usually rests with the advertising department.
(d) Requesting and outlining window and interior displays, including signs, and arranging for display and advertising aids and allowances from vendors.
(e) Making decisions or recommendations about floor or fixture position and space to be given to specific products.
(f) Requesting and outlining bulletins and display pages for informing stores about available goods and urging their purchase. This function is peculiar to resident and central buyers.
(g) Furnishing information about the selling virtues of merchandise to salespeople, bulletin writers, advertising, display and sign writers, and all others who may be responsible for promoting the sale of goods. This is a *universal function* of buyers in retailing, whether or not they are otherwise involved in the selling function.

[14]Discussed more fully in Chapter 15.

5. **Planning and Control,** as associated with the work of the buying-selling cycle, includes the coordination of all the tasks previously described in order best to cater to customer demand at a profit. The work is sometimes assigned to staff specialists; sometimes it is the reserved work of the buyer's superior; sometimes the buyer must do most of it personally; usually it involves other divisions of the business. Whatever the case, the buyer, if not responsible, still participates actively. The work of the major planning and control functions referred to here includes:

(a) Participating in the formulation of and finally ascertaining the firm's policies and objectives about:
  (1) The consumers whose patronage is desired.
  (2) How to serve them with respect to pricing policies, quality and styling standards, fashion position, price lines, brands, depth and breadth of assortments; and ancillary services like charge accounts, delivery, display, and decor.
  (3) Promotional emphasis, techniques, and programs.
  (4) Sales, margin, expense, profit, and turnover.

(b) Analyzing and forecasting demands and requirements of desired customers involve:
  (1) Estimating conditions and trends in the general economy and in specific areas or communities, in the procurement market, and in competitive structure and practice.
  (2) Learning characteristics of desired customers as individuals and groups, including their shopping habits and motivations.
  (3) Determining their trends in merchandise and service requirements and preferences.

(c) Budgeting sales and stocks involves:
  (1) Formulation of estimated dollar sales by selected categories and time periods.
  (2) Estimating dollar stocks required at selected points in the time periods and reconciling them with turnover goals.
  (3) Building up estimates of unit sales and reconciling them with dollar plans.
  (4) Building up model stocks by units to picture the composition of the assortment and the depth of individual elements—reconciling the whole with dollar stock plans.
  (5) Computing, from sales and stock plans, the required purchases ("open-to-receive") by selected periods.
  (6) Allocating funds for purchases at the start of selling "seasons" to provide for later fill-ins of the planned assortment and for special promotional purchases.
  (7) Estimating and setting objectives for markon, markdowns, and other elements of margin; also certain expenses and levels of profit.

(d) Control involves:[15]

[15]Because planning and control are interactive, it is sometimes hard to tell where one ends and the other begins. But (a), (b), and (c), as outlined, are commonly listed under the planning function. The section under 2 (c) (Stock-keeping—inventory control) in this outline illustrates some specific control tasks associated with the problem of maintaining inventory assortments at a planned level.

(1) Checking on the performance of subsection 2C on inventory control.
(2) Setting up check points, standards, and guidelines for all operations from the previously mentioned forecasts and budgets.
(3) Setting up methods, systems, and procedures for measuring condition and performance against plans.
(4) Measuring and projecting deviation from plan and recommending or making required adjustments in the operation or the plan itself.

Examples of the control function at work are found in later discussions on "open-to-buy" control, which governs the placement of orders against the "open-to-receive" plan, and on how the buyer achieves the planned markon by controlling the "mix" of markons which result from the pricing of individual items.

part II

What to Buy

chapter 4

Consumer Demand

ANTICIPATING DEMAND

The prime objective of the buying function is to *anticipate* the needs and wants of customers; the word "anticipate," as used in this text, means being ready to gratify a customer's product desire on demand. Stringent limits on the size of the inventory that can be prepared for this purpose necessitate that the desires be forecast with some accuracy and that the goods be procured expeditiously and promoted in such a way that customers become aware that their needs and wants have indeed been anticipated.

This concentration by makers and sellers on what the consumer will want is the basis for what has come to be known since midcentury as the *marketing concept*, referred to in Chapter 1. Basically, this credo includes three elements: (1) that producer and distributor alike must be consumer oriented, searching out and meeting consumers' needs and wants; (2) that marketing activities like promotion (media, personal selling, and other) be closely coordinated with procurement; (3) and that the effort aims at a profit that will enable the business to recompense capital invested and attract new capital for growth.

Over the long run, it is the consumer who dominates both retailers and their suppliers, because it is the consumers who accept or reject what is hopefully laid before them. This does not mean that a new product cannot be launched successfully until an active demand has been *expressed*. Only part of our wants are conscious; many remain subconscious or *latent*. Nor are all conscious wants expressed so that a buyer may be aware of them. Actual sales are expressions of today's wants by those who purchased the goods.

From sales analysis, and from other sources of information, inferences must be made about future demand.

When electric refrigerators were first put on the market, the need had to be inferred: from conscious and expressed desires for the things it could do and from the latent desire for just such a mechanism. Maintenance of the ice supply, drainage of water, poor and uneven cooling, all contributed to make the icebox irksome and inefficient. A machine that would reduce household labor and better protect foods fitted in perfectly with the kind of lives housewives wanted to lead—freedom from drudgery, better food protection, and better, easier meal preparation. No matter how much retailers may have wanted to buy such equipment, or to get it made, they were frustrated until pressure of consumers' latent needs mothered the invention and Frigidaire actually put one on the market. Once out, copied, and improved, almost every model was swept up in the voracity of demand. As production accelerated, demand became more satiated and consequently more selective. Each new wanted product tends to follow this pattern.

Before mass production began, there was such a scarcity of products and so great a demand that customers were not very exacting. As a result, manufacturers' efforts were directed toward making what could be produced cheaply, in large quantities and with a potential market, rather than toward analyzing demand closely to determine what would have the best chance of acceptance. It was assumed that promotional efforts would "put across" any style the designer elected to produce and that if the producers in any field would agree on what was to be the fashion, the consumer could be forced to fall in line.[1]

The history of promotional campaigns is strewn with items that were failures because they ran counter to customer demand, and there are also notable examples where a product with little promotion has been much sought after because it was just what many people wanted: Word-of-mouth advertising carries the news of availability to people who are ready for the new product. This is not to say that promotional effort cannot sell some of almost anything; but it can be a costly effort. In the main, *the residual profit or yield on promotional effort tends to vary with the acceptability of the thing promoted.*

Examples of Success

A case where a successful product grew from a concept of consumer want based on a perceived central idea was Ford's Mustang. It evolved around the notion that there might be a good market among young families for an

[1]The chairman of Proctor and Gamble, giant among makers and marketers of consumer products, was quoted as saying: ". . . if a new product can't pay out in a very short time we don't push it. The only way you can succeed in this business is with a good product. You can't do it with advertising." ["The Spectacular Rise of the Consumer Co.," *Business Week*, July 21, 1973 (pp. 48–56).]

Italianate, sports-type compact if it could be made practical for family use—and cheap enough. Consumer reactions were then tested for 2 years as the specific car evolved from the central idea. Other examples were: "Crest," "the first therapeutic dentifrice," and "Ultra-brite" toothpaste, which stressed cosmetic and sex appeals; "Arm & Hammer's" use of plain old baking soda as a "nonpolluting phosphate-free detergent";[2] and the "unisex" vogue in the subsequent popularity of pants for women and necklaces for men.

Merchants and makers alike are quick to put promotional effort behind products with a seemingly strong generic demand. Even though the cost of promoting the new product may be great, there is the hope of recouping on the success of a likely winner. Sometimes it backfires, like the tremendous promotional effort behind DuPont's long struggle to gain acceptance for the leather substitute called *Corfam*; or like the disastrous failure of the effort to cash in on "the need for change" in garments with "midi"-length skirts in the early 1970s. Consumers apparently did not yet strongly feel "the need for change." For the retail merchant, the disaster was compounded: it is not only that customers refused the overstocks of new longer lengths, but sales were lost because of stocks inadequate to anticipate the demand for the old short lengths.

CONSUMER MOTIVATION

Plainly, if the retail merchant is to anticipate the needs and wants of consumers, even to the point of starting the process before the consumers are consciously aware of their desires, then a lot must be learned about these consumers: who they are, where they are, and what characteristics make it possible to group them as markets and submarkets. How do their individual characteristics affect their shopping behavior, and how are they influenced by group pressures? What appeals are most likely to attract their patronage and yield the most profitable reward for effort expended?

Out of the need to answer these questions, a whole interdisciplinary study of consumer motivation and behavior has evolved, using mathematics, economics, psychology, sociology, and cultural anthropology. Sometimes practical application does not keep pace with progress in research methodology; sometimes line executives and researchers don't tell each other clearly what is wanted, what can be gotten, and how it can be used. The result is then a sort of information overkill in which success is proclaimed more by

[2]The phosphate-free detergent was aimed at the growing and very vocal interest in ecology. A new awareness of the power of its basic ingredient (baking soda) to satisfy a nostaligic vogue for the simple and old-fashioned prompted Arm & Hammer to expand into other household cleaning products, refrigerator deodorants, and then personal deodorants.

those who authorized the research expenditures than by those who have to use the findings.

We cannot, in this book, dig at all deeply into the disciplines mentioned. We point out some of the more important things to look for and how they affect the job of anticipating consumer demand. It may be that more will be learned from the examples of application than from the explanation of the theories behind them.

Motivation is a much used term in explaining why people act as they do. As we use the term, it refers to "all those inner striving conditions variously described as wishes, desires, needs, drives and the like."[3]

Primary and Secondary Motivations

Motives are often classified as "primary" and "secondary." The "primary" group is said to stem from those physical needs, the gratification of which is imperative for survival (hunger, thirst, mating, etc.) The "secondary" group is a learned or psychogenic group of drives, not demonstrably needed for material survival (acquisitiveness, recognition, exhibition, etc.)

Primary motives, however, are not *primary* in the sense that they always take priority in governing our behavior. Their gratifications may be postponed and even renounced in favor of the so-called secondary or social motives (cf. Ghandi and Joan of Arc for extreme cases). Indeed, social and psychological motives often determine the specific form in which the primary motives get expressed.

Individual customers are just that, individuals: Each has a unique set of drives and a set of priorities for satisfying those drives. Neither drives nor priorities are stable or necessarily logical or rational. Under one set of circumstances, one might drag a weary mile for a glass of water and, in another situation, spurn any liquid refreshment other than Bourbon—and that of a particular brand, served in a particular way. This specific demand may be the result of an exquisite sense of taste, of a desire for social acceptance and conformity or of the need to demonstrate sophistication and economic status.

Another case in point where primary motives are not *primary* is the food selection of the human adult: heavily based on fad, taste, class conformity, whimsy, convenience of purchase, and ease of preparation, with relatively little attention to nutritional values. Important to merchant buyers is the fact that *they are there to anticipate these wants as perceived—not to sit in nutritional judgment.* They must be alert to countertrends, which indicate the formation of separate market segments. A trend for "natural" foods may be just as illogically faddish as the main trend and may be carried to extremes

[3]Much of this and following material on human behavior reflects concepts in *Human Behavior, an inventory of scientific findings,* by Bernard Berelson and Gary A. Steiner, published by Harcourt, Brace, New York, 1964.

by its practicioners, but if they represent a large enough market to be profitable, they become a market to pursue.

Predisposition and Patronage

A powerful influence on consumer purchasing decisions is *predisposition*, a built-up attitude toward the product and the seller. Over the long run, the merchant's goal is to woo predisposition toward the firm and constantly to reinforce the ties that bind. This union is known as "patronage loyalty;" we prefer the term *patronage constancy*. It is rooted less in logic than in that built-up set of opinions, attitudes, and beliefs that can form a strong habit but not an unbreakable one. Some great "carriage trade" stores of the past died because they failed to recognize the changes taking place in their chosen market segments and in the times. Conversely, witness the modern versions of carriage trade stores like Neiman-Marcus and Bloomingdale's, who learned how to anticipate the changing needs of their markets and the new markets they decided to court.

Perception

Basic to all these actions and reactions is the process of "perception," defined as "the process whereby people select, organize and interpret sensory stimulation into a meaningful and coherent picture."[4] For example, a dress in the window may be perceived by a particular customer as a pretty garment that will cause pleasure in the wearing of it and will confer a certain amount of status because of the designer's or the store's label.

Perception is in part determined by motivations, needs, and values. Under normal conditions, the major effect of motives on perception is *what* will be seen (i.e., by *selection*) rather than *how* it will be seen (i.e., by *interpretation*). In short:

> . . . Perception is selective and can be so to the point of rejection.
> . . . Perception is interpretative and can be so to the point of distortion.

To the buyer, the central ideas of *perception* may be more usefully expressed in terms of application. For one thing, the ideas of *selectivity* and *interpretation* are inherent in the nature of perception. They generally take the form of "we see (hear, feel, smell, taste) what we want to see and even how we want to see it." Who sees one perfume as enchanting may see another as repugnant when, really, neither is either. One person just won't have copper pots as cooking utensils; another would use nothing else.

[4]Ibid., p. 88.

The interpretative perception of risk may be strong enough to thwart many a purchase by many a customer, and the same perception may be a prime determinant for inducing continued patronage of the store or department or brand that provides the comforting security of peer approval. That puffed and tufted velvet couch may not appeal to the aesthetic tastes of the buyer and may be summarily rejected as a decorative piece by some of the customers. But there may be some to whom that piece looks like a thing of comfort and beauty. The buyer must learn to see it in all these lights, and if the class of customers who would "love" that couch are a sufficient part of the store's clientele, it should be bought and displayed.

From these notions of perception stem two cardinal precepts for buyers.

1. *Always have typical customers in mind and see all products and all promotions through their "eyes."*
2. *What the customer perceives as the total benefit of a proposed purchase may far transcend the physical attributes or the obvious characteristics of a product. This is discussed more in Chapter 5.*

Egocentricity

The customer's perception of himself or herself is a major buying motive. With an increasingly affluent society and expanding discretionary income, an increasing number of consumers are expressing an attractive image for themselves by what they wear, how they decorate their homes, what they drive, and how they use their leisure time. While fashion in clothes has, from time immemorial, been a self-expression of the affluent and the mighty, most consumers today are able to build their self esteem by impressing other people with the personality images they have chosen. Today youth has a tremendous appeal with its physical vigor, exciting activities, and ready acceptance of the new. It is emulated by middle and even old age.

Some of the newer ways consumers are expressing themselves are in the use of cosmetics and wigs by men, elaborate equipment for use in sports, pocket calculators, citizen band communication equipment, health foods, contemporary furniture, and *objets d'art.*

While some moralists may decry the preoccupation with the self, it has been established that one must think well of the self if he or she is to function well and usefully in society. As the buyer caters to ego building in the assortments he provides, he may be catering to a more wholesome society.

CONSUMER INFORMATION IMPORTANT IN BUYING

National retailers may want to know about the distribution of consumers in demographic, economic, sociographic, and other detail for local communities, states, regions, and the country as a whole. The local department store is less concerned about states and regions than about its SMSA[5] county and surrounding cities and with census tract and block data within those cities. Smaller, neighborhood stores focus on the makeup of the census tracts and blocks that map their more immediate trading area.

But all merchants have some interest in consumer doings in all areas, large and small, near and far. For the chain store as well as for the neighborhood store, a change in the ethnic composition of a few city blocks can bring changing style or food preferences as well as changing size scales. And the economic status of whole regions, like the prosperity shift from north and east to south and west, can affect every retailer, large and small.

What we have to know about those characteristics and groupings of the population in a given trading area that are subject to statistical analysis are called *demographic studies*. Most of those in Table 4–1 are of this kind, being subject to counting. Information about motivations and life styles (Item 15 in the table) may be called *psychographic studies* and are less subject to statistical review. In addition, the buyer should be aware of geographic features, climatic conditions, transportation facilities, institutions, and other factors that affect the requirements and demands of the population. A few of the factual groupings listed in Table 4–1 are discussed in the following subsections.

TABLE 4–1
Facts to Know About Customers

1. Number–population
2. Age and sex distribution
3. Marital status
4. Household and family formations
5. Ethnic distribution
6. Religion and politics
7. Occupation
8. Residential characteristics
9. Employment conditions
   (a) Working wives
10. Income distribution and purchasing power
11. Expenditure patterns
12. Levels of education
13. Mobility and shifting trends
14. Purchasing patterns, habits, and customs
15. Life styles, attitudes, and tastes

---

[5]A "Standard Metropolitan Statistical Area" (SMSA) is a geographical subdivision of great value to all engaged in marketing activities. By sales management's definition (roughly), an SMSA must include one city with a population of at least 25,000, which, when combined with contiguous places having a density of 1000 or more people per square mile, will have a population of at least 50,000 (provided that the city and contiguous places are in a county or counties with a population of at least 75,000).

Population

The population of the United States is known as a *mobile* population. Individuals and households change their addresses with relative frequency; two-thirds of the moves being within the same town or county, one-sixth to another county within the state and one-sixth out of state.[6] But two broad secular trends have emerged in the last 50 years: (1) from rural to urban and from urban to suburban, and (2) from the eastern and northern part of the nation to the western and southern regions.

And one might add a third trend: (3) a dramatic slowdown in the exodus from the country to the city. Congested cities and their "suburban sprawl" have led to overcrowding, pollution, crime in the streets, sudden stoppage of vital services, high taxes, and a deterioration in the quality of education. These negative developments are moving many to try living in small towns and villages and even in rural areas. This trend is moving retail merchants to look to these areas for expansion.[7]

Age Distribution

The proportions of various age groups in the population keep changing as science and culture combine to slow down influx at the birth end of the aging cycle and to resist departure at the exit end. Figure 4–1 is an example of projected population mixes to the year 1985. Figure 4–2 carries ages and birth forecasts into the next century. For the retailer who would use this kind of information, the warning flags are up.

1. For one thing, it must be born in mind that these are national figures. For the nation as a whole, the over-65 population for 1973 was estimated at a little over 10% of the total; but in Johnson County, Iowa, the proportion was 7%, and it jumped to 29% in Sarasota, Florida.[8] Moreover, the Sarasota merchant who sees no infant's and children's market for pleasingly expensive infant's and children's goods among all those grandparents is deaf to the whisper of opportunity's wings.

2. Another danger is in overemphasizing the perception of a growing bulge in one segment of the population. For example, although it is true that 29% of the Sarasota population is over 65, it is equally true that 71% is under 65; and 40% is under 35. Another example of exaggerating bulges came in

[6]Conference Board, New York, A Guide to Consumer Markets, 1973–74, p. 39.

[7]See *Sales Management's 1974 Survey of Buying Power*, "Rural Markets Show Signs of an Upswing."

[8]The national figure was extrapolated from Conference Board data; the figures for Johnson County and Sarasota came from the 1973 estimates of the *Survey of Buying Power*.

FIGURE 4–1 The changing age mix

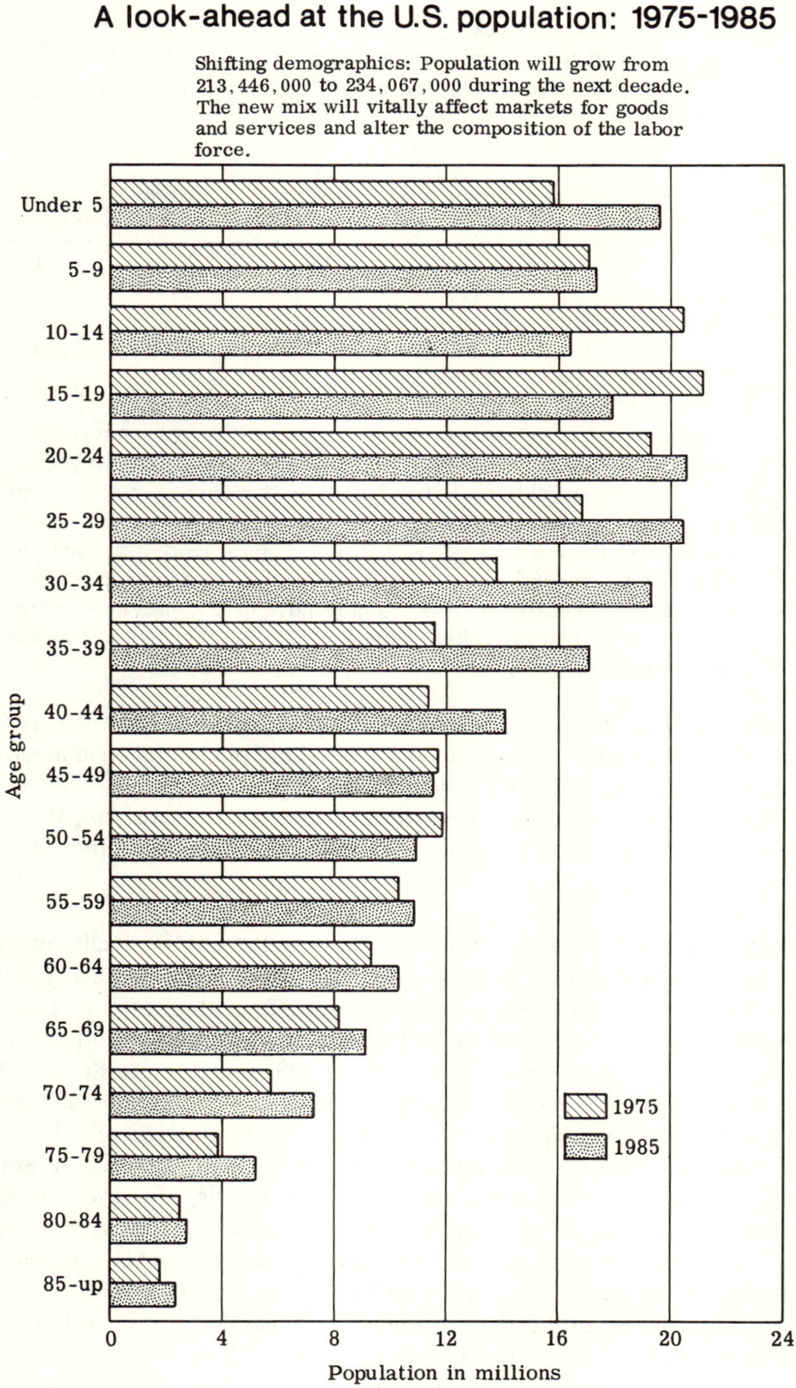

FIGURE 4–2 Trend toward an older population

The Bureau of the Census' National Center for Health Statistics presented early in 1977 the following projections of the United States' population:

Median age level		*Fertility birth rate (Births per 1000 women 15–44 years of age)*		*Percent of population Over 65 years of age*	
1900	22.9	1940	79.9	1900	4.1%
1950	30.2	1950	106.2	1950	8.1
2000	34.8	1960	118.0	2000	11.7
2050	37.0	1970	87.9	2050	16.1
		1980	66.7		

With an approach to a zero rate of growth, with fewer children, and adults in the productive years, and with nearly one-sixth of the population over 65 years old, some 70 years hence, there are likely to be major changes in customer demand for goods and services. Among the probable changes are less baby foods, more medicines, more furnishings for small apartments and homes, and smaller college enrollments. America may be more conservative and less innovative in fashion. The economic problem of supporting older people weighs heavily on the middle-income working group.

the 1950s and the 1960s, when a noticeable tide of teen-agers washed over our population statistics. Many retailers treated the phenomenon as a veritable tidal wave, which it wasn't. Inventory resources, styling, especially merchandise and store ambiance was overconcentrated on satisfying this age group—often to some neglect of the needs and desires of the other 80% of the population.

Again in the early 1970s there was increasing talk about the declining birth rate. Baby food companies began to back off and diversify, maternity shops began to woo the trade of nonpregnant women, and producers of baby toiletries suddenly discovered the efficacy of their products on other members of the family. Apparently, not much thought was given to the fact that the number of women of child-bearing age was projected for increase as the 1970s wear into the 1980s and that, therefore, although the *rate* of births is projected to decline, the total number might hold up pretty well. An example of the danger in overemphasizing statistical trends, not involving age-segment changes, occurred when the successive waves of sportswear "separates" and pants invaded the women's apparel markets; many merchants hyperbolized the preference shift into the notion that dresses were disappearing from the apparel fashion scene even though they were still of great importance. Exaggerating such trends can bring vicious cycles of vanishing returns. If dresses are not made or stocked adequately, the prophecy becomes self-fulfilling: sales fall off, followed by further cuts, and so on. Helen Galland of Bonwit Teller commented: "The supposed demise of the dress did not occur—except by default and because we let it happen. Them what had them in good assortment sold them" [At the National Retail Merchants Association (NRMA) seminar on fashion merchandising, June 4, 1974].

Income Patterns

For the buyer, trends in income and expenditure are of major importance in the vital and continuing process of market segmentation. In fact, general knowledge about segmentation is an important subject of marketing and economics, with a vast literature of its own. For purposes of this book, we stick to our practice of pointing the way and giving some examples of application.

Growth of Middle and Upper Income

The information behind Figure 4-3, for example, helps to show how more and more families are becoming people of "substance," less concerned with the exigencies of subsistence. It causes wonderment at the persistence and prevalence of *price-competitive* techniques as opposed to the host of available *non-price-competitive* techniques. It is a point of reference for later discussion on assortment, market selection, and pricing.

It should be observed, however, that 10% of the families of the country in

FIGURE 4-3 The changing income pyramid: total families each year—100- based on 1974 dollars

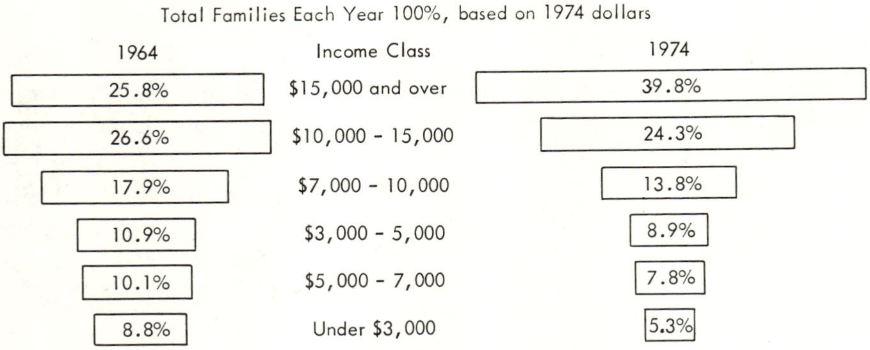

Source: Figures and tables in this section, unless otherwise labeled, are from "A Guide to Consumer Markets," 1976/77, published by The Conference Board, 845 Third Avenue, New York, N.Y. 10022 with data from the Department of Commerce.

FIGURE 4–4 Supernumerary income: after-tax figures in 1974 dollars

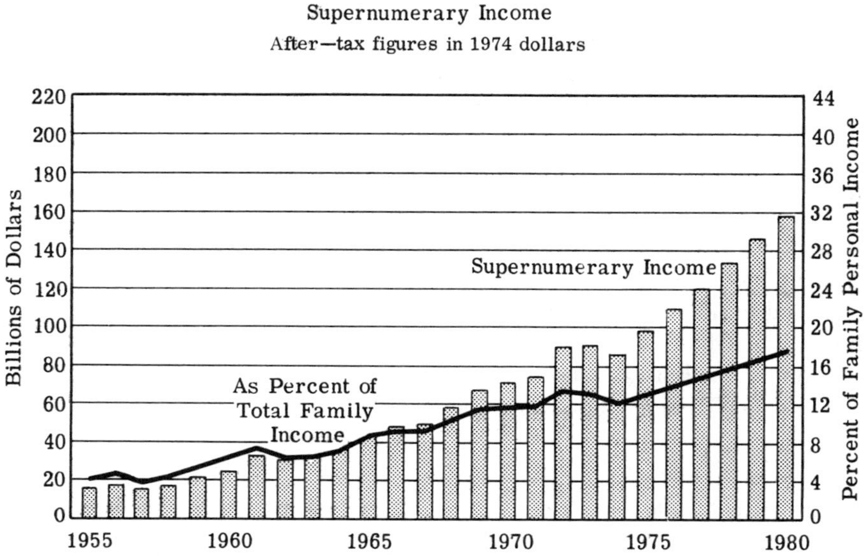

Note: Dates are preliminary. The term *supernumerary income,* as used here, refers to that share of consumer income that is not needed for the essentials and is available for optional spending. Specifically, it consists of all income in excess of $20,000 a year flowing to each family unit. The supernumerary income series represents a general measure of rising consumer affluence. Projections are based on a 4 percent annual growth in real personal income.

1974 still lived in poverty, with incomes of less than $6,000 a year.[9] Many of these poor live in communities inadequately served by retail stores. This situation poses a major social problem that government, with the active cooperation of merchants, must attempt to solve.

Supernumerary Income

With the exception of short recession jolts, our whole economy has reflected a tendency toward buying "the most wanted" rather than "the most needed." In no small measure, this comes from higher incomes, working wives, more leisure time, smaller families, and comforting "kitties" in the form of savings of all sorts,[10] including social security and pension plans. A general measure of rising consumer affluence is represented by Figure 4–4. However, buyers are warned that these conditions vary markedly by locality.

[9]These figures are not directly comparable with the data in the chart (Figure 4–3) because they are limited to families of four, where the price index adjusted for the poverty level in 1974 was $5950.

[10]The savings cushion also acts as a stimulus for credit buying.

Consumer Expenditures

Some help in forecasting demand may also be obtained from information like that exhibited in Table 4–2. At best, these are only rough indicators and should be replaced with *local* data wherever possible. (See comments at end of this section.)

The *income elasticity ratio* in Table 4–2 is derived as follows: (1) divide the growth rate for each item in the 1960–1974 column by 4.2 (growth rate of disposable income 1960–1974); (2) divide the growth rate for each item in the 1967–1974 column by 3.6 (growth rate of disposable income 1967–1974). The resulting income elasticity columns show that food purchases apparently respond sluggishly to income changes (indexes .53 and .26), women's and children's clothing respond more actively (.85 and 1.09), and toilet articles still more actively (1.50 and 1.05).

TABLE 4–2
The pattern of growth in consumer spending, 1960–1974
Average annual growth rates and income elasticity ratios, selected items, based on constant dollars

Item	*Average annual growth rates* 1960–1974	1967–1974	*Income elasticity ratios*[a] 1960–1974	1967–1974
DISPOSABLE PERSONAL INCOME	4.2	3.6	1.00	1.00
PERSONAL CONSUMPTION EXPENDITURES	4.0	3.5	.95	.97
Durable Goods[b]	6.2	5.5	1.48	1.53
Automobile purchase	4.5	3.3	1.07	.90
Tires, tubes, accessories, parts	4.9	7.1	1.17	1.96
Furniture, bedding	4.0	3.6	.95	.99
Kitchen, other household appliances	6.2	6.9	1.49	1.90
China, glassware, other durable house furnishings	7.0	6.7	1.67	1.86
Radios, TV, records, instruments	12.5	9.2	2.99	2.53
Wheel goods, durable toys, sport equipment	10.0	8.1	2.39	2.25
Nondurable goods[b]	3.0	2.4	.71	.66
Food, beverages at home	2.2	.9	.53	.26
Purchased meals, beverages	2.0	2.0	.49	.55
Food only (excl. alcoholic beverages)	2.0	.9	.48	.25
Alcoholic beverages	2.6	2.4	.62	.67
Tobacco	.9	1.5	.22	.42

cont'd.

TABLE 4–2 (cont'd.)	*Average annual growth rates*		*Income elasticity ratios*[a]	
Item	*1960–1974*	*1967–1974*	*1960–1974*	*1967–1974*
Shoes, other footwear	2.7	2.6	.64	.71
Women's, children's clothing	3.6	3.9	.85	1.09
Men's, boys' clothing (incl. military)	3.6	3.3	.86	.90
Gasoline, oil	4.7	4.7	1.13	1.31
Toilet articles, preparations	6.3	3.8	1.50	1.05
Semidurable housefurnishings	6.2	6.1	1.46	1.68
Household supplies, preparations	5.9	4.0	1.40	1.10
Drug preparations, sundries	5.5	5.6	1.31	1.55
Services[b]	4.3	3.9	1.02	1.06
Housing: owner-occupied (nonfarm)	5.0	5.0	1.18	1.39
Housing: renter-occupied (nonfarm)	4.7	4.4	1.11	1.21
Household operation services, total	4.3	3.6	1.02	.99
Electricity	6.0	5.9	1.43	1.64
Gas	3.3	1.6	.78	.45
Telephone	7.9	7.2	1.87	1.99
Auto transportation services	4.9	4.9	1.18	1.36
Purchased local transportation	−2.8	−3.1	−.67	−.87
Purchased intercity transportation	6.0	2.7	1.43	.75
Medical care services	5.5	6.1	1.31	1.68
Personal care services	− .1	−3.4	−.02	−.93
Admissions to spectator amusements	1.0	1.5	.21	.41
Higher education	5.0	2.9	1.18	.80
Foreign travel, U.S. residents	5.7	3.6	1.37	.99

Note: Growth rates are based on exponential trend growth.
[a]Percentage change in personal consumption expenditures for each 1% rise in real disposable personal income.
[b]Includes items not separately listed.
Sources: Department of Commerce; The Conference Board.

Psychographic[11] Segmentation and Life Styles

Psychographic segmentation represents a prodigious, involved, and still controversial part of marketing research. Here are some specific changes in demand preferences stemming from demographic and psychographic changes in the population:

[11]"Psychographics" involves a wide range of characteristics including opinions, attitudes, beliefs, interests, and activities—often reflected in so-called life styles.

1. As a children's bulge in the age mix moves into a teen-age bulge, the "wheel goods" buyer must *gradually* shift inventory and promotion from tricycles to bicycles. Note the emphasis on "gradually": The change will not happen some night when the store is closed but rather over a period of time, which will give the *alert* buyer time to cash in fully on the developing opportunity in bicycles while gently trimming the investment in tricycles to suit a lessened but still lively demand.

2. Harder but still possible to anticipate is the change in life style that makes the multiple speed "gussied-up" bike or moped an important possession for teen-agers, young adults, and even older members of society.

3. More important than the change in population numbers may be the forecast about whether an age group like teen-agers will carry their life styles, attitudes, and cultural mores over into adulthood. And, if so, how will they be expressed? Will an antimaterialistic attitude of youth be reflected in smaller cars and less formal and elaborate costumes and home furnishings of adult life? Or will the anticult be expressed in ever more elaborate motorcycles, smaller but racier looking autos, and clothing and furnishings that may look more casual but still conform tightly to a new ritual.

4. "Americans are discarding the traditional eating utensils and three-meals-a-day for a new, more casual life style which (among other things) includes more "finger food."[12] Add to the list "fast food" eating places, "take home" eating places, and "TV dinners" at the freezer counters.

5. There is a new wave of attention to "bean-pot" slow-cooking devices, which permit a meal to be set up in the morning and cook all day if need be, and concomitantly, microwave ovens, which cook with startling rapidity.

6. There are expanding markets developed in the mass electronics industries, the amateur photo industry, various participating sports, and do-it-yourself activities, resulting in any and all devices designed to cut down the amount of work required to run a household.[13]

Changes in Life Styles

Changes in life style, interests and activities, attitudes, opinions, and beliefs thread through all these demographic and psychographic elements, both springing from and causing them. For example, one of the causes behind the trend to smaller households and smaller families is the desire to control and reduce childbirth and all the devices and practices that spring from it, all of which makes it necessary to interpret data most carefully.

Business Week[14] points out that although the trend is toward smaller families, the large number of women arriving at child-bearing age between

[12] *Marketing News*, American Marketing Association (May 7, 1976), p. 2.

[13] Credited with accelerating some of these trends are the growing number of working women who prize convenience, speed, utility, and automatic performance.

[14] Issue of January 12, 1976, p. 75.

1975 and 1985 will mean a lot of "first children" for whom new equipment and apparel has to be purchased (as opposed to hand-me-downs used for successive children). And it is reasonable to guess that, with two parents working with fewer children and with more affluent grandparents, those purchases could well be at higher price lines.

HOW ONE STORE ADJUSTED TO CHANGE

A "market" for any one retailer has to be a segment of the population described in a *combination* of demographic and psychographic terms. The magazine *Time* summed Bloomingdale's "major market" as follows: "young, affluent, fashion-conscious, traveled, professional people. They are attuned less to refrigerators and washing machines ('Bloomies' sells neither), more to clothes of fashion and quality, stereo equipment and wacky gadgetry for the compact Manhattan society of small apartments, crowded schedules and casual relationships. These consumers, to Bloomingdale's profit, go for such baubles as yogurt makers, $30 peanut-butter-making machines, 'male chauvinist pig' neckties and even 'Pet Rocks'."[15]

This may not be an accurate description of that market and may not include all of its distinguishing characteristics. It might be that the description fits a relatively small core of the market, which is then swelled to its great size by the multitudes who think of this core as a reference group with whom they can identify. In any event, some such concept provides a good bull's-eye for targeting a whole merchandising and promotional approach.

Nor should it be imagined that a store like Bloomingdale's lives on cake alone. Behind all its "trendy," avant-garde merchandise is a basic stock of goods with much more universal appeal—even for the far-out segment of trade. The great and growing middle classes bustled around the Manhattan store in 1975 and deposited some $350 annual sales per square foot (over three times the NRMA average), with a reportedly much better profit ratio than the average.

DISCUSSION QUESTIONS

1. (a) If the fashion industry agrees to promote a new style energetically, can it create a fashion, accepted by the public, even though the style itself has no marked attraction to the public? Give apparent examples, if any.
   (b) When the promotion of a new item is a success, is it fair to say that the style met an existing customer demand, even if only a latent one?

[15]"Trendy Bloomingdale's," *Time* (Dec. 1, 1975), pp. 73–80.

2. What so-called secondary buying motives can you suggest in addition to those mentioned in this chapter?
3. Give examples of how the perception of an article of merchandise differs with different customers and customer groups.
4. Suggest examples of a customer buying a "little piece of heaven" when he or she purchases an article of merchandise.
5. Which of the consumer changes depicted on the demographic charts are changing the buying and promotion practices of store buyers?
6. Suggest names of great firms that have gone out of business, and conjecture about the reasons.
7. Why is it important for buyers to be so objective about their judgments concerning the goods they buy for their firms?
8. Has the increased mobility of the U.S. population had an important effect on consumer buying?
9. In how many product lines can projected demographic changes have an effect on size ranges in merchandise? Explain.
10. Do food stores and stores that handle basic commodities have an obligation to provide as low prices and as good service in depressed areas of the city as they do in middle-class neighborhoods, even though shoplifting and vandalism make their expenses in these areas high?
11. Table 4–3 on page 106 is a sampling of some items of information taken from the 1974 edition of the *Survey of Buying Power* published annually by Sales Management, the Marketing Magazine. If you were a merchant in one of the cities included, what facts gleaned from Table 4–3 would be of special importance to you if you deal in (a) foods, (b) general merchandise and apparel, (c) furniture and appliances, and (d) drugs and cosmetics?
12. Some economists are convinced that the concept of consumer freedom and sovereignty is a myth, that consumers are being coerced and manipulated in the buying decisions they make.
    a. What evidence is there for this belief?
    b. If the concept were accepted by retailers, how would it change their buying and selling practices?
    c. Should retailers adhere firmly to the attitude towards consumers presented in this chapter?

TABLE 4–3
Retail Sales by Store Group—1973

Iowa Metro Area/County	Total Retail Sales ($000)	% of U.S.	Food Total ($000)	Food Super-markets ($000)	Eating & Drinking Places Total ($000)	General Merchandise Total ($000)	General Merchandise Dept. Stores ($000)	Apparel Total ($000)	Furn.-House.-Appl. Total ($000)	Furn.-House.-Appl. Furn.-Home Furnishings ($000)	Auto-motive Total ($000)	Gas Station Total ($000)	Lumber-Bldg.-Hdwre. Total ($000)	Drug Total ($000)
Cedar Rapids Linn	426,489	.0830	88,623	84,192	38,310	97,953	92,559	14,543	28,590	14,996	73,583	34,455	21,309	13,004
Davenport - Rock Island - Moline	889,930	.1731	173,068	151,200	94,933	142,836	124,685	31,423	41,987	29,996	177,833	75,998	47,265	30,043
Henry, Ill.	136,420	.0265	23,805	16,349	11,488	6,999	1,059	4,337	5,539	4,072	25,935	12,735	16,253	3,819
Rock Island, Ill.	424,875	.0827	82,202	71,143	49,845	64,393	55,329	13,492	19,184	12,357	90,197	36,107	17,929	15,355
Scott, Iowa	328,635	.0639	67,061	63,708	33,600	71,444	68,297	13,594	17,264	13,567	61,701	27,156	13,083	10,869
Des Moines	788,097	.1533	172,045	163,439	64,408	158,102	127,048	42,099	35,498	17,769	157,867	64,542	35,864	20,521
Polk	746,038	.1451	161,471	153,397	61,484	157,333	127,048	39,780	34,015	16,952	147,583	59,223	30,673	19,869

Retail Sales by Merchandise Line—1973

Iowa Metro Area	Groceries, Other Foods Mdse. Lines	Groceries, Other Foods In Food Stores	Cosmetics, Etc. Mdse. Lines	Cosmetics, Etc. In Drug-stores	Women's, Girls' Clothing Mdse. Lines	Women's, Girls' Clothing In Dept. Stores	Men's, Boys' Clothing Mdse. Lines	Men's, Boys' Clothing In Apparel Stores	All Footwear Mdse. Lines	All Footwear In Apparel Stores	Major Appliances Mdse. Lines	Major Appliances In Appliance Stores	Furn., Sleep., Etc. Mdse. Lines	Furn., Sleep., Etc. In FHF Stores
Cedar Rapids	79,818	76,748	17,486	8,557	43,707	27,027	14,074	1,905	8,103	5,410	20,898	10,916	14,074	5,668
Davenport - Rock Island - Moline	169,087	151,781	33,817	17,846	55,506	33,955	27,588	10,684	13,349	6,316	29,368	9,629	24,918	14,548
Des Moines	155,255	146,238	26,795	12,990	62,319	34,811	28,371	12,293	14,974	8,630	32,312	14,183	23,643	7,356
Dubuque	37,215	35,784	8,391	5,297	18,987	10,742	6,193	1,590	3,996	2,168	8,790	4,077	5,594	1,836
ΔIowa City	32,447	31,199	7,022	5,057	7,194	4,593	5,148	2,540	2,231	1,536	4,463	2,700	3,148	2,083
Sioux City	52,581	50,559	10,768	5,563	23,120	14,709	10,768	4,749	5,101	2,249	11,052	6,446	8,218	1,941
Waterloo - Cedar Falls	59,764	56,158	9,419	5,171	20,864	13,865	10,069	4,077	5,847	3,416	13,967	5,555	10,069	4,010
Total Above Areas	586,167	548,467	113,698	60,481	231,697	139,702	102,211	37,838	53,601	29,725	120,850	53,506	89,664	37,442

chapter 5

The Merchandise Assortment: Product Differentiation and Policy Considerations

DIFFERENTIATING THE PRODUCT

The inherent elements that differentiate one product from another, and that form the basis for ultimate selection or rejection by the consumer, are complex and often subtle. Following is a partial listing of the most common and easily recognizable elements to which we shall frequently refer as "selection factors." These are the factors that make a product specially suitable for a particular end-use, i.e., for a given purpose, occasion, customer, or group of customers.

1. Basic or generic style or silhouette (such as single-breasted as opposed to double-breasted suits, or Swedish glassware as opposed to Venetian).[1]
2. Decoration or trim, or pattern of print, weave, or embellishment.
3. Material or fabric, which may in turn be differentiated by factors like thickness, weight, texture, transparency, durability, and finish and by basic components such as yarns, threads, metal, wood, glass, and chemicals.
4. Packaging of the product.

[1]There is no point in making precious distinctions of classification. Specific details like long versus short sleeves could be called versions of silhouette or could just as well be classified as determinants of primary utility. This kind of problem will confront us when dealing with "crew" necklines as opposed to "jewel" or "boat" or "keyhole" lines, or in separating "hobnails" from other categories of spreads. Terminology is understandably confusing: versions of generic styles or silhouettes are called "models," "types," "styles," and other names. The context has to define meanings as used. (See also the section on Classification NRMA in Chapter 6).

5. Sensory factors such as color, odor, sound, texture, and taste or considerations like tenderness or juiciness.
6. Construction or workmanship, which includes the final finishing touches and quality control that distinguish grades from "clean" to "sloppy."
7. Size, which is usually a factor of low substitutability except within a narrow range.
8. Ease and cost of maintenance: "no-stick" surfaces, elasticity, crease retention, and washability.
9. Health and safety factors like diet and nutritional considerations, natural versus synthetic components, and allergenic and carcinogenic properties.
10. Social considerations, like effect on the environment, biodegradability, etc.
11. Ability to save or conserve energy in use. This is the basis for (a) the gadgets, devices, compounds, and materials designed to decrease work, and (b) the size of automotive vehicles and the speed regulations that govern them.
12. Utility or versatility (including a variety of end-uses).

The list of specific selection factors can go on and on.

Some, like the last three on the list, are specific virtues that may depend, at least in part, on factors previously listed. Some become controversial, because it is not known how much they influence customers in making a final selection decision. To conclude, the list is ended with two more factors that need further discussion:

13. Brand, a shorthand description of a group of standards of grade or style.
14. Price, the exchange value of the sum of all other selection factors.

Brand

A brand may identify one maker's[2] or one seller's version of a given product, or it may identify a line of products from one seller. In this case, the brand is an outgrowth of the "hallmark"—an identification of the maker's pride in his or her product and an assurance that certain uniform standards are maintained.

This kind of assurance becomes especially important to the customer when the product is hidden in a package (as in drugs, beverages, groceries, cigarettes, etc.), when the rational determinants of value are complex and hidden (as in automobiles and other mechanical devices), when customers generally doubt their abilities to judge values (as men often feel about their clothes), or when the expenditure is high and the perceived risk is correspondingly great.

But some brands—especially those associated with high prices—come to

[2]It is common in the pharmaceutical industry, for example, for one common or "generic" product to appear under as many different names as there are manufacturers making it.

stand for symbols of status. For some purchasers, the labels have a worth quite apart from the virtues of the products themselves. Some retailers have built their reputations to the point where their private labels on the goods they sell materially enhance the value of those goods to certain purchasers.

A great many products are sold without any brand label at all or without a label of established significance. For these products, the reputations of the retailers who offer them are, again, important selection factors.

Price

To be an important factor in the purchasing decision, a selection factor must be significant and observable. Price is one of the most observable selection factors and may have considerable significance. However, its importance as a decision factor may easily be exaggerated.[3] Purchase is made on a combination of selection factors, in which the position of price may rank all the way from dominant to insignificant. When all else is equal, purchasers drift to the lowest-priced product or to the retailer who offers lowest prices.

Retailers have always used this fact as a simple, direct sales-promotional device. To bolster the effectiveness of the low-price claim, retailers have sought products wherein the other selection factors are highly identifiable (or observable) and therefore comparable. Branded, strongly advertised product lines have been prime ammunition: Drugs, books, and groceries are common examples. Products where some single selection factor has become the symbol of value are used similarly to establish "identity" of goods for price-cutting purposes; such products are sterling silver, and any other material that stands for obvious price identification. Technological innovations are prime candidates for the pricing guillotine; an example is the spectacular drop in price lines of electronic caculators and digital watches soon after their introductions. In these cases, however, the drop in prices resulted from savings through mass-production technology as soon as acceptance swelled.

The larger the amount to be saved through lower prices, the greater the effort that customers will make to earn the savings. The amount on each item of groceries is small, but the aggregate on a week's purchases becomes significant. "Discounters" who flourished after World War II made use of this principle. In out-of-the-way locations, they promoted "big" savings on expensive merchandise: electrical appliances, tools, cameras, typewriters, luggage, and silverware, to name some. These were highly standardized,

[3]Quality of product and services won out over lower prices in a nationwide survey conducted by Citicorp, the nation's second largest bank holding company. Of 1407 persons polled, 72% claim that they look for quality rather than lower prices, although most of them add that products and services are overpriced [*Business Week* (July 12, 1976), p. 62].

strongly advertised, branded products; hence, the selection factors were easily identifiable. There was no question about comparing the values of B brand, style number x00 refrigerator in two different stores. The products were obviously identical, price being the only difference—and a substantial one.

As a matter of fact, the term "discounters" stemmed from the fact that they promoted their wares simply by offering them at various discounts from the manufacturer's "list" prices. Originally these represented the normal retail price in traditional retail outlets. The cost to retailers was quoted as so much "off" list. In time, most stores were selling at prices below list; no one sold above list. Therefore "list" became the upper limit of "value" for price comparison.

The big discount stores and chains that later developed did not confine themselves to these highly identifiable goods, although they used them heavily to promote their "low-price" image. These were really "cut-price" department stores. In their less identifiable product lines, they tended to sell merchandise in the lower price ranges at bargain prices: "cheap goods cheaper." These competitive practices change as new forms of retailing discover that *price is not the dominant selection factor for large segments of consumers who are somewhat rigid about their demands for certain product qualities and services and who are quite willing to pay for them.*

Within a range, other factors may be more important than price in the decision to buy one particular version of a product. The customer who asks about or vaguely intends to buy a $10 shirt may willingly pay $12 or even $14 for one with an especially appealing color, pattern, fabric, collar design, or combination of these factors. Or the customer might buy more than one if a suitable combination of selection factors is available at $8 or less. Thus specific price within a range can be a selection factor of low demand rigidity. In other words, *price lines within a range are quite substitutable, one for another.*

The Combination of Selection Factors

Except for custom-made goods, products cannot profitably be made or stocked in the infinite permutations represented by all the desires of all the possible customers. The solution is a great compromise. Products are made in *combinations of selection factors* designed to appeal to the core preferences of a reported group of customers "somewhere out there." And the members of each group settle for products that come close to satisfying their individual combination of desires.

These are the ideas behind the processes known as "market segmentation" and "benefit segmentation." And these are the concepts behind the growing proliferation of versions of products: more styles, more patterns, more colors, all in the attempt to make attractive combinations of selection factors, and all contributing to a growing problem of inventory management.[4]

Customers' selection decisions are not always conscious and *rational*, being influenced—and sometimes dominated—by *emotional* considerations. And much quarrel can ensue over which is which. The buyer does not have to untangle the philosophical roots of the problem: he or she should weigh the selection factors individually and in combination as *appeals to purchase*. That will be hard enough. And the buyer must keep in mind that what the customer buys is not a cold sum of factors but a concept of utility. The psychologists have a word for this common phenomenon wherein the whole is something more than the sum of its parts: It is called the "configuration" or "gestalt" of the whole. In the activities of selling, skilled practitioners know—and sometimes take advantage of the fact—that what the product seems to be may be more important to the consumer than what it "really" is by less imaginative measurement. The customer who buys a new refrigerator may be getting more than a practical, efficient food storer. The right kind of refrigerator may be "a little piece of heaven," and heaven only knows how much that may be "worth." Nor can the aggregate utility of a product be measured at the time of purchase. Its final utility becomes available over time, and its ability to continue to function effectively in use is an important element in that utility.

A product itself or some version of it may stand as a symbol of status. It may be due to size alone: very large as in a diamond, or very small and precise as in a watch. Some products or versions are symbols of conformity. This is a very special problem in anticipating the faddist demands of young people in their teens or in college. In fact, this is an important basis for the whole phenomenon of popular fashion, mode, or fad with consumers of all ages. Whatever the motivation, emotional appeals are selection factors; they contribute to final utility, and are therefore significant and observable value determinants.[5]

ELEMENTS OF MERCHANDISE POLICY

Success in retailing depends on repeat and expanding patronage. A major way to realize this goal is to develop a definite character, personality, or image that lifts one out of the competitive ruck. This character, or totality

[4]For a good, detailed treatment of the subject see: Chester R. Wasson, Frederick D. Sturdivant, David H. McConaughty, *Competition and Human Behavior* (New York: Appleton-Century-Crofts, 1968), "Purchase Behavior, Product and Economic Competition," pp. 4–25.

[5]The Kwakiutl Indians of Vancouver were an "affluent" society for the time and place. Precious "coppers" and other objects of great value were often destroyed in festive potlatch fires simply to shame a rival who did not have a like amount to destroy. Reported by Ruth Benedict, *Patterns of Culture*, chapter 6, a Mentor Book, published by the New American Library in 1934 and followed by many reprints.

of "look," depends on policies as expressed in plant and facilities, service, pricing, promotion, and nature and in assortment of merchandise offerings (recall the Bloomingdale story at the end of Chapter 4). We are here concerned with the merchant's assortment policies growing out of a study of the consumers in the trading area, the choice of segments wanted for customers, and the determination of their merchandise preferences.

Factors Requiring Policy Decisions

In stores that have departmental buyers, management must make policy decisions in regard to the following attributes of the assortment and must instruct buyers to express these policies as they assemble the selection factors and combinations that make up their stocks: (1) quality, (2) price ranges, (3) merchandise standardization versus exclusiveness, (4) taste level, (5) timing of fashions (a leader or a follower), (6) continuity of product lines (maintenance of a basic assortment), (7) variety of product lines permitted in the store and in each department, and (8) relative emphasis on breadth and depth of the assortment.

Quality

Quality can be limited to best materials and workmanship available or serviceable quality consonant with low-price lines, or it can conform to some set of standards in between. Where standards are concrete, there may be policies about testing goods for conformance. Definite policies about the use of "irregulars" and "seconds" may also be needed.

Consumer interests had long been protected in a somewhat desultory way by a combination of governmental laws and self-regulation.[6] Then, in the countercultural movement of the 1960s, "consumerism" was spurred by a consumer protection apostle named Ralph Nader and was adopted by politicians as an article of faith. Because the passion lasted, a flood of legislation appeared in the name of consumerism, and liability laws were changed and spruced and lengthened so that their provisions impinged on all levels of the producing, manufacturing, and marketing systems. See the section on Federal Regulations and Laws on Consumer Protection at the end of Chapter 15.

Retailers must now be more perceptive of product faults to the point of being charged with the responsibility of promptly notifying producers or makers. And all states now support the dictum that every product carries with it an implied if not an expressed warranty. It should also be noted that some of our largest retailers place great stress on quality specifications and control and have made their names synonymous with "implied warranty" in customers' minds.

[6]The work of the American Standards Association in setting industrial standards for consumer goods deserves special mention.

Price Ranges

Price ranges interact with quality. Although there is no specific correlation between price and quality, with the most serviceable merchandise often not the most expensive, there is general correlation. Top-quality policy is usually associated only with top-price lines, and "serviceable" quality imposes a limit as to the bottom of the price range. Goods at the very lowest price lines are likely to be shoddy and are therefore not generally recommended as a policy requirement. Only the very largest retailers can come even close to spanning the whole range. Therefore management should set a range for each product line.[7]

Standardized Offerings Versus Exclusiveness

In this regard, the policy of a store may range from one of dealing only in highly standardized goods (vendors' brands available to competition also) to one of private design and specification. The latter is a most sophisticated device to take an inventory out of direct competition.

A store may also attain exclusiveness by becoming the sole agent in the trading area for a nationally branded specialty product, by prevailing upon vendors to confine certain styles and patterns to one store, and by buying abroad from sources not tapped by competitors.

Exclusiveness is a characteristic that many stores would like to have but is not easily obtained. It is most difficult to keep lines and styles out of competitors' inventories or to have these lines incorporate truly exclusive features of design or utility to distinguish them from competitors' offerings. It is also imperative to avoid becoming involved in "a conspiracy in restraint of trade." Legal counsel is advisable. Nevertheless, the buyer should be informed by management as to the degree of exclusiveness to be sought. For many popular stores, the policy is to carry standard goods along with private brands that measure up in all material respects except price to the national brands. Specialized versions of a product, containing exclusive features not available elsewhere, are not sought.

Taste

Taste is hard to define and express in a policy. Good taste involves an aesthetic appreciation and a degree of sophistication that recognizes a purpose or point of view in the design and color of the article. Although the experts do not wholly agree on what is in good taste, it may be said that it involves the avoidance of extremes, the appropriateness of the design to its functional purpose, and the freedom from sham (where an article masquerades as being something it isn't; an iron bed painted to simulate wood, for example). However, there are many who insist that it is less important for

[7]See Chapter 15 for other elements of pricing policy.

the buyer to make value judgements about taste (good and bad, high and low) than to learn to recognize that aesthetic components differentiate tastes.

For commercial purposes, some merchants insist that "good" taste is that which appeals to a retailer's chosen clientele; "bad" taste describes that which they reject. Although this may be pragmatically true, it must be recognized that with increased education, leisure time, and discretionary income, many consumers are attempting to develop more sophisticated standards of taste. Accordingly, a sound policy may be to aim at a taste level slightly "above" that of the typical customer. Of course, best-sellers will be stocked in depth, but there will also be an adequate assortment of "better" designs and perhaps more fashionable colors. These will add tone to the assortment and allow discerning customers to find something better than the "run of the mill." It must also be recognized that even customers who think they have no appreciation of design and color often respond instinctively to the better. A large mail-order house redesigned the label on a can of a material used by farmers in line with the principles of aesthetics. A great increase in sales resulted with no other change and no special promotion. Consumers simply liked the new can better and bought and reordered more. Many probably didn't know why.

Fashion tends to be a great leveler of taste preference. Great masses of people who prefer simple, tailored goods will buy the rococo and the fussy when they are in fashion. Nevertheless, there are still gradings in the degree to which different groups accept these characteristics.

Timing of Fashions

Timing of fashions in the introduction of new goods is a vital element of policy. The question is whether to undertake leadership, to be a close second, or to wait until the new trend has become an accepted fashion. The buyer for each department or line needs a policy guide as to when to experiment with the new, how quickly to risk deep-ending the stock, and how soon to drop the prevailing mode.

In an address at the NRMA Seminar on Fashion Merchandising, June 1975, Sidney A. Mayer of Saks Fifth Avenue named "three types of successful retailers" in terms of fashion leadership:

"The one who *recognizes* fashion (scouts, predicts and buys adequate stocks) but does not establish preeminence in the community. The second kind *anticipates* fashion (by scouting, predicting and buying aggressively). He makes mistakes, but the rewards for being right more often than being wrong are great. The third *influences* fashion. These are usually principals of very successful specialty shops, individually owned, where the owner has a very strong fashion point of view and uses it with suppliers."

Continuity of Product Lines

The maintenance of regular assortments is a must for staple convenience goods with a short consumption–replenishment cycle like foods, for example. It is essential also for shopping lines, such as open-stock china and glassware, where the same pattern must long be available for replenishment. A continuity of brand in both shopping and specialty goods is also essential if the brand is an important selection factor for customers. Even in fashion goods, where it may not be necessary to maintain continuity of individual styles, there must be a continuity of "central ideas" like type, basic colors, sizes, and price ranges.

Other lines, however, may be sold on a bargain basis from stocks composed of remnants, remainders, and other odd lots. "Bargain basements" have characteristically featured such merchandise or dealt exclusively in it. Some great stores were built on this policy; few have survived. The tendency has been for bargain stores or bargain basements to build maintained assortments of regular merchandise, using the odd lots as traffic pullers.

Most "upstairs" stores also follow the policy of maintaining regular assortments for their "bread and butter" business and of adding "promotional" merchandise when available for extra volume. How much effort to devote to the maintenance of regular assortments and how much to devote to "promotional" effects is an important decision that serves to differentiate stores.

Variety of product lines

These may be sharply limited as in specialty stores or widely covered as in department stores. Specialization may go so far as a decision to carry only one size type, like Tall Girl stores or King Size retailers catering to large men, or knit goods only, or antiques, or exotic foods. Buyers must be clearly informed as to the limits to the variety of lines they may carry.

Breadth and depth of the assortment within product lines

A store may have a policy of carrying only the most popular selection factors, such as a few colors, a few sizes, a few materials, a few prices, a few brands, or a few variations in style details. Another store may decide to provide a wide variety of the many selection factors so that its customers may inspect a number of different items that will meet their basic requirements and from this variety select the one or more that provides them an extra bonus of satisfaction, growing out of the special combination of factors inherent in the item or items selected.

Because space and money, along with time, are the major factors limiting decision, a policy of broad assortments automatically limits the average depth to which items can be stocked; and conversely, if a given depth is desired for a given product, its versions must be limited.

Wide variety and shallow depth may lead to frequent out-of-stock conditions, whereas narrow variety in depth may not permit customers to find just what they are looking for. Thus a balancing of these two factors of inventory becomes the central problem of merchandising and will be given detailed study in this chapter and the next.

BREADTH VERSUS DEPTH

A clear set of policies determines the kind of merchandise that buyers will stock in anticipation of customer wants. They know the product lines for which they are responsible and the price ranges in which they must buy them. They know the standards of quality and styling that will govern selections. They know the degree to which they must buy or avoid standardized goods and seek exclusiveness, and they know requirements for meeting and beating competition. They know what is expected of them in timing the introduction and development of experimental goods, fashions, and seasonal merchandise and in the maintenance of continous assortments. Within product lines, they know what their firms expect by way of variety of selection factors, but they are also given inventory limitations that presumably contain implied selection policies in budget form. They are now ready to plan the composition of the inventory, its breadth and depth.

FIGURE 5–1 Breadth versus depth in an inventory of 16 units. Letters represent different selection factors, such as different colors or patterns. Numbers represent number of units stocked of each different selection factor.

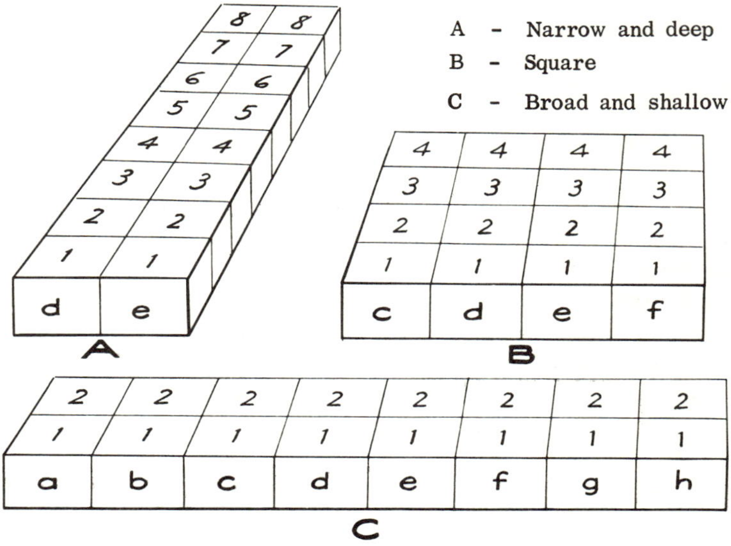

The Model

Figure 5–1 diagrams three ways of composing the stock for a product limited to 16 units of inventory. The letters *a* to *h* represent one or a combination of selection factors that create different versions of the product. The alphabetical factors, for example, may represent color alone or a combination of color and material.

Inventories in the diagram are shown in one plane, as on a shelf (although the numbers beyond 1 could symbolize any reserve stock). The first row of product versions is the "face" of the stock—that which the customer sees and which therefore characterizes the selection as "broad" or "narrow."

Boxes behind the first row measure "depth"—the dimension of inventory that determines its capacity to fulfill the promise implicit in its face. Only an alert (and costly) system of reordering can keep all the versions of C in stock.

Inventory A is described as "narrow and deep." Only two selection factors are carried but average eight each in depth. Inventory C is "broad and shallow"; desire to show the product in eight versions (*a* to *h*) limits their average depth to two units. Inventory B may be considered as characteristic of normal, typical, or common compromise; in line with the concept, it may be described as a "square" inventory (four by four).

Obviously, within the limits of inventory budget, a decision about width is critical with respect to depth, and the desire for depth governs the permissible width. Nor can decisions be based on *average* depths. Each selection factor, such as each color, may have a different rate of acceptance, or sales velocity. Figure 5–2 shows how the buyer constructs a model to account for variance in salability of selection factors.

The models A, B, and C correspond to the types A, B, and C in Figure 5–1. Assume that the selection factors *a* to *h* represent eight colors in which a typewriter is available. Color *d* is the known best-seller; *e* is second; *c* and *f* are third; and *a*, *b*, *g*, and *h* are colors that appeal only to a few.

The price-competitive buyer might stock *d* to a depth of 10 units and *e* to a depth of six units as shown in Model A. He or she has composed the inventory of 16 pieces into the narrow and deep inventory, which is theoretically most efficient from a *cost* point of view. The next chapter will show how faster turnover results from this approach. It is easier to stock and uses less room for display. It is easier to order, check, receive, mark, and handle only two colors. Counting and/or recording for control is simpler. Markdowns due to obsolescence and spoilage resulting from slow-selling colors are avoided.

But the buyer for a firm noted for the breadth of its assortments and for high-fashion colors to suit the most discriminating taste may carry all eight colors, in varying depths as shown in Model C. Model B represents the middle or "standard" form of compromise.

The buyer of Model C is aware that 25 percent of the inventory is "sunk" in four colors that may yield only 5 percent of the total sales of that typewriter—and that the four colors may eventually contribute most to the

FIGURE 5–2 "Model" stocks showing depth of each selection factor balanced to estimated sales. A "broad and deep" assortment would be represented by C stocked to a greater average depth. But this would require a larger inventory allowance than the 16 units currently permitted. A high inventory could be justified only if higher sales could be predicted. Otherwise, the increased depth would produce only costly sludge in the inventory reservoir.

A

A is the "narrow and deep" assortment averaging 8 units of depth per selection factor.

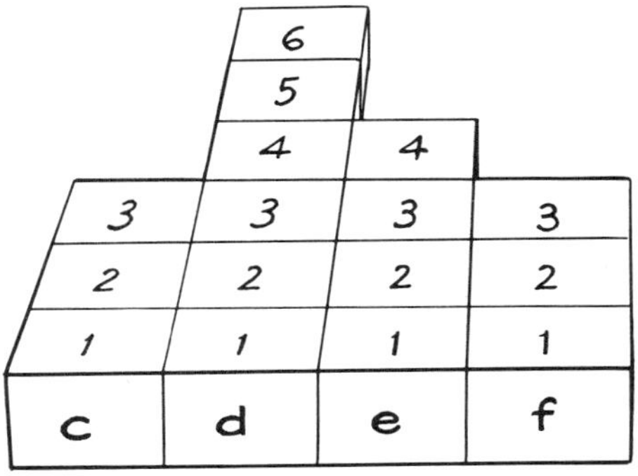

B

B is the "square" assortment averaging 4 units of depth per selection factor.

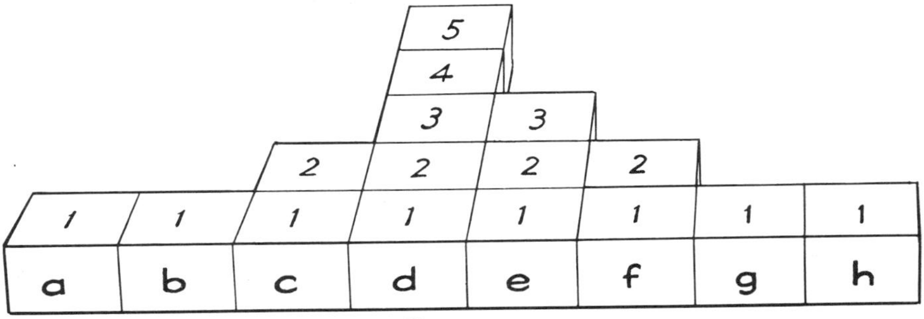

C

C is the "broad and shallow" assortment averaging 2 units of depth per selection factor.

markdown record of the product. But the buyer also knows the effect of those four colors in the window and in departmental displays. He or she knows they have stopping and pulling power, even over those customers who finally buy colors *d* or *e*.

Shallowness does, however, require alert and frequent reordering. *The ultimate test of a stock is its capacity to satisfy the demand of the one customer standing at the counter.* If that customer wants color *f*, momentarily out of stock, the whole assortment loses some of its impressiveness, although the customer may still accept one of the remaining wide selection as a satisfactory substitute.

FACTORS THAT DETERMINE BREADTH

The required breadth of selection varies with: (1) the kind of clientele, (2) time points in the seasonal selling cycle, (3) the productivity of increased breadth, and (4) competitive practice and the type of store.

The Kind of Clientele

In the fight for patronage, *breadth of assortment is an important non-price-competitive weapon.* For many people, the excitement of the bazaar is still a strong impellent, and variety is in itself a magnet. The heightened chance of making a choice "nearer to the heart's desire" is another obvious attraction of wide selections.

The more a retailer's clientele is dominated by mass thinking, the more it is insensitive to differences in detail, the more it becomes advisable to emphasize depth at the expense of breadth.

But the customer who is more discerning, more discriminating, more fashion-conscious, or just more rigid in demand, requires a wider choice. For example, the customer who seeks high fashion or who wants to "mix or match" a sweater with a particular skirt—or even with the color of eyes or hair—is more likely to find the article in the collection of eight colors than in the two that satisfy the great bulk of customers.

Even those who buy the selection factors most in vogue often like to make their choice from a wide range. The presence of high-fashion selection factors also tends to lend an air of fashion authenticity to the whole assortment.

Time Points in the Selling Cycle

In the commodities subject to volatile fashion or seasonal changes, the opening assortments are wide and shallow. There are many new selection factors on the market, and their ultimate degree of acceptance is not yet known. The buyer must use a lot of judgement in a preliminary culling of the marketing offerings. When in doubt, the dubious items must be added to the early collection for testing.

But once the early customer response reveals likely[8] concentrations of demand, the stock will be reduced in breadth and expanded in depth. This does not preclude the purchase of those selection factors that the demand pattern indicates were mistakenly rejected in the preliminary cull or preclude the inclusion of new selection factors that were not available in early showings.

The process of narrowing and deepening continues into the peak of the season, after which narrowing proceeds at a faster rate than deepening. Toward the end of a season, most of the remaining regular stock should be concentrated in the lowest price lines and on the most popular selection factors. Those elements that could not be forced into this orderly liquidation procedure will remain as "broken assortments." These may, in turn, be fused with special price promotions of vendors' overstocks, which are brought in to bolster sales volume late in the season.

Two theories about consumer demand govern these programs. First, *customers for higher-priced goods tend to buy in the earlier part of the season.* Second, *customers become less discriminating as the season advances toward and past the peak.* Their willingness to accept substitutes for original, specific demands is reinforced by their awareness that they are shopping at a time when assortments are diminishing in all stores.

When a selling cycle is marked by some calendar date that acts as a cutoff,[9] the breakup of assortments begins almost coincidentally with the beginning of a peak demand. This kind of cycle is marked by a sharply peaking demand curve followed by a precipitate decline. The assortment required to maximize sales at the peak would create a too costly markdown problem afterward. The burden would also be too great to permit carrying over inventory into the next selling cycle; or the obsolescence or spoilage factor would make it impossible.

The assortment planned for the early part of the season and for peak selling may be called an "elected model." Breadth and depth are chosen and reflect balance to sales expectancy. The assortment at the end of a season has two components: (1) a *basic model,* satisfying minimum requirements of assortment, and (2) the leftovers of the season's operation, representing an unbalanced and technically excessive stock.

[8]Remember the warning that customer preference in the early part of the season is not necessarily a true harbinger of preference by later purchasers.

[9]Merchandise subject to such cutoff dates includes: women's accessories on Mother's Day, certain men's furnishings on Father's Day, back-to-school clothes on Labor Day, turkeys on Thanksgiving, toys on Christmas, produce on Saturday night.

Productivity of Increased Breadth

The breadth of an assortment may be expanded by adding product lines or by adding versions of a product line. The results of the two maneuvers are quite different. The first tends to bring wholly additional or *supplementary* sales; the second brings *complementary* sales that may be shared with other versions of the product line.

Adding product lines

The addition of new product lines is less likely to cause diversion of sales from the established assortment; the effect on total sales is largely or wholly supplementary. Thus, when shoe stores added hosiery to their stock, the hose detracted nothing from the sale of shoes; hosiery sales were wholly additional. As a matter of fact, the new product line was priced to bring traffic into the store and thereby increase the sale of shoes. The "pulling power" of this added factor to the store's assortment should be remembered. It will form an important part of subsequent developments.

The tendency toward this kind of expansion is apparent also among departmental buyers; they crowd policy limits set for their lines as much as interpretation and market practices will allow. One need only contemplate the emergence of the old notions department from its little cell of buttons, safety pins, and hairnets to a sprawling complex of giftware, closet accessories, and home furnishing.[10] Stationery and housewares departments have not been slow to follow. The gift department, a natural "catch bucket," has characteristically "pirated" from many specialized departments, only to face the day when these departments are themselves becoming gift centers.

Apparently buyers also will "mine" a given assortment only to the point where it seems that *marginal productivity from further exploitation can be exceeded by the marginal productivity of added product lines.* Homogeneity with established lines is no longer very important; "scrambled merchandising" is commonplace.

Buyers, like the stores they represent, seek a mixture of benefits from added product lines. They may produce added sales, added traffic, higher profit margins, or any combination thereof.

Adding product versions

The addition of selection factor variants to an *established* product line does not bring wholly additional business. *Each added selection factor—be it color, material, brand, style or price—will add to total sales volume of the*

[10]The start of the 70s saw the start of movements in many stores to "break up" the notions department and incorporate its parts with related categories.

line but commonly at a diminishing rate of speed.

Each worthwhile addition presumably has some complementary selling and pulling power. But there is an increasing tendency to share sales with the variants already in stock. An example may be drawn from a sweater assortment. Assume that a buyer had an initial assortment of six colors, selling at the rate of 144 per week, or averaging 24 per week for each color. If six more colors were added, the sales would not be likely to double.

What actually would happen depends on many circumstances surrounding the individual case. Here is what might very well happen: The presence of the seventh color might add six sales per week to the total sales of the category. That would be the "net marginal productivity" of the seventh color. But this does not mean that recorded sales would show six units for the new variant. It might actually sell at the rate of eight per week. But three of the sales credited to it might have been made from the first six colors if the seventh had not been available.

In other words, the new color is substitutable with one or more colors in the initial assortment and therefore "shares" demand with them—depending on the whim of the individual customer or the salesperson. Up to this point in the analysis, the "complementary" effect of the seventh color is represented by the net of five units (eight recorded sales minus three shared sales).

In addition, it may be assumed that the seventh color, by its very act of increasing the size of the assortment, has exerted an added pulling power. This may be represented by one additional sale in one of the six original colors. Adding this one additional sale to the five complementary sales gives the six sales, noted above, which represent the marginal productivity of the seventh color.

An eighth color might sell at the rate of six units per week, with three shared sales and one pulling-power sale, giving it a net marginal productivity of four. Jumping now to the tenth color, it is possible that all its sales are shared with the nine prior colors, giving it no complementary effect. If it still produced an extra sale for the nine prior colors, its presence in the stock would have to be justified or rejected on the basis of that factor alone. An eleventh color might not even add pulling power to the assortment, thereby netting a marginal productivity of zero—and becoming completely unjustified.

But somewhere along this process, a peculiar phenomenon may take place. The addition of a twelfth and thirteenth color may make the assortment so wide as to give it the character of a "dominant competitor" as opposed to a "competent competitor." At this point, added colors may share almost wholly with prior colors. But the pulling power may increase sufficiently so that additional increments have a rising marginal productivity.

Theoretically, this phenomenon will continue briefly, until the effect of diminishing returns makes itself felt again. By the time an eighteenth color is added, the marginal productivity may have shrunk back to zero.

Graphic representation to the productivity of line expansion

Figure 5–3 shows a still more simplified illustration of the workings of the marginal productivity concept. A single variant of a product line sells at the rate of four. It doesn't matter whether the rate is four per week or per day or whether the illustrated variant is color, style, brand, price, or any other selection factor.

FIGURE 5–3 Total productivity and Marginal productivity

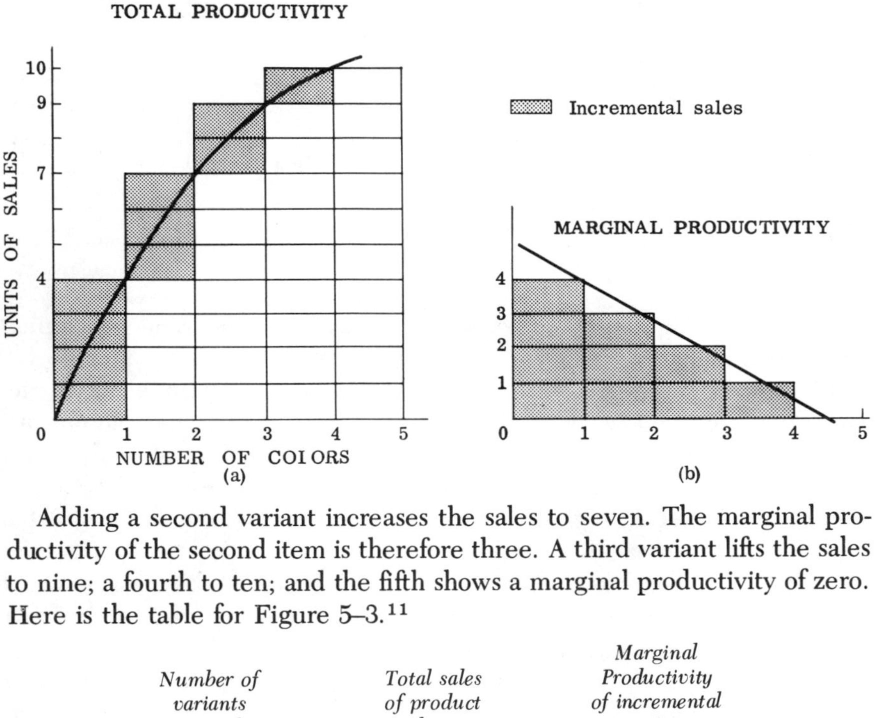

Adding a second variant increases the sales to seven. The marginal productivity of the second item is therefore three. A third variant lifts the sales to nine; a fourth to ten; and the fifth shows a marginal productivity of zero. Here is the table for Figure 5–3.[11]

Number of variants in stock	*Total sales of product line*	*Marginal Productivity of incremental variant*
1	4	4
2	7	3
3	9	2
4	10	1
5	10	0

Figure 5–3(a) shows the cumulation of total sales as variants are added. The shaded areas indicate the net amount added to sales by each variant. Notice how the curve of sales slopes upward at a decelerating rate until it flattens out at the fifth increment.

[11]The reader is referred to *Economics*, Paul A. Samuelson, 10th ed. (New York: McGraw-Hill, 1976), to see how analogous this concept is with economists' laws of marginal utility.

FIGURE 5–4 Total productivity of a dominant assortment

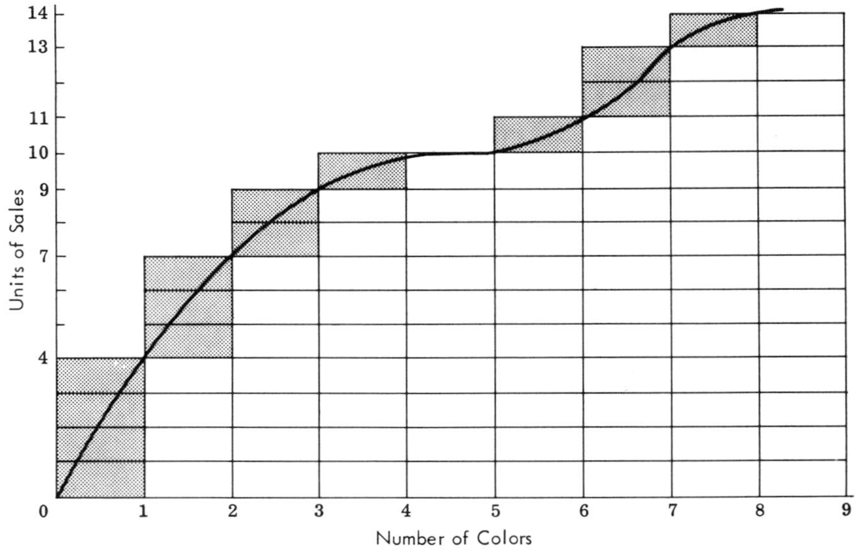

Figure 5–3b shows the net added sales of each increment as its marginal productivity—starting with four and vanishing to zero.

Figure 5–4 shows the effect of the dominant assortment phase in the continuous addition of increments. Notice that the first five columns are identical with Figure 5–3(a). At the sixth increment, marginal productivity rises again, from zero (at 5) to one. It climbs to two at the seventh increment, falls back to one at the eighth, and becomes zero again as the ninth variant is added to the assortment.

Marginal productivity is very hard to measure. But the buyer who would build an efficient, productive assortment must understand the concept and measure or estimate effects with whatever tools and data are at hand.

Adding variants beyond the point of zero productivity does not increase the selling power of a stock: It merely creates a pseudo-assortment. And before this point is reached, the buyer must try to estimate whether added variants will produce enough added sales to defray incremental costs.

Competitive Practice a Determinant of Breadth

What constitutes a competent or dominant assortment depends on the merchandise, the store, and competition. A supermarket with a comparatively meager health and beauty aids section may offer one brand of nail polish in eight or ten of the most wanted shades. Due to materials-handling problems in the warehouse, it cannot afford the open or split carton handling necessary to support the low sales velocity of added shades. The buyer works on the assumption that sales from these few shades represent the optimal profit situation.

Buyers for cosmetics departments in department or specialty stores or large drugstores may feel that 50 shades in at least two brands are necessary to be "in the business" at all. They realize that a large part of the sales volume comes from relatively few shades. But the wide assortment seems to be the minimum competent assortment in the face of practice by their most direct competitors.

There was a time when the color card for a women's silk hosiery manufacturer contained about 40 or more colors. And buyers stocked a great many of them, ignoring the fact that many were such minute variations of beige as to be barely distinguishable by experts.[12] The wasteful extravanganza was finally boiled down to three or four shades. Then came a demand for some of the more chromatic colors, and the cycle may repeat—perhaps in diminuendo.

The search for volume is a restless surge, and adding product versions, like lowering price lines, becomes addictive. The hosiery spectacular has since been repeated in sheets and pillowcases and in towels, to name two once plain, mostly white, staple standbys. Another example is to be found in the size assortments of shoes in department stores, where a given style number may come in 40 or more combinations of length and width. Chain shoe stores halved and quartered these combinations by carrying one principal width, "medium," with sometimes a second width, which may be "narrow" for some styles and "wide" for others.

Size is a factor of very low substitutability, and addition of certain sizes, especially at ends of the scale, produce sales of a relatively high supplementary value. Nevertheless, a high proportion of sales is usually contributed by the few "heart" sizes of a size scale. And the buyer who moves out toward the fringe sizes will find distressingly low marginal productivity. Sometimes the need to carry such sizes is dictated by store policy. The buyer for a women's shoe chain might decide to dispense with size four shoes on the assumption that the few potential sales are unprofitable and can therefore be easily surrendered. But a department store, at the other end of the spectrum, may have to reckon with the fact that this potential purchaser may be a highly profitable customer for heart-stock goods in 20 other departments of the store.

It can be stated as a fairly generalized principle that, all *else being equal, the width of assortment in a given product line should vary somewhat directly with the number of product lines carried.* In multiple-product retailing, considerations concerning the individual product or category must be secondary to the profitability of the mix.

[12]Compounding the nonsense was the fact that in those days of "silk stockings," no two dye lots of the same color ever came out the same way.

The discount houses may be an exception to the rule. In spite of many product lines, their managements know full well that a few items comprise most of the sales opportunity as far as their price-conscious clientele is concerned. Hence, they carry deep and narrow stock assortments: "Thick on the best, to hell with the rest." But as they grow in size and attempt to expand their customer markets, they find it necessary to broaden lines. The number of customers who forego assortments for price is limited, especially when other outlets of the same kind begin to use wider assortments as a competitive device.

Marks & Spencer, the great English chain, succeeded in building one of the world's largest apparel businesses on narrow stocks, even confining itself to most popular size ranges. But the image it created is not one of low price alone. The company designs much of its own merchandise and observes high-quality standards. By concentrating on key items, it has been able to bring distinctiveness and quality to the masses. But few stores could hope to emulate successfully a policy so long, carefully, and consistently nurtured.

DEMAND RIGIDITY: A FACTOR IN DEPTH

Nature of the Problem

In the process of providing the proper depth for each variant in the product line, the buyer must be fully informed about the relative demand rigidity of the selection factors. He or she must be aware that wants are not always clearly defined in the mind of the customer and that elements in the stock may overlap in their capacity to satisfy an expressed demand. It is quite possible that the customer who asks for a solid-colored necktie may, in the end, be more than satisfied to buy a simple "under-knot" pattern; and the customer who asks for a heavy woolen blanket may be happier with a lighter electric blanket, even at a somewhat higher price. Thus it may be more important to have an adequate assortment of woolen *and* electric blankets than a broad and deep assortment of one or the other. This is another example of anticipating the central idea rather than a specific item of demand.

Consumers as individuals display a bewildering variance of rigidity about their expressed wants. As customer groups, however, they exhibit discernible patterns that can be employed in constructing the assortment.

Reasons for Analysis

In planning the assortment, it is important to determine the order of rigidity of the various selection factors for the following reasons:

1. It is essential to plan a full assortment in each of the selection factors that are rigid, whereas the assortment may be less complete in the factors that are flexible. Thus the shoe buyer must carry a full assortment in each of the popular colors and sizes of shoes but may not have to have full assortments at all prices, in all materials, or in all brands. Stock-control records and replenishment procedures must be set up to facilitate keeping up the assortments at all points at which demand is rigid.

   Once again, it is important to remember that the principle should be a guide and not a rule. It is, for example, not always practicable to work assortments by order of demand rigidity because of variables beyond the buyer's control—one variable being the problems of fast and convenient coverage of a market where assortments may be presented in arbitrary classes and price lines, not strictly based on customer end-use.
2. The physical stock should generally be arranged according to demand rigidity, especially in self-selection fixtures, to facilitate customer selection and also to make it easy for salespeople to select what to show the customer. For example, if, within a budget street-dress department, size is found to be the most rigid factor with price line second, the stock should be arranged that way, with prices grouped within each size.
3. Displays will be more effective and the customer influenced to buy more than one item, because all the merchandise in a single location meets primary or more rigid requirements.
4. The planning provides a basis for determination of how to set up unit stock controls. It is both expensive and time-consuming to analyze all sales and inventories by every possible selection factor. Records must be kept that reveal the sales and stocks of the rigid selection factors so that goods incorporating these elements may always be in stock. Flexible factors may be handled more informally, by judgment at the time of selection and by a visual inspection of stock.
5. Where there can be agreement among stores as to the best order of breakdown, statistical interchange will be of value in improving one's own assortment and promotional emphasis. If a group of stores agree, for example, as to the major (most rigid) subdivisions of a women's sweater classification,[13] useful comparisons can be made.

Influences Determining Relative Rigidity of Demand

These influences, among others, include:

1. The primary and specific utility of the product.
2. Secondary considerations in product utility, such as aesthetic value.
3. Typical purchasing habits related to the product as a convenience, shopping, or specialty good.
4. Price lines within a product class.
5. Urgency of Purchase.

[13]This classification is analyzed in detail in Chapter 7.

Primary and specific utility

At the level of primary utility or customers' intended end-use, distinctions are usually quite clear, demand quite rigid, and the compartmenting of a retail stock quite easy. Neither in planning the assortment nor in controlling its content does the retailer have much difficulty in distinguishing among food, furniture, and women's apparel (among sardines, dining tables, and dinner dresses).

But confusion can and does start at the first subdivision of the generic categories. Unless sales records are kept by requisite subclasses, the demand for sardines can be estimated only within the demand for canned fish—and the latter estimated only within the category of canned groceries. Without sales records by subclassification, there is no way to determine at all accurately the total demand for sardines and, consequently, the number of variants and depth that may be profitably carried.

In an economy of extreme scarcity, such as might prevail in time of war or famine, it might be assumed that the demand for sardines is essentially a demand for the primary utility of protein food—and that almost any meat, fish, cheese, or similar product will be accepted, however reluctantly, as a substitute.

A situation of lesser scarcity would demand that canned fish, at least, be separated from meat products, soups, cheese, and all other food categories for purposes of planning and control. Lacking sardines, the grocer could hope to substitute only with some other product in the canned fish assortment.

In an economy of abundance, the more specific utility of sardines, as distinguished from all other canned fish, would become an area of high demand rigidity. Sardines would then have to be classified separately and procedures devised to assure an adequate assortment of variants within this particular product line.

Similarly, to optimize the breadth and depth of a dining table assortment, it is imperative to separate it from the rest of the dining room category or from the even broader class of "case goods."

Secondary considerations in total utility

On the whole, demand rigidity softens as we move down the scale from primary specific utilities and into the other considerations that make up the total utility of a product.

A HANDBAG EXAMPLE A customer seeking a handbag for formal evening wear wants something more specific than a "wearable" container for her costmetics, keys, handkerchief, and money. Generally, this kind of handbag must be small in *size* and conform to certain requirements with respect to *material* and *color*. Beyond these limitations, substitutability of requirements becomes more possible.

If gold is a color in high demand for formal handbags, there must be a selection of gold in the assortment. But a gold brocade may, for some customers, do just as well as gold sequins or beads. And a gold satin may be highly substitutable with gold peau-de-soie. But, within these groupings, the buyer must have gold represented in combination with other colors, such as gold with black, white, green, etc.

White and black must be separately treated in the handbag assortment because they are basic—always in appreciable demand. Other colors combined with gold may be treated more cavalierly, as a group, on the assumption that a demand for one that is temporarily short in stock may be filled from the fully prepared assortment of combinations.

A MEN'S SHIRT EXAMPLE Size, in categories such as clothing, is a factor of high demand rigidity. A customer may accept substitution in brand, fabric, price, and even in collar style of a men's dress shirt. But a size 16 collar is most unlikely to satisfy the demand for a 15½ or 16½. Only slightly more substitutable is a 1-inch departure in required sleeve length. The buyer must recognize this order of demand rigidity in classifying a shirt stock for planning and control purposes.

Again, it must be emphasized that these problems become acute because the capacity for keeping detailed records is limited.[14] Convenience in record-keeping and reordering sometimes results in good data being kept about brand demand in a situation where brands may be more substitutable than collar styles. This is questionable practice.

Where there is no brand rigidity, the first classification under "dress shirts" should be collar styles.[15] If only one set of complete or formal records can be kept, it should be under this heading in order to ensure that assortment and depth are related to the variable demand for styles of collars. This order of classification becomes a source of contention with vendors in many categories, especially where the vendor's salesperson assumes some of the functions of stock-counting and record-keeping for reorder purposes. Vendors prefer data systems wherein all items of their brands are grouped.

Typical purchasing habits

It would seem that the more important a purchase becomes, the more thought would be devoted to it by the customer and the more rigid would be the specification demands. This is only partly true. There are complex elements involved.

[14]Even with the use of modern machines and procedures, the cost problem has not disappeared from inventory control. Today's equipment can do wonders with respect to sorting and analyzing data. But the data to be processed and the reports to be made and studied must still be carefully considered for cost versus value, not only in preparation but in use.

[15]The knotty problem of controlling individual sizes and sleeve lengths can usually be handled by following a standard scale in reordering.

Convenience goods are generally bought with a minimum of thought and effort, and promptly, as a recurring need develops. Examples are ordinary drug and cosmetics products, cigars and cigarettes, newspapers, and most of the items found on the grocer's shelves. The category can be expanded to include articles with a longer consumption–replenishment cycle, such as many of the items in notions, stationery, and housewares categories.

Many of these products are branded and presold by manufacturers. Brands often become a rigid requirement and must be planned separately in the assortment. Deeply ingrained tastes and preferences are involved. Habits are strong. All of which tends to widen the assortment requirement. Quick and effortless purchase must not be confused with indiscriminate purchase.

The sardines previously mentioned are a good example. To begin with, there are several basic kinds: French, Portuguese, Maine, California; large, brisling, and a very small one called "cross-pack"; whole, skinless and boneless—and more. Each is sold under various brands and in various price lines. Most customers are quite rigid in their demand for a specific type and brand. Price lines may vary by brand and type. In selecting the breadth of assortment, the buyer must give close heed to depth, because substitution will not satisfy most customers.

In the fashion goods field, habit also plays an important role in the relative rigidity of such factors as color. In nail polish, for example, there are certain basic colors that must be planned separately and stocked in depth, because there is little substitutability among them. This is also true of the more discriminating customers with respect to the more subtle color variants. But many less discerning or less meticulous shoppers will manage to make a selection even if some of the colors are temporarily out of stock. These colors may therefore be planned in groups with individual colors subsequently controlled by "eye." It is not worth either the effort or the added investment to protect each color against possible depletion.

Price lines

Flexibility about price tends to increase with ascending price lines. At the very bottom of the price spectrum for a given commodity, shoppers may be quite unyielding in regard to the price they will pay because of the economic necessity, frugality, and penuriousness, or because of their notions about what constitutes a "bargain." Moving up the spectrum, shoppers become more sensitive about other selection factors and more willing to pay for some desired combination thereof.

The customer seeking a "cheap" saucepan would be more flexible about material, and even size, than about price. There may be a limited amount available to spend, or the purpose is not limited by exacting requirements, or the consumer does not know and/or care about the more exacting requirements of the purpose. Price-cutting retailers have a strong tendency to aim their assortments at this market, whether it be for saucepans, blankets, socks, or dresses.[16] It is quite likely that the size of the market for undiscerning purchase of cheap goods has often been exaggerated. In an abundant economy, there is a much wider market (certainly in terms of dollar expenditure) that is sensitive to the gamut of selection factors other than price. To them, "cheap" means only "cheap for the quality."

Urgency of purchase

Customers who buy well in advance of their needs tend to be more selective than those who wait until the last minute. This phenomenon is important to the buyer who must prepare and protect wide assortments for the peak of a short selling season, followed by a sharp drop in demand. Spring-season clothing is a good example in some climates; so are fans and air conditioners in hot "summer" climates and greeting cards for Mother's Day and Father's Day. In so-called "Christmas merchandise," it would be impossible to maintain stocks right up to the day before the holiday without incurring a subsequently heavy markdown penalty.

Fortunately, as customers delay purchases in these crucial periods, they become less selective. They know that stocks are depleted in all stores and that prolonged search for precisely what they want may prove fruitless. They frequently must and do settle for substitutes. Because the situation is most common in lower price lines, buyers learn to concentrate their stocks in these ranges as the season progresses past its peak.

A similar situation prevails with respect to advertised "sales" at bargain prices. Customers who respond with reasonable promptness are justifiably resentful when inadequate preparation leaves them only broken assortments from which to make a selection. Those who come late are conditioned to expect depleted stocks and are therefore more amenable to suggestions for altering their preconceived combination of wanted selection factors.

CHOICE OF POLICY

Determinants in Choice of Policy

Which combination of policies a retailer should adopt depends on:

1. *The nature of merchandise lines carried.* A policy of fashion leadership is plainly more important to a women's specialty store than to a drugstore. This is not, however, the same as saying that a drugstore has *no* interest in fashion. Much of its stock is staple, but in cosmetics, for example, new

[16]This is more true of old-fashioned "bargain stores" and early discounters, both of whom relied strongly on "cheap goods cheap" where they could not cut prices on highly identifiable better goods, then protected by "fair trade."

products and new versions are not infrequent. Last year's vogue in lipstick color may be this year's slow-seller.

2. *Characteristics of trading area.* Although it is true that retailers may select the groups to which they cater, choice may be limited by the general character of the trading areas—as was indicated in the preceding chapter. Large areas usually have room for all kinds of retailers; smaller communities may present definite limitations. They may be very poor or very rich, thus limiting the scope of quality, price, and fashion policies. Concentration on good assortments of staple goods and lower-priced fashions and novelties may be forced by nearness to a large city that offers too much competition for other kinds of goods.

3. *Community need.* Nevertheless, a close study of customers and their preferences may reveal the need for merchandise with special attributes of taste, quality, price, size, and other selection factors. This is certainly true in large trading areas. Even in small communities, it may serve to develop specialized stocks that can compete with the "big city" stores and their big suburban branches.

4. *Competition.* The creative way to beat competition is to compare the services it provides with the needs and wants of the trading area, remembering always that requirements may be latent and waiting for offerings to evoke awareness and response. Certainly competition must be aped to some degree. What they carry and what they do that is successful may well be copied. But what they don't carry and what they don't do represent the possibilities for creative, distinctive enterprise.

It may be all right to meet price-cutting head on. But when standards of service and quality are lowered in the process, a store begins to lose character—or clear image in the minds of customers. Meeting competition in this case may call for emphasizing differentiation of products and services. When retailers who are initially successful with the appeal of low price draw the inevitable inrush of like operations, they themselves begin to use other, non-price-competitive techniques to pull away from direct competition.

5. *Personal capabilities of the merchant.* To undertake the task of appealing to a sophisticated or highly discriminating clientele without sufficient experience is to court disaster. Again, untried ventures tend to rush into new forms of retailing that depend primarily on price appeal, and they too court disaster. A merchant should clearly limit merchandise policies to those that can be implemented successfully.

6. *Capital resources.* It takes time to make customers aware of certain policies. Broadened assortments and new kinds of styling may not produce quick response. Sound financing permits strong promotion toward hastening recognition and acceptance and absorbs the costs of increased inventories and markdowns during the waiting period. Programs undertaken without adequate financing may fail for want of time alone. Retailers with limited

finances, or those who use their capital for rapid expansion, usually adopt policies that lead to fast turnover of stocks, such as narrow assortments of key selection factors.

Need for Clear-cut but Mutable Policies

To the extent that all these policy decisions are designed to give the retailer a distinctive personality, it follows that their implementation in different departments should reflect the desired, unified image. This requires that management have clear ideas about what it wants, which means that abstract notions have to be expressed in concrete detail but not set in concrete, and preferably be in writing. Implied also is the need for all merchandisers and buyers to ascertain these policies with equal clarity and to implement them with equal firmness.

Unforunately, these requirements are more often met with pious obeisance than devout observance. Few retailers have detailed central policies and still fewer have committed them to writing. Interpretation of abstract policies becomes too varied, with some departments catering successfully to customer groups that patronize other departments very little. As a result, there is conflicting and wasted effort.

This danger of conflict does not apply to cases where different departmental policies are deliberately planned. For example, a popular-priced department store may open a deluxe department for women's clothes or for furniture. Or a higher-priced store may open a budget department. In either case, several of the listed policies may be modified for these departments, catering to hitherto untapped occasional preferences among the store's own customers or reaching out for other groups in the trading area.

There may be deeper reasons for such moves. They may be intended to accentuate or modify some feature of the store's character; if so, the deluxe shop might serve to lend authenticity to the store's fashion position. Or the budget shop may serve to modify a popular impression that the store's prices are prohibitive. Sometimes these moves are trial balloons, or opening wedges in a general campaign to trade up or down.

Changes in Policy

Although it is true that policies should be firm and consistent, they need not be immutable in a changing world. Nor should they go forever unchallenged by analysis of the trading area and consequent hypotheses concerning its wants. *Just as policies are aimed at definite groups, so policies themselves determine the groups that will patronize the store.* This is one of the common feedback relationships of retailing.

The truism that "a retailer gets the trade he or she deserves" is aimed directly at the one who follows a worn groove of action without regard either to fresh opportunity or changing circumstances. Such a merchant's favorite phrase is, "not for my customers." And he or she may be quite right! Having once amputated all sizes above 8 from the women's shoe sizing scales, the merchant cannot have customers among consumers with big feet. On the other hand, if ethnic shifts in the population of the trading area have produced a new complement of such consumers, the merchant becomes dead wrong when he or she says, "not for this town."

Although it is true that policies need not be firmly set in concrete, changes should be deliberate and directed at specific objectives. Danger of becoming one of the mob lies in the direction of frequent, capricious changes in policy, of policies too broadly beamed at the trading area,[17] policies that are too vague or at too high a level of abstraction, or no policy at all. There are records of once great stores that failed because, during times of stress, the owners brought in new managements who were free to discard established policies and to try new ones. But when the new ones failed to bring prompt sales results, management was again replaced, and the store started off on a new tack. And sometimes top management itself is ambivalent, one member of the team working with one store image in mind and another engaged in developing a very different one.

Examples of policy change and development

Many retail organizations have gone through a cycle of policy change, beginning with rock-bottom prices, little service, and limited assortments of basics, followed by a broadening of merchandise lines, more service, and rising expenses and prices. The supermarket is the *archetype* of this development. It began as a bargain store featuring staple grocery products on improvised pine-board shelving in low-rental lots. The swift favorable public response led to a swarm of imitators who put pressure on the already low prices of the innovators and made operations generally unprofitable. This led to the addition of produce and meats which increased volume and higher markup opportunities. Although expenses went up, the added margin was temporarily rewarding. But as each competitor sought distinction from the rest, assortments of groceries were expanded, price lines traded upward, and plants and fixtures made more attractive but also more costly. Price remained the dominant competitive tool. To maintain this image, costly promotions were backed with costly "leaders": 5 percent markups on coffee, sugar, and cigarettes with each item taking its turn on the altar of the great price image.

The rising expenses associated with these moves again squeezed profits and again led to the search for new product lines that would provide higher

[17]This luxury can best be afforded by very large, dominant retailers in a community.

markups. The answer was found in nonfoods: drugs, cosmetics, housewares, toys, magazines, garden supplies, and apparel and their accessories. Some became *superstores,* a combination of supermarkets and discount department stores, catering to the consumer's total needs for "routine purchases."[18] The former bargain appeal was replaced with fast and convenient purchase opportunity to satisfy all basic needs at competitive prices.

Other types of stores have gone through a similar cycle. Discount stores, for example, began as small stores (often in run down or abandoned buildings in high rent areas) carrying samples of big ticket household appliances, with customers' orders filled from the wholesale distributor. But competitive pressure and the need to broaden the market led to the carrying of key items in depth for immediate delivery. Seeking distinction, the leaders began to build costly showrooms and provide costly services. Assortments of selection factors became wider, lines more continuous, and price lines higher. The discount store has found that the American market for "cheap goods cheap" was somewhat limited. As in the case of the supermarket, imitators proliferated and new, more costly ways of competing for patronage had to be found. Among them are longer hours and Sunday openings. It is possible that these may provide "incremental sales volume," because working people with their added spending power find these hours well suited to their shopping requirements.

Similar changes are taking place in other retail areas. The success of the great mail order firms in attracting customers who find it pleasant and convenient to shop by catalog perusal rather than by store visit has led many traditionally over-the-counter stores to distribute catalogs and to run ads in both the newspaper and broadcast media soliciting sales by phone or mail. Catalog stores and catalog desks in over-the-counter stores also make it possible to broaden the market and the assortments made available, with relatively little increase in the inventory required for the purpose.

DISCUSSION QUESTIONS

1. What elements can you add to the "selection factors" listed at the beginning of this chapter?
2. Discuss "price as a surrogate of value" for consumers.
3. Does modern society reflect, at all substantially, Thorsten Veblen's ideas on "Conspicuous Consumption"?
4. (a) How is the wave of "consumerism"-generated laws progressing?
   (b) Discuss the governmental management structure to enforce these laws.
   (c) How should store policies relate to these laws and to their enforcement?

[18]See Walter J. Salmon, R. D. Buzzell, and S. G. Cort, "Today the Shopping Center, Tomorrow the Superstore," *Harvard Business Review* (Jan.–Feb. 1974).

5. Aside from differences in brand names, do many stores actually achieve exclusiveness in their trading areas?
6. Can "good" taste be measured objectively, or is it the subjective valuation of (a) a group of customers, or (b) a group of designers or sellers?
7. There is a combination of pressures on retailers to increase the variety of product lines stocked. Give some examples, by store types, of yielding and of resistance.
8. Adding to the number of colors in which a product is carried is clearly an example of added versions, where each addition is likely to produce a smaller net sales increment than the previous addition. What other selection factors are likely to be controlled by the same principle in the case of (a) pots and pans, (b) women's skirts, (c) sheets and pillowcases, (d) brands of cereal, and (e) another of your choice?
9. Why does a shoe department in a department store need greater breadth than a specialized shoe store of similar volume?
10. Why is the policy with respect to breadth likely to be critical with respect to depth?
11. Why were supermarkets spoken of as "archetypes of policy development"?
12. How does "scaling" solve a knotty problem of classifying a rigid demand factor like size?
13. Relate the concept of "substitutability" to assortment planning and control and give examples of lowered demand rigidity late in the season.

chapter 6

Forecasting Customer Demand

STUDY OF PAST SALES

Making Sales Records Meaningful

For the established retailer, no source of information is more rewarding than a study of his or her own sales records: of sales made and lost, of sales returned, and of complaints about goods sold. Many records and systems can be made available for the purpose: unit controls, special records of promotions, want slips, charge accounts, and adjustment bureau files, as well as personal observation on the selling floor and personal conferences with salespeople.

The sales of many product lines fluctuate with seasons of the year—many quite sharply. It is customary to examine records of "last year" and even prior years as a base for planning sales in any given season. Unfortunately, too many records fail to show special or nonrecurrent factors that may have influenced sales in a particular period—memory being trusted to fill the gap. But memory is an untrustworthy servant. As a result, records are often misinterpreted; poor planning results, and errors may be perpetuated. The dead hand of yesterday may fall heavily on plans for progress.

Diary notes

There are safeguards. For one thing, every sales record should have diary notes that tell about the big storm, the rainy week, the fine hot weather for swim wear, the bus strike, the shortage of inventory, and the "big promotion" in the department, in nearby departments in the store as a whole, or in the competitive area, etc. Also, the buyer should exhibit enough curiosity about sales potentials to (1) examine all sales results if possible—or at least unexpectedly large or small sales—in the light of inventory, service preparation, and other factors such as those just mentioned, and (2) to make appropriate notes in the records.

Again, *sales activities should be summarized at the end of a seasonal or holiday period* in preparation for the following year. This is the time when so much that affected sales is still fresh in the mind, the time when good resolutions may be implemented with good interpretative analysis. Buyers should not attempt to carry too many details in the head for too long a time. Nor should important guiding data be buried in a welter of current reports. They should be summarized in seasonal or monthly diaries as suggested.

Figure 6–1 shows how one store analyzes its seasonal staples as a basis for next year's buying. The sales and stocks of toy table-and-chair sets for Christmas are analyzed with comments on the goods. This record is invaluable in planning the purchases for the following Christmas.

FIGURE 6–1 Analysis of sales of table and chair sets

Vendor	Style No.	Cost	Retail	Quality	Styling	Color	Sales Period	Rec'd	Sold	O. H.	Comments
A	31291	8. 50	15. 94	Fair	Fair	Maple	12/6--	337	240	97	Finish on top not good. Came in late. Not very saleable.
B	1242	12. 50	24. 98	Good	Excellent	Wheat	10/3–12/15	325	325	0	Went very well.
C	31269	16. 50	34. 98	Good	Good	Wax	11/15	42	15	27	Price changed to $29. 94. Oval table not practical.
D	21235	10. 80	19. 98	Fair	Good	......	8/14–11/16	150	150	0	Sold well. Weak cleat.

Systems for Analyzing Sales[1]

Most systems for keeping track of sales and stocks are variants of the following four basic methods.

1. Immediate record of each sale

This may be obtained by means of stubs on price tickets, duplicate copies of sales checks, control cards (one placed in each box containing a number of

[1]For a detailed account of unit-control systems, see *Retail Merchandise Management*, a companion volume by John W. Wingate, Elmer D. Schaller, and F. Leonard Miller (Englewood Cliffs, N.J.: Prentice-Hall, Inc., 1972), especially chaps. 18, 19, and 20.

units of an article and removed when the box is empty), tally records kept by salespeople or by the cashier and by the newer automatic recording devices at the point of sales. Any one of these methods provides the basis for a "perpetual inventory" system where the stock on hand can be calculated continuously by means of the formula:

Inventory at the start of a period + purchases −
sales as recorded = inventory at the end of the period

The perpetual inventory method presents the following difficulties in arriving at correct inventory figures: (1) errors are cumulative, whereas with the periodic system described shortly, they tend to be self-correcting, each time the stock is counted; and (2) stock shortages and unrecorded sales are not accounted for, and their accumulation tends to overstate the inventory. In fact, stock counts are taken from time to time in order to get a true inventory picture.

Sales recording used to be considered too expensive a method for "unit control" to be used on any but high-priced and fashion merchandise. But the continued development of sophisticated POS (point-of-sale) devices has made it feasible to record all sales transactions as they occur. Manufacturers are providing price tickets or labels with bar charts readable by POS equipment from punched cards or special type font. These developments make it possible to record enormous amounts of data at low cost instantaneously.

2. "Periodic inventory" system

By counting the stock of each item at intervals, it is possible to tell how many have been sold by the following formula:

Inventory at the start of the period + purchases −
inventory at the end of the period = sales

(Technically, the result is "disappearance," but it serves the purpose of a "sales" figure.)

This is the commonly used method for lower-priced and staple goods. But, as stated previously, developments in electronic data processing (EDP) is tending to crowd out this form of control. In fact, great progress has been made in "automatic reorder systems" for staple goods based on data gathered by EDP machinery and processed to calculate reorder quantities, according to programs laid down by the buyer. See Chapters 7 and 8 for more on this subject.

3. Visual control

This involves assigning to each item a stock space that holds a predetermined number of pieces. The section is filled periodically, and, at any time, the unfilled space in each section measures the number sold since the last replenishing date. Basically, this is a version of periodic-inventory control.

Some small stores find simple but effective a combination of visual control and a record of receipts. The buyer has a loose-leaf notebook with a sheet or more devoted to each class of items. Records are kept only of orders and receipts, but an inventory of the stock at any time, compared with the number received to date, reveals the sales. Figure 6–2 illustrates the system as used by one store for reordering scatter rugs. A simple record like this does not reveal what the stock level was on any given date. For example, in the case of item number A-721 LZ, it can only be assumed that the stock levels on March 10 and April 5 were low enough to prompt orders of 18 and 24 pieces respectively. And, during this time, B-90 LY never got low enough to justify a reorder. If the item is selling better than expected, the stock on hand will tend to run out before the new order comes in. Mainly, the buyer relies on the number of circled transactions (frequency or order) to indicate slow sellers, like B-90 LY, in Figure 6–2, and fast sellers, like A-721 LZ (Figure 6–2). Sometimes, with these simple systems, a predetermined standard order is automatically placed when the stock gets down to a predetermined level.

FIGURE 6–2 Simplified unit control form

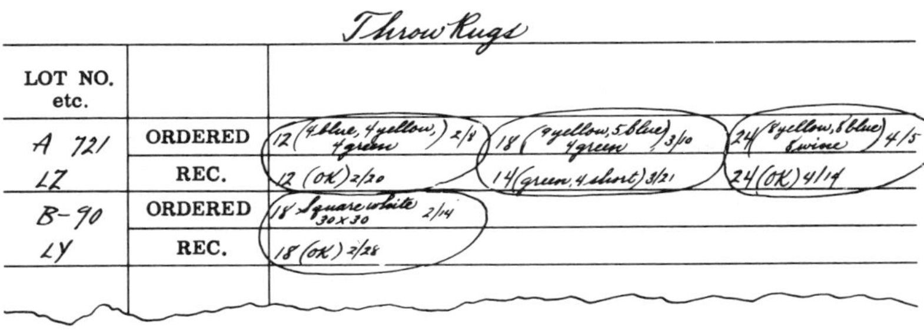

4. Record of all disbursements from a reserve or warehouse stock to forward stock.

This is regarded as a measure of sales. When the forward stock is built up daily or weekly to a standard quantity, the disbursements closely approximate sales to the store's customers. If the requisitions are recorded daily and subtracted from receipts, the system is one of perpetual inventory.

Many buyers who are not expert in formal planning and control and who do not have specialized staff assistants prefer simple systems, such as 3 and 4. However, an increasing number of buyers with varying expertise are learning to use much more elaborate sales and stock status analysis, as illustrated in Tables 8–4 and 8–5.

Staple Stock Lists

On a basis of sales information revealed by any one or a combination of the above methods, it is possible to develop a staple stock list. This may be in two parts: first, purely staple items that always should be carried; and second, seasonal items and novelities that should be in stock at certain times. The list is obtained from past sales and from purchase and inventory records. Every item that has sold in sufficient quantities to show an active demand may be included. In a chain, for example, the joint sales experience of all the units is used to develop a master list of items to be carried regularly and in season, and each new store unit is stocked with these.[2] Other items, not generally carried throughout the chain, may be tested; actual sales results will allow gradual adjustment of the stock to local demand. Once a staple and assortment list has been developed, what to buy may be readily determined by checking the actual stock against the list. Additions to and subtractions from the original stock list may be made by watching the sales carefully. If certain classes of goods are selling well, but salespeople report that customers want bigger style, color, or size assortments, additions will be made. If items sell slowly or only during certain seasons, they may be dropped or included in stock only during certain months of the year. If items are in very active demand, they may be starred or put on a special *never-out* list. It is then required that ordering judgments err on the side of *overordering to protect the sales potential* and reduce customer disappointment to a minimum.

Analyzing Sales by Selection Factors

The four methods for analyzing sales and wants are described previously in terms of every different *unit sale* down to the SKUs, or stock-keeping units. The SKU narrows the variants of a product down to one particular combination of selection factors such as style number, size, color, material, etc. Thus we can follow and manage the stock of Brand Xs 10¾-oz.-size can of cream of chicken soup. Such detail may serve a good purpose, because it is with such particularity that we buy and sell the product. But, as noted in the previous chapter, it may be useful to plan and control on a broader basis, watching the data not on particular items but on the central ideas or generic or primary demands behind them. This would require the use of broader controls, for example, on chicken soups as a whole, or cream soups as a whole, or on all

[2]In large chains, where store units vary considerably in size, a number of lists are sometimes made out, one for each store size classification.

canned soups as a whole. Such systems are commonly known as *classification controls*.

Sometimes there is so much substitutability for particular products in a group of products serving the same purpose that it becomes more important to ensure a good assortment in the classification as a whole than to ensure the presence of any specific component of the group. In fact, it is important for buyers constantly to review the individual products they sell to see if demand patterns are developing—or receding—around common denominators of significance. These are the central ideas that serve as the basis for both assortment planning, and promotion. Examples are:

1. "No work" or "less work" in performing a specific task for mothers or working wives.
2. A vogue for cowls or decorated T-shirts.
3. Disposable diapers without safety pins.
4. The "masculine look" or the "peacock look" in men's apparel.
5. A brand as a symbol of quality and excellence.

This type of analysis is particularly important for apparel and seasonal goods. Although certain styles, known as runners, may be reordered a number of times and reported like staples on best-seller lists, the chief problem is to maintain not a permanent stock of specific items but rather an assortment of styles that—although constantly changing—conform to certain characteristics in fashion at the time and that serve the same basic common need. Even in high-fashion merchandise, there are certain characteristics that continue to be in demand longer than the demand for a particular style number. These are brands, including designer names, classification, type, size, price range, some colors, silhouette, material, and vendor (source).

Brands

As discussed in Chapter 5, brand preference is an important factor in the consumer's choice. It is especially important for staples and, to a growing degree,[3] in the choice of fashions. It is not enough, then, to watch the sales movements of each individual item: All sales of all goods of one brand should be summarized in order to determine the relative importance of brand families.

There is always likely to be some intermittent demand for any brand that has been advertised to the consumer, and the store is faced with the problem of what and how many brands to carry to satisfy the demand of the majority. Generally, a few well-selected brands will be enough—one or two, perhaps, in each of three price zones: low, medium, and high. For example, a grocery

[3]Closely related to brand identification is that of designer names—domestic as well as foreign—a growing practice in the apparel and home furnishings industries.

study in Minneapolis showed that the stores surveyed carried a total of 77 different brands of tea, but that 65 percent of all the sales were on one brand, 13 percent on a second, and 3 percent on a third. If a store carried these three brands only, it would cater to over four-fifths of the consumer market. By adding two or three more of the brands that are particularly popular in the neighborhood and that cover important price zones of demand not covered by the popular leaders, it should be possible to satisfy nearly everybody. Where slow-selling brands "must" be carried for one reason or another, it may be well to consider them as a unified group and to merchandise size, color, and other selection factors as an aggregate within the group. This requires less stock than would be needed to protect the selection factors within each brand. The effect would be that of a calculated risk of being caught short in specific colors or sizes within a specific brand of this group and to hope for substitutability.

No store is large enough to carry every brand on the market, and yet small stores sometimes try it and fail. In the zeal to follow customer demand, a merchant may put in a dozen of a new brand or item whenever there are a "couple of calls" for it. This practice piles up a large stock of slow-selling odds and ends that eat up the capital and space needed to keep up an adequate stock of the proven best sellers.

Which of the many brands on the market to stock is not easy to determine. Most stores have found out by the trial-and-error method, experimenting with a new brand if the product looks unusually good, if the markup obtainable is above average, if a large number of customers ask for it, or if the manufacturer submits evidence that he or she is about to launch a major advertising campaign directed toward the consumer.

Classification and type

In the case of classification, the relative demand for sportswear, afternoon wear, and evening wear, for example, changes less rapidly than do the individual styles. If past sales are analyzed according to these classifications, it is not hard to forecast the relative future sales in each. The terms *classification* and *type* are often used interchangeably, but it is useful for this discussion to consider *classification* as a generic or end-use designation and to limit the term *type* to more specific selection factors within the class. For example, dresses as a class may be typed as conservative and extreme, youthful and matronly, tailored and ornate, or "fussy." If sales are analyzed these ways, it may appear that 30 percent of the department's customers like extreme clothes and that 70 percent prefer conservative. In buying, then, the buyer will try to adhere to these proportions. Likewise, 50 percent of women's dress sales may be in distinctly youthful styles, indicating that one-half of new purchases should be of this character rather than of the matronly type.[4] Because many manufacturers specialize in one or two types of dresses, it is easy to know where each type may be found. Once again we must caution against thoughtlessly equating actual sales with potential demand. For example, a store may have sold very few "fussy" dresses because few were carried in stock, even though 30 percent of the customers might have preferred that type.

Size

As in the case of classification and type, the demand by sizes is nearly constant, even though odd variations are sometimes reported. In general, if past sales show the proportions in demand, it is probable that customers will buy in the same proportions in the near future.

In a misses' dress category, for example, sales analysis might yield the following size scale as a guide for future buying:

Size	8	10	12	14	16	18	20
Percent of total sales	4	13	23	25	18	15	2

Of course, some changes in size do take place. The fashion for a boyish figure increased sales of small sizes somewhat. Increased interest in active sports over a period of many years resulted in the sale of a greater proportion of large shoes. Then, too, the measurement specifications for a given size may change. For example, the athletic life of many young women so developed their shoulders and arms as to necessitate more room in armhole and sleeve than was once considered standard. Again, sizes established as standard may not be suited to a large proportion of customers. For example, analysis of sales in misses' sizes (16 to 20) has showed that many alterations had to be made, that many had to buy a size too large and have the waist made narrower in order to procure sufficient room in the hips or bust. This fact resulted in the development of junior sizes (now 3 to 17) and half sizes (now 10½ to 24½) especially suited to persons who are shorter than the professional model type and larger in hip or bust.[5] In some stores, these sizes outsell the regular misses' sizes. Some stores opened "Tall Girl" shops with sizes to fit women who are above average height.

But all such changes are gradual, and *occasional periodic analysis of sales by size* should serve to determine what sizes to buy and in what proportions.

[4]"J.C. Penney Co. has analyzed its customer base and broken it down into three segments: young juniors, who are highly fashion-conscious; contemporaries, who spend more than any other segment on high-quality clothes; and conservatives, who are interested in comfort and value." From "Department Stores Redefine Their Role," *Business Week* (Dec. 13, 1976), p. 48.

[5]Junior petites have been added in sizes 3–13. Women's sizes 38–50 are still available but the half sizes meet the same basic need.

It must not be concluded that the sales of an individual style will always correspond to the typical proportions established in the past. Some styles appeal to older, more mature women who may wear larger sizes, and other styles appeal to younger women who may wear smaller sizes.

Men's clothing also has size variants such as long, short, portly, etc. Sometimes these figure types vary with region or area due to ethnic or occupational factors. Sales analysis will not show the relative demand among these types unless experimental stocks and promotions have been instituted to test it.

Although changes in demand for sizes in clothing tend to occur slowly over time, they must nevertheless be watched for trend, because size is a selection factor of low substitutability. Nevertheless, there has been a long-time trend toward condensing elaborate size scales into designations like medium and narrow in shoes or small, medium, and large in many other items of appparel.

Sizes are important also in other than clothing lines. Changes in window styles or in the fashion of their hangings and coverings produce demand for changed sizes in curtains, draperies, shades, blinds, etc., and reach into the very hardware accessories that accompany them. As the growing population of "senior citizens" and "singles" moves into smaller living quarters, demand increases for smaller sizes in pots, pans, and packaged groceries. Advertising campaigns may produce sudden changes in demand for "economy size" large packages in food and drugs. Sales analysis is distorted unless the analyzer is aware of the new pressure and accounts for it in his or her interpretation.

Price range

Price is normally a fairly stable selection factor, so sales analysis provides reliable guidelines for planning. But depression or inflationary pressures can cause wild changes. Some fluctuations are due to seasonal and fashion changes. Another cause of sharp change is the downward movement as improved technology and increased production bring down the price of a new product—a classic case being the pricing of minicomputers and digital wrist watches in the mid-1970s. And always there are the fluctuations that accompany special glut or scarcity so common in food stuffs.

It is true that in price, as in other selection factors, *random purchase does tend to concentrate at specific points*. Nevertheless, price demand is not as rigid as it would seem. As explained in the section on selection factors, *demand is quite flexible within a price range*. Sales analysis should carefully account for this tendency. It should also be devoted to experiments with "price endings." Competition permitting, it is a waste of markup to price at \$2.95 or \$2.98 that which could be sold just as effectively at \$2.99 or even \$3.00. The difference is much more significant to the store than to its customers.

Color

There are three other selection factors in merchandise that are not as stable as those mentioned previously but that do change gradually enough to be predictable at least in broad groupings. These are color, silhouette, and material.

For forecasting purposes, clothing colors may be grouped under three heads: (1) black (or white in the summer), (2) the season's basic colors, and (3) high shades. In clothing, the relative importance of black over the previous year is likely if not sure to be duplicated during the present year. The same is true of basic seasonal colors such as brown, wine, and dark green in the fall, and navy, beige, and gray in the spring.

The situation is different in the case of high shades. If Tyrian purple or soldier blue was good last year, it is not likely to be good this year. But even here current sales can be a guide for future buying. Early in the season, the buyer can try out a number of the high shades that manufacturers and fashion publications are sponsoring. By watching customer response closely, it will be possible to determine which colors are catching on as the season's fads and which are being rejected. To make this judgment effective, however, it is necessary to learn how the preferences of one's early customers differ from those of later shoppers.

Color has become important and variable in lines other than clothing. There was a time when white was the immutable color for kitchens, with red as the one big accent color. In recent years, kitchen colors have ranged the spectrum, and if white and red ever regain their lost importance, it will be temporary—as a fad. Color in home furnishings generally is not as volatile a demand factor as it is in women's clothing, but sales must nevertheless be watched for trends in preference.

Tints, tones, values, and other attributes associated with color also have their demand cycles: some with season, some with fashion. It does not do to analyze sales by hues alone (viz. red, orange, or yellow). Orange in the fall may be deep, dark, and saturated. In the spring, it may appear in less chromatic form, with a lot of white added. This last touch produces the "pastel" colors. The dark somber colors of early fall may give way to vivid jewel colors in the winter holiday season. These are sharp changes of demand and require constant analysis of sales to determine trends. Less sharp may be the transition of demand from versatile pastels or even muddy colors to purer chromatic versions. Each may have its sway in customer preference over a period. Achromatic versions of color governed demand in men's clothing for 4 or 5 years, to the point where all suits "looked black." When the "peacock look" began to emerge, it was subtle and escaped detection by all who were not watching for it in sales analysis or who failed to inject enough of the new colors into experimental efforts. When the elements of the peacock look are rejected, the change may come more suddenly than the onset.

It is important that colors in different departments be coordinated. All departments should carry ample stocks of the basic colors and also, of colors to supplement the basic ones. Also, buyers should try to agree early in the season as to the probable winners among the high shades and should carry adequate stocks of them.

Silhouette and basic pattern

The generic silhouette in clothing, particularly women's apparel, often has a life of several years, generally of at least one year. Consequently, if sales are analyzed according to the general lines of a garment, customer demand for some time ahead can be determined. For example, dress sales may be analyzed according to the prominence of the shoulders, the shape of the neckline, the line of the sleeves, the degree of tightness at the waist, the placing of the belt line, the closeness of fit at the hips, the flare of the skirt, the length of the skirt, and the degree of evenness of the hemline.

Frequently, many of these specific factors in silhouette can be summed up in a type, and sales may be analyzed accordingly. For example, after separating skirt suits from pant suits, preference may be expressed in recognized silhouettes or types such as the dressmaker, boxy, softly-tailored, semifitted, bloused back, bolero, suit plus blouse, stole suit, and skirt-stole costume. As in the case of color, the trend in silhouette, as noted during a period of successive weekly or monthly analysis, is more important than the current percentage.

The general prevalence of one silhouette may forecast the gradual appearance of a new silhouette, although the fact that a change has occurred is suddenly and often belatedly discovered. For example, as Mary Jane Dowd of Bloomingdale's, N.Y., observed: " 'short' follows 'long' or 'ease' must follow 'tight fit'—'fussiness' had to be replaced by 'stark simplicity'." But the question always is: How long will the vogue last, and how quickly can we spot the change.

Some years ago, very short skirts were the vogue. Instead of a sudden transition to long skirts, the trend was gradual toward a long even hemline. But by 1963, short skirts were again popular, and the cycle was ready to be repeated. But through the '60s, skirts kept getting shorter than ever before. By 1970, the fashion pundits thought the cycle had run its course and nearly all got aboard the disaster-bound "midi" bandwagon. The pundits were partly right: The cycle had practically run its course but was not ready to brake quite so convulsively.

Material

The vogue for a particular material or class of materials may last for a season or longer. For example, dress fabric sales may be classified as silk, wool, cotton, lace, linen, rayon, acetate, nylon, polyester, other new synthetics, and blends and mixtures; and each of these may be broken down into specific materials.

The central idea behind demand is more quickly apparent if sales are classified as follows: lightweight, medium weight, heavyweight; soft, medium stiff, stiff; dull, medium bright, shiny; plain, small pattern, large pattern; and smooth or textured. It is not as important to know that figured flat crepe is popular in dresses as to know that all dress materials that are lightweight, soft, dull, and patterned are wanted. Fundamentally, customers are interested in effect and not in the particular name or construction of a material, although specific materials like velvet, denim, tafetta, or challis may enjoy a vogue because they are particularly suited to prevailing silhouettes or perceived life-style demands.

Sales analysis, in other than the apparel field, may reveal that some particular material is going out of style; nevertheless, there may be a steady and persistent, if small, demand for it. Aluminum cooking utensils, and later other metals, replaced enamel to a large extent. Nevertheless, a small demand for enamel persisted, and those who maintained their assortments, albeit in little depth, were rewarded by loyal patronage. And those who experimented with imports of enameled cast iron and analyzed their sales for trend discovered that changing styles and interests in cooking had produced a demand for a new kind of cookware that was really the revival of a very old kind.

Vendor analysis

There are other factors that may be used as a basis for sales analysis in forecasting demand. It is often useful to study sales by vendors to determine those manufacturer's styles that sell best and at a reasonable profit and those that sell poorly and at a loss. Such a study is called a *vendor analysis*. Some manufacturers are very successful in turning out styles that will sell. A buyer's chances of correct style selection are enhanced by patronizing the resources that have demonstrated best results in sales analysis. The warning is: Even "good" resources may have "bad" seasons.

Merchandising to Aesthetic Elements in Demand

Many of our examples are taken from the "fashion" clothing field, because it is the prototype of goods in mutation—of burgeoning consumer acceptance followed by swift rejection. What is said about preference analysis in this field applies to others—the difference being chiefly one of speed in change.

Aesthetic emotion has been expressed as an increasingly important element of utility, or power to give satisfaction. Some industries find it costly to change basic silhouettes. Automobiles are an example. Another may be found in shoes, where the lasts on which they are shaped are costly factors.

To buy a new set represents a serious capital investment for the manufacturer: therefore, fashion changes are relatively slow in basic shape and much faster in color, material, heel and style of the uppers. Gifts and housewares have similar problems with respect to tools and dies. Nevertheless, even their basic designs are not forever static, and colors can be changed with comparative ease.

Greeting cards can swing from square to extremely elongated shapes; window coverings from pull shades to Venetian blinds and back to shades again; curtains from tailored to ruffled to café types; shirts from long collars to short to button-down to tab; deodorants from liquid to paste to roll-on balls and to sprays; shoe laces from cotton to leather; and luggage from leather to cotton.

Analyzing Special Sales

Owing to the seasonal nature of the demand for staple as well as fashion items, records of special sales events, in addition to an analysis of regular sales, are fruitful in determining what to buy. If a special sale of toilet goods and drugs was successful in May this year, it is likely to succeed again next year; and the particular items that sold well are likely to be again in demand. This is also often true of merchandise not advertised.

Records of each advertised promotion

Records should be kept of each advertised promotion indicating the following:

1. Date or period of sale.
2. Weather.
3. Exact description of the merchandise, including price and markup.
4. Advertising media used: newspapers, direct mail, electronic media, with quantity and cost of each.
5. Supplementary publicity media.
6. Sales of the item or items in dollars and in units for 2 or 3 days following the advertisement.
7. Ratio of advertising cost to direct sales of the item.
8. Reasons for success or failure and suggestions for making a repetition of the sale more fruitful, including an evaluation of inventory preparation.

With such a record, the buyer has an excellent guide not only as to what to buy and promote at different times of the year but also as to what past buying mistakes to avoid. Unless sales are recorded, a buyer will fail to repeat many successful events of former years and will continue to make many of the old mistakes.

Preliminary Sales Tests

In addition to analyzing sales of merchandise that has been stocked in the past, the sale possibilities of new goods may be determined by preliminary sales tests. A new article may appear on the market, and past sales in the store may throw no light on the demand that can be developed for it. Various preliminary sales tests have been tried as indicators of demand. For a firm like Sears, catalog sales can be an excellent harbinger of demand. A buyer may obtain a daily record of catalog sales shortly after a new catalog is delivered. Indeed, in the first week, with only 30 percent of the catalogs delivered, the buyer can often get a fix on the final sales volume of a line. Advance indications sometimes save buyers from over-ordering items. They do not, of course, save the buyer from the first order,[6] a risk that must be taken as a part of the "batting average."

Mail-order firms generally make good use of sales tests. For example, with a mailing list of 50,000 potential customers, the store may buy 250 pieces of an apparently attractive article on the condition that thousands of additional items can be procured from the seller at short notice.[7] Five thousand mailing pieces may be sent out on this item to a random sample of the 50,000 list. If 200 orders are received, the article will probably be deemed an excellent one for promotion to the rest of the list. A commitment may then be made for nine times the quantity sold, or 1800, and 45,000 more promotional pieces may be sent out.

If the sample mailing is scientifically chosen, and if the large mailing is made promptly before seasonal or economic factors change materially, the initial returns provide an excellent barometer of how many to buy. What percentage of return to demand from the sample mailing in order to justify further purchase and promotion varies with the dollar markup on each article and the direct expenses involved. Typically, a 2 to 4 percent return is likely to be regarded as satisfactory.

Other kinds of retailers rely on less sophisticated tests. Sometimes one unit only can be used to gauge demand. Salespeople may be required to report all customer comments made about the item before it is sold. It is often possible to sell the one piece with the proviso that it remain on display for a specified period and to take orders for others to be delivered in a few days by the manufacturers. If a considerable number of orders are placed, or if sufficient interest is shown, the store may decide to put in a stock.

Of course, nearly every purchase of a new style or line is a type of preliminary sales test. No practice will do more to minimize mistakes in buying than cautious purchasing of anything new. If the small quantity moves out

[6] "Sears Makes it Look Easy," John McDonald, *Fortune* (May 1964).

[7] The key to this sort of testing is in the back-up supply, which is not always available and still less often reliable. Stores often use a newspaper advertisement in the same way.

rapidly, it is safe to buy more. If it does not, even a heavy markdown on the few items ordered will not represent a serious loss. But the buyer is faced with a recurrent dilemma. It is true that hesitant experimentation will minimize the losses from error, but it will also reduce the profit possibilities and leadership reputation that can come only with aggressive exploitation of the successful innovation.

Moreover, it is easy to talk of deepening stocks with quick reorders if the response to an early offering is good. But every buyer knows how hard it is to get reorders of an item that has "taken off." The chances are that it has done so for many, and the manufacturer is swamped. This is one place where size of store and corresponding buying power count; where good relations with suppliers, built over time, count; and where association with a good buying office helps materially.

OTHER INTERNAL INDICATORS OF CUSTOMER DEMAND

The methods of determining what to buy discussed so far in this chapter are all based on an analysis of actual sales to date. In the established store, they may be the most important sources, but they are not sufficient alone. Customers supply a store with much buying information that is not reflected in their purchases. Every failure to buy is almost as important in determining demand as is every purchase. Not only do lost sales give information as to what not to buy again, but they have positive value, because customers often outline to the salespeople fairly exact descriptions of the goods they want but fail to find.

Some fundamental changes have been taking place in the classes of goods that sell in different kinds of stores and departments. This makes flexibility of mind an essential quality for today's buyer, because decisions as to what to buy cannot be rigidly based only on what has sold in the past or on the lines of goods customarily handled in this type of store or department. As indicated in Chapter 5, the variety of goods carried are tending to broaden with examples like raincoats in auto supply stores and women's apparel in men's stores.

Information from Salespeople

Because salespeople are continually receiving information from customers about wants not reflected in sales, the salespeople become a major source of buying information. Moreover, they are frequently typical customers themselves, and their reactions to new goods presented by vendors are often a true index of sales possibilities. Even when salespeople's personal likes and dislikes vary from those of the customers, they frequently judge sales possibilities correctly because of their knowledge of their customers.[8] The buyer must be careful, however, not to place too much reliance on salespeople's opinions because of their frequent inability to distinguish clearly between their personal likings and those of their clientele.

Direct communication and want slips

There are two ways of obtaining information from salespeople about demand not reflected in actual sales: the personal and the impersonal. Under the former plan, the buyer or sales manager maintains close contact with every salesperson and discusses customers' requests and comments with each. Frequent open meetings are held with free discussions regarding what should be in stock. Furthermore, the salespeople are called upon to inspect new samples and give their opinion as to whether or not they should be bought. Sometimes they are asked to judge a reasonable retail price for the new merchandise without knowing the cost. This is a most useful device to avoid buying goods that prove unsalable because of a price that is too high (or even too low).

The impersonal method of obtaining information is to establish a reporting system, wherein each salesperson fills out a daily form, called a *want slip* (see Figure 6–3). This lists every request for merchandise not in stock and tells whether or not a substitute article is sold. The information may be analyzed by the buyer as follows:

- Merchandise regularly carried but out of stock.
- Merchandise carried elsewhere in the store.
- Merchandise that should not be carried because it is definitely outside the purchasing power or range of interest of the group to which the store is trying to cater.
- Merchandise that should be stocked if a sufficient number of wants or calls for it appear.

In addition to listing the specifications of wanted merchandise that is not in stock, the want slip would have space for customers' comments or criticisms in regard to existing stock. Bare sales records do not tell the whole story: A color or size or price may not sell simply because it is inadequately represented in the stock. A mattress cover may get in bad repute because of a skimpy tuck-under panel; a shoe may sell poorly becuase of the fit in the heel; a jacket may not sell because of a tight armhole. These are deficiencies that a good want-slip reporting system can reveal. The buyer or the buyer's assistant should be required to make some disposition of every want slip turned in, and this disposition should be made known to the salesperson turning it in. Some stores list possible dispositions on the form, so that the

[8]Furthermore, if a store is committed to personal selling—as opposed to self-service—this is a way of getting supplemental benefit from that costly sales force.

FIGURE 6–3 Want slip form

If no sales have been lost—Write "I LOST NO SALES TODAY"

"CUSTOMER WANT" SLIP

PUT DOWN EVERY CALL EVERY DAY

Dept.______ Date.______

Name.______

Number.______

	ITEM AND SUBSTITUTES	STYLE	COLOR	SIZE	PRICE	NO. OF CALL	BUYER'S DISPOSITION
ITEM							
SUBS							
ITEM							
SUBS							
ITEM							
SUBS							

Items LOW in STOCK or OUT of STOCK

Salesclerks Suggestions and Customer Comments

Form 850 3-36-200M-E

buyer merely checks the action, such as "will order," "not available," "on order," "already in stock," or "unseasonable." Other stores give each disposition a code number, which the buyer writes on the slip. The explanation of the code system is on the back. A personal word to salespeople and thanks for suggestions acted upon, however, are more effective than formal reports.

It must not be thought that the functioning of a good want-slip system makes it unnecessary for the buyer to maintain other contacts with salespeople and customers. Even though specific wants may be carefully reported, suggestions, observations, and customers' criticisms seldom are. And yet, it is this information that may be the basis for creative merchandising—for developing new or improved products that will sell.

Information from the Adjustment Department

Customers bring the store information as to what to buy not only through their purchases and their wants but also through their complaints. These may be presented directly at a central adjustment bureau or to the sales manager or sales people on the selling floor. In either case, all complaints may be recorded and tabulated according to merchandise reasons and service reasons.

By determining the chief merchandise reasons for complaint in each department, repetition of the buying errors that lead to complaints may be avoided. For example, if many of the complaints in a shirt classification involve shrinkage, it is evident that the store should seek a more reliable resource or set up specifications limiting possible shrinkage to certain limits of tolerance. Unfortunately, many look on the adjustment department as wholly a service department to correct wrongs that have already occurred. An equally important function is undoubtedly to direct the way to avoidance of mistakes in the future, not only in service but also in the nature of merchandise offered for sale. This becomes increasingly important as the retail merchant's role and responsibility in regard to product liability increases.

Charge Account Records

Stores study charge accounts to find out why individual customers patronize one department more than others. Sometimes letters or interviews are used to arrive at answers. It is common to write inactive charge customers asking in what respect the store may have proven unsatisfactory. Results are obtained when such letters are signed by the store president. Some of the answers point to errors in merchandise selection as well as service. A novel method was employed by a large store during the Christmas season. Letters were written to charge customers asking to whom they planned to give gifts. The store then wrote to these potential recipients asking them what they wanted for Christmas and stating that friends had asked it to find out. The lists of desired gifts obtained in this manner were sent to those who wanted to know what to give, and the store's ability and readiness to provide these gifts was pointed out. Thus the store acted as a go-between among friends without the embarrassment of disclosing the giver's identity to the recipient in advance. Again, although this was a promotion scheme, it did reveal the type of gifts that were in particular demand and ensured an adequate stock.

Closely analagous is the practice of having brides register at a store, stating the brand and pattern of silver, china, etc., that she is collecting. This enables customers to buy one or a few settings or special pieces toward a full service.

DIRECT CONSUMER SURVEYS

Interviews

Besides drawing on internal records of sales wants and other data, there are other ways to find out about customers and their preferences, where interest tends to focus more specifically on:

1. Tastes.
2. Standards of living as related to kind and quality of merchandise and services.
3. Habits and customs.
4. Interest in fashion timing.

One way of getting this information is to interview consumers directly—either on a visit to the store, at their homes, or in other places where they congregate. The survey may take the form of opinion or intention research or observation of what they do, wear, or use. The first involves personal interviews and is a highly specialized job that should be done by experts. Properly conducted, the method can yield useful information.

An example of what may be gained from customer research occurred when a store quizzed customers as to the use they made of studio couches. The department buyer had assumed that they were used mostly as extra beds, but the survey revealed that most were used as inexpensive living room couches and that the styling of the covers was not wholly suited to this use. This led to a restyling of the line with a consequent increase in sales.

In its more complex and scientific form, this kind of consumer survey is a task for skilled specialists, and the procedures are outside the buyer's ken or need and therefore outside the purview of this book. In fact, consumer surveys may be too costly for one store to undertake. Sometimes they are undertaken as a cooperative venture by competitors with an enlightened view of their common interests—perhaps under the aegis of a board of trade, chamber of commerce, or research center. Daily newspapers in many large cities and some magazines make surveys or buy the reports of surveys made by other agencies. Buyers get such reports or the gist of their findings from trade sources.

The Consumer Panel

Another source of information is the customer panel. The panel is a representative group of customers organized by a manufacturer, advertising or research agency, newspaper, or retailer to furnish facts and opinions about consumption. It may express opinions about advertising copy, radio or television programs, sketches or samples of styles under consideration, store assortments, or store services.

There are five varieties of such consumer panels:

1. The customer advisory group, organized by a store or a merchant's association to make suggestions in regard to store policies, services, and merchandise assortments and to learn something of store problems.
2. The consumer jury, which expresses opinion on copy, radio programs, or sketches of styles. If organized by the store, this group may consist of the same people who comprise the customer advisory group.
3. The consumer experience group, which reports on performance of products in use, shopping habits, and brand preference.
4. The home inventory group, which reports on the goods they have on hand according to brand.
5. The continuous-purchase record, whereby customers record their purchases in certain commodity classes and make monthly reports on their family purchasing.

The *customer advisory group* is perhaps the most important, because it is associated with a particular retailer or community and serves a double purpose by giving the community a sense of participation. Customers feel that deep concern is being displayed about their preferences. For some, there is an aura of authenticity about merchandise offerings, which have apparently been strongly influenced by their own, directly expressed desires—especially when these expressions seem to stem from those who are viewed as leaders in the community. Nevertheless, stores have been slow to make use of such groups—except for high school and college "boards" in connection with their "young" ready-to-wear departments.

It may be advisable to encourage such customer groups to expand their council into community safety problems, ecology, price control legislation, and other matters identified with special community interest. This would not commit the firm, but the provision of a forum would reenforce the firm's identification with the community.

Consumer experience groups are a testing device used by manufacturers. They may put samples of a new product into the hands of a group of consumers to determine how it performs before it is placed on the open market.

Home inventory and continuous purchase panels are used to gain information about trends in consumer preference through study of what they have in their homes or by keeping a continuous record of their purchases. This kind of survey may be initiated by newspapers or manufacturers, or by private agencies that sell the results. Information may be gained about brand, price line, and other preferences as well as about store type and individual preference for stores within a type.

Observation and Counts

Valuable information about what to buy may be obtained by observing individuals and groups in the local community rather than interviewing or questioning them. A great deal of business would be lost if nothing were bought until customers demanded it. Local newspapers report in detail costumes and decorations at social functions, and a store may send representatives to attend these affairs. Whatever is worn or displayed by social leaders gives indications about what may achieve popular demand. Quick experimentation may save otherwise lost sales and may serve to establish a reputation for alertness.

Because fashions are determined by the kinds of lives that people lead, undoubtedly the more the buyer can find out about the people that make up the local community, the better he or she will be able to buy for them. Sometimes, and perhaps most fortuitously, the source of information is no further away than the traffic in one's own store or on the sidewalk outside.

Whatever the source and whatever the method, one warning always applies: beware of jumping to quick conclusions from wrong sampling and wrong interpretation. To the extent that there is some cultural lag, observations about those in higher socioeconomic strata may be expected to reflect subsequent demand in lower strata. However, demand may eventually focus on watered-down or extremely exaggerated versions of the original. Observations of customers at the stores' own levels may serve two purposes:

1. To show what is in apparent demand but has been overlooked in preparing the assortment, and
2. To show trends in preference.

The first may have already become apparent through examination of want slips or through watching competitors' offerings. The second purpose is best served if the timing of observations is carefully analyzed. With respect to seasons, for example, the increasing prevalence of white accessories in June does not indicate a particular trend to white as much as it indicates that summer is waxing. In general, it may be said that *the peak of use or wear comes after the peak of selling.*

Tabulating observations

Because some of these observations may be made on a homey, do-it-yourself basis, a few words on methodology are apropos. In the case of clothing, observation of the tastes of the local community has been put on a statistical basis. An observer can record what people are wearing, and this information can be analyzed in much the same manner as sales are analyzed. Although it is hardly possible to determine size and price; classification, pattern, styles, color, and material can be studied. If these studies are repeated at regular and frequent intervals, the trend of demand becomes apparent if the previously mentioned seasonal factors can be ironed out. Certain colors, for example, are seen to increase in popularity and others to decline. This information acts as a check on sales information. Sales may not show that a certain color or type of merchandise is becoming more important, because the store may not have a sufficient stock. Although want slips should have revealed the deficiency, customers may not have gone to the trouble to ask for the wanted items when they did not see them in stock. The fashion count shows what customers have bought from all the stocks in the community or even from outside sources. It is thus not warped by the incompleteness of one merchant's stock or by the failure of wants to be openly expressed and recorded in a store.

Where a number of factors exist, it is sometimes wise for the observer to count only one at a time. For example, in handbags, one observer may count only the type-classification of the bag at a time. Two other people may work on the team, one observing the material and another the color and size of the same bags. Or a single observer may first count materials and then count an additional group of women to obtain data on colors. The reason for considering one factor at a time is that practically every person passing a given point can be included this way; whereas, if each bag or shoe must be analyzed for a number of factors, only a few can be "caught," and the observer tends to include those that appeal to him. This bias caused by unconscious choosing of people or merchandise to include in the sample leads to an inaccurate picture of actual use. If it is important to know about ensembles or other combinations of factors, however, each passerby should be so studied by using a code designation for each factor, even if checking is slowed up. All of these observations in the store and the community must be regarded as late intelligence.

Observations in major centers

In order to anticipate fashions that are spreading, fashion observations should be made not only in the store's community but also in fashion and market centers. When visiting their buying markets or their large regional cities, buyers make note of what is being worn or used and what is being offered in the big stores. In all these surveys, it becomes important to have a good idea of the time lag for changing preference between the observed centers and one's own customers and of the differences in the two groups. Some stores encourage their buyers to adopt apparent successes from these belle-weather stores, forgetting that by the time they have placed orders and received delivery they may be presenting "ho-hum" goods to their own clientele.

In sum, buyers should train themselves to be habitual observers of the pertinent aspects of the social scene of constant change. And it always is important to determine the underlying theme or central idea that becomes apparent in one or a few products and ends up spawning a host of products, be it "the stubby look" or "the long look," the egalitarian look of denim and hopsacking or the foppishness of elegant broadcloths and silks, or, for that matter, the sudden turn from synthetic to the natural in food and textiles, or vice-versa.

TRADE SOURCES OF CONSUMER PREFERENCE

In addition to interviews, panels, and direct observation, retailers seeking information outside their own records have recourse to various trade sources. Other stores, resident buying offices, manufacturers and wholesalers, trade and consumer publications, trade services, and reporting agencies may all be drawn upon, because they report the demand as evidenced in different parts of the country.

Shopping Competing Stores

Data collected from other stores may be from both competing and noncompeting stores. Reports from other stores may show the demand expressed elsewhere before the articles purchased appear in use. Again, they throw light on the demand for many articles that could not be reported by means of counts or observations of store representatives. By watching these reports, buyers are able to base their buying not only on the movement of their own stock but also on that of other stores' stocks.

Competitors' sales may be determined in four ways. The first is by studying competitors' advertisements to see what they have to offer. What they offer represents their judgment as to what people want and is based partly on their past sales.

The second is by studying competitors' windows to see what they are displaying. Care must be exercised to determine the store policy in the use of its windows. Some use them for goods above the best-selling price lines that give prestige to the store but bring in little volume. Others put their best sellers in the window on the theory that it is wise to push what sells most readily without pushing. Many put their newest merchandise in the windows to establish a reputation for fashion leadership. Finally, some put *bait* in the windows: standard or apparently standard merchandise at abnormally low prices, with the purpose of getting people into the store and then selling them something else or, at least, something in addition to the bait. From the standpoint of buying decisions, it is important to recognize these differences both in advertisements and displays and to use the information judiciously. If, for example, the goods promoted are very new, they indicate what that store is betting on experimentally, not necessarily what its customers are buying.

A third way to determine competitors' sales is to study their stock. The buyer, a salesperson, or a professional shopper may go to the other stores, look over merchandise like any customer, and possibly make purchases. What the competitors *have* represents their expectations to some extent. Price comparisons are important in order in order to determine whether or not the home store's prices reflect its competitive policy. Comparisons of assortments are important to show whether or not the home store is competitive in variety of salable styles. Study of competitors' stocks aids in selling as well as in buying; methods of displaying the goods and good selling techniques may be learned.

The fourth and best way to determine competitors' sales is to observe them as they actually take place. The buyer, a comparison shopper, or the representative of a reporting organization may visit competing stores at busy times of the day to see at what counters the greatest sales activity is taking place. This will show what actually is in demand, not what others want to sell. The buyer often will find that goods not carried in the home store are in active demand or that goods in stock would move readily if differently displayed or changed in price.

In the small store, watching competitors must be done by buyer and salespeople, but a larger store can afford to employ a special group of shoppers (known as a "shopping" or "comparison" staff) to relieve the selling departments and to cover competitors' offerings more completely. It may also subscribe to an outside shopping service. Sometimes each regular salesperson is allotted occasional time to shop certain competitors and to make a report to the buyer. With an intimate knowledge of the goods and the department, the salesperson may bring in some data missed by the professional shopper.

A word of caution must be given regarding comparison work, whether performed by a specialized staff or by the selling departments directly. So much time may be spent watching competitors that there is little left for work at home. Few stores are wholly successful if they merely ape someone else. Frequently the leading stores, which are doing the creative, original jobs, have better sources of inspiration than those their competitors provide. They do the least comparing for general information about customer preferences although they may shop prices thoroughly.

Some stores have found that it is not necessary to watch every price and make adjustment each time a competitor makes a change. They try to build a reputation on the reasonableness of all their prices rather than on the alleged rock-bottom nature of every price in the house. Others have advertised policies that make it imperative to "meet or beat" competition's prices on all identifiable merchandise.

Information from Noncompeting Stores

Information as to what is selling elsewhere and may soon be in demand locally may be obtained directly from other stores or through some reporting agency. Noncompeting stores are frequently organized into groups and exchange information regularly. Every successful and unsuccessful promotion in one store is broadcast to other members of the group. Model assortment lists of merchandise are jointly worked out, so that each store has a standard to guide its buying. Because buyers for any one line normally go to the central market at the same time, they frequently get acquainted in a hotel, restaurant, or manufacturer's showroom. The personal contacts formed become a major source of buying information. Because the buyers are not competing, they are frequently happy to exchange information freely. This interchange is fostered and usually formalized by resident buying offices.

As previously noted, buyers profit greatly from studying the merchandise offerings of the stores in big market or regional cities. On a day-to-day basis, this program can be supplemented by reading one or two key newspapers from these cities.

Studying Advertisements

A store may obtain information about nearly any store in the country by studying advertisements. For example, a store in Youngstown, Ohio, noted that a large Detroit store repeatedly advertised lace curtains at a price that had been considered too high to prove popular, but the Detroit store's evident success, as shown by repeat advertisements, led to the Ohio store's purchasing a supply and featuring them in a window. Almost a hundred curtains were sold with no advertising.

A store will do well to subscribe to leading newspapers in the great cosmopolitan centers in this country, as well as in the city that dominates the section of the country in which it is located. For this purpose, the following nine districts with their central cities may be set up, although other cities in each district are excellent guides for smaller cities near them.

Region	*Cities*
New England	Boston
Middle Atlantic	New York City, Philadelphia
East North Central	Chicago, Detroit, Pittsburgh, Cleveland
West North Central	St. Louis, Omaha, Minneapolis-St. Paul
South Atlantic	Washington, Baltimore, Atlanta, Miami
East South Central	Memphis
West South Central	Dallas, Houston
Mountain	Denver, Phoenix
Pacific	Los Angeles, San Francisco, Seattle, Portland

It is important that a store recognize the district it is in, the city or cities that dominate it, and also the stores that are the leaders in those cities. What is selling well in Atlanta may sell well in Jacksonville but not in Minneapolis. What is selling in Boston may sell in Manchester, New Hampshire, but may be a failure in Omaha, Nebraska.

Information from Vendors and Market Representatives

Vendors

Manufacturers and wholesalers present new goods coming on the market and are in close touch with the designers of new styles and with sales results in other stores to which they sell. Again, vendors are particularly anxious to pass on useful information and are well organized for the purpose, because their success in obtaining orders depends partly on the quality of the reporting service they render. Information from vendors can be obtained in four ways: (1) direct from their sales representatives, (2) from catalogs and price lists, (3) from style services or bulletins issued by them, sometimes at regular intervals, and (4) from showings.

Salespeople often inform retail buyers as to which styles other stores have ordered or reordered. Because a reorder usually reflects customer acceptance, a buyer finds knowledge of reorders of great value but must be sure that the store in question caters to customers whose preferences are similar to those of his or her trade. The buyer should also ascertain that the vendor is a competent and unbiased analyst of the data. For a more detailed account of vendor's help, see Chapter 9.

Trade associations sponsor fairs or expositions commonly called shows, often as part of the association's seasonal conventions. Manufacturers buy space in the form of booths and exhibit their wares, often quite elaborately. Some of these shows fill great auditoriums, or several floors of a hotel. Couturiers, too, assemble their seasons' offerings in special style shows, attended by manufacturers as well as by retailers. What is shown at these exhibitions frequently, though not necessarily, become the vogues of the forthcoming season. These creators are close students of social trends and frequently are successful in reflecting the interests and attitudes of the times in dress, home decoration, and automotive and sports equipment.

The major trade show of the French ready-to-wear industry is known as the *Pret a Porter* and is held semiannually just outside of Paris.

Market representatives

Market representatives are posted in wholesale markets to assist buyers in selecting resources and merchandise. They generally serve a group of stores. Because of their close contact with vendors and with other stores in the group, they are able to provide a great deal of buying information and have become important for buyers of fashion goods. As a source of buying information, market representatives are superior to vendors in so far as they represent the stores and are not trying to sell a particular product or style. Moreover, they frequently have more complete information than any one vendor as to what other stores in the group are selling and buying. How they operate has been discussed in detail in Chapter 3.

Trade Papers

Nearly every line of merchandise has its trade organ. These carry vendors' advertisements and report all the information they can as to what is new, what stores are selling, and what appears in use. *Women's Wear Daily,* issued by Fairchild Publications, is dominant in the women's apparel field; *Drug Topics* is outstanding in the drug field; *Daily News Record,* in textiles and men's wear; *Retailing Daily,* in home furnishings; and *Footwear News,* in shoes. Among interesting facts frequently reported in these papers is a list of items in different lines that are selling best in stores at the time or that store buyers are seeking in the market. Some of the facts need interpretation to be of use.

Reporting and Research Agencies

Some of the trade papers, newspapers, consumer magazines, resident buyers, and special reporting organizations undertake market research of value to buyers. These often take the form of weekly and monthly reports. Reference has already been made to the special editions of magazines and to dealer panels. The Fairchild organization has a large worldwide reporting staff that sends in fashion news and forecasts for apparel and accessories as well as for furniture and home accessories. There are also a number of organizations that specialize in fashion reporting and spot-news information on what is selling in the stores. Prominent among these is the famous Tobe fashion center, RAM Reports and the Retail News Bureau. The last provides merchants with a barrage of confidential reporting services on developments in major markets like New York City, California, Dallas, and Florida, as well as with spot-news on ideas, developing trends, fashion forecasts, resource information, and promotions in the stores (see Figure 6–4).

Noted market researchers in the field of convenience goods like food and drugs, are the A. C. Nielson Company and Market Research Corporation of America (MRCA). The first, through dealer panels, and the second, through consumer panels, maintain a continuous audit on product sales and associated store activities and on consumer purchases by product and place of purchase. These reports are available on a national and regional scale and, in many cases, for even smaller geographic subdivisions and firm sizes. Another organization, the George Newstadt Company, has made a national reputation for its analysis of retail advertised merchandise by price line and month in which the advertising appears.

DISCUSSION QUESTIONS

1. (a) What system of sales determination is likely to be used for each of the following: women's better sweaters, sewing notions, towels, oriental rugs, canned foods?
   (b) What factors, other than the nature of the goods, help to determine the system to use?
2. Why is it dangerous to assume that sales analyzed by the various selection factors truly reveal customer demand?
3. Summarize the case for and against a want-slip system.

FIGURE 6–4 Retail News Bureau confidential reporting service report

RETAIL NEWS BUREAU

'A *Confidential* Reporting Service'

ITEM (S)— JUNIOR SUITS
SIZES: 5-13
$29.00

RESPONSE*			
FAIR	GOOD	STRONG	SELLOUT
			X

CSJ RESOURCE

EVAN ROBERTS
1410 BROADWAY
NEW YORK CITY, N.Y.

REPORT NO. SFG-M00621-10

STORE SAKS FIFTH AVENUE

PAPER TIMES 6/17

AD. SIZE FULL PAGE

WEATHER CLOUDY

*Shopped 3 Times

DETAILS: REPEAT PROMOTION ON JUNIOR PANTSUITS.....

STYLE #4500R: FOUR POCKETED SAFARI SUIT IN CAMEL OR WHITE COTTON. SIZES: 5-13, $29.00.
STYLE #4319R: SHORT SLEEVED SUIT WITH LACE POCKET TRIM. IN CAMEL OR WHITE COTTON, $29.00, 5-13.
STYLE #4599R: TWIN POCKETED SHIRTJACKET WITH MATCHING PANTS. YELLOW, WHITE, GREEN OR BLUE COTTON. SIZES: 5-13, $29.00.

ADVERTISED MERCHANDISE DISPLAYED ON FLOOR RACKS, YOUNG DIMENSIONS IN SUITS ON SEVEN. THIS IS A REPEAT AD ON A PROMOTIONAL GROUP--SAKS HAS USED ALMOST 20,000 UNITS. THIS MERCHANDISE IS SOLD UP. EVAN ROBERTS WILL OFFER A FALL PROMOTIONAL GROUP OF SUITS PRICED TO RETAIL AT ABOUT $40.00. ORDERS MUST BE PLACED ON THAT MERCHANDISE BY AUGUST 15TH FOR AN END OF OCTOBER DELIVERY.

Errors subject to correction

● MERCHANDISE REPORT OF **RETAIL NEWS BUREAU**, 232 MADISON AVE., NEW YORK N. Y. 10016 ●

Copyright An Independent Agency Reporting the News of Retailing—Promptly, Accurately, Completely. MU 6-7134

4. Discourse on the "central idea" in merchandising, using categories in question 1 (a) as examples.
5. (a) What selection factors do you think can be merchandised by "scaling"?
   (b) And what is the current trend with respect to the proliferation of selection factors like sizes and colors?
6. When and how should seasonal goods' sales be analyzed as a basis for future buying?
7. What outside reports about customer acceptance of merchandise should be followed by a dress buyer? A furniture buyer? A supermarket buyer? A cosmetics buyer?
8. Evaluate the practice of a buyer who seeks to minimize the losses from error by a consistent policy of buying cautiously as compared with the one who risks many failures in order not to miss a big sales winner.
9. Evaluate the practice by buyers in smaller cities of getting a large part of their information from selected stores in large regional cities or in market cities.
10. How can information from a vendor in regard to trends in demand be scrutinized to make sure it is not distorted by his or her own production commitments?

chapter 7

The Merchandise Assortment: Quantitative Considerations

SECTION 1. MERCHANDISE PLANNING AND CONTROL

TOP-DOWN VERSUS BOTTOM-UP PLANS

Merchandise planning is approached from two directions, which may be described as "top-down" and "bottom-up." The top-down approach starts with comprehensive budgets covering broad segments of operation and/or broad segments of time. These plans are then subdivided into smaller segments—often by applying percentages based on experience and judgment. Thus the parts automatically sum up to the 100 percent whole of some predetermined broad plan.

Figure 7–1 illustrates such a plan for a five-store chain of infants' and children's apparel shops. Top management has forecast sales of $225,000 for the forthcoming quarter. This amount has been distributed down to the five stores [Plan (a)] and three departments [Plan (b)] within the framework of the planned total: $225,000.

The bottom-up approach to the same set of budgets is illustrated by Plans (c) and (d). In Plan (c), each store has been studied for its potential sales in the planning quarter and a resulting forecast entered on the plan. The chain total for this plan comes to $234,000 or $9000 more than the top-down plan. Because the latter [Plan (a)] acts as a guide or control, the two budgets must now be compared and reconciled. The difference is not great (4 percent), but it is centered on two stores. The built-up plan for Store A shows a sales budget of $3,000 more (about 6.5 percent) than the $45,000 allotted to it in

FIGURE 7–1 Top-down and built-up sales plans for a chain of five stores with three departments

SALES BY STORES

	Plan (a)		Plan (c)	
Store	% Total Chain	Dollars	Dollars	% Total Chain
Total Chain	100	225,000		
A	20	45,000	48,000	20.5
B	16	36,000	37,000	15.8
C	20	45,000	45,000	19.3
D	26	58,500	57,000	24.4
E	18	40,500	47,000	20.0
Total Chain			234,000	100.0

Plan (a) is a top-down or generic plan which apportions $225,000 sales among 5 stores.

Plan (c) is a built-up plan of sales for each store which adds to $234,000 for the chain.

SALES BY DEPARTMENTS

	Plan (b)		Plan (d)	
Department	% Total Chain	Dollars	Dollars	% Total Chain
Total Chain	100	225,000		
Girls&Teens	30	67,500	78,000	33.0
Infants	50	112,500	112,000	47.5
Little Boys	20	45,000	46,000	19.5
Total Chain			236,000	100.0

Plan (b) distributes the $225,000 sales budget over 3 departments by estimating the normal percentage each would be expected to contribute to the total.

Plan (d) is a built-up plan for each department which adds to $236,000.

SALES OF STORE "A" BY DEPARTMENTS

	Plan (e)		Plan (f)	
Department	% Total Store	Dollars	Dollars	% Total Chain
Total Store	100	45,000		
Girls&Teens	30	13,500	16,000	33.3
Infants	50	22,500	23,000	48.0
Little Boys	20	9,000	9,000	18.7
Total Store			48,000	100.0

Plan (e) picks up the $45,000 budget for store A from plan (a) above, and distributes it by departments.

Plan (f) is a built-up plan by departments which adds to $48,000.

the control plan. Store E shows a much wider discrepancy: $6,500, or 16 percent.

This will undoubtedly result in some debate. If the store planners can justify their figure with convincing reasons, it may be accepted, and the control, or top-down, plan may be revised. Otherwise, the plans for Stores A and E will have to be revised. Or some compromise decision will result in revision of both sets of plans. The student should scrutinize departmental sales Plans (b) and (d) in the light of the foregoing discussion. The built-up plan of $236,000 is $11,000, or nearly 5 percent, higher than the control plan with the increase concentrated in girls' and teens' wear.

Plans (e) and (f) show how each department's sales have been distributed within Store A. Note that in the control Plan (e) the sales sum up to the store's planned total of $45,000 in Plan (a). That is because they were derived by *starting* with $45,000 and apportioning it down to the three departments according to their past relative performance in contribution of sales. Plan (f) is the built-up plan wherein each department was studied separately and planned separately on the basis of possible improvements in merchandising or promotion, which could yield increased sales. It is apparently on this basis that girls' and teens' wear has been budgeted for sales of $16,000 as opposed to $13,500 in the control plan. It is also likely that this was an argument advanced for planning Store A's sales potential at $48,000 [Plan (c)]. Because it will be observed that in the built-up planning procedure, the sales of Store A [Plan (c)] *result* from the detailed budgeting in specific Plan (f). This is just the reverse of top-down planning wherein the details of specific Plan (e) result from the distribution of a figure already determined in generic Plans (a) and (b).

Reconciling Plans

Good planners use both approaches to get two different perspectives. There is an underlying assumption that wherever both sets of plans agree, both are likely to be good estimates. This is not necessarily true but serves as a practical working assumption. *Buyers and merchandisers learn to work with likelihoods as opposed to certainties. Likelihoods,* as appears later, is synonymous with *probabilities*—and probabilities are a sound working law unto themselves.

In all merchandise budgeting, only one statement may be made with certainty: "When control plans and built-up plans do not agree, something is wrong somewhere"—and the two sets of plans should be reconciled to a point of reasonable agreement. Generally, the laws of probability are on the side of control plans, because they deal with broader, larger segments: And *big figures are less subject to the vagaries of pure chance than are small figures.* But *intimate knowledge of the operation usually rests with the detail planners.* The buyer, for example, is in the best position to appraise past mistakes and may reflect their intended correction in an improved performance. This reflection should appear in his or her budget and be backed with forceful presentation based on sound conviction. To take another example: If a new item or expected change in style may result in greatly improved sales, the buyer should budget his or her expectations. Otherwise, all stock and promotion plans (which are based on the sales budget) will be too skimpy to permit exploitation of the expected sales potential.

THE GENERAL MERCHANDISE PLAN

Figure 7–2 illustrates a common type of departmental dollar plan.[1] The four basic elements provided in this example are:

1. Last year's performance, labeled LY;
2. This year's plan, labeled PL;
3. Revisions of plan, labeled RV; and
4. Actual performance this year, labeled ACT.

FIGURE 7–2 A departmental or classification seasonal plan in dollars

Store ———

*DEPARTMENT 4 #43 Blouses and Sportswear** *Season: Spring*

Spring 19 / *Fall 19*		*Feb.* / *Aug.*	*Mar.* / *Sept.*	*Apr.* / *Oct.*	*May* / *Nov.*	*June* / *Dec.*	*July* / *Jan.*	*Total* / *Total*	*% of* / *Change*
Net Sales	LY	45	55	53	60	97	40	350	
in $1000	PL	48	60	58	65	106	41	378	+8.0
	RV								
	ACT								
Markdowns	LY	5	4	4	4	9	18	44	
in $1000	PL	6	4	5	6	10	14	45	+2.3
	RV								
	ACT								
								EOM	
Retail Stocks	LY	157	172	176	184	208	166	162	**2 ST
B.O.M.	PL	155	170	178	185	212	165	160	2.16 ST
In $1000	RY								
	ACT								
Retail Purchases	LY	65	63	65	88	64	54	399	
in $1000	PL	69	72	70	98	69	50	428	+7
	RV								
	ACT								
Direct	LY	7	8	8	8	10	6	47	
Expenses	PL	7	8	8.4	9	11	7	50	+6.6
in $1000	RV								
	ACT								

*Data in thousands. **ST = Stockturn.

Approved ______________________________
(Buyer)

Approved ______________________________
(Merchandise Manager)

Sales are always planned first. By various methods, stocks in dollars are then set for the beginning of each month. Probable markdown requirements are also entered in months when they should be taken. "Retail purchases"

[1]See John W. Wingate, Elmer O. Schaller, and F. Leonard Miller, *Retail Merchandise Management*, (Englewood Cliffs, N.J.: Prentice-Hall, Inc., 1972), chap. 17.

indicates the amount of merchandise that should be received into stock each month to maintain the level of the inventory reservoir, if sales and markdowns occur as planned. The formula for computing planned purchases, also called "planned receipts," is as follows:

> Sales for the month, plus markdowns for the month, plus stock required at the end of the month (start of the following month), less the stock provided at the beginning of the month.

EXAMPLE: AS PRESENTED IN THE MERCHANDISE PLAN (FIGURE 7–2):

Planned sales—February	$ 48,000
Planned stock—end of February	170,000
Planned markdowns—February	6,000
Total provision required	$224,000
Less planned stock—beginning February	155,000
Planned retail purchases—February	$ 69,000

Inventory as a Reservoir

A plan like this views the department inventory as a reservoir from which may be drawn the goods required to meet an ever changing and not always predictable customer demand. Unfortunately, it is a reservoir that cannot be maintained at comfortingly high levels of safety. The penalty for attempting to do so is a costly accumulation of stagnant contents and sludge—unneeded reserves and unsalable merchandise. But the penalty for letting the level run too low is even more costly—in lost sales, in loss of customer good will, in expensive emergency measures, and in a lowering of employee morale.

The level must be maintained at a somewhat delicate balance between expected demand, or outflow, and anticipated receivings, or inflow. Both are hard to measure precisely. In the end, the measurement of both always contains elements of estimate. Skill in estimating requires some talent and may be improved with training and good practice.

During the course of a planning season or year, the amount of stock put into the reservoir is roughly equal to sales plus whatever may be required to cover markdowns and other shrinkage. But it is the *rate* of receivings, or *rate* of input, that becomes the key to management of the inventory level and mix.

It is this *rate* of flow that is the subject of so much planning. In fact, some planners prefer to arrive at the total requirements (purchases) for a planning period and then distribute the total directly among the component months or weeks on the basis of many considerations of requirement and probable availability. In this case, the first-of-month stocks must be computed and become the result of a built-up plan. Nevertheless, the planner must be prepared to defend his or her position if resulting inventory plans produce a turnover rate at substantial variance with the turnover objective embedded in the company's generic merchandise plan. The setting of this objective is discussed later in this chapter.

Open-to-Buy

The system that regulates this flow of goods into the stock is known as the open-to-buy control.[2] Purchase receipts are controlled for each month (or week) by subtracting the outstanding orders for delivery each month (or week) from the planned or revised retail purchases for that period. The heart of the system is illustrated by the example (Figure 7–2), which computes the Planned Retail Purchases for February at $69,000. In this case, the data is all in "planned" figures, because it is taken from the 6-month departmental plan (Figure 7–2). However, as the season wears on, most recent available actual (ACT) performance figures along with revised (REV) future plans are used to project future purchases. Thus:

1. If planned sales for April were revised to $52,000, from $58,000,
2. and if the stock planned for the end of April (beginning of May) was revised to $175,000,
3. and if markdowns for April were revised to $8000,
4. and if actual stock at the beginning of April turned out to be $180,000,
5. computation of planned purchases for April would be as follows:

Planned sales—April	$ 52,000
Planned stock—end of April	175,000
Planned markdowns—April	8,000
Total provision required	$235,000
Less actual stock—beginning of April	180,000
Revised retail purchase—April	$ 55,000

Contrast this with the original plan of $70,000 for April, as shown in Figure 7–2.

Furthermore, if by the first of April $50,000 worth of orders at retail had already been placed for delivery in April, the open-to-buy (OTB) for that month would now be only $5000 (55,000 − 50,000). That is to say: only $5000 more in orders should be placed for delivery in April. That $5000 will be

[2]For a detailed treatment of OTB control, see the companion volume to this work: *Retail Merchandise Management, Ibid.*

needed to realize the sales plan for April and provide a balanced inventory at the end of the month. As further orders are placed for April delivery, the OTB will be reduced to zero or thereabouts. If more than $5000 worth are placed, the department will be "overbought" by the amount in excess of $5000.

The rigidly conservative controller's view that the $5000 OTB is a fixed limit, and the prodigal buyer's disdain of it as theoretical clap-trap, are both wrong. The OTB reading at any time serves as an extremely useful guide or diagnostic aid. If it shows less than the buyer seems to need, it may indicate any one or a combination of the following:

1. wrong forecasting or other planning errors;
2. improper distribution of the merchandise mix or other errors in buying;
3. unsuccessful promotions;
4. late receipt of goods or other timing errors.

If the OTB for a period shows more than can be effectively ordered and received in that period, it may be due to errors in planning or buying or to:

1. unexpectedly successful promotions; or
2. failure to place needed orders in time.

In any event, an unsatisfactory OTB situation cannot be corrected either by rigid adherence to the arithmetic or by disdain for it. The root causes must be determined and dealt with—promptly. If a men's furnishing stock is overbought because of a surfeit of pajamas, the condition can't be cleared by running short of shirts.

It must also be noted, unfortunately, that buyers who run short of open-to-buy will often resort to skimpy reordering programs instead of rooting out the stocks that are really causing the trouble. This process has been called "spinning the middle" because it results in excessive turnover of the middle, or better selling goods, while the "dead-ends" turn sluggishly.

Degree of Detail in Planning

Obviously, the profitable sales-yield capacity of the stock reservoir at any level depends on the nature of the components in the mix. Just as total inventories are planned for specific dates, so may their parts be planned. A *model stock* is a quantitative picture of that mix. A *buying plan* is a schedule of things to buy, when to buy them, and when to have them delivered so that model stock plans may be fulfilled.

How detailed plans should be depends on many factors and calls for the continual use of trained judgment. Practicability is a powerful consideration. Detailed plans are costly: They take time to prepare, to analyze, and to follow. Before embarking on them, it is wise to consider *whether their value will merit the cost*. In the planning illustration shown in Figure 7–1, it would certainly be necessary to subdivide the department Plans (b) and (d) into smaller categories or classifications of merchandise. In some cases, plans might well be developed by units of items for monthly intervals and for key weeks. But plans like (e) and (f) for each store may be left at the department level—in dollars—and subdivided by months. It is left to the chain's "distributors" to plan and fill individual store needs by units of specific price lines or other small categories. In a small chain where the stores are near enough to each other and where merchandise is in open display, visual control and direct communication may substitute for a certain amount of formal planning. This is even more true when the buyer operates in a single store—and still more true when the store is small.

Following examples show that still other elements should color judgment about the detail with which planning should be conducted. These elements include the buyer's capacities and assistance, the length of time for which he or she must make commitments, the severity of penalty for mistakes in merchandising, the need for speed versus the desire for accuracy, and volatility or stability of customer preference.

The buyer with highly developed powers of visual observation and memory will require relatively less paper work to chart a course of action. Those who lack this special talent may be equally successful by substituting more formal programing and control. Their most serious mistake is to emulate the buyers who just don't happen to need as much formalized guidance. It is also *wasteful to prepare elaborate or sophisticated material for buyers who lack the time and/or the capacity to use it.*[3] The buyer who is furnished with a team of assistants, clericals, and specialists obviously is able to prepare and use more elaborate plans than is the buyer less blessed with help.

Demand curves affect planning detail

Sometimes action is too swift for detailed analysis. A sportswear buyer at the peak of a selling season may spend much time in the market fitting individual items into a broad plan of price lines, colors, or types. Accurate planning of specific variants must yield to the need for speedy fulfillment of the overall requirements. Further diminishing the importance of accurate selection, among the individual items of sportswear, is their substitutability in filling the overall requirements of most customers (cf. preceding chapter).

The buyer of women's shoes who procures most of the goods from jobbers is in a somewhat similar position with respect to planning and selecting individual styles. But shoe buyers for large stores, chains, and mail-order catalog houses must plan in great detail and far in advance. For one thing,

[3]Inability to use such material is becoming constantly less excusable as the use of data-processing equipment becomes more prevalent.

they buy directly from factories that, in this industry, have delivery periods that are long in relation to the swift obsolescence of the selection factors involved. Also, these buyers often have shoes made up with special details, thereby becoming committed to purchase a specified quantity of the particular styles.

Furthermore, the multiplicity of sizes (a selection factor of very low substitutability) heightens the importance of keeping down the number of other variants. Therefore, the number of styles to be included in the model of a given category is carefully worked out long before the opening of a season, and specific styles to fit the model are then chosen. New styles that turn up later are carefully and sparingly introduced. And one of the perennial problems is to save enough open-to-buy from the enthusiasm of early buying to provide for these later styles. The depth in which these specific items will be stocked is the subject of successive model stocks which reflect the mix at the start of a season, at its peak, and near its end.

Where more stable demand patterns prevail, it becomes less necessary to plan a succession of model stocks. An assortment framework showing the number of greeting cards to be carried in each type and at each price would be adequate for controlling the model stock of birthday cards. Methods for filling in can be routinized as will be shown later. New numbers can be fitted in smoothly in a continuous pattern without undue urgency about the selling-off of discontinued numbers. A moment's thought will show how this differs from the problems presented by cards for Christmas, Easter, Saint Valentine's Day, Mother's Day, or Father's Day. The key difference appears in their steeply fluctuating demand curves.

Standardized Merchandise Classifications

The trend is in the direction of planning and controlling sales and stocks in greater detail than by departmental totals. For department stores, these classifications have been standardized so as to facilitate exchange of data and to provide a better knowledge of trends in customer demand leading to quick adjustment of stocks to change.

In 1969 the National Retail Merchants Association published its "Standard Classification of Merchandise," designed to classify the universe of consumer goods from the viewpoint of their consumer end-use. As a guide, this is neither simple nor rigid. To quote Frank Burnside, chairman of the committee to develop a standard classification plan:

> End-use changes with changing manners and customs, with the individual's mood and circumstances, and with the powerful feedback drive of manufacturers' search for product versatility and consumers' urgent, if latent, desire for

products with versatile end-use. The sweater designed for ski wear soon became part of the general sweater wardrobe—and how much of a television console, a table, or a bedspread is functional and how much is decorative?

The guiding principle in setting up the order of classification is to secure greater homogeneity within a class as it becomes a lower order of subdivision: that is, the different products within the class become more and more substitutable for each other in satisfying perceived end-uses. Table 7–1 is an example.

The names of the successive orders of classification—demand center, sub-center, class, sub-class and category—refer to the code numbers appearing in lines beneath them. Thus, classes are 742 and 743; sub-classes are 7421 and 7426 and 7431.

As Emerson Tolle of J.C. Penney points out in the manual:

> A small store may elect to keep classification records on only the second level breakdown, "demand centers." A medium-size store may elect to carry some of its less important lines at the demand center level while sub-dividing more important lines down to the 3rd and 4th levels (sub-centers and classes). Still larger stores may use still more levels. Large stores also have the problem of similar stocks in different departments, shops, or boutiques. If such a product is once logically identified as a member of a single class and so labelled with a code number, its activities may be tracked and summed, whatever its physical location.

Classification control is not a new idea in merchandising. But all these improvements in standardizing and coding have interacted beautifully with recent developments in the management of inventories through electronic data processing, discussed throughout and summarized in Chapter 8.

STOCKTURN AND THE PRODUCTIVITY OF THE INVESTMENT

An increasingly important consideration in planning the assortment, both by department and by classification, is to make each dollar invested in merchandise productive of both sales and profit. The customary index used to measure this is called *stockturn*. It is the sales for a period of time, divided by the average inventory carried during the period. For example, if the sales for a year in a department or classification are $100,000 and if the average retail stock carried during the year is $25,000, the stockturn is 4.[4] The

[4]If a store keeps its inventory records only at cost prices and not at retail prices, the stockturn may be calculated as the cost of the goods sold, divided by the average inventory at cost.

TABLE 7–1
Classifying within the Merchandise Group: Home Furnishings (No. 700)*

U.S. comm. dept. c.c.#	*Your dept or code*	*Demand center*	*Sub-center*	*Class*	*Sub-class*	*Category*
		740 Window and furniture coverings				
			741 Ready made draperies, slip covers, wall hangings, piece goods, supplies and accessories (spreads, canopies, vanity skirts, pillow shams, etc. which are matched to draperies go here; otherwise in 750).			
202				742 Draperies, matching spreads and accessories		
					7421 Draperies	
						7422 Lined
						7423 Unlined (include liners)
						7424 Open
						7425 Open
					7426 Matching spreads, accessories and ensembles	
						7427 Spreads and canopies to match draperies
						7428 Matching vanity skirts, pillow shams and other accessories including valances
						7429 Ensembles
				743 Slip covers and throws (including those for studio beds and other convertibles)		
202					7431 Slip covers and sets (e.g., with bolster covers)	
						7432 Open
						7433 Open

*Page from NRMA manual: *Standard Classification of Merchandise*.

average stock is sometimes roughly calculated as the average of the opening and the closing stocks for the period, but it is more accurate to make use of monthly or weekly stock figures to calculate the average. For example, the average of $25,000 given above may be obtained by adding together the stock on hand at the first of each of the 12 months, adding the closing stock, and dividing by 13. The monthly inventory figures may be obtained by counting the stock each month or by using book figures where a perpetual inventory system is used, as explained in Chapter 6.

The buyer's ability to reduce his or her average inventory without decreasing sales or to keep the inventory nearly constant while sales increase (both reflections of a higher stockturn) shows that every dollar of investment is providing more sales than it did before. If, by careful planning and control, an investment of $20,000 rather than $25,000 will produce $100,000 in sales, $5,000 (at retail) is made available for productive use elsewhere, and the faster turn will probably reduce markdowns and provide fresher stocks that are more attractive to customers. A danger for the buyer to guard against is cutting the inventory assortment so low that it reduces the sales opportunity and thus sacrifices potential profits.

Some of the ways that have been used to keep inventories low without sacrificing sales appear below, but all the items listed are not applicable to every situation.

1. Prepare basic stock plans that are the outgrowth of planned sales.
2. Reduce the number of price lines carried, if they are unnecessarily close.
3. Avoid styles and brands that duplicate one another.
4. Concentrate on key items, eliminating items and lines that contribute little to sales volume.
5. Buy more frequently in smaller lots, provided that the extra ordering and shipping costs are not excessive.
6. Carry smaller reserve stocks if they are higher than needed to guard against running out of stock before the goods can be replenished.
7. Introduce and follow a system to avoid the accumulation of slow-selling merchandise.

Slow-selling stock is commonly controlled by (a) marking the day or month of receipt of every item on the price ticket or package and then checking the stock at frequent periodic intervals, (b) setting a period of time for each classification of goods, at the end of which, items remaining are to be regarded as slow selling, and (c) either taking markdowns when this period is reached or giving special promotional attention to the slow sellers.

If a perpetual unit control system is used for each unit of sale, the record can show when each item in stock was originally introduced, and thus report slow sellers without periodic counting. Electronic data processing is ideal for this purpose.

The Stock-Sales Ratio

Another way to measure the ratio between sales and stocks is the monthly stock-sales ratio. This is usually calculated by dividing the total stock at retail at the first of each month by the sales for that month. Thus, if in a merchandise classification the stock on February 1st is $20,000 at retail and the sales for February are $5,000, the stock-sales ratio is 4. The usual goal is to decrease the stock-sales ratio, not to increase it as in the case of stockturn.

The ratio is useful as a planning device. A goal for each month's ratio may be set based on past experience and on the experience of other similar stores with whom data is exchanged. For example, if the stock-sales ratio for November is set at 3 and if the sales for November are planned at $12,000, the planned stock for November 1st would be set around $36,000. To depend upon such ratios is unwise but they do provide some guidance for experienced buyers.

Productivity Measured in Gross Margin (Profit) Rather Than in Sales

A more sophisticated way to measure the productivity of the investment in a department or classification is to determine the gross margin return for each dollar of investment at cost. For example, with sales of $100,000 for the year, the gross margin realized may be $37,500 and the average inventory carried at cost may be $15,000. The gross margin return per dollar of investment then is $37,500, divided by $15,000, or $2.50. These calculations may be made monthly, or even weekly, for some fashion merchandise. The goal is to obtain, for each dollar invested, an adequate margin to contribute towards expenses and profit. With the current high costs of obtaining the money to finance inventories, this measure is of great importance.

SECTION 2. STAPLE STOCK CONTROL

PERIODIC FILL-INS OF STAPLE STOCKS

The model stock plans and buying procedures that are now detailed as examples are based on three distinct types of operation:

1. Periodic fill-in of staple stocks, i.e., models that are continuously replenishable by item.
2. Fashion goods that are subject to long opening commitment and subsequent adjustment by reorders.
3. Stocks that are subject to long commitment with relatively little reordering.

The first is discussed in this chapter, and the other two are discussed in Chapter 8.

Continuous Replenishment Procedure (Plan 1 for Staple Stock)

Regardless of the system used, certain data must be provided for a reordering program, and an orderly procedure must be followed. The facts necessary for the control of each staple item carried are: a listing of the items, determination of the probable rate of sale for each, the delivery period, the reorder period or frequency, the reserve to provide for sales exceeding the estimated rate of sale, and the stock currently on hand and on order. With this information, it is easy to calculate how much stock should be on hand and on order at each reorder period (known as the provision or maximum) and how much more to order (the unit OTB). Following is an example of a step-by-step procedure.

STEP 1. LISTING In the case of merchandise bought from resources that stand ready to fill orders promptly, the first step is to make a list of all the items that should be carried. For a new store, it is wise to consult reliable vendors for advice in drawing up the initial list. In the going store, the list is initially compiled and subsequently amended from purchase records, inventory, or direct sales information. This will be the assortment framework and should follow the principles advocated in the preceding chapter.

The listing should include all pertinent ordering data, such as, but not limited to, price, minimum pack required by vendor, shipping weight where freight is important, and normal delivery time. Figure 7–3 shows such a

FIGURE 7–3 Periodic inventory control sheet (delivery period—DP—one week)

Checking and Reorder Periods (RP) 2 and 4 weeks

Can Openers (wall)	Cost / Retail	Pack	Weekly Unit Sales	RP in Weeks	*P	Order Pack if Over	4/2 OH / O	4/16 OH / O	5/1 OH / O	5/15 OH / O	5/29 OH / O
Brand A	1.50 / 2.50	6	2	4	17	2	9 / ~~8~~ 6		11 / ~~4~~ 6		10 / ~~7~~ 6
Brand B	1.75 / 3.00	12	6	2	28	3	16 / 12	13 / ~~15~~ 12	11 / ~~14~~ 24	21 / ~~14~~ 12	22 / ~~10~~ 12
Brand C	2.50 / 4.00	6	3	2	16	1	10 / 6	13 / ~~3~~ 6	11 / ~~8~~ 6	11 / 6	10 / ~~7~~ 6
Brand D	3.50 / 5.50	6	1	4	10	3	6 / ~~4~~ 6		10 / 0		7 / ~~3~~ 6

*P=Provision or maximum in units

listing that was extracted from a housewares model stock. The can openers listed come in prepacked cartons of 6 and 12—with colors assorted in each carton—but are sold by the piece. Because of the constraints set by size of pack, the buyer is not able to order exactly up to the planned provision or maximum quantities. For example, in Brand A the buyer has 9 pieces on hand and intends to build up to 17. But she must order packs of 6, so she buys one pack, building up to 15 pieces rather than 17.

STEP 2. THE RATE OF SALE[5] The rate of sale, usually calculated on a weekly basis, may be averaged from recent records, provided goods sell fairly steadily throughout the different seasons of the year. If sales fluctuate sharply in different periods, recourse must be had to the records of prior years in order to plan expected sales for each period. A good practice is to establish *relationship factors* among selling cycles. May, June, and July, for example, may be indicated as the average of February, March, and April plus 40 percent. Electronic data processing is a great boon to the determination of sales for individual items and is discussed later in this chapter.

These factor relationships, once established, show the normal seasonal variations in the rate of sale and save repeated reference to prior years' performance. In this way, there is also an automatic adjustment to current trends. These are best evidenced by most recent activities. If sales for February, March, and April happen to be running 10 percent ahead of sales in the same quarter last year, the addition of 40 percent to their average automatically adjusts for the expected 10 percent increase in May, June, and July. Thus, if sales in the first quarter were 130 units, the second quarter's sales might be projected 40 percent higher, or 182. With 13 weeks in the quarter, the projected average rate a week is 14. The buyer must also be alert to coming conditions in economic factors, market changes and innovations, store events, and other elements that can alter the normal, arithmetic projection of sales.

STEP 3. RECONCILING SALES PLANS The buyer now has a built-up plan that will have to be reconciled with some top-down plan. Calculations may be made in the following order:

1. Group the expected weekly sales rates by price lines.
2. Total each group and multiply by the retail price. This gives the expected weekly rate of sale in dollars.
3. Convert to monthly figures, and compare with the generic plan for the category.

Several possibilities may develop from the comparison. Two may be discussed as examples. The aggregate of planned sales by units in a category may be at the rate of $8000 a month, whereas the generic plan estimated

[5]The sales unit used in staple stock control is usually the number of individual items sold, but if certain items such as tennis balls are usually sold in cartons of 3, the carton or box becomes the unit of control.

$6000. A previous caution should be repeated: The generic plan is more likely to be right. If so, it will be necessary to review the specific plans for apparent error of estimate. If errors are found and corrected, the resulting buying plan figures will have to be changed. This is the time to learn a fundamental rule of procedure in all merchandise planning.

> *First, plan sales on which all else depends. Reconcile them where necessary, and obtain approval of the sales plan before proceeding with other elements.*

It may also turn out that specific sales plans reflected changed conditions that were not accounted for in the generic plan. To that extent, evidence is then supplied for needed changes in that plan.

STEP 4. DELIVERY PERIOD Estimate conservatively the normal interval that elapses between the time the order is written and the time goods are received in stock, ready for sale. If 3 days are likely to elapse before the order leaves the house and reaches the vendor, if the vendor rarely requires more than 2 weeks to get the goods to the buyer's receiving point, and if 2 or 3 days are required to get the goods processed and down to the selling department, it is well to assume a 3-week delivery period. The *reserve* discussed later is not meant to cover fluctuations in delivery time but rather to provide for chance increase in sales above normal.

STEP 5. REORDER PERIOD A common practice in staple-goods categories is to count stock at regular intervals. To avoid making the counting burdensome on certain days, a good plan is to stagger the counts. For example, there may be 1000 items that should be checked every 2 weeks to determine the items for which reorder points have been reached. Rather than count all 1000 items on 1 day, the counting may be spread over 5 days of each of the 2 weeks. Thus 1000 is divided by 10, and approximately 100 of the 1000 items are counted each day. These items are listed on cards or sheets that are kept in a tickler file. After each day's check, the card is put in the back of the file so that in just 2 weeks it will work itself up to the front to be checked again.

The checking frequency depends on the rate of sale and conditions such as minimum pack. The general rule is to count most frequently for best sellers and less often for poor sellers. In the example of can openers, this rule is followed. Actually, it would have been better to count Brand D every 6 weeks, so as to make the average expected sales in the reorder period equal to the minimum pack. This would enhance the likelihood of placing an order for six more items when counts were taken. But strict adherence to this principle could result in a confused staggering schedule. Therefore the item was placed with others in the 4-week rotation—at the cost of a few more occasions when zero orders will turn up at checking time. If there were enough items like D in the category, it would be advisable to add another checking frequency, say every 8 weeks, to the 2- and 4-week periods already established. There is frequently justification for checking very fast sellers weekly—or even semiweekly, as in many grocery items—and daily in the case of produce and other food perishables. If practical, reorder periods should be no less than delivery periods to avoid the confusion of open orders at checking time.

In deciding on the reorder period, the buyer attempts to balance the advantages of a low stock against those of buying large quantities infrequently. If the buyer reorders every few days, in small quantities, he or she will have a smaller average stock and therefore will cut down interest and insurance expense, reduces the risk of markdowns to a minimum, and economizes on storage space. If the buyer reorders infrequently in large quantities, he or she may obtain lower cost prices and reduce transportation costs and clerical and handling expenses, and more easily meet minimum pack requirements.[6]

A counting or checking schedule could therefore be made up on the following basis:

1. Volume sellers to be reordered every week.
2. Fast sellers to be reordered every 2 weeks.
3. Average sellers to be reordered every 4 weeks.
4. Slow sellers to be reordered every 2 to 3 months.

STEP 6. SETTING THE REQUIRED RESERVE Whatever the method or frequency of reorder, it is a step preparatory to computing the amount of stock to be provided at each reorder time so that expected sales during the following lead time may be *protected* by adequate inventory. Projected sales are really an estimated average. In actual performance, sales will fluctuate over and under the average, as illustrated by the weekly sales record in Figure 7–4. Sales for the 20 weeks listed total 120 for an average of 6 per week but range from a low of 2 to a high of 11. If the delivery and reorder periods total 6 weeks, the normal sales expectancy during this lead time are 36, and this calls for a reserve of 8 (according to the table of short reserves in Figure 7–5 and explained in the technical appendix to this chapter. With long reserves, also explained in the technical appendix, the reserve is 14.)

The reserve may be computed in several ways, including the simple one of noting actual variations of demand in past sales records. The reserves used in the reorder table in the technical appendix are based on the laws of probability that indicate chance variations in sales from a norm that may occur over a period of time in which a certain sales volume is estimated to be most

[6]The theoretical optimum or economic order quantity (EOQ) is achieved by the following formula:

$$\text{EOQ} = \frac{2 \times \text{annual unit sales} \times \text{cost per order}}{\text{annual rate of carrying cost} \times \text{cost value per unit}}$$

This formula is more widely used in manufacturing than in distribution trades, where it is hard to get accurate figures on costs per order and on inventory carrying costs.

FIGURE 7–4 Example of a 20-week reordering program to illustrate foregoing 10-step procedure with P (maximum) 44

Week No.	*1*	*2*	*3*	*4*	*5*	*6*	*7*	*8*	*9*	*10*	*11*	*12*	*13*	*14*	*15*	*16*	*17*	*18*	*19*	*20*	
Sales	*6*	*4*	*6*	*5*	*7*	*3*	*2*	*6*	*5*	*9*	*11*	*4*	*6*	*7*	*3*	*5*	*8*	*9*	*8*	*6*	*Total 120*

Weeks	1 to 4	5 to 8	9 to 12	13 to 16	17 to 20
Period	I	II	III	IV	V
Opening inventory	21	23	26	15	23
Order placed	23	21	18	29	21
First half sales	10	10	14	13	17
Second half sales	11	8	15	8	14
Receipts	23	21	18	29	21
Ending inventory	23	26	15	23	13
Low Point Inventory (Opening inventory less first half sales):	11	13	12	2	6
High Point Inventory (Low point plus receivings):	34	34	30	31	27

FORMULA

Sales per week, average: 6			
Reorder Period (RP):	4 weeks	Reorder Period Quantity (RPQ)	24
Delivery Period (DP):	2 weeks	Delivery Period Quantity (DPQ)	12
Lead Time (LT):	6 weeks	Lead Time Quantity (LTQ)	36
Reserve (R) from "short list" in Figure 7–5			8
Provision (P) or maximum quantity (order up to)			44

probable. These reserves augment both the stock on hand and the provision to protect against stock depletion. Stress is placed on *the need to prevent basic or staple goods from running short* rather than on the danger of becoming temporarily overstocked.

STEP 7. SETTING THE PROVISION[7] The provision, more commonly called the "maximum," is the sum of projected sales for the reorder period, the sales for delivery period, and a reserve. It is the quantity that must be made available (on hand and on order) at any reordering point. It must be sufficient to cover sales expected during the lead time with a reserve for extra sales that might materialize during this period. In the workout in Figure 7–4, the provision consists of the lead-time sales expectancy of 36 plus the reserve of 8, for a total of 44.

STEP 8. THE ON HAND (OH) AND ON ORDER (OO) At the time the previous steps are being instituted, the goods on hand may have already been determined by the periodic count that is used also to establish the rate of sale for the period just past. Or, in the case of a perpetual inventory system, the on hand has been routinely computed as previously described. Goods on order are determined by reference to the open-order file.

[7]Provision often written as *M*, which stands for "maximum." In other words, provision made at the time of reorder is the maximum commitment in terms of goods on hand and on order. Following developments demonstrate that the stock itself seldom reaches this amount, because sales occur before the reorder is received.

FIGURE 7–5. Provision required to protect against random fluctuations in demand

LTQ	*P: order up to* *With short R*	*With long R*	*LTQ*	*P: order up to* *With short R*	*With long R*	*LTQ*	*P: order up to* *With short R*	*With long R*
1	3	3	26	33	38	51	60	68
2	5	5	27	34	39	52	61	69
3	7	7	28	35	41	53	62	70
4	8	9	29	37	42	54	63	71
5	9	10	30	38	43	55	64	73
6	10	12	31	39	44	56	65	74
7	12	13	32	40	45	57	66	75
8	13	15	33	41	47	58	67	76
9	14	16	34	42	48	59	68	77
10	15	17	35	43	49	60	69	78
11	16	19	36	44	50	70	80	89
12	17	20	37	45	51	80	90	101
13	18	21	38	46	53	90	100	112
14	20	23	39	47	54	100	111	123
15	21	24	40	48	55	150	161	178
16	22	25	41	50	56	200	212	233
17	23	27	42	51	57	250	264	287
18	24	28	43	52	59	300	315	340
19	25	29	44	53	60			
20	26	30	45	54	61			
21	28	32	46	55	62			
22	29	33	47	56	63			
23	30	35	48	57	65			
24	31	36	49	58	66			
25	32	37	50	59	67			

STEP 9. OPEN-TO-BUY Because goods on hand and on order comprise *provision already made,* their amounts should be subtracted from the calculated provision. The quantity that remains is the amount that should then be written as the new order. This is the quantity known as the unit open-to-buy (OTB). In terms of formula shorthand, this last step may be presented as:

$$\text{OTB} = \text{P} - \text{OH} - \text{OO} \quad \text{or} \quad \text{OTB} = \text{P} - (\text{OH} + \text{OO})$$

STEP 10. RECONCILING THE STOCK PLAN By calculating average inventories, (see Technical Appendix) and multiplying by price lines, it is possible to view these unit stock plans in dollars and then to compare them with classification top-down plans. If there are important differences, the two plans should be reconciled.

The build-up unit plan may, for example, total to considerably more than the top-down dollar plan. Unless the buyer can justify this excess, it may be necessary to trim the unit plan. This may be done in several ways. Shorter reserves may be established on the basis of relying more on demand substitutability or on the basis of a somewhat chancier risk on protecting against very sharp fluctuations in demand. Reorder periods may be shortened. Or some doubtful, slow-turning items may now yield to the hard voice of necessity and be eliminated from the assortment. The last two steps are preferable to shortening the reserve on the assumption that it may be better to say that "we don't carry" the marginal item than to pretend to carry it and present a moth-eaten stock.

THE MAXIMUM-MINIMUM SYSTEM OF STAPLE STOCK CONTROL

A variation from the standard control plan discussed previously involves the way the reorder period is determined. A stock-on-hand point at which a reorder should be placed (called the *minimum*) is set. Whenever the stock level of the item drops to this point, as determined either by inspection of the stock level as sales are made or by means of a perpetual inventory, the buyer (or in some instances the computer) is notified that a reorder should be placed. Thus the length of the reorder period is not fixed but rather varies with the fluctuation in the rate of sale. For example, with unit sales estimated at 10 a week, with delivery in one week, and with the reorder quantity a normal 4-week supply or 40 units, the minimum (reorder point quantity) may be set at 27. This provides not only for the expected sales of 10 during the delivery period but also for a reserve of 17[8] to allow for chance increases in the sales of 50 normally expected in the lead time of 5 weeks (the sum of the delivery period quantity and the reorder quantity).[9] The provision (maximum) is, accordingly, 27 + 40 or 67. In actual operation, the stock may drop to the minimum in less than 4 weeks if sales exceed plan or in more than 4 weeks if sales are below plan. Thus the stock is built up to the provision not exactly at 4-week intervals but whenever the minimum is reached.

The goal is to "catch" the stock level when it falls to 27 and then to order 40 more, or somewhat more or less depending on the vendor's packing unit. Should this be 6 units, 42 rather than 40 would be reordered. Should there

[8]This reserve may be checked in Figure 7–5, where the LTQ (lead-time quantity) is 50. With the long reserve, the provision is 67, yielding a reserve of 17. The minimum, with the short reserve, would be only 10 + 9, or 19, rather than 27.

[9]Theoretically, where the minimum system is used, it is not necessary to set the reserve to allow for sales increases above normal during the reorder period, rather only during the delivery period, because the reorder period may be much shorter than normal, and the risk of running out of stock is limited to the delivery period. But minimum stocks may not be reported and acted upon promptly. And with an unexpected sales spurt, reorders would be very close to one another.

be a delay in notifying the buyer that the minimum has been reached, the actual inventory below the minimum is reported, and the reorder is placed for the difference betwen the provision and the actual inventory.

Except where a perpetual inventory is kept for each sales unit, the stock inspection at the right time may be facilitated by the following procedure: Whenever an order is received, 27 units may be bound with tape or marked off with a separation card. Whenever the basic 27 are reached or broken into for sales purposes, an order suggestion may be noted or the card turned in. Sometimes it is possible to arrange layers in a bin or compartment in such a way that when a certain layer is reached, the item is up for automatic reorder. In other cases, control is kept over reserve stocks; when they reach a certain point, a reorder is placed.

The minimum system is hard to supervise and control. Most operators find that reorders can better be controlled by having set times for checking stock rather than depending on sales and stock personnel to "catch" every item when the stock reaches its action point. However, with a computer operation, reorder points for each item controlled can be reported as soon as the stocks reach these points. The computer can also be programmed to compute the reorders automatically, subject to buyer review.

The minimum system presents another problem. It is expensive and time consuming to order each unit separately. All staples from the same resource that fall into either a slow- or fast-selling category should be ordered at the same time. Thus, when the minimum is reached for a fast-selling item, it would become necessary to determine the stock on hand of other fast-selling items from the same resource that have not yet reached their minima and to reorder them as well.

CALCULATING STOCKTURN WITH STAPLE STOCK CONTROL

Under perfect or "ideal" conditions, actual sales during RP and DP would be exactly as estimated, and the reserve would not be depleted. As a matter of fact, the reserve would not be needed. But, in the real world, sales are sometimes higher and sometimes lower than estimate. Therefore, remaining stocks at the critical point will sometimes be less than the reserve, and the buyer will be thankful for having provided it. At other times there will remain the whole reserve plus the amount by which sales fell under the estimate.

Over time or over a great many individual items, the remaining quantity at the critical or low point (just before the reorder comes in) will average out to the amount represented by the reserve. Thus "ideal" conditions prevail "on the average." And that is why the average inventory and turnover may be predicted for a given ordering procedure. The average inventory will tend to equal the quantity represented by one-half the reorder-period sales quantity plus the reserve: Av Stock = ½RPQ + R. (Average of high and low stocks.) Stock tends to fall to the reserve when the reorder is received. It is then built up to R + RPA but falls back to R when the next order comes in. Thus the average approximates R + ½RPQ.

The annual rate of stockturn is then calculated by dividing the estimated annual rate of sale for the year by the average stock as calculated. Referring to the data in Figure 7–4, the following is the stockturn workout:

1. When the delivery comes in halfway through the reorder period, the stock will be at its low point. This point over time averages out approximately to 8 units.
2. The amount delivered over time equals planned or average sales for the reorder period (RPQ) averaging approximately 24 units over time.
3. The sum of R plus RPQ marks the inventory high point, which may be expressed as 8 + 24, or 32.
4. Dividing by 2 to average the high and low points gives
   $\frac{(8 + 32)}{2} = \frac{40}{2} = 20$, the average inventory in units.
   (also calculated as $8 + \frac{24}{2} = 20$).
5. Sales at 6 per week would be 312 per year.
6. Dividing by the average inventory of 20 yields 15.6 turns per year.

In general, the higher the rate of sale of a unit the higher the stockturn, since the reserve is relatively lower due to the "inertia" of large numbers.

ADJUSTMENTS OF STAPLE CONTROL TECHNIQUES TO HETEROGENEOUS UNITS

In the discussion above and in developing Figure 7–4, it has been assumed that the unit under control is homogeneous, that all articles comprising the unit are identical. Accordingly, the reserve needs to be large enough only to avoid a reasonable probability of running out of stock. But the unit may be heterogeneous. For example, it may consist of three different colors, all in the same style. If each color must be protected from depletion, that is, if the colors are not readily substitutable, a larger reserve is necessary for the style than if all the units in the style were the same.

For example, suppose the style (treated as a homogeneous unit) sells at the rate of 12 a week, with 3 weeks for delivery and 4 weeks for reorder. The lead-time sales, then, are 12 × 7, or 84. According to the provision table with long reserve in the Technical Appendix to this chapter, the provision is 106, and the reserve is 22 (106 − 84). But the style consists of three nonsubstitutable colors. If they are deemed to be equal in sales probability, each would sell at an average of 4 a week and the lead-time sales for each would be 4 × 7, or 28. According to the table, the provision is 41, and reserve is 13 (41

– 28). For the three colors combined, then, the reserve would be 39 and the provision 123 (39 + 84). This compares with a reserve of 22 and a provision of 106 for the same sales volume in a homogeneous unit. Accordingly, it should be observed that the provision for a heterogeneous unit having the same rate of sale as a homogeneous unit is always higher and the resultant stockturn always lower.

Provision may be made for different rates of sale of the elements in the heterogeneous unit. For example, with three colors in the style, one may account for about one-half of the sales with the rest fairly evenly divided. Thus, with a total of 12 sales a week, the following workout may be made:

Colors	*Weekly sales*	*Lead-time sales (7 weeks)*	*Reserve*	*Provision (see Figure 7–5 with long reserve) (LTQ + R)*
A	6	42	15	57
B	3	21	11	32
C	3	21	11	32
Total	12	84	37	121

The reserve and provision are somewhat smaller than would be necessary if all colors were equal.

Allowance may also be made for ease of substitutability. Suppose that Colors B and C are readily substitutable but that A is not. B and C combined, then, may be treated as a homogeneous unit, and the following workout is prepared:

Colors	*Weekly sales*	*Lead-time sales (7 weeks)*	*Reserve*	*Provision (see Figure 7–5) (LTQ + R)*
A	6	42	15	57
B and C	6	42	15	57
Total	12	84	30	114

The smaller reserve does not fully protect both Colors B and C from running out of stock but assures that 99 times out of 100 at least one of the two colors will be on hand.

Additional Variants in Control Units

The foregoing reasoning may be applied to more complicated homogeneous units: different sizes and patterns as well as different colors. For example, the style selling at the rate of 12 a week may consist of 5 sizes in 3 colors, a total of 15 variants. If the sales expectancy of all are about equal, the rate of sale of a single variant is 12/15, or 4/5. Seven weeks' supply would give lead-time sales of about 6, calling for a provision of 12 (see Figure 7–5 with long reserve) and a reserve for each of 6, or a total reserve of 90 compared to only 22 if the style were homogeneous.

Placement of the Open-to-Buy

It does not follow from the foregoing that every variant in a heterogeneous unit is to be separately controlled. The style number may be treated as a unit in determining the provision, but the reserve will be set as indicated in the workouts. Thus, in the previous example, the provision for the style is 90 (the reserve) plus 84 (the lead-time sales), or 174. From this is subtracted the number on hand and on order every 4 weeks to determine the OTB. If the commitments are currently 100, the OTB is 74. The buyer or the control clerk will now study the actual assortment of colors and sizes within the style and distribute the 74 pieces in order to keep a reasonable balance of sizes and colors. It would be too much work to set a separate provision for each variant, and it would be very hard to make an accurate forecast of the sales of each. Because of the law of inertia of large numbers, the sales of the style as a whole can be much more readily forecast.

Integrated with these procedures is a concept called "Part Time Staples." It is explained as follows:[10]

> We try to treat as much of our assortment as possible as though it were "staple" even though sold in a "fashion department" or in demand for only part of the year.
>
> We assign in-stock periods to each item by week numbers; thus there is nothing more "staple" in our stock than an assortment of snow shovels in weeks 36 to 52; or lawn mowers in weeks 6 to 26; or black patent shoes in weeks 1 to 13, white calf in weeks 13 to 26 and brown calf in weeks 26 to 44. Same with short-sleeve shirts, winter-weight sleepwear, and many other seasonal categories.

During their "staple" periods, all these categories enjoy the advantages of planning and control by the aggregate of the central idea, instead of or in addition to control of individual SKUs within the group.

Application of Staple Stock Control to Fashion Goods

It may prove desirable to group a number of styles all within a basic type, color, and size category. For example, all *classic black dresses* may be combined into summary records. Reserves may then be applied to each size within the group and the open-to-buy computation completed as shown previously. Individual styles may be bought at will as long as they fall within the size requirements of the group as a whole. However, outstanding sellers should not be mixed with poor or mediocre styles in such groupings.

In these cases, it may be wise to add a special basic reserve large enough

[10]Adapted from an address to the NRMA in 1973 by Frank Burnside, president of Fowler, Dick and Walker. Mr. Burnside was one of the pioneers in the development of P.O.S. and general computer technology for individual department stores.

to contain a minimum representation of styles at the very lowest point. For example, 67 may be the provision for a lead-time quantity of 50 black dresses in size 12 with the reserve of 17. But there will be times when the stock will drop almost to zero before the next reorder arrives. This would provide an inadequate style representation. Therefore, it might be wise to raise the reserve from 17 to 24 or 30.[11]

In pursuit of this technique, Fowler, Dick and Walker of Wilkes Barre, Pennsylvania, has established what they call their "synthetic SKU." This involves an assortment plan by sizes within each class (e.g., Junior Raincoats), each size within a class being treated as an SKU. The year is divided into eight blocks of 6 or 7 weeks, and assortment by SKU is planned and controlled within these periods.

EXPEDITING THE STAPLE-STOCK CONTROL PROCEDURE

These procedures threaten so much dull, grinding, time-consuming work that neophytes should be advised of hidden but more beneficent aspects.

1. Much of the work involved, like drawing up the initial assortment framework and fitting the figures for expected sales, reorder frequencies, and reserves, is a big "one-time" job. Maintenance of an established program is much easier. The hard initial work becomes a sort of capital investment, producing a working tool that then makes life easier, work more efficient, and results more valuable.
2. Experience with a category of merchandise develops a sixth sense about its figures of performance. Rates, requirements, and other schedules are drawn up with increasing facility and guided by instinctive rules of reason, which often do not require formal summing procedures to keep them in line with generic plans.
3. In many large retail firms and especially in chains and mail-order houses, a lot of this work is done by staff experts, guided by the special knowledge and judgment of the buyer.

In many discount stores, individual departments are often leased to syndicates operating regionally or nationally. Headquarters sets a provision for each unit, and store managers take periodic counts. In some instances, they place orders for the difference between the provision and the on hand (plus on order, if any), and in other instances, the central office computes the OTB, adjusting the provision when the rate of sale so dictates.

A good many stores, including discount houses, often rely on vendors'

[11]The basic theory here is that, within a category, size may be a less substitutable factor than style, color, material, etc.

detail men to determine reorders at their periodic visits and stock checks. Although this service cuts down on expense to the store, the buyer should insist that the detail man follow a sound procedure in figuring reorder quantities.

In general, it must be remembered that *businesses undergoing a rapid rate of growth have a great capacity for absorbing error*. That is why discount stores during their great growth period could order somewhat casually—with a minimum of restraint. As their volume of business stabilized, they came to realize the benefits to be derived from carefully controlled ordering procedures.

4. The small buyer, burdened with many other responsibilities of storekeeping, often feels that he or she cannot keep records of the sale of each item or apply a formula to determine how much to reorder. Yet no buyer's operation is too small to keep a record of how many of each item received into stock since the beginning of the year or other control period, and to count how many on hand before ordering more. The amount bought minus that on hand is, roughly, the sales total. Knowing the time that has elapsed since the first of the period, the buyer can express sales in terms of a weekly rate. Next, the buyer can train him- or herself to think in terms of provision for a predetermined number of weeks' supply. This may vary from a fraction of a week's supply in the case of milk and bread to as much as 26 weeks' supply in the case of an infrequently selling nonperishable that has to be ordered long before time of delivery. A rough but usable estimate of how many weeks' supply to carry in any given case can be arrived at by analysis, as explained, by exchange of information, and by advice from a buying group to which the merchant may belong or from trusted vendors.

Some buyers maintain a controlled ordering system without ever formally computing sales. Figure 7–3 is, in essence, that kind of control. It is based on the assumption that, however roughly, stocks are always counted before a new order is placed. If the items are listed in an assortment framework, the counts can be entered right on the checklist and orders noted thereon as shown. These two procedures require no *extra* work—only methodical work. It is then assumed that orders placed have come in or will soon be in. Exceptions may be noted, but they would usually be for some item that is about to be discontinued or is subject to other self-cancelling conditions.

Sales can be quickly calculated or noted, if desired. For Brand B in Figure 7–3, there were 13 on hand as of April 16. Because there were 16 on April 2 and 12 placed (presumably received), sales must have been 16 + 12 − 13 = 15 for the two prior weeks. Whatever method is used to "guess" at the required order, the fact remains that at least the stock and order data is spread before the eyes, in orderly fashion, and the buyer can judge whether too much or too little is being ordered or if the frequency is wrong.

Where the buyer is unsure about the accuracy of the planned weekly rate of sale, it is wise to recalculate the weekly rate every time the inventory is checked and to adjust the planning rate if actual sales deviate considerably from plan. Special promotions can be allowed for very simply by ordering for them not only the normal reorder quantity but enough more to cover the extra quantity that is likely to be in demand during the sale.

Technical Appendix: **REORDER TABLES**

Figure 7–5 presents a table based on a statistical probability distribution for readily determining P (provisions, also called maximum) for varying rates of sale during a lead-time period—that is, the sum of the delivery and reorder periods. The amount sold during this period is called the lead-time quantity (LTQ). The table presents two P columns. The second, labeled "with long P," limits inadequate reserves to only one out of 100 *reorder periods*; or, at any given time, one out of every 100 items may be out of stock.[12]

The first of the two P columns, labeled "with short P," is designed to protect against more than 1 percent loss of the *unit sales* potential. Except for very slow rates of sale, the provisions in the first column are smaller and the stockturn potential higher than with the second or "Long P" column.

For example: If the average sales during the lead-time period are 25, it would require a safety stock of 12 to prevent running out of stock in more than two out of 100 reorder periods. But to prevent losing more than 2 percent of the sales possibilities, a reserve of seven will be adequate.

Although the "long reserve" table ensures that stocks will not run out in more than one of every 100 order periods, perhaps a more meaningful figure would be an out-of-stock tolerance based on actual "lost sales" potential. This involves weighing the unfilled demands that can occur during "out" periods by the frequency of the demand occurrences.

For example, if the lead-time quantity to be protected was 6, a long reserve of 6 would be added, bringing the provision up to 12. The random chances of demand being greater than 12 in an average expectancy of 6 would appear in a Poisson distribution as follows:

[12]The "long" reserves are based on the Poisson Distribution where the reserves to provide protection against running out of stock in about 99 percent of the reorder periods is 2:326 lead-time sales. This reserve takes care only of chance variation in sales. Delays in delivery are best handled by setting the delivery period somewhat longer than normal expectancy. The square root relationship reflected in the formula means that a quadrupling of lead-time sales simply doubles the reserve. The application of the Poisson Distribution to inventory control was first presented by Thomas M. Whiten, *The Theory of Inventory Management* (Princeton, N.J.: Princeton University Press, 1953).

"Long Reserves"

Chance of demand	% of lead-time periods
13	0.5
14	0.2
15	0.1
16 or more	insignificant
13 or more	0.8

In computing the "short reserves," we note the amount of unfilfilled demand (or "lost sales") in each such period and weight that amount by the percent of times that that particular period is likely to occur. Thus, with a lead-time quantity of 6 and a short reserve of 4, the maximum provision for each period would be 10.

"Short Reserves"

In periods when demand is	*Sales lost in each period*	*% of periodic loss likely to occur*	*Total sales lost as a % of the potential sales overall (100%) of the periods*
11	1	2.25	2.25
12	2	1.13	2.26
13	3	0.52	1.56
14	4	0.22	0.88
15	5	0.09	0.45
16	6	0.03	0.18
17 or more	insignificant		—
Total sales lost		7.58	
Total unit sales potential (6 × 100)		600.00	
Lost sales as a % of the potential		1.3	

The total sales potential for 100 percent of the periods, at an average of six per period, can be described as 600. By stocking up to only 10 pieces, seven or eight (roughly 1.3 percent of the sales potential of 600) is lost (7.58 ÷ 600). The short reserves in Figure 7–5 have been calculated in this manner.

A similar but not identical result can be achieved more simply by aiming at 95 percent protection—stock inadequate in one out of 20 periods. The reserve requirement for this is $1.6 \times \sqrt{\text{lead-time sales}}$. With six as the lead-time sales, as in the previous example, its square root is 2.45. Multiplying by 1.6 gives 3.9, rounded out to 4. Thus the maximum is 10, as in the table of "short" reserves. As the lead-time quantity increases, the reserves so calculated are somewhat more than those used in the table. Thus, with lead-time sales of 49, the reserve would be 1.6 × 7, or 11, and the maximum would be 60 compared with 58 in the table of "short" reserves.

DISCUSSION QUESTIONS

1. Consider the departmental-sales plans (b) and (d) in Figure 7–1.
   (a) What differences merit reconciliation?
   (b) What circumstances would affect your decisions in changing either plan?
2. For controlling aggregates of merchandise, most stores use the formula:

   planned purchases = planned sales for the period (usually a month) + planned closing stock − opening stock

   and

   OTB = planned purchases − commitments (on order + receipts during period)

   The formulas established in this chapter for unit planning are:

   provision = reserve + delivery period quantity + reorder period quantity

   and

   OTB = P − (on hand + on order)

   To what extent are the terms of the two formulas equivalent to each other?
3. Comment on the contrasting views of buyers and controllers in regard to data-based open-to-buy.
4. Is classification planning and control likely to replace departmental planning and control?
5. Suggest merchandise classifications for men's furnishings and for chinaware that are based on the end-use concept.
6. While merchandise classifications and controls are generally breakdowns of departmental data, how may a computer be used to assemble classification data from a number of departments that carry similar goods, such as boutiques? What is the value of combining such data?
7. In what ways may an increase in stockturn reduce expenses of operation?
8. Even though high markdowns are often associated with fast-turning fashion stocks, should an increase in the stockturn of a specific department or classification be expected to reduce its markdowns?
9. In developing an index of "profit" per dollar of cost inventory, why is the profit figure generally used the gross margin rather than the operating profit (after expenses)?

10. What are the buyer's responsibilities in connection with electronic data processing? Is the buyer concerned with the technical aspects of programming and of collecting the data?
11. Relate both perpetual versus periodic inventory and SKU versus classification planning and control to the inventory management of each of the following:
    (a) inexpensive costume jewelry
    (b) medium-priced blouses
    (c) branded canned soups
12. A staple housewares article sells at the rate of 13 a week, delivery takes 1 week, and the planned reorder period is 4 weeks. The reserve to provide for chance increases in sales above expectations is calculated as 2.3 times the square root of the lead-time sales. At the current reorder date, 45 pieces are on hand. Find the:
    (a) lead-time sales
    (b) reserve
    (c) provision (maximum)
    (d) OTB (current reorder quantity)

    If reorders must be in units of 12, adjust the OTB. What is the minimum (important if the maximum-minimum system were used)?
13. In Figure 7–4, a reserve or safety stock of 8 pieces was used. What other choice was available in Figure 7–5? What evidence is there to defend the choice of 8?
14. Is all this formal planning and control relevant for the small merchant?
15. Data available for a staple stock item

Weekly sales	14
Delivery period	3 weeks
Reorder period	4 weeks
Reserve	$2.3 \times \sqrt{\text{lead-time sales}}$
On hand at reorder period	40

Using the above data, calculate the:
(a) lead-time sales
(b) reserve
(c) provision (maximum)
(d) reorder quantity (O.T.B.)
(e) minimum (normal quantity on hand at time of reorder)

chapter 8

The Merchandise Assortment: Quantitative Considerations for Fashion and Seasonal Goods

Once a selling season is under way, fashion "runners" may be reordered by periodic check-up as described for staple goods. The sales rate, however, will not be as even as that of can openers, because sales velocity speeds up rapidly into the peak of a season and may fall very sharply thereafter.

But, before the season really starts, a new stock of styles and colors must be provided while remainders of the previous season's stock are being cleared. Furthermore, in the apparel fashion trades, these seasons are no longer three or four a year. The number and character are subject to product, store, and regional variations, but for each season there is the same, repeated wavelike trio of procedures: introduction, full-selling, and clearance, as illustrated in Figure 8–1.

BUILDING THE MODEL AND THE PURCHASE PLAN

The Model Stock Plan

One way of contending with these seasonal waves is to plan model stocks for each critical point. A model stock plan is a charting of a unit assortment, kept within dollar control limits, that is distributed in such a way as to best satisfy expected customer demand at a specified time. There are three preliminary steps in the preparation of a model stock:

1. A decision must be made as to the selection factors to be provided: classifications, types, prices, colors, sizes, etc.

FIGURE 8–1 Fashion calendar

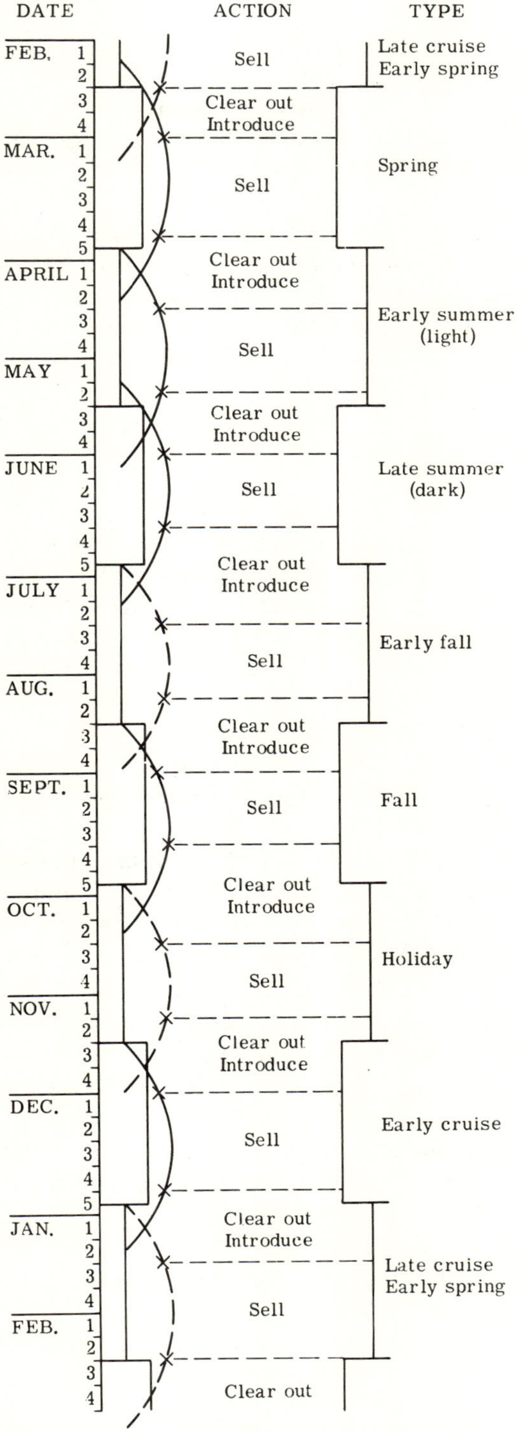

Source: from NRMA Seminar, June 4, 1975, by Joseph B. Siegel, vice-president and general manager, Bloomingdales, Hackensack, New Jersey.

2. The important dates in the season for which model stocks are to be constructed must be determined.
3. Sales for the months preceding and following the date for which the model stock is to be set should be planned in units, and the total should be translated into dollars to check against the dollar departmental classfication plan.

The actual planning of the model involves deciding on how many items to have on hand in the major breakdowns, such as price line, types, and basic style. This is done by studying the sales expected in the month (or months) immediately following the model stock date and applying stock-sales ratios based on previous experience and outside comparisons.

The Buying Plan

To implement the model stock, it is necessary to develop a buying plan. This involves adding to the model the expected sales during the buying period preceding the model date and subtracting any purchases already made. For example, if the model for November 1 in a certain price and type is 100 units, and if sales during the preceding September and October are estimated at 150 units, provision should have been made for 250 units on September 1. If the stock then on hand and on order was 120, the OTB was 130. If delivery takes well over a month, most of this should have been ordered very early in September. If some of the requirements could be obtained at short notice, only a portion of the total of 130 needs to be ordered well in advance.

The portion of the OTB to be ordered well in advance of November 1 would be scaled according to size and color ratios established on a basis of past experience and current trends. Adjustments should be made for currently unbalanced stocks. For example, of the 130-unit OTB, 30 percent, or 39, might normally be in black. But the stock of 120 currently on hand and on order may contain 50 percent, or 60 units, in black. The total stock in black should be 30 percent of the total provision of 250, or 75. If 60 units already committed for are in black, only 15 more rather than 39 more need to be ordered.

The buying plans for each segment of the model assortment must be assembled into a compact chart that can be checked off as actual orders are placed to ensure that the plan is realized.

As the market is covered and orders are placed, it may prove wise to modify the model. However, the buyer must resist market pressures to disregard advance plans. And once again, the buyer is admonished to place orders promptly so that the goods are in stock at the planned model date.

An example

In order to interpret the foregoing generalizations in terms of a specific plan, the procedures suggested are applied in the following to an autumn sweater assortment. Some buyers may change the order of the steps given or may leave out some steps. But we are presenting one orderly approach to the planning of models and resultant purchases. Although the beginner may find the figure analysis arduous, every experienced buyer knows that buying decisions are full of risk that may be diminished by rigorous planning.

STEP 1. PROFILING THE ASSORTMENT For convenience, we have decided that the cardigan assortment will be grouped around three price lines: $15, $20, and $30.

The assortment is planned under two major classifications: cardigans and pullovers, the latter including vests.

Cardigans are divided into "bulky" and "regular" knits. Bulky knits are generally made of coarse yarns of less than 7 gauge and are being watched separately because they represent a fashion trend.

Bulky and regular cardigans are each subdivided into two categories. The first represents another upcoming fashion, "coat sweaters." Full coat sweaters are generally belted and pocketed, 3/4 length or more, and with large collars, many featuring hoods. All other cardigans are grouped into a class called "modified."

Further, to keep a close eye on fashion development, bulky coats have been subdivided into two categories: hooded and all other (mostly collared).

The major color is expected to be honey, with black second. The balance of sales is expected to fall among navy, gray, green, red, and brown. These are the base colors, often combined with others.

STEP 2. DETERMINING CRITICAL DATES AND LEAD TIME The buyer would like to have a representative assortment in the store by early July. Because sales of autumn sweaters will be meager during that month, it is not expected to have good reorder information much before August, except for possible outstanding performers in the early assortment. Experience has taught that, in this case, 4-week delivery should be allowed between the time of placing first reorders and the receipt of reordered goods on the selling floor.

This means that reorders should not be expected until early September. Therefore, opening purchases should be planned to cover sales for a lead time of 2 months (July and August) and an inventory at the end (August 31). Because this should be a planned inventory, a model is built for September 1.

Later, successive models could be planned for the first of each succeeding

TABLE 8–1A
Distribution of Cardigan Sales by Type and Price

Type	July and August						September					
	$15		*$20*		*$30*		*$15*		*$20*		*$30*	
	LY	*TY*	*LY*	*TY*	*LY*	*TY*	*LY*	*TY*	*LY*	*TY*	*LY*	*TY*
1. Bulky Coat	30	40	50	50	35	35	40	40	50	55	35	40
2. Bulky mod.	40	30	40	50	50	60	40	35	45	55	55	65
3. Reg. knit coat	65	65	90	90	60	60	75	70	100	100	60	65
4. Reg. knit mod.	65	65	70	80	85	95	70	70	75	110	85	100
5. Total units	200	200	250	270	230	250	225	215	270	320	235	270
6. Total dollars	3000	3000	5000	5400	6900	7500	3375	3225	5400	6400	7050	8100
7. Total—All prices			LY $14,900						LY $15,825			
8. Total—All prices			TY $15,900						TY $17,725			

month. Thus they would coincide with the dates of the "6-month" top-down, or control, plan against which they should be matched. But it may not be necessary to build a model for the first of each month. A model may be set up for September 1, another for November 1 (to approach the holiday season), and a third for January 1, as a target for reducing the assortment at the end of the winter season.

STEP 3. BUDGETING SALES AND RECONCILING WITH CONTROL PLAN The first step in actual budgeting is to estimate sales. Table 8–1A shows one approach to the task. Cardigan sales for last year (LY) are examined and used as a base for estimating sales this year (TY). July and August are combined, because they form the lead-time period for opening purchases. September sales are planned to provide a basis for estimating the inventory model that should be prepared for the first of September.

Note that price lines form an important part of the plan, because they form a useful bridge between units and dollars. Lines 1 through 4 represent units, which are totaled on line 5. Multiplying the units on line 5 by the price lines they represent translates the unit sales into dollars, as shown on line 6.

This plan is made for cardigans only. A similar plan is made for pullovers, and the two are brought together in a classification total in Table 8–1B.

The figures on line 1 are picked up from the totals in line 7 (rounded to the nearest 100) of Table 8–1A. Similarly, line 2 of Table 8–1B would have been picked up from the detailed pullover plan.

The planned sweater sales are now in dollars, comparable to whatever top-down departmental or class plans are available. For purposes of proceeding with our example, we have to assume that the buyer was able to justify the plans as shown in Tables 8–1A and 8–1B during the reconciliation process.

STEP 4. BUILDING THE MODEL FOR SEPTEMBER To conserve time and space, further illustration will now be confined to the bulky coat category.

TABLE 8–1B
Recap of Sweater Sales Plan for July, August, and September

Classification	*July and August*		*September*	
	LY	*TY*	*LY*	*TY*
1. Cardigans	$14,900	$15,900	$15,800	$17,700
2. Pullovers	9,000	10,000	12,500	15,000
3. Total sweaters	$23,900	$25,900	$28,300	$32,700

Having estimated unit sales for September, the buyer has assumed that a 2-month supply (in terms of September sales)[1] would provide a sound opening stock for the month. Plainly, this yields a quick figure for checking with the dollar stock for September, as shown on the control plan.

Table 8–1C shows such a model for bulky cardigans plain. The totals, it will be noticed, are just double the TY unit figures for September (the three price lines combined) in line 1 of Table 8–1A. The figures for hooded and collared styles were determined by comparing the proportion as they existed last year, in recent periods, or as market and fashion intelligence dictate. At the bottom of the plan are notes to govern the number of styles that will compose the model and that present ideas about promotional spots.

Selecting the *number* of styles to comprise the assortment is governed by the basic philosophy of the buyer, within the requirements of store policy. As described in a preceding chapter, the limitation of available inventory prevails. Should the buyer elect to buy two styles of bulky collared sweaters at $20, where the model calls for 30 units, they would have to average a depth of 15 each. This would call for a shallow spread of colors and sizes. There would be more room for two styles in the 55 pieces allocated to hooded collars at $30. But the buyer has evidently elected to carry only one style in some depth. This represents a rigorous application of a narrow and deep assortment policy.

STEP 5. BUDGETING THE PROVISION TO BE COVERED BY OPENING PURCHASES Table 8–1D is taken from the detailings of Table 8–1A (cf. line 1, July and August, TY). Apparently, Table 8–1A was used as a top-down plan within which the buyer estimated the proportions that should be allotted to hooded and collared styles.

The buyer is now ready to compute the purchases that must be made to cover expected sales during the lead time (July and August) and to provide for an inventory at the end of that time (September 1). The common open-to-buy formulas, used in the 6-month plan in the last chapter, may be used here.

> Planned stock at end of period *plus* planned sales during the period *less* stock on hand and outstanding orders *equals* the open-to-buy.

Because the buyer is concerned with an opening purchase for a new seasonal line, there is no stock on hand and there are no orders already outstanding. Therefore, the amount to be purchased equals the lead-time sales plus the planned-model stock at the end. Table 8–1E shows the addi-

[1]The number of week's supply to include in the model varies with the nature of the goods and the store's policy in regard to breadth of assortment. A planned annual stockturn may be used as a guide, with higher monthly turns in busy seasons than in dull ones. The 2-month supply in the example, if maintained throughout the year, would result in six stockturns.

TABLE 8–1C
Excerpt From Model Stock Plan, September 1, Bulky Coats

	$15	$20	$30	Total
1. Hooded	20	80	55	155
2. Collared	60	30	25	115
3. Total	80	110	80	270

Note: One style in each neckline with promotions at $20 hooded and $15 collared.

TABLE 8–1D
Sales Plan for Bulky Coats, July and August

	$15	$20	$30	Totals
Hooded	10	35	25	70
Collared	30	15	10	55
Total (from Table 8-1A)	40	50	35	125

TABLE 8–1E
Provision Required to September 1 for Bulky Coats: Hooded and Collared

Hooded	$15	$20	$30	Totals
1. 9/1 Model	20	80	55	155
2. Sales July, August	10	35	25	70
3. Total Provision	30	115	80	225
4. 60% (OTB)	18	69	48	135
Collared	$15	$20	$30	Totals
5. 9/1 Model	60	30	25	115
6. Sales July, August	30	15	10	55
7. Total Provision	90	45	35	170
8. 60% (OTB)	54	27	21	102
9. Current OTB Hooded and Collared	72	96	69	237

tion of these two factors as totaled on lines 3 and 7. In a going operation, there would be some carry-over, not provided for here.

At this point, it is customary to hedge a little in order to "buy time." As previously stated, there may not be enough time to conduct a complete reordering program between the start of the season and the first of September. But some style, type, or color *may* receive *very strong* customer preference in early sales, probably at the expense of other selection factors. Should this happen, the buyer would not like to be caught in a position of no choice because early plans had been completely filled with merchandise commitments.

It must always be recognized that plans are no more or less than estimates—reflecting the best use of available information and judgment. Error is accepted as likely, as something to be handled as plans are reviewed and revised. For these reasons, the buyer has elected to place immediate orders on only 60 percent of the required provision, as indicated on lines 4 and 8 of Table 8–1E.

Now the buyer is tactically poised to take advantage of further developments.[2] Because the remaining 40 percent must be committed by the first of August (if it is to be in stock by September 1), there *may* not be enough data in July sales to guide further placement. In this case, the buyer will have to place the remaining orders without that help, but in the time between this preseason planning and early August, there will probably be fresh information from the market itself. Reactions from salespeople after the first shipments come in may give some clues as to customer preference.

In any event, nothing is lost and much may be gained by leaving some margin for correction of error. Therefore, instead of purchasing immediately the 225 hooded and 170 collared cardigans shown on lines 3 and 7 of Table 8–1E, the buyer will purchase 135 and 102 units as shown on lines 4 and 8 (totaling 237 units of bulky hooded coat sweaters).

STEP 6. "SCALING" COLORS AND SIZES Once the buyer has developed a control plan for certain types or styles, it is possible to determine selection factors like colors and sizes by a top-down method: applying predetermined percentage distributions to the planned types or styles.

Within a given article, the demand by sizes is likely to be fairly constant, changing slowly over time, or changing because of changes in type of customer or because of other predictable factors like cut of the goods or introduction of new size ranges. In this case, the buyer knows from analysis of past sales that sweaters of this type are likely to sell by size in the proportions or "scale" noted in Table 8–1F (percentage line). If these percentages are applied to the total immediate purchase plan of 237 units (sum of totals on lines 4 and 8, Table 8–1E), the distribution of units by size is obtained, as shown on the unit line of Table 8–1F.

[2]Provisions of this sort come under the generic title of "contigency plans."

TABLE 8–1F
OTB Distributed by Size: Bulky Coat Cardigans

Size	*34*	*36*	*38*	*40*	*Total*
Percent total category	18	24	30	28	100
Units	43	57	71	66	237

TABLE 8–1G
OTB Distributed by Color: Bulk Coat Cardigans

Color	*H*	*B*	*N*	*Others*	*Total*
Percent total category	33	20	14	33	100
Units	78	48	33	78	237

Colors are much more volatile than sizes—so much so that the buyer hesitates to make a prediction. But it must be made, so the buyer decides to start by ordering one-third of the units in the much-touted honey, (H in Table 8–1G) another third in black and navy (B and N in Table 8–1G), and the remaining third in four other colors. These are the proportions that roughly determine the unit distribution of colors in Table 8–1H.

Size and color scales form an overall guide as individual styles are being ordered. There is an assumption that some degree of substitutability exists among price lines and collar types. Therefore, if the distribution of sizes and colors over the category as a whole is in line with averaged customer demand, there is a better chance of satisfying the individual customers who come in to shop.

Some buyers do not find it practicable to work out plans in the detail shown here. They will arrive at the planned purchase of 237 units by working with broad totals. They will then scale them for size and color as just shown and proceed to buy selection factors such as type, kind, and neckline, "by ear," making certain that colors and sizes accumulate according to the broad scale plan. This procedure is not recommended for inexperienced buyers, for those who cannot marshal a lot of detail in their heads, and for those who believe that time spent in careful planning pays in the end—by shortening time spent on actual procurement, by yielding better balanced stocks with consequently improved sales and stockturn, and by reduced markdowns.

STEP 7. SUMMARIZING THE BUYING PLAN Table 8–1H summarizes all other

TABLE 8–1H
Final Distribution of Purchase in Bulky Coat Cardigans

STYLE	PRICE	UNITS	HONEY		BLACK		NAVY		GREEN		RED		BROWN		GREY	
Hooded				34·36·38·40		34·36·38·40		34·36·38·40		34·36·38·40		34·36·38·40		34·36·38·40		34·36·38·40
a	15	(18) 20	12	2 3 4 3	8	2 2 2 2										
b	20	(69) 72	24	3 6 8 7	12	2 3 4 3	12	2 3 4 3	8	2 2 2 2	8	2 2 2 2			8	2 2 2 2
c	30	(48) 48	12	2 3 4 3	12	2 3 4 3	8	2 2 2 2			8	2 2 2 2	8	2 2 2 2		
Subtotals		(135) 140	48		32		20		8		16		8		8	
Collared																
d	15	(54) 58	18	3 4 6 5	12	2 3 3 4	12	2 3 3 4	8	2 2 2 2			8	2 2 2 2		
e	20	(27) 24	8	2 2 2 2	8	2 2 2 2					8	2 2 2 2				
f	30	(21) 24	8	2 2 2 2					8	2 2 2 2			8	2 2 2 2		
Subtotals		(102) 106	34		20		12		16		8		16			
Totals		(237) 246	(76) 82	14 20 26 22	(52) 52	10 13 15 14	(33) 32	6 8 9 9	24	6 6 6 6	24	6 6 6 6	24	6 6 6 6	8	2 2 2 2

plans in a single diagram that almost serves as an instruction sheet for writing the final orders. It is based on a Model Assortment Plan, with the initials of the three words fortuitously spelling the word MAP. This is just what the plan is: a map to guide the buyer in the market. What is actually found there may cause some alterations in detail, but the overall guides should be followed quite closely unless extraordinary, unexpected developments dictate change.

Note that the proposed styles are designated by letters *a* through *f*. Actual styles will be selected to fulfill the purposes designated for each of these lettered styles. The circled figures in the column headed *units* correspond to lines 4 and 8 in Table 8–1E. The circled figures at the bottom of the columns labeled "honey," "black," and "navy" correspond to the distributions developed in Table 8–1G. All these figures are entered first to serve as guides for the juggling process that follows as the buyer tries to distribute colors and sizes among the six planned styles and within the desired framework of the scales in Tables 8–1F and 8–1G.

Notice, for example, that colors are distributed in a cross-supporting pattern. By planning to buy eight pieces of red, Style *e*, the buyer is filling a color gap in Styles *d* and *f*. Because the $20 price of *e* is considered substitutable with either the $15 price of *d* or the $30 price of *f*, the three together form a selection for the choice of an individual customer. Apparently, the buyer is dubious about gray, buying only eight pieces in Style *b*, and concentrates the limited purchasing power of other colors in green, red, and brown.

As the colors and sizes are tentatively entered, the buyer compares the totals with the circled figure for the style. Originally, the buyer may have planned to buy one of the last four colors in Style *a*, but even eight pieces would have pushed the total for that style to 28. Not wanting to exceed the control plan of 18 by that much, the buyer eliminated the color and bought Style *a* only in honey and black. It still exceeds the control figure by two units, but such differences are not significant in this kind of planning, provided that overall goals are not exceeded.

Size quantities are totaled in the bottom line and compared with the scale guides of Table 8–1F. Adding across the line reveals the following comparisons:

TABLE 8–1I Final Purchase versus Original Plan

	34	*36*	*38*	*40*	*Total*
Size totals (Table 8–1H)	50	61	70	65	246
Size totals (Table 8–1F)	43	57	71	66	237

There is some discrepancy between the sizes as plotted in Table 8–1H and those prescribed by Table 8–1F, especially in sizes 34 and 36. This arises from the buyer's policy of not buying fewer than two pieces of even the poorest sizes in a style. As a result, the total purchase for these sizes runs over plan, and the total quantity comes to 246 units instead of the planned 237.

This is just another illustration of how a built-up plan can differ from a top-down plan. And it also illustrates the kind of adjustments or reconciliations that are too insignificant to be worthwhile attempting. Subsequent reordering will make the needed adjustments. The controls have served their purpose as guides; there is no need to treat them as iron limitations.

STEP 8. ADJUSTING PLANS TO MARKET CONDITIONS It is assumed that a preliminary survey of market offerings preceded all this planning. In fact, experienced buyers often place some portion of their orders before plans are completed, care being taken not to commit so heavily that adjustments cannot be easily made as the plans formulate. But, with plans completed, the buyer is ready to implement them by completing the actual selection of specific items in their various selection factors.

If market offerings and rumored trends indicate the need for major changes, the plan should be reexamined. It may be that the latest styles and colors or new information may *necessitate* a change in plans; earlier judgment may have been faulty. But reexamination of the plan is more likely to reveal it as being quite logical. This is when the buyer must suspect that market pressures and whims have been mistaken for valid changes.

STEP 9. PLACING ORDER PROMPTLY Need is urgent and deliveries are long. Therefore it is more than whim to include again the warning that, whatever the degree or elaboration of planning, orders must be placed *promptly*—especially for important styles such as *b*, *c*, and *d*. Late delivery will result in lost sales during the early period and delays in getting test information for the reorder program, which should be under way in August.

STEP 10. FILL-INS DURING THE SELLING SEASON As the season advances and customer preferences become better known through analysis of sales records, a reorder program, not unlike that for staple goods, takes over the task of balancing the stocks to demand. In fashion goods, it may develop that one style becomes a "runner," in which case it may be ordered several times on an RP + DP + R basis. Special care must be taken, however, to reduce the size of orders as the selling season nears the end. Especially if the end is swift, it does become necessary to carry small reserves. Any attempt to protect the sales of individual items under these conditions will result in remainders out of proportion to the capacity of succeeding weeks' sales to absorb them.

Successive models, as previously noted, may be set up for critical dates in the season. By estimating sales between dates, a reorder open-to-buy is formulated in much the same manner as was done in Table 8-1E. Where periods are long (as between Sept. 1, Nov. 1, and Jan. 1 models), an open-to-buy can be worked out for the entire period and used as an overall guide. Portions of the plan may then be reordered from week to week and records of purchases accumulated against the plan.

There is one very important difference between the reorder of fashion goods and the reorder of staples. The latter takes the form of continual filling in of specific items. In fashion goods, except for runners, fill-in is done on the basis of central ideas or selection factor types. For example, collared cardigan lines may prove to be better than expected. This does not mean that Styles *d*, *e*, and *f* will be reordered over and over. Other styles may be chosen as long as they have the principal characteristics of line, design, texture, etc., that distinguish Styles *d*, *e*, and *f*. This practice reaches its height in fast-running goods like sportswear and dresses.

There are merchants who have a "strictly no reorder" policy with respect to individual styles of items like dresses and blouses. On the other hand, chains that work a narrow and deep assortment like to reorder specific styles. For one thing, they have to be displayed in windows, and it becomes impracticable to keep changing the items too often because of insufficient sizes or colors in stock to back up the window number. Again, many retailers feel that working too many styles produces too much remainder stock in odd sizes and colors, with never enough depth to support promotions of successful items.

THE BUYING PLAN FOR SLOW-TURNING FASHION AND SEASONAL STOCKS

A considerable portion of the goods handled in many stores cannot be ordered by the methods that have been outlined. In many lines, vendors do not carry stocks, and the earlier orders are placed with them, the better the quality and workmanship obtainable. Nor do styles change so rapidly as to make it imperative that a continual flow of new styles be maintained through the season. The merchandising of such lines must be accomplished less by weekly fill-ins and more by seasonal orders. Examples of such goods are men's and boys' clothing, shoes, furniture, and piece goods. In these lines, most of the buying is done well before the season commences. Although there is some filling in, this may represent only a small fraction of the buying, whereas, in the case of staples and fashion items discussed, most of the season's buying takes place at weekly or other periodic fill-ins. Success in buying goods of this third class depends on the accuracy of long-range forecasting.

An example

An example of seasonal buying is taken from boys' clothing. The classification is jackets and blazers. They may be subdivided into two color groups: navy and fancies (all other than navy). The former is handled largely as described for staples, because the manufacturer carries a stock and stands ready to make prompt deliveries as periodic reorders are received. In the case of fancies, however, the buyer must plan in November the probable sales for the entire spring season, February through July. This is done by price lines, as shown in Table 8–2.

It will be noted that all of the better coats that the buyer thinks will be

TABLE 8–2
Probable Spring Sales by Price Lines
Feb. 1–July 31

Price $	*Last Year Spring Sales*	*This Year Planned Sales*	*Increase or Decrease in Stock Desired**	*Quantity to Buy*	*Percent of Season's Requirements to Order in November*	*Number to Order in November*
40	50	60		60	100	60
30	150	170	+30	200	80	160
25	200	220	−20	200	60	120
20	100	100	+10	110	50	55
	500	550		570		395

*The carry-over from the previous season and carry-over into the next season must be considered. At $40, this buyer wants as many suits at the end of the season as at the beginning. At $30, the stock at the beginning is too low to provide an adequate assortment even on July 31, so he plans to buy 30 more than he expects to sell. At $25, he plans to have 20 less on July 31 than on February 1, and at $20, he plans to have 10 more.

needed are ordered months in advance. This ensures good workmanship and quality materials that may not be available during the season. Lower-priced merchandise and job lots will be available, so it is not wise to be committed for the entire season's needs at $20. Again, markdowns will be necessary; thus the lower price lines may be partly filled in from the higher ones. The number that the buyer plans to buy in each price will be further broken down into types, colors, sizes, and month of delivery. Most of the advance orders will be scheduled for delivery before Easter.

Forecasting Styles, Colors, and Sizes

To the uninitiated, it may seem very difficult to anticipate in November just what styles, colors, and sizes will sell next spring and how many of each. But the experienced buyer, backed by adequate records of past sales, does not find the problem insurmountable. Last year's sales by price give him or her a clue to this year's sales. These may then be distributed by size according to the size distribution last year. Next it is a matter of selecting outstanding styles. The buyer has a mental picture of the details of the garments that have sold best, and there are many manufacturers' samples to inspect. These samples incorporate the features that each believes will be in demand during the coming season. The buyer's knowledge of past demand in his or her own store, supplemented by newly gained information as to what features most vendors agree on, give an adequate basis for selection. Because the styles are not going to change during the season, the buyer who can begin the season with a carefully planned assortment of leading styles and good values has little to fear, even though most of the stock has been bought before any sales have been made. Of course, some mistakes will occur, but the original markup allows for markdowns on the occasional style or color that fails to sell.

It must not be assumed that prior years' operations are the sole guide for forecasting. Recent trends, although not in comparable fabrics and colors because of seasonal differences, may nevertheless throw light on the interpretation of data from other years. In the case of topcoats, for example, recent trends may indicate that raincoats with zip-out linings are being used increasingly as between-season coats. Therefore, topcoats may be due for a decline and require drastic action to correct error caused by reliance on previous performance.

Summary of Planning Procedure

In principle, the method of planning is simple and not beyond the scope of even the smallest operator:

1. Determine how much was sold during the season last year.
2. Estimate how many you will sell this year.
3. Decide whether you want more or less stock at the end of the season than at the beginning.
4. Decide on how many to order in view of 2 and 3 above.
5. Spread number to order over types, styles, colors, and sizes in proportion to the anticipated sales.
6. Decide when to order this amount by considering both manufacturers' requirements and the possibility of unexpected sharp changes in sales expectations.

Plans for Sets and Open Stock

Home furnishings departments, such as furniture, china, and silverware, have to contend with the problem of selling goods in various "set" combinations. Table 8–3 illustrates the season's sales plan for a model assortment of stainless steel flatware. Here, the sales plan is virtually the same as the buying plan, except that the latter may allow for difference between an opening and a closing carry-over stock.

The standard "place setting" consists of one teaspoon, one soupspoon, one dinner fork, one salad fork, and one knife. There is a wide variation among the prices of the individual pieces when sold separately (in "open stock"). For example, the open-stock prices for the $4.95 place settings may be: 69¢ each for teaspoons, 99¢ for soupspoons and forks (both dinner and salad), and $1.59 for the knife. Thus the five pieces would total $5.25 if bought individually but are offered at $4.95 in the combined place setting.

Another favored combination is the 24-piece "service for 6." It is an inducement for customers to start collecting the particular style, additions being bought later from open stock.

The 50-piece[3] service for 8 is a common promotional device in the lower-to-middle price lines. It appeals to customers who can afford to buy a whole service at once or who are looking for a useful gift-giving set. Similarly, a 74-piece set provides a service for 12. The addition of serving pieces may make a 75-piece, 76-piece, or larger set. In Table 8–3, these services for 12 are listed in the column headed "Special Sale Services."

Another device, commonly used in higher-price sets, is to induce multiple purchase of place settings by putting special prices on sets for 6, 8, and 12 (30, 40, and 60 pieces, respectively). Added pieces are chosen by customers from open stock, which contains gravy and soup ladles, cold meat forks, carving sets, and cake turners, among others.

[3]The compostion of sets is governed more by "common practice" than by "standard" practice. A 50-piece set, for example, could be made up of 8 dinner forks, 8 salad forks, 8 knives, 8 soupspoons, 16 teaspoons, 1 butter knife, and 1 sugar shell.

TABLE 8–3

Legend: Price / Unit Sales

SALES PLAN: STAINLESS STEEL FLATWARE

FALL

PATTERNS	5 Piece Place Setting	24 Piece Service for 6	50 Piece Service for 8	Special Sale Services	Place Settings for 6	Place Settings for 8	Place Settings for 12	Open Stock $ Sales	Total Dollar Sales
Light Embossed Scroll		$7.50 200	$15 300						6,000
Free Flow Sculptured		$10 200	$20 200					2,000	8,000
Light Embossed Floral 74 pc.				$25 200					5,000
Classic Embossed Crest	$2.80	$12 200	$25 200					2,500	9,900
Nylon Handle			$25 200						5,000
Free Flow Etched Floral	$3.30 300	$14 100	$30 150					4,000	10,890
Undecorated Danish	$3.30 500				$19 100	$25 100	$37 50	3,000	10,900
Free Flow Sculptured 75 pc.				$40 200					8,000
Undecorated Danish	$4.40 300		$40 50		$25 50		$48 50	2,000	8,970
Heavy Embossed Sterling Type	$4.40 300		$40 50		$25 50		$48 25	2,000	8,970
Sleek Sculptured Swirl	$5.50 200				$32 25	$41 25	$60 25	2,000	6,425
Very Slender Free Flow	$5.50 200				$32 25	$41 25	$60 25	2,000	6,425
Severe Danish with polished bowls and blades and satin handles	$6.60 200				$37 25	$49 25	$72 25	2,000	7,270
									101,750

Buying to Plan

Having made up a preliminary assortment plan and estimated the sales potential of each element, the buyer may proceed to plan what portion of the season's requirements for each item to order each month, allowing of course for stock already on hand or on order. As in the sweater case, he or she may set up model stocks for specific critical dates, estimate sales between those dates, and thereby set up a buying program. And, as with the sweater case, three things should be kept in mind when actually buying:

1. The styles are described in abstract terms and must now be implemented with actual selections in the market.
2. In the process of selection, there may be some valid reasons for making some changes: minor departures, either from the descriptions or from prices, noted in the plan.
3. Subsequent developments may show that the quantities listed in the plan were in error. Time buys information: As market news and sales information show the need, plans may be revised so that future reorder placements may adjust the stocks to newly conceived sales potentials.

Buying Plans in a Seller's Market

The preceding discussion has been predicated on the assumption that the buyer can procure what he or she orders—that he or she operates within a normal market. When there is a marked scarcity of goods, however, the decision as to how much merchandise he or she will get may be made by the seller, not by the buyer. In spite of the poorly balanced stocks that would result from the retailer's inability to control buying, the avid demand for goods might enable retailers to sell whatever they had. At any rate, the penalty for error is reduced in a market of scarcity.

HAND-TO-MOUTH BUYING

An important policy that every buyer must determine in making the buying plan involves the size of the order and the time it is placed in relation to the delivery date desired. Hand-to-mouth buying involves two concepts: first, the placing of many small reorders rather than a few large ones, and second, the ordering of goods for immediate delivery rather than well in advance of delivery date desired.

Advantages and Disadvantages

The following outline gives the advantages and disadvantages of hand-to-mouth buying from the retailer's standpoint.

Advantages

1. Constant flow of fresh goods, leading to stimulation of business as a result of up-to-date styles.
2. Economical use of capital. Capital and credit requirements for financing inventories are lightened.
3. Elimination of the risks of commitments long in advance of needs that lead to returns to vendors and cancellations.
4. Reduction of inventory risks of obsolescence.

Disadvantages

1. Increased cost of merchandise resulting from loss of quantity discounts plus higher transportation costs for small shipments.
2. Increased expense of ordering and handling.
3. Frequent necessity of a jobber between manufacturer and retailer. The retailer could buy direct if he or she would order further in advance and in larger quantities.
4. Loss of sales resulting from inadequate or incomplete stocks.
5. Increased dominance of seller over buyer.
6. Lower merchandise standards possible, as speed in production and delivery is put ahead of quality.
7. Possibility that, on a rising market, higher cost prices would have to be paid for much of the goods purchased.

A Recurring Problem

The practice of limiting orders to immediate and recurring needs rather than placing them on a basis of seasonal sales expectations is not a new development. It recurs during periods of falling prices and when there is great uncertainty as to whether coming sales will follow established patterns. Buyers hold off buying until the last minute, when they believe that the longer they wait the lower the price will be or the less the danger of committing themselves to the wrong merchandise.

During periods of rising prices, particularly for staples, and of clear upward trends in demand, hand-to-mouth buying is curtailed, because the early buyers get the best prices and often a better markup if they price their goods on a basis of replacement cost. Although such buying savors of speculation, merchants find it advisable to make advance commitments when there is evidence of increasing demand for specific goods in restricted supply.

For fashion goods, however, there is always a great risk of obsolescence leading to markdowns. Here the buyer must take whatever risks are needed to ensure the timely build-up of fashion-right stocks. A degree of proficiency in this guessing game is necessary for survival. An attempt to rely on many small reorders for immediate delivery is not likely to succeed with the assortment badly depleted.

Technical Appendices

A. PLANNING DATA FOR MODEL STOCK AND BUYING PLANS

Table 8–4 depicts a stock status report prepared by electronic data processing equipment. It reports weekly the activity in the various price lines within a merchandise classification (# 2) within a selling department. For each price line, the following facts are reported: the total unit receipts and sales season to date, the current on hand and on order, the sales last year for two 4-week periods (the coming 4 weeks and the following 4 weeks), the sales this year for the past 4 weeks, the percent of increase over the like 4-week period last year, and last year's coming 4-week sales on a weekly basis.

With such complete data, the buyer is able to forecast sales for the coming 8 weeks with considerable accuracy. This forecast permits planning stocks for at least a month ahead and calculating how much to buy in each price line.

For example, sales in the $5.98 price line are 13 percent ahead of last year for the past 4-week period and 12 percent ahead for the season to date. Sales in the coming 4 weeks last year were 235, and 82 in the next 4 weeks, and the forecast might be made for 258 in the coming 4 weeks this year and 90 in the following 4 weeks (an increase of 10 percent). With sales at a peak during the next 4 weeks, followed by a sharp decline, the buyer might decide to reduce the stock to 180 pieces (two times the following 4-weeks' sales) at a point in time 4 weeks from now.

With a planned closing stock, then, of 180 pieces with projected sales of 258 pieces, provision must be made for 438. With 356 on hand and none on order, the OTB would be 82 for the coming 4-week period.

Where orders have to be placed further ahead, stock may be planned for 2 or 3 months ahead rather than for 1 month ahead.

How this OTB should be spent is partially determined by the unit net sales report (Table 8–5). This reveals that two styles are involved at $5.99 (same as $5.98). In Style 599, 577 have been sold season to date, and in Style 500, 736 have been sold. In Style 599, 60 pieces are now on hand, and in Style 500, 296. Even though Style 500 is outselling Style 599, the stock on hand of the former is disproportionately large. With 82 more units to order most should be alloted to Style 599 to keep up size and color assortments.

Individual styles that are clearly runners may also be controlled by the formula developed in the last chapter for building each unit of sale up to a provision or maximum. For example, if reorders are planned for 2-week intervals and delivery takes 3 weeks, the sales for the coming 5 weeks can be forecast for each style and to this added a reserve to take care of unexpected sales and a minimum assortment of sizes and colors. Subtracting from this provision, the number currently on hand and on order will yield the OTB for the style number.

TABLE 8–4

DEPT NO XXX

Stock Status Report *

	Cl	Price	Total Rcpts	Total Sales	Total On Hnd	Total On Ord	On Hnd & On Ord	Projected Sales Next 4 Weeks	Projected Sales Foll. 4 Weeks	Sales Past 4 Weeks	% Inc. Past 4 Weeks	Last Year Sales by Weeks #1	#2	#3	#4	#5
TY	2	4.98									%					
LY								8	95				1	5	2	
TY	2	5.98	1669	1313	356		356			198	11.0%					
LY			1493	1173	320			235	82	175		112	22	37	24	40
TY	2	6.90	2124	1693	431		431			162	7.0%					
LY			1901	1512	389			175	92	151		83	3	18	50	21
TY	2	7.98	123	95	28	36	64			32	2.0%					
LY			110	83	27			45	1	31		37	2		4	2
TY	2	8.98	336	296	40	160	200			99	1.0%					
LY			301	263	38			138	160	98		45	16	22	28	27
TY	2	9.98	535	406	129		129			46	4.0%					
LY			478	272	206			57	3	44		21	6	6	11	13
TY	2	10.98	313	257	56		56			18	1.0%					
LY			280	139	141			29	15	17		4	5	8	11	1
TY	2	11.98	533	346	187		187			102	3.0%					
LY			476	307	169					99						
TY	2	12.98	1199	763	436		436			276	2.0%					
LY			1072	680	392			355	34	271		108	62	45	60	80
TY	2	15.00	525	374	151		151			81	1.0%					
LY			470	333	137			109	5	80		37	20	16	16	20
TY		Total	7357	5543	1814	196	2010			1014	6.0%					
LY			6581	4762	1819			1151	417	966		347	117	127	186	174
TY	Markdowns		390	281	109			147	100	72	2.0%CR	89	6	21	16	15
LY			401	277	124					74						

* By permission of Hochschild, Kohn & Company, Baltimore, Maryland.

TABLE 8–5

Unit Net Sales *

WEEK ENDING xx/xx/xx DEPT. NO. xxx

				Current Week		*Season to Date*									
Cl.	*Ven*	*Style*	*Price*	*Rec.*	*Sales Tot.*	*Rec.*	*O/H*	*Sales Tot.*	*#1*	*#2*	*#3*	*#4*	*#5*	*Remarks*
2	124	1606	1198			37	24	13	6	1	2	3	1	
2	750	599	599		9	637	60	577	271	87	32	72	115	
2	932	2620	798		3	60	14	46	14	6	5	10	11	
2	932	2690	698		2	72	9	63	17	12	10	11	13	
2	932	2750	798		1	60	14	46	16	6	6	13	5	
2	932	3038	1198		31	217	70	147	62	14	21	21	29	
2	932	3050	1198		5	108	22	86	28	8	15	16	19	
2	1160	250	690			14	2	12	11				1	
2	1160	260	690			29	16	13	7	5		1		
2	1160	400	699		63	1560	339	1221	522	113	137	238	211	
2	1160	450	898			307	36	271	84	43	44	52	48	
2	1160	471	998		10	277	133	144	50	17	25	29	23	
2	1160	477	998		3	112	30	82	43	7	11	8	13	
2	1160	500	599	72	51	1032	296	736	323	52	70	141	150	
2	1160	481	998		47	146	66	80	20	11	16	18	15	
2	1160	2530	690		3	51	13	38	11	4	11	2	10	
2	1160	2708	690			66	1	65	24	9	9	11	12	
2	1160	2910	690			52	8	44	20	6	7	6	5	
2	1160	2930	1500		10	252	114	138	31	23	24	28	32	
2	1160	2932	1298		11	223	133	90	35	8	13	14	20	
2	1160	2960	1500			208	3	205	70	23	28	35	49	
2	1160	2962	690			38	11	27	7	6	2	9	3	
2	1160	2965	690	24		88	36	52	17	10	7	10	8	
2	1160	2966	690			8	6	2				1	1	

* By permission of Hochschild, Kohn & Company, Baltimore, Maryland.

B. DEVELOPMENTS IN ELECTRONIC DATA PROCESSING

Whatever their virtues, analyses similar to the stock status report above are more voluminous than sophisticated. What buyers need is some kind of magic carpet that can whisk them in an instant from selling floor to stockroom, to warehouse, to order check, to receiving and marking, and to delivery platforms. Their days are bedeviled with problems that need "now" information, fast calculations, and instant solutions. Recent sharp switches in the directions of computer technology promise some relief.

Much of it was born of electronic miniaturization; of semi-conductors, of micro-processors, or "computers on a chip." NCR says: "Today it is not uncommon for a small micro-processor to provide as much computational power as some of the early giant computers." Computer makers saw the need and the wherewithal and welded them into a system of point of sale or point of service (POS) terminals connected to relatively nearby mini-computers, which, if need be, could be connected to some big central main frame computer or to an outside rented service computer.

The result is an interactive communications network of distributed processing (as opposed to centralized processing). Service terminals can hold conversations with mini-computers about individual transactions and, in larger organizations, mini-computers can send daily batches of information to master computers for more elaborate analysis. And the conversations can now be held in a language more common to all users—as opposed to the specialized language of computers, which requires a lot of special training.

As with digital watches and little hand and desk computers, the cost comes down as the capability goes up. For retailers, the result will be that many smaller ones will be able to make considerable use of computer technology. Furthering this probability as well as the developments previously discussed will be the rising tide of "software"—programming that makes the little wonder-children do their tricks.

Developments at the point of sale have included the following four steps:

1. Provision by the retailing industry of coding systems for identifying consumer products so that POS terminals can read them.
2. Devices for displaying the coded identification on merchandise tickets, wrappers, or packages.
3. Devices for machine-reading this information at the point of sale and translating it into modes suited to use by computers.
4. Point-of-sale mini-computers to perform this function and start the merchandise information system (MIS) on its electronic processing course.

The food field provided the Universal Product Code (UPC), a series of vertical bars with printed numbers that could be read by a POS terminal when moved over or past a scanner in the terminal. The code reports the product, brand, and size or weight of the packaged item. Current prices for the item are kept up to date in the computer and are automatically matched with the product information. See Figure 8–2.

The sales register part of the terminal then issues a detailed sales slip with description and price of each item and the transaction total and sales tax. The computer cumulates total sales for each SKU, providing information for inventory control that hitherto could not be economically obtained. In addition, the terminal can verify charge account balances and report new charges to the appropriate accounts.[4] While supermarkets have been somewhat slow to introduce the new system because of the high cost of the equipment, its future is bright.

It should be noted that consumer groups oppose having prices marked

FIGURE 8–2 The Sweda Superscanner, below reads UPC label (inset) on a can of vegetables.

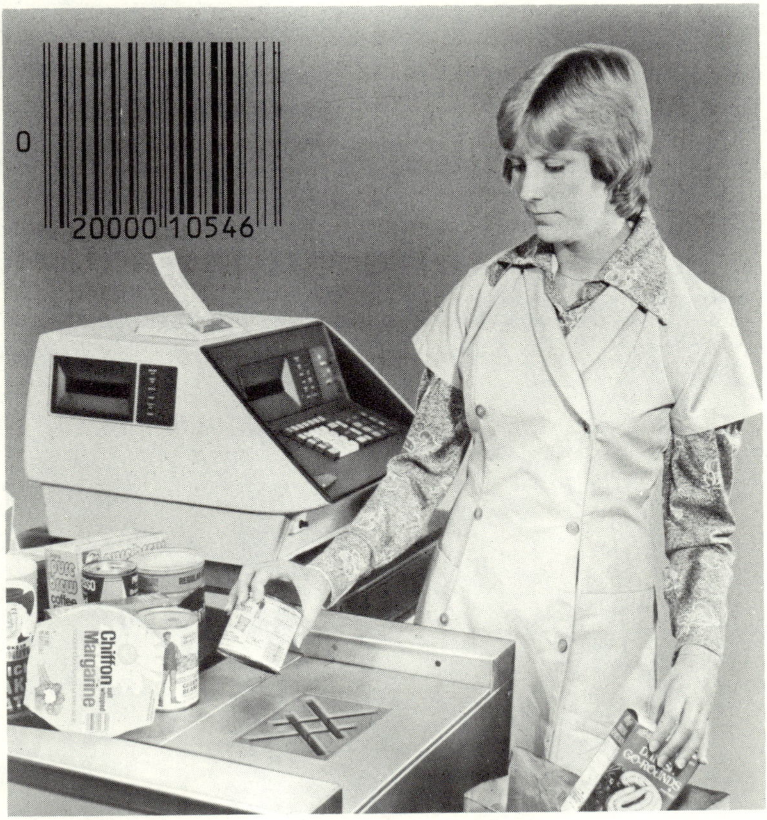

Photo courtesy of Sweda International, Inc.

[4]NCR states that "the 2151 retail terminal, with its own powerful micro-processor and extensive memory, is a full-fledged data processing unit which can be tailored to meet a store's changing needs."

only on the shelves and not on each item. But retailers could save a great deal of marking expense and assure that prices are current if they store the prices of each item in the computer and not mark each item. But unions, too, oppose the idea because of its work-threatening implications.

"Soft goods" merchants developed a classification code under the aegis of the National Retail Merchants Association and express their code on tickets or packages with numbers and letters that can be read by customers as well as by the computer. This is called "Optical Character Recognition—Font A (OCR-A)." See Figures 8–3 and 8–4.

FIGURE 8–3 Tickets in optical character font as produced by the Ticket Unit of an IBM Merchandise Information System

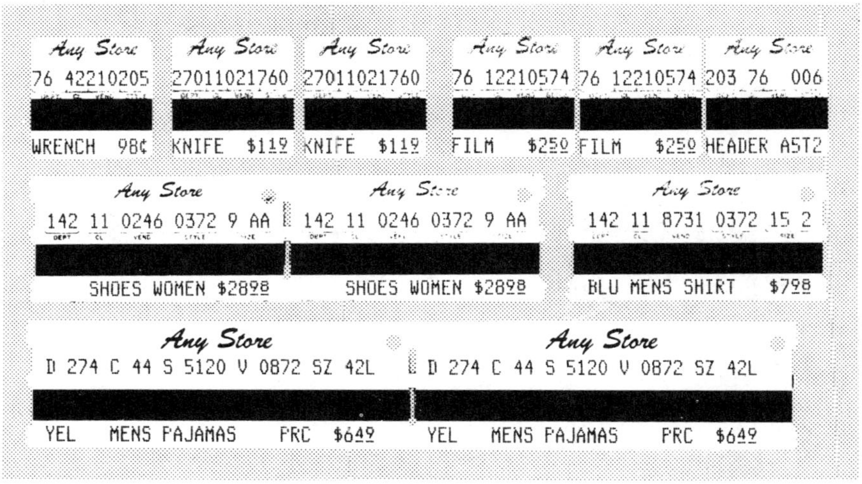

FIGURE 8–4 The Kimball KODE 310's version of a machine readable merchandise ticket in Optical Character Recognition symbols

DISCUSSION QUESTIONS

1. Why is it necessary for management to have a clear policy about "tolerable" out-of-stock conditions when setting up a reordering formula?
2. Except at the time of placing initial orders for a season, what quantities have to be subtracted from the total provision calculated for a period in order to determine the OTB?
3. In the sweater example, a unit of OTB is calculated on each neckline style (hooded and collared): within each price line ($15, $20, and $30), within each knit (bulky coat, bulky modified, regular knit, and regular-knit modified), and within each type (cardigan and pullover). Sizes and colors are then scaled. By what factors and in what order would you plan OTB for at least two of the following: handbags, millinery, hosiery, men's suits, men's hats, handkerchiefs, women's shoes, dresses?
4. Some stores arrange their dress stocks primarily by size ranges rather than by classifications. Thus the junior sizes are in one place, the misses' sizes in another, the women's sizes in a third, and the tall women's sizes in a fourth. Within each group are found the various classifications, materials, prices, and so on. What advantages and disadvantages does this arrangement have?
5. Suggest the most desirable "order of breakdown" (stock arrangement) for men's shirts. Be sure to include all of the following factors: colors, materials, neck sizes, sleeve lengths, collar styles, and prices. Note that stock arrangement does not necessarily follow the order of breakdown in the buying plan.
6. As indicated in the text for sweaters, plan a minimum stock assortment for some price line in some classification of any other line of merchandise with which you are familiar.
7. You have in black, size 16, a stock on hand of five garments, and six are on order. The stock wanted on hand after the next order is received is 10. It will take 3 weeks before a new order can be received into stock, and sales are three a week. How many should you order?
8. Stock for May 1 is planned at 200. Sales for March are estimated at 100 and for April at 125. Delivery takes 1 month. On March 1, stock on hand is 170 and on order 110. How many should be ordered for April delivery?
9. If one-quarter of April's requirements in question 8 is to be ordered during the first week in March, how should the purchases be distributed if the following data are at hand?

Class	*Model (%)*	*On Hand*	*On Order*
A	50	70	60
B	30	45	50
C	20	55	—
	100	170	110

10. In which direction do fashion buyers err?
    (a) Buying too many different styles, few of which are ever reordered.
    (b) Buying a few styles, most of which are reordered in depth.
11. (a) To what extent do toy sales at Christmas give the buyer an adequate basis for planning the stock assortment and purchases for next Christmas?
    (b) Does the same answer apply to men's suits, china and glass, and handbags?

part III

Where and How to Buy

chapter 9

Merchandise Resources

FACTORS IN CHOOSING A RESOURCE

Key Resources

Although it is desirable to have the broadest possible market contacts, a large part of the buyer's purchases should be concentrated with a few key resources in order to qualify for lowest prices and best service. The exact proportion of purchases to be so concentrated depends in large measure on total buying power. With the object being to make oneself important to the key resources, the buyer for a very large firm can accomplish this aim with more spread than is possible for the buyer of a small firm.[1] Furthermore, a certain amount of purchasing power *should* be spread in order to broaden market contacts, to experiment with new goods and new sources.

Freedom of choice is sometimes limited. Examples are found later in discussions of the need for credit and in the case of a vendor who has gained theoretical monopoly. A buyer's firm may prize its continuity of relationship with certain resources. In this case, the buyer is not necessarily forced to patronize these vendors but will probably have to show cause for not doing so. Less urgent, but not ignored by the realistic buyer, are the resource preferences of the superiors in the firm.

[1]Sears Roebuck reported recently that it buys from over 12,000 merchandise resources. Nearly one-half of these each provide over $50,000 worth of goods a year.

A Variety of Considerations

Beyond these limitations, buyers select resources on the basis of their own evaluation of what the resources can do for the firms the buyers represent. They basically are interested in increasing sales volume and profits—in meeting budgets for sales, markon, margin, contribution after certain direct expense charges, and inventory turnover. Preferred resources are the ones that identify themselves most closely with these interests. They must help in the fight for customer patronage. Therefore, the buyer is interested not only in their goods but also in their marketing policies, because both affect the need to meet, beat, or avoid competition. They may help in selling efforts, in inventory management, and in lightening procurement work. Their prices and terms must enable the buyer to price competitively within markon requirements and to satisfy policies of the firm with regard to financing.

A classified list of factors that a buyer should examine in selecting resources appears in Table 9–1.

Suitability of merchandise to the buyer's clientele

This factor refers to basic quality and styling and to price ranges. These may suit the preferences of a large part of the clientele or have special appeal to certain groups. If neither, choice stops right there, and none of the following factors matters very much. To be suitable, the goods must also be offered at a price that permits them to be resold at a figure that fits the pocketbook of the store's clientele and that provides an adequate markup. A manufacturer whose lowest price is $72 a dozen will not suit a store whose highest retail price is $5.95.

In some respects, the following factors are elements of "suitability," because they do depend on the nature of a buyer's clientele.

Distinctiveness

Buyers of convenience goods often need vendors of highly standardized products, especially vendors of branded goods that have been presold to consumers or goods to which consumers have become partial through long usage. In most cases, however, the buyer looks for those vendors who differentiate their products: partly to avoid direct competition, but most importantly, to obtain features of superiority or originality. Sometimes the difference may be only in the packaging.

Especially in goods of fashion volatility, a given manufacturer may be "very hot" in any one season but "very cold" in other seasons. Some buyers try to hop from one such resource to another. Other buyers prefer to patronize those vendors who are consistently good rather than occasionally spectacular. The probabilities are that the uniformly good ones will produce their share of spectacular success over time.

TABLE 9–1
Factors in Choosing a Resource

Characteristics of merchandise offerings
1. Suitability—type and price
2. Distinctiveness
3. Timing
4. Brands
5. Specifications
Competitive policies
6. Distribution policy
7. Efforts to maintain retail prices
8. Clearance policy
Inventory Procurement
9. Output and shipping quantities
10. Delivery
11. Method of contact
12. Breadth of assortment
13. Dependability
14. Control of store inventories
Selling aids
15. Advertising policies
16. Dealer help
Price policies and terms
17. Pricing
18. Terms of sale
19. Shipping arrangements

Timing

Involved here are elements of fashion leadership and speed of innovation as well as the speed with which seasonal changes are introduced, exploited, and dropped. The buyer whose volume business comes in the normal "mid-season" cannot afford to concentrate purchases with those vendors who start discontinuing their lines shortly after the "season" is under way. Similarly, the buyer who wants a reputation for fashion leadership cannot achieve it with vendors who do not produce in depth until a new fashion or other form of innovation has developed proven acceptance.

The alert and knowledgeable buyer often combines the two types of resources. He or she establishes sufficient contact with the first kind to get goods for early testing operations and to meet the demands of the early-demand clientele. The buyer can then buy the midseason and later requirements from the second type of vendor. The merchandise may not be the same, but the "knock-offs" or copied variants may be even better suited to the mass, or late-buying, element of the clientele.

Brand policies

The manufacturer who has created demand for a product through preselling techniques has a theoretical monopoly: The buyer has no choice. Some brands, however, are merely devices for a type of differentiation or for identifying goods to encourage repeat patronage. A single manufacturer may have two or more such brands—often called "labels." He or she may sell to two competing retailers, under two different labels, virtually the same product with some slight differentiation that serves merely to avoid direct identification.

Some manufacturers of brands also sell unbranded goods or put a retailer's private label on them at a lower price. Although the unbranded article may be changed somewhat with the idea of avoiding direct competition with the branded version, the buyer must be very careful to see that the changes have not lowered the quality of the article or made it less attractive to his customers.

Specifications

Buyers who set specifications for their goods must be certain that the resource is not only willing but able to follow specified details. A few big retailers go so far as to help a manufacturer with the purchase of required raw materials and equipment and with the industrial techniques for producing the wanted goods at the wanted price. Sometimes buyers merely want details altered to remove the product from direct competition, to bring it down to a wanted price, to make it more attractive at the original price, or to build it up to a more profitable, higher price line.

Manufacturers tend to develop definite characteristics about the quality and styling elements of their products. One, for example, may produce suitable goods in the middle or lower price lines but not in the higher ranges. Into these may be put better materials, more ample proportions, and more decoration. But the result may still reflect workmanship and styling geared to the manufacture of low-end goods. The very nature of the design and added decorations may make the new product unsuitable to the tastes of customers in the higher price ranges. In such cases, the buyer is often better advised to *develop higher ranges from the low-end price lines of a higher priced manufacturer.*

Distribution policies

Buyers commonly strive to get a vendor's line confined to their outlets in their trading areas. But many vendors, especially those who make presold convenience goods, will have a policy of wide distribution. Buyers who need these goods have little choice. Some vendors sell more than one retailer in a trading area but only to outlets of a predetermined price and status level. They call this "selective distribution." A special warning bears repetition at this point. The buyer who seeks a hard-to-get brand, or exclusive representation, must be careful not to commit him- or herself to excessive purchases or to other arrangements that will prove to be hampering or restrictive. This does not preclude the acceptance of such burdens on a short-run basis if benefits over the long run promise to outweigh temporary losses or inconvenience. One of the problems faced by the buyer is that of "tie-in sales" in various forms. For example, a vendor may press the buyer to take some unwanted shampoo item at half price in order to get a highly desirable hair rinse. Another form of such tie-in is to insist that a buyer take all styles in the line in order to get that line at all.

Efforts to maintain retail prices

Until recently, many manufacturers of national brands had the policy of controlling the resale prices of their store customers. They entered into contracts with their retail accounts, setting the minimum retail prices at which their products could be resold. Such contracts were legal in most states, protecting the parties from antitrust violation, and the federal government legalized such contracts in connection with commerce among the states that had their own "fair-trade" laws.[2]

The manufacturers who took advantage of the opportunity to fix minimum retail prices were those who depended on retail merchant cooperation to move their products, particularly the small stores and the larger retail establishments that stressed service rather than price. These stores were fearful of price competition that would erode their margins above cost. On the other hand, there were heavy national advertisers of popular products who were much more concerned with getting customer preference directly than with helping retailers to sell. They were not interested in protecting the retailer's market and gave concessions to volume retailers who, in turn, cut the retail price. These vendors depended on customer demand to force retailers to stock their products. Sometimes they set resale prices, not to protect the retailer, but rather to ensure that the resale price would be low enough to

[2]Early in 1976, only seven states still had laws permitting general price maintenance: Arizona, Delaware, Illinois, Maryland, North Carolina, Virginia, and Wisconsin. But federal legislation has made them operable only in intrastate commerce.

attract volume patronage. Chains, popular-priced department stores, and discount houses that depend on large volume at low retail prices preferred this type of resource.

In spite of the desire to protect small merchants, most state legislators became convinced that "fair-trade" was keeping retail prices above competitive levels, and they either rescinded their price maintenance laws or made them inapplicable to merchants who had not signed a contract to maintain prices. And Congress in 1975 repealed its laws permitting price maintenance among the states.[3] Thus price maintenance of brands sold across state lines is now illegal. But some manufacturers of branded lines still use indirect methods to control and maintain retail prices, such as refusing to sell to price cutters. The small merchant and the service-oriented larger store are no longer legally protected against price cutting. However, loss-leaders sold below cost, including direct expenses, are still illegal in many states, and a vendor may choose to sell the entire line or certain of the brands on an exclusive basis in each trading area. It is still possible for the vendor to distribute on consignment, retaining ownership until the goods are sold to the consumer.

Clearance policies

Many buyers of regular goods at regular prices are offered "irregulars" or "seconds" or manufacturers' clearance lots at special prices. Buying the regular line may be a condition for getting their share of such goods. Some resources dispose of such goods to a few preferred accounts; still others sell them to price-promotional outlets that are not regular customers.

Output and shipping quantities

The buyer who needs only a few items at a time is precluded from vendors who ship only in gross lots. Conversely, the buyer who needs large quantities is often unable to patronize excellent but small resources that have neither the stock nor the manufacturing facilities to provide enough goods. As noted previously, some retailers may provide the financing and other assistance in order to build up such a manufacturer.

Delivery and order-filling practices

The reliability of a vendor in meeting promised delivery dates is important to all buyers. Speed of delivery is most important when it is difficult or inconvenient for the retailer to anticipate sales far ahead or to warehouse or finance heavy reserve stocks. In such cases, buyers may prefer nearby vendors or those with nearby warehouses and those who carry a ready stock of

[3]The Miller-Tydings Act of 1937 and the McGuire Amendment were repealed in 1975 by the Consumer Goods Pricing Act.

finished or nearly finished goods. Some manufacturers have set up regional distribution centers as a means to expedite delivery. Quick delivery in small lots is one of the prime functions of wholesale intermediaries. In fact, several of the factors that follow are important determinants in a decision to buy from wholesalers instead of directly from manufacturers. These wholesalers commonly deliver by means of their own trucks, and it is important from the retail merchant's view that these arrive at the right time of day, that they unload in the right spot, and that they avoid blocking customer traffic.

Other practices among vendors with respect to filling orders should be considered by the buyer:

1. Requirement of blanket orders.[4]
2. Stretched-out deliveries such as "as ready, complete by ________".[5]
3. Splitting shipment into small lots without the buyer's consent. This practice can increase freight and other costs, such as receiving, marking, and order checking.
4. Ability and willingness to carry stock and make shipments to fill the orders of the store's individual customers. This practice is discussed in Chapter 12.
5. Willingness to provide fast service, such as by air, when needed.

Method of contact

Some vendors send sales representatives on frequent visits to the store or office. Others visit less frequently, depending partly on ctalogs or bulletins. Some have nearby branch offices; others can be visited only at distant home offices or factories. Some sell only through local or regional distributors. Small store buyers tend to purchase from those resources that assume the cost of the contact. They also prefer salespeople who call at regular intervals, follow up their requests meticulously, and help to maintain stock assortments. For fashion goods, most manufacturers expect retail buyers to come to them, as a follow-up either to a representative's visit or to a recommendation of a resident buying office.

Breadth of assortment

The small merchant, in particular the one who handles many convenience items, prefers to buy from a wholesaler or manufacturer who handles a family of products. This is also true of buyers for large retail firms with respect to minor categories of such merchandise.

[4]See Chapter 11.

[5]This refers to the practice of shipping goods as they are finished in the factory, promising completion by some future date. Many buyers are insistent about the rate at which goods should be shipped in the intervening period.

Dependability

Resources vary in dependability not only with respect to delivery but in other factors of dealing, including the attributes of the very goods they sell. Some shrewd and skilled buyers may take risks on a vendor's dependability, relying on their own acumen to forestall any advantage the vendor may seek to gain. Most buyers prefer a resource of proven integrity that can be relied upon to fulfill all specific promises and their implications—the game of caveat emptor is not for them.

Following are some of the elements about which a buyer should determine the dependability of a resource.

1. Shipping goods according to sample or description.
2. Shipping selection factors like style, color, and size as ordered; substituting only with the advice and consent of the buyer.
3. Uniformity of product in successive shipments. Policies vary sharply with respect to the amount and standards of inspection, or "quality control."
4. Authenticity of the intelligence that the resource conveys to the buyer about the market and demand.
5. Accepting responsibility for defects in merchandise and failure in delivery, making adjustments promptly and even graciously.
6. Efficiency in billing customers, seldom making an error in invoicing.
7. All factors previously discussed under the headings of *timing*, *specifications*, and *delivery*.

Control of store inventory[6]

When a buyer has to spread purchases over many lines or is negotiating an exclusive agency for a quality line, a resource who will keep track of the store's inventory is welcomed. This service may include preparing reorders and making transfers. One manufacturer of foundation garments receives sales data collected by computer at the point of sale and replaces the items sold or substitutes these items with other more seasonal styles.

Advertising policies

A vigorous controversy has grown out of the practice of granting cooperative advertising allowances to retailers. Because this matter is discussed in detail in Chapter 12, at this point it is necessary only to list some of the major variations in practice:

1. Payment of all or part of the retailer's newspaper advertising. Some vendors demand that their cuts and layouts be used; others specify only certain elements; others make no demand about presentation.

[6]See Chapter 12 for details.

2. Some vendors demand "tear sheets" of actual advertisements and pay allowances only on presentation. Others give "advertising allowances" based on some standard such as quantities of merchandise bought.
3. Some vendors furnish advertisements for mailing insertions. Others contribute toward special promotional circulars and catalogs made up by stores or buying offices.
4. Some vendors help retailers with their entire promotional programs, either by incorporating them in a master plan or by giving counsel and guidance.

Dealer helps at point of sale

Not only in advertising but at the point of sale, there is a great variation in the way resources participate in selling their products. The small store, especially, prefers resources that furnish signs, counter and window display units, fixturing, and other point-of-sale helps, but these must meet the store's practical needs.[7] Many large stores prefer the uniformity of their own presentations. But even large retailers are partial to vendors who take an active interest in the resale of their products by helping in any of the following ways.

1. Recruiting and training skilled demonstrators, often reimbursing the store for their salaries. This practice is common in the cosmetic trade.
2. Holding meetings with the sales force to train them in product knowledge and selling techniques.
3. Sending out "detail" or "missionary" people, who check stock, make out suggested orders, fill fixtures from reserve, set up displays, and "keep house." This service is welcomed by supermarkets and by buyers of staple goods for very large stores.
4. Cooperation in the provision of "universal vendor markings" of merchandise in computer readable fonts as noted in Chapter 8 and also assistance in developing computerized inventory controls.
5. Providing efficient installation, warranty, and repair services. Few stores are equipped to set up and maintain the necessary repair and installation departments; they prefer to purchase lines where the wholesale distributor assumes these functions and has a proven reputation for quality and speed in performing the servicing required.

There are many who contend that retailers who seek these helps are abdicating their proper responsibilities. Nevertheless, the practices are common and constitute a consideration in choosing a resource.

[7]See Chapter 3 on associated buying arrangements and Chapter 12 on dealer helps.

Price policy

All buyers are interested in a vendor's prices and terms but for different reasons. In many fields, price lines are standardized among sellers, and the chief buying problem is to get the best combination of all the preceding factors at fixed prices. The buyer should determine whether the vendor's policy is to sell at (1) the market price, (2) the "market plus" price, or (3) the "market minus" price. The second means that the vendor asks a higher price on a basis of special and distinctive features of the product; a "market minus" price indicates that the policy is to undersell, possibly simplifying or skimping the product or services somewhat to do so. The "market minus" seller's goods may be satisfactory for basement and discount stores but may not meet the requirements of a discriminating clientele. A "market plus" seller may try to explain the extra charge by pointing to slight and even imaginary advantages that do not justify the difference in price. The unusual features should be *significant and observable* to the store's customers to warrant a "market plus" price.

Some sellers have a policy of maintaining steady prices throughout the season, offering clearances only toward the end. Others offer special price inducements at frequent intervals. These may take the form of "free deals,"[8] or of reduced price "deals." The promotional policy of the store tends to determine whether or not to seek out highly promotional manufacturers. The mass buyer may prefer to develop his or her own deals, but most of the smaller buyers are eager to patronize vendors who offer frequent special deals: lower prices for a specified period, tied in with special promotional aids.

Terms of sale

Although the well-financed store wants substantial cash discounts and anticipation, the store with limited resources may want considerable time to pay and may look for vendors who grant advance dating and longer than ordinary terms. But it should be noted that if long terms mean loss of substantial discounts, the store is unwise to defer prompt payment if money can be borrowed at low enough interest.

Credit is often a very important determinant in the choice of a resource. The buyer for a retail firm in straitened circumstances may be severely limited—forced to buy only from those who will grant credit. It has also been common practice for swiftly expanding retailers to finance, in part, with money gained from long credit terms.

Shipping arrangements

In many lines, freight costs are high in relation to selling price. Buyers of such lines may prefer resources that have nearby shipping points or shipping routes that reduce freight costs. All buyers are interested in getting "pre-

[8]See Chapter 11.

paid" freight terms or least costly FOB points. In fact, lower transportation costs are one of the primary advantages of local and regional wholesalers.[9]

Weighing the Selection Factors

The relative importance of each selection factor in the list varies with many circumstances, some of which have been noted. Buyer must weigh the combination of factors just as their customers weigh the whole utility of the goods they buy from the stores. Depending on factors such as the kind of firm they serve, the categories of these goods, the competitive situation, and their own qualifications, each buyer must determine a scale of values as the attributes of possible suppliers are studied. Conflicting needs and desires preclude maximizing the benefits of all: Decision must be toward the familiar optimum—the best compromise.

The housewares buyer may find that in a category like "gadgets" or small household hardware, it is best to buy from a vendor with a complete line. It might be possible to get more distinctive goods or more favorable prices by shopping the market, but extra sales and extra markup may not be worth the time spent. Measured in the scales would be the "opportunity costs" resulting from less time devoted to categories like cutlery, cooking utensils, hampers, and others.

Even in the factor of "suitability of merchandise," there is some room for compromise. Discriminating customers are not immune to the appeal of a bargain. That is why a buyer may sometimes deal with vendors whose material is quite superior to their workmanship. The material may be much more significant and observable to customers than is the workmanship—and the lower price may be a bargain.

Vendor Analysis

On a basis of such factors as those already presented, stores are finding it profitable to analyze the vendors from whom they have purchased in order to eliminate the undesirable ones and to concentrate volume on the better ones. As already indicated, those that are found most satisfactory for regular purchases are called "key" vendors, and it is desirable to obtain the great majority of purchases from them.

There are various ways of analyzing vendors. Each may be rated in relation to each of the factors just discussed. It is more common to limit the analysis to an accounting of the sales and profits realized from the purchases for each vendor. Figure 9–1 has been used for this purpose. This virtually provides a complete operating statement for each vendor's merchandise and is based on the retail method of inventory. The chief statistical facts to analyze by vendor are sales, markup obtained on purchases, markdowns,

[9]See Chapter 11 on how to reduce transportation costs.

FIGURE 9–1 Vendor analysis form

VENDOR ANALYSIS

MERCHANDISE	STYLE NO.	SEA-SON	BEGINNING OF SEASON				NO. REC'D	O. H. End of Season	NO. SOLD	COST PER UNIT	ORIGINAL		MARK DOWN		TOTAL SALES	TOTAL COST OF MDSE. HANDLED	UNIT RETAIL END OF SEASON	CLOSING INV. RETAIL	CLOSING INV. COST	COST OF MDSE. SOLD	G.M.	G M. %
			O. H	UNIT RETAIL	TOTAL RETAIL	TOTAL COST					UNIT RETAIL	No. Sales	UNIT RETAIL	No. Sales								
			1	2	3	4	5	6	7	8	9	10	11	12	13	14	15	16	17	18	19	
					1X2	3XA	7+6-1								9X10 +11X12	4+5X8		6X15	16XB	14-17	13-18	
TOTAL																						

SEASON	FALL OR SPRING YR.	FROM TO	DEPT NAME DEPT NO.		BEGIN	END	VENDOR'S NAME VENDOR'S NO.	GROSS MARGIN PER CENT
				CUM. M.U. %				
				COMPLEMENT	A	B		

maintained markup, inventories, and resultant turnover. Vendors whose products afford a large sales volume, coupled with an adequate maintained markup, are generally included on the key resource list.

Group evaluation of vendors

A method of obtaining a group evaluation of the performance of vendors of national brands has been developed by the National Retail Merchants Association.[10] A questionnaire is sent to the member stores asking them to grade the manufacturers from whom they buy (1) as excellent, good, fair, below par, and poor on overall performance, and also (2) on three criteria: quality of merchandise, compliance with the purchase order, and return policy. The results are converted into percentages for each of the five degrees of performance, with excellent weighted 5, good 4, fair 3, below par 2, and poor 1. These weighted scores for each manufacturer are arrayed in rank order so that the outstanding vendors, in the opinion of the store buyers, are readily separated from the scores of the mediocre and unsatisfactory vendors. In one of the first of such evaluations completed, 45 junior sportswear vendors of national brands and also 69 vendors of misses sportswear were rated by a total of 335 store respondents. Of course, no one store rated the entire list.[11] Not only were outstanding vendors identified, but it was also found that the vendors tended to rank lower on compliance with orders and with returns than they did on merchandise quality.

MANAGEMENT POLICY AND RESOURCE CHOICE

Because most buyers work in both an employee and agent capacity for a store organization and not as independent entrepreneurs, they need to be provided by top management with directives as to the goals they are expected to reach and the priorities involved. The goal given top priority most frequently is perhaps a combination of sales volume and markon. This means that the buyer is to seek out vendors and particular offerings that will provide

[10]Stores Magazine of the NRMA, October 1975.

[11]The statistical technique followed in developing each vendor's total score was to total the number of excellents, goods, fairs, etc., each obtained and to divide the number in each of the five classes by the number of stores reporting on that vendor. The ratio for excellent was then multiplied by 5, that for good by 4, etc., and the scores so determined for each quality were totaled to give the total ranking for each vendor. The rankings for merchandise quality, purchase order compliance, and return policy were similarly handled. For example, if 200 stores rating a single manufacturer assigned 100 excellents, 50 goods, 30 fairs, 20 below pars, and no poors, the ratios for excellent would be 50, for good 25, for fair 15, and for below par 10. Weighing by 5, 4, 3, and 2 gives an overall score for this vendor of 415.

the largest product of these two factors. However, it is not possible to estimate volume on competing lines precisely, and there are other policy matters to be weighed. For example, management may set a controllable profit goal for the department (gross margin minus direct expenses). This makes the buyer responsible for markdowns, shortages, and expenses that his or her department incurs directly rather than through proration of overhead. In this case, the buyer must estimate which line is likely to lead to more markdowns and which will involve more handling expense or more difficulty in making returns.

But management may have another immediate goal that takes priority over controllable profit. This may be to build an image of quality, broad assortments, or exclusive merchandise (not available elsewhere in the community), or it may be concerned primarily with increasing the return on the merchandise investment; this means reducing the inventory relative to sales. If a higher stockturn is the goal, the buyer may select the vendor that can provide fill-ins the most quickly and that replaces slow-selling goods with new items. Again, management may want advertising of the department increased but at minimum expense. This means giving preference to vendors who provide allowances.

Unfortunately, management frequently fails to direct buyers clearly along such lines, leading to buyer uncertainty as to what results are expected of them as they select vendors and items.

Store-Owned Merchandise Resources

A management policy in connection with sources of supply is whether to manufacture some or all of a store's merchandise or to buy wholly from the outside. Virtually all small stores and most large ones prefer to specialize in retail distribution and to be free to select from the best resources available without any long-time commitment, growing out of ownership. Most stores prefer to keep most of their capital in liquid assets and not to become involved in the maintenance of large fixed assets.

However, many chains and mail-order houses do have their own factories or are owned by manufacturers or by common holding companies. This is especially true in the case of men's and women's apparel, hosiery, shoes, and household drugs and toiletries. Such integrated arrangements make it possible to adjust factory production closely to customer demand. The central buyer acts not only as a selector but also as the product planner for the factory.

To depend on one's own factory solely, restricts assortments and opportunities to take advantage of promotional merchandise that may be available on the market. Chains that do considerable manufacturing usually plan to purchase a substantial portion of their requirements from outside sources.

Franchised retailers and other forms of integration are subject to regulatory restrictions and restraint-of-trade laws.

Even in the case of private store brands, outside sources are generally preferred. First preference is usually for the manufacturer of a well-known brand who is willing to sell identical or similar goods to the store at a lower price for private branding. Next is the meticulous contractor who can be relied upon to follow store specifications carefully and continuously.

BUYING FROM THE MANUFACTURER DIRECT VERSUS BUYING FROM WHOLESALE MIDDLEMEN

A decision sometimes set by management policy, sometimes by the buyer, and sometimes by the resource is whether to buy directly from the manufacturer or from a wholesaler or other wholesale distributor.

Policies of the Manufacturer

In many cases, the decision is not for the buyer to make. The manufacturer of a nationally advertised convenience product may sell only through agents or wholesalers, and the manufacturer of a shopping goods line may sell only through regional representatives. Some textile houses, for example, wish wider distribution than they can hope to achieve by direct retailer contact at a reasonable cost. The wholesaler provides them this wide distribution at a moderate markup. He or she may provide special promotional aid and other helps to push the products. The manufacturer can create retailer demand by national consumer advertising and by the use of missionary salespeople or detail people who contact retailers on behalf of the manufacturer or agent but channel resultant orders through the wholesaler.

Again, in the food field, many manufacturers of a limited line of food products sell exclusively through regional food brokers who are actually manufacturers' agents, representing noncompeting food lines and selling to chains, wholesalers, retailer cooperatives, and institutional buyers. Because these brokers take over the selling function for the manufacturers they represent, and because they can usually sell at a lower cost than could the manufacturers were they to set up their own selling organizations, they do not add to the cost of distribution.

On the other hand, most manufacturers of specialty products will sell only directly. They may prefer to set up a relatively few franchised retail dealers, sometimes on an exclusive agency basis. They maintain a close working relationship with their selected outlets, making sure that store stocks are complete and up-to-date, that planned promotions are executed, that salespeople are properly trained, and that the product is properly installed and serviced if required. Under federal law, the manufacturer is barred from contracting with the buyer (as distinct from an agent) to prevent the latter from handling competing goods; but on his or her own volition, the buyer may avoid competing products in order to become identified as the local headquarters for a well-known specialty line.

Such arrangements often work out well for the store, but certain contingent dangers must be recognized before the buyer enters into such arrangements:

1. The manufacturer may set a sales quota most difficult to attain as the price for permitting the buyer to retain the franchise.
2. The manufacturer may insist on a large merchandise investment and thus limit the buyer's opportunity to exploit other lines, when his entire operation is not franchised.
3. The manufacturer may attempt to dictate the amount of promotional attention the goods are to receive and may disrupt a balanced promotional plan.
4. The seller's suggested retail prices may not continue to provide an adequate markup for the store.

The Case for the Wholesaler

Where the buyer has a choice as to whether to buy from a wholesaler or direct from the manufacturer or a selling agent, the decision is based on a combination of factors. In buying a convenience goods item that is to be replaced in relatively small quantities at frequent intervals, a local wholesaler is the usual choice. This resource will maintain a broad assortment ready for quick delivery and will accept small orders. Most small stores and many expanding retailers that carry the products of many manufacturers must of necessity operate with minimum inventories, and even these must be partially financed by liberal credit terms. Nor are they in a position to plan their merchandise requirements far ahead or to buy large quantities at one time. The wholesaler is literally made to order to this set of requirements. Although the prices will be somewhat higher than direct prices from the manufacturer shipped in large quantities, the extra cost will probably be more than offset by the savings in inventory carrying costs, in the avoidance of lost sales due to delay in obtaining replenishments, and by savings in freight costs.

Wholesalers have come to realize that their success is dependent on the success of the smaller independent merchants. Accordingly, they are ready to act as strategists for their customers' competitive battles. They provide them point-of-sale promotional material and special merchandise for promotion. They provide merchandising and managerial assistance and aid in layout and store fixturing. Many wholesalers, especially in the food and drug fields, have set up voluntary chains by entering into contracts with their retail customers to supply them with most of the services that the chain provides its units, in exchange for the assurance of continuing patronage covering the store's major requirements.[12]

When large stores use wholesalers

Even large retailers find buying from the wholesaler profitable under special circumstances. One is in the buying of fringe items where even large stores handle small quantities. Even the largest stores and chains carry many products of low unit value and small customer demand that cannot be economically ordered direct. Another special circumstance is in getting quick shipments where direct orders would take too long. The wholesaler maintains a wide choice of staples accessible to the store and ready for immediate delivery and makes it possible for a retailer to fill in stock quickly when sales of some item exceed estimated expectations. This makes maximum sales with a low stock possible. Many large retailers place opening orders and some large reorders directly with the manufacturer. They then use the wholesaler for emergency fill-ins or for interim requirements needed to balance out sizes or other selection factors. Imported goods are commonly bought through wholesalers, because both of these circumstances exist.

An example of the use of wholesalers by a large retailer is illuminating. A buyer of woolen goods in a large department store reported that he buys half of his requirements from wholesalers for the following reasons: (1) He can obtain short lengths on patterns, whereas manufacturers sell only in lengths of 35 yards or more. (2) He can obtain goods for immediate delivery that would take a few weeks to obtain direct. (3) He can return all pieces in excess of remnant lengths for full credit, whereas manufacturers will accept returns only under unusual circumstances. (4) He can obtain some desirable material sold under the wholesalers' private brand that he cannot obtain from manufacturers. (5) He can often pick up job lots below the manufacturers' prices. (6) He pays very little more for the new goods than he would have to pay if he bought direct from the manufacturer, especially in view of the freight differential, because the local wholesaler delivers FOB store.[13]

Use of rack jobbers

As supermarkets extended their operations into nonfood lines, particularly cosmetics, toiletries, and housewares, many of them found buying from a special type of wholesaler superior to direct buying from the manufacturer. This is the rack jobber who carries a limited line of nonfoods particularly adapted to the supermarket trade, who is assigned by the store a rack or shelf space, and who undertakes to keep a rack well stocked with quick-turning goods. He or she visits each of the stores by truck once or oftener each week

[12]Discussed in Chapter 3 under section on voluntary chains.

[13]The reader will note certain services that are performed by both wholesalers and resident buyers, especially in regard to market scouting, helping to maintain a steady flow of goods with smaller stocks, and providing promotional and management aids.

and restocks the shelf. A number of rack jobbers service each store, each handling different lines. Note how similar this is to the duties performed by detail people or route personnel.[14] Sometimes manufacturers provide special sizes of nonfood items to avoid direct competition with the standard sizes sold to traditional outlets.

The rack jobber usually makes better use of the space than would the store manager, who may be primarily a food merchant, unskilled in nonfood merchandising and prone to neglect a segment of the business that may be relatively small.

Because the rack jobber sells to many markets, he or she is able to generate sufficient volume to buy at lower prices from the manufacturer than could the supermarket unless it were a member of a chain or cooperative organization. He or she also receives jobber's discounts that may be denied the chain.

Typically, the rack jobber purchases a $1 retail seller from the manufacturer for 55¢ and sells it to the supermarket for 65¢. Although the market could buy the article direct for about 60¢, it would be achieving a cost savings at the expense of all the benefits gained from the rack jobber's services. Many chains, after getting started in nonfoods with supermarket rack jobbers, have decided to buy direct as they become expert in the nonfoods field.

Wholesale resources for fashions

There are at least two classes of fashion goods that even large stores commonly buy through wholesalers. These are furs and millinery. In the case of furs,[15] the wholesaler remains important largely because of the high degree of specialization among fur manufacturers themselves, most of whom are very small and financially weak, without enough capital to extend credit. Each generally produces only one or two kinds of fur garment or fur. Fur wholesalers, on the other hand, carry a wide assortment, offer extended credit, allow goods to be sent on memorandum, and can be better relied upon to stand behind their merchandise.

The Case for Buying Direct

Even though wholesalers remain important sources for convenience goods, large stores and multiunit operations are buying in increasing quantity direct from manufacturers.

In the fashion goods fields, with the exceptions noted, buying direct from

[14] A spectacular example of combined detail people and rack jobbers is the *L'eggs®* hosiery racks in supermarkets and drugstores developed by the Hanes hosiery people.

[15] The fur garment industry is largely concentrated in New York, but Los Angeles, Chicago, Milwaukee, St. Paul, and Detroit have important fur markets.

manufacturers has become the accepted rule, even for smaller stores in the big cities. There has been a tendency on the part of customers to shop in larger cities where broader assortments can be provided for clothing and home furnishings—assortments that are sold on a basis of "look-rightness" rather than of utility alone. These stores, often highly specialized, do a large enough volume with each source of supply to make it economical to buy direct and thus receive newly created styles more quickly than they could obtain them through a wholesale intermediary. Direct buying may result in lower prices too, because it is not necessary to pay a wholesaler a margin of profit or to pay for unneeded storage.

Wholesalers might get more reorder business except that their fashions are likely to be somewhat classic and geared to smaller stores. Fashion life is too short to stand the strain of an intermediate, time-consuming operation.

Again, there is much seasonal variation in customer demand for fashion goods. For example, in some parts of the country less than 3 percent of the year's sales of women's coats and suits may occur in June, and nearly five times as much in March. Storage by wholesalers is successful when production is irregular (as in the case of agricultural products) and demand is fairly constant. Where demand varies greatly, however, both quantitatively and qualitatively, it is not practical to make major use of the storage function. Fashion goods have to be produced just before the selling season; they cannot be produced regularly and held by wholesalers until the customer-buying season arrives.

Although the chief factors that have motivated retailers to buy direct are newer styles and lower prices, manufacturers also have sought out retailer patronage. Through direct contact with retail customers, they hope to prevail upon retailers to give more promotional attention to their lines, because the interest of most wholesalers is spread over so many items that no one item is likely to receive special promotional emphasis. If the manufacturer can deal directly with the retail merchant, however, he or she may obtain special display or advertising attention and may even have an opportunity to "sell" the merchant's salespeople on the desirability of pushing the product. Where a product is of a technical nature and requires installation and servicing, it is particularly important to the manufacturer that a direct line of communication be maintained with retail dealers. If distribution is too wide to make direct factory contact practical, the manufacturer can sell through regional or district distributors who specialize in the line or at least handle no competing products.

Buying convenience goods direct

Although buying direct from manufacturers or through distributors is the usual practice in the case of fashion goods and specialty goods, the retailer may also purchase some convenience merchandise directly, under the following circumstances:

1. When the goods are perishable and must reach the retailer directly with a minimum of handling to avoid deterioration. Most agricultural products, however, can be distributed with adequate speed through middlemen, who are able to provide a more complete assortment at all times than can most farmers.

2. When the retailer is able to buy in large wholesale lots, as in the case of chain, mail-order, and large department stores, and in the case of buying offices for a group of department or specialty stores.

3. Where the manufacturer produces such a wide line of goods or family of products as to make selling costs per typical retail store order low. The line of the General Foods Corporation is a case in point.

4. Where the wholesalers carry competing brands of their own and accordingly neglect the manufacturer's product.

5. Where many retail stores handling the line are located in a small compact area and can be easily contacted by the manufacturer.

6. Where public merchandising warehouses have been established to take on storage and shipping functions without taking title or negotiating sales. By taking over some of the wholesale functions, these warehouses can sometimes replace the wholesaler. They are particularly successful in the case of convenience goods that are thoroughly established or that are sold direct from manufacturer to home consumer and are not sold to retail dealers.

7. When the retailer wishes to develop his or her own private brands in order to acquire repeat patronage for him- or herself rather than for a manufacturer whose branded products may be carried by competitors. This policy requires direct dealing with manufacturers on the basis of specifications. Many wholesaler middlemen have established their own private brands and, unless they control manufacturing plants, are not in a position to fill requirements under specifications.

SOURCES OF INFORMATION ON WHERE TO BUY

In making contacts with possible resources for merchandise, the buyer has the following sources of information, listed roughly in order of importance:

1. *Past Experience* This is best made available for future reference by maintaining a resource file where a card record (see Figure 9–2) is kept for each resource with which the buyer has had contact. A more detailed record may also be kept of the specific items and quantities of each purchased in the past from each vendor. (See Figure 9–3, a page from a notebook called a "buyer's Bible" that is used in the ready-to-wear field.)

2. *Market Representative* If the buyer's store is a member of a resident

FIGURE 9–2 Resource card

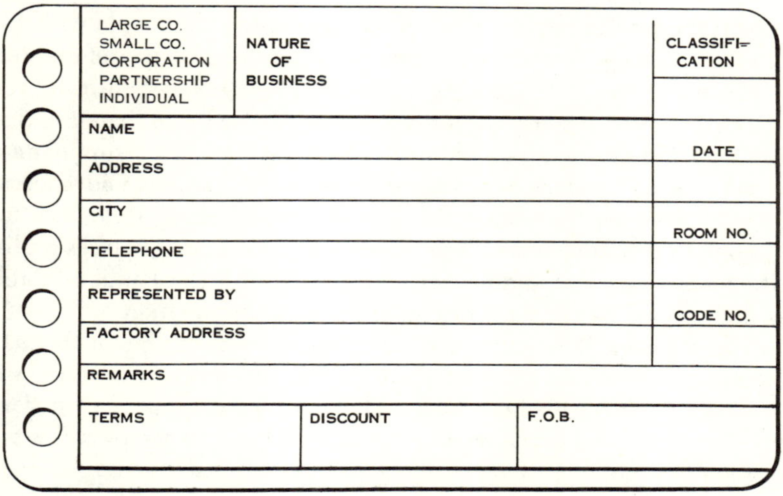

FIGURE 9–3 Buyer's bible

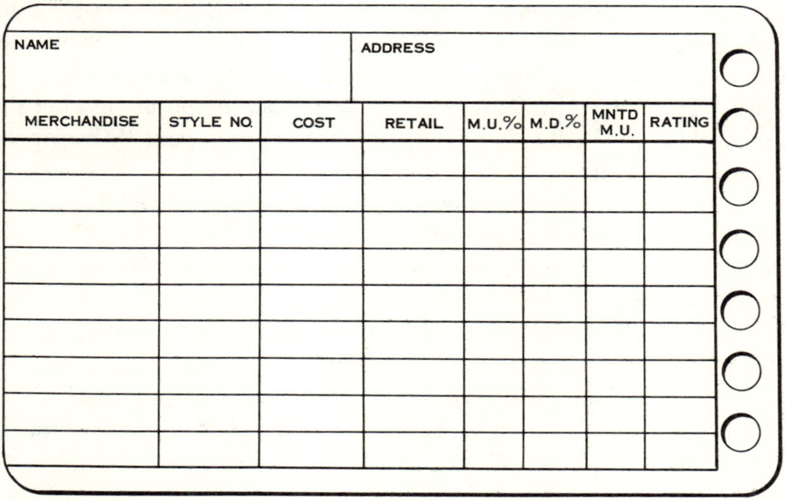

buying office, the resident buyer for this line is always on the lookout for new sources of supply and for new offerings by established resources.

3. *Salespeople* Manufacturers' and wholesalers' salespeople, selling representatives, and merchandise brokers are still the chief reliance of the smaller store. They often represent a number of noncompeting manufacturers and are often able to steer a buyer to a resource handling merchandise that does not compete with their own lines.

4. *Shopping Competing Stores* If comparison shopping reveals that a

product is selling well in another store, it is usually possible to determine its source. If the producer's name is not on the goods, salespeople with whom the buyer is already in contact can usually locate the producer of the item.

5. *Reporting Services* Agencies such as the Retail News Bureau[16] report on important new resources and also on advertised merchandise that is selling well in various retail centers and on the resources supplying this merchandise. See Figure 9–4. Fashion magazines, too, have advance merchandising editions that name the manufacturers whose styles are to be featured in forthcoming issues. For most buyers, the major services probably are the trade magazines and newspapers, such as those of Fairchild Publications, that provide a constant stream of resource information.

6. *Other Buyers* Buyers from stores in various cities frequent the market at the same time. They stay at favorite hotels and meet in vendors' showrooms and in resident buying offices. Where the buyers represent stores not in direct competition, exchange of information about resources and product innovation flows freely.

7. *Visits to Market Centers* Many wholesale markets are highly concentrated. A single building may be devoted to the showrooms of toy, furniture, or popular-priced dress manufacturers. By just walking through such a building, the buyer can contact many new resources and make a quick evaluation of their potential by inspecting the lines exhibited and talking to the persons in charge. The buyer also finds it important to visit temporary market shows where an exhibition hall or hotel may be taken over temporarily by representative wholesale sellers.

8. *Trade Advertising* By following the advertisements in the consumer and dealer press and reading direct-mail pieces, with which he or she may be flooded, the buyer can make the acquaintance of scores of new resources and approach those that are of interest.

9. *Trade Directories* Classified directories of wholesale dealers and manufacturers, generally compiled by trade papers, provide a convenient list of the resources available in the various markets and may prove useful when new resources are being sought. However, they are used mostly for addresses and phone numbers.

DISCUSSION QUESTIONS

1. Is it better to buy the cream of many vendor's lines or to carry in considerable breadth and depth the lines of fewer vendors?
2. If want-slips indicate a demand for a type of sport shoe that a store does not carry and that the buyer has not seen in the market, how can a resource for it be located? Indicate other sources of information, in the order of use, that should be tried if this source fails.

[16] 232 Madison Avenue, New York, N.Y. 10016.

FIGURE 9–4 Retail News Bureau report

BULLETIN... BULLETIN... BULLETIN... BULLETIN... BULLETIN...

NEW RESOURCES

BULLETIN... BULLETIN... BULLETIN... BULLETIN... BULLETIN...

MCG-WEEK ENDING AUGUST 20, 1976 ATT: MISSES SPORTSWEAR BUYER

CLAUDE
1407 BROADWAY
NEW YORK CITY 10018 (212-869-9050)

SIZE RANGE: 6-16
PRICE RANGE: $9.00-$15.00
DELIVERY: 9/30-10/30

THIS IS THE FIRST SEASON FOR CLAUDE AND IT SHOULD BE A TERRIFIC ONE, BECAUSE THEY ARE FEATURING QUALITY FASHION LOOKS AT A PRICE

THE DESIGNER LOOK SKIRTS ARE DONE IN POLYESTER AND RAYON WITH THE LOOK AND FEEL OF WOOL GAB. TOPPINGS ARE AVAILABLE IN SOLID OR PRINTS IN WASHABLE POLYESTER-CHIFFON.

HERE ARE SOME OF THE FAVORITES...... Priced at $12.00 is the slimmer skirt with tab watch pockets and slit front. Getting a good response is the gaucho with fly-front and tab waist at $11.00. A must on all orders and also priced at $11.00 is the a-la Polo skirt with button/tab slit pockets and detailings. All the skirts are done in the poly/rayon menswear fabric in khaki, bone, gray, black, rust, or skipper blue.

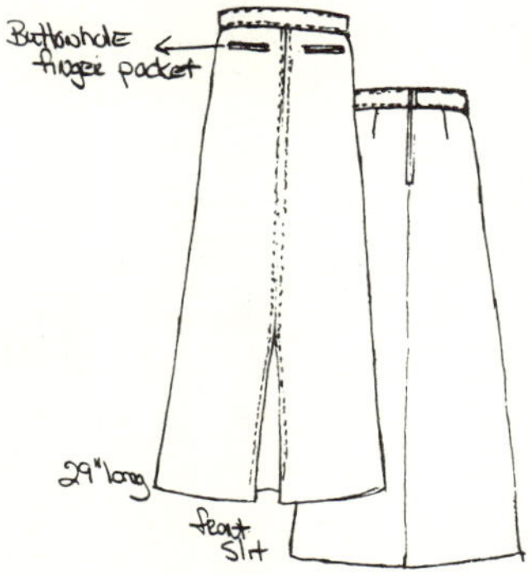

TOPPINGS........... Four styles are available in solids or prints.....The tunic with mandarin neck and long sleeves at $15.00. A blouson with keyhole detailing; $12.00. Stock-tie top with long sleeves; $12.50. And wrap tunic at $15.00. The solids are slightly lower in price. A group of skirts and pants known as the Disco Dancing group is made of slinky polo/silk in black, red or royal. Prices range from $12.00 to $13.00 in detailed styles.

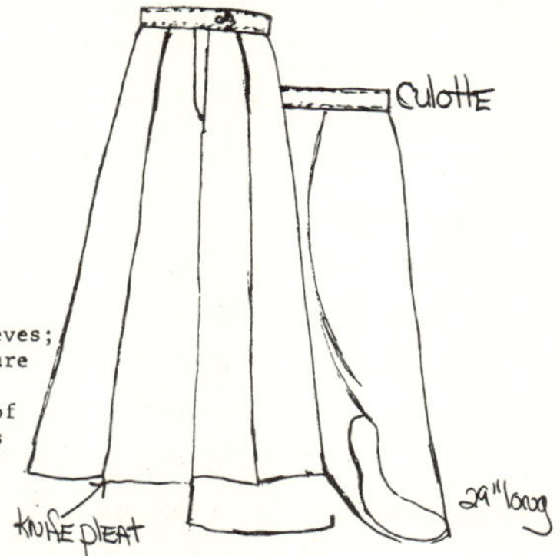

(SEE OTHER SIDE......)

A CONFIDENTIAL REPORTING SERVICE . . . ITEMS . . . IDEAS . . . RESOURCES

RetailNewsBureau 232 MADISON AVENUE • NEW YORK, N.Y. 1001

NEW YORK REPORTS • CALIFORNIA REPORTS • DALLAS REPORTS • FLORIDA REPORTS

3. Of the factors to consider in choosing a resource, which are most important in each of the following lines: men's suits, women's coats, mechanical refrigerators, kitchen utensils, blankets, millinery?
4. A vendor analysis at the end of a year reveals that one vendor's goods accounted for 25 percent of the entire sales. The margin (gross profit) on the goods, however, was only 20 percent, whereas the average expense

rate for the department was 30 percent of sales. The margin on purchases from other vendors was about 35 percent. Would it be wise to stop buying from this vendor? What justification may there be to continue the line?

5. Does it really make any difference to the buyer whether the resource chosen is a manufacturer or a wholesaler as long as the resource provides good merchandise and services?
6. Can the wholesaler afford to sell at as low a price as can a manufacturer who chooses to sell direct to retailers?
7. Are rack jobbers a temporary phenomenon, or are they likely to continue as an important factor in the distribution of nonfoods to supermarkets?
8. What sources of information regarding merchandise resources with which the buyer has as yet had no dealings would be of particular value for: (a) a small gift shop, (b) the central buying office of a supermarket chain, (c) a large independent furniture store, and (d) the sweater buyer for Sears?
9. What risks are faced by the buyer who has placed orders for stretched-out delivery to be completed by dates specified?
10. (a) Should the purchases of distress stocks from other retailers who have gone bankrupt be regarded as an important and profitable source of merchandise for retail store buyers?
    (b) If so, in what lines are there likely to be exceptional opportunities?
11. In analyzing the attitude of retailers to their wholesale suppliers who deliver by means of their own trucks, a research team grouped questions under the following headings:
    (a) Management knowledge and integrity
    (b) Pricing and discounts
    (c) Service responsiveness (keeping up retailers' stocks and handling complaints and returns and accuracy in billing)
    (d) Delivery (keeping promises and delivering at the right time and place)
    (e) Sales responsiveness (regular visits by sales personnel, follow up of requests, and sound advice)[17]
    Compare this classification with the one followed in this chapter. Which do you prefer? Why?

[17]From F. Kelly Shuptrine and J. Robert Foster, "Monitoring Channel Conflict and Evaluation from the Retail Level" *Journal of Retailing* (Spring, 1976).

chapter 10

Techniques of Merchandise Selection

Selecting the actual merchandise to implement the buying plans discussed in Chapters 7 and 8 is a *process of elimination:* of winnowing the chaff, of successive cullings. The "one right item" is not likely to pop up and announce itself; more often it must be discovered from among many that are nearly right. Before choosing, it is necessary to have a clear image of what is wanted, or at least as clear and concrete an image as creative planning can produce. Then it becomes easy to sort out all the items that do not conform at all closely to the image. Culling becomes increasingly difficult as the remaining choices come closer to satisfying the demands of the image. Often it becomes important to remember, after a line has been so narrowed down to a few things, that no single one is preferable to the others. This is the point where the indecisive buyer dawdles too long, fails to make a choice because nothing is quite right, or chooses too many things.

In one dress manufacturer's showroom, a buyer may have to view 30 different styles in one price range of one classification in order to select one or two; and there still remains a choice of colors. The buyer of a food chain may have to view more than 100 items in a typical week. The choice may be limited to two or three. On a market trip it may be necessary to inspect 1000 or more items to select 50. In a shoe show, housewares show, or toy fair, a buyer has to cover hundreds of vendors showing thousands of items, and all in 2 or 3 days.

There never seems to be enough time, space, money, or data to accommodate the requirements of decision making. Nevertheless, decisions must be made—constantly, swiftly, and firmly. What to choose and how strongly to back the choice is a challenge to wisdom. But wisdom can be cultivated. And one way to do it is to follow a set of rules for good procedure, to follow them very conscientiously and meticulously until such time as good habits and good judgment become ingrained—and good decisions spring from deep wells of trained intuition.

We have discussed rules for selecting resources. There are further rules for handling contacts with vendors, for market timing and trips, and for the selection of new items. These are the subjects of this chapter. Future chapters deal with rules for negotiating prices and terms, for handling orders, and for following up to expedite delivery.

MAKING BUYING CONTACTS

There are three ways of making market contacts:

1. By visiting the vendors' place of business.
2. By interviewing visiting sales representatives.
3. By mail, telephone, or telegraph.

Buying by Visits to the Market

Visting the market, with the help if possible of a resident buyer, is the best way to be sure of getting the best styles, the widest selections, and the lowest prices, and it is the best way to make contacts with new resources that have no well-developed selling organizations.

In spite of its importance in direct procurement of goods, the trip to market should be primarily for the purpose of getting ideas. Although new items or things should be procured, the actual ordering should be done back in the store or central office, away from high-pressure salesmanship.

Timing market visits and deliveries

Clothing and some home furnishings sales are much influenced by seasonal changes in demand. Manufacturers of these lines often set opening dates for the showing of their new seasonal lines. Table 10–1 indicates a use of these market opening dates for sportswear that determine when buyers should visit the market. See also Figure 8–1 for a general fashion calendar.

Buyers of women's wear formally place orders for one-quarter to two-fifths of their season's requirements at or following their visits shortly after manufacturer's openings. Reorders are depended on for volume but today are not always assured.

In spite of the fact that in most clothing and in some home furnishings lines, manufacturers make use of seasonal openings, there is a trend toward

TABLE 10–1
New York Market Date for Sportswear

November*	Market weeks for spring goods Heavy ordering
January	Ordering of spring goods completed Early inspection of summer goods
February	Ordering of summer goods completed Trips made abroad
April (post-Easter	Early inspection of fall goods
May*	Market weeks for fall goods completed
August	Ordering of holiday merchandise
October	Ordering of resort wear Early inspection of spring goods

*Major dates for those buyers who can make very few market visits. Buyers in stores near market cities may visit the market as often as every week.

having new styles available throughout the year. Retailers have been most successful when they have maintained a continuous flow of new merchandise roughly proportionate to the outflow to customers. The arrival of new styles every week is more conducive to customer interest than are two or three retail openings throughout the year with in-between offerings largely confined to reorders.

Final delivery dates

From the buyer's viewpoint, the final date for allowing delivery from the manufacturer is just as important as the opening date. For example, even though manufacturers of sportswear show their fall lines in May, deliveries are being made all through the summer. Intelligent buyers, however, set schedules, such as insisting that delivery of early fall apparel ordered in May and June be at least 70 percent complete by July 31, with the remainder delivered before the end of August. See footnote 5, Chapter 9.

Failure to schedule deliveries upsets monthly open-to-buy plans and leads to deliveries that are too late for selling need and productive only of markdowns.

Seasonal buying schedules

Ownership groups may provide buyers with seasonal buying charts for each type of highly seasonal merchandise. Table 10–2 presents a schedule for back-to-school bags.

Many seasonal staples and novelties, as well as fashion lines in clothing, are bought on a basis of periodic trips. For example, a toy show is held in New York in early February, and toy buyers place orders there for delivery

Table 10–2
Example of a Seasonal Buying Schedule in a Centrally Merchandised Chain: *Back-to-School Bags*

Collection of samples from the market	Jan.–Feb.
Decision on items	Early Mar.
Orders	late Mar.–early April
Shipments to stores	May
In stores	June 1
Reorders	June–July
Mass selling	July–Aug.
Close-outs	early Sept.

the next fall. The idea of this is that with the Christmas season fresh in their minds, they will be able to plan intelligently for next Christmas. The peak of the fall buying season is usually in May and June and, except for fill-ins, fall buying is completed in July.

Again, in the case of piece goods, fall buying starts in March with the inspection of import lines; it is at its peak in May and June and is over early in July. Spring buying starts in September, is at its peak in October and November, and is over early in January. Manufacturers' openings are even earlier.

Procedure in making the market trip

The procedure followed by a store buyer in making a market trip for apparel or home furnishings may be explained in 12 steps, many of which apply to the central buyer, also, when visiting resources; see Table 10–3.

Buying from Visiting Sales Representatives

In spite of the trend for retailers to go to the market rather than wait for the market to come to them, buying from visiting sales representatives remains an important method even for the larger stores and for central buyers. Because many resources—proven best by years of experience—send salespeople to the store or buying office, it is not necessary to insist on a complete canvassing of all other possible sources before placing an order.

Once a buyer has found that a vendor maintains a consistently high standard of quality and style and that the products find ready acceptance with the buyer's customers, choices will be made at periodic intervals and as a matter of course from the assortments provided.

However, a buyer must periodically check all resources to keep fully informed of developments in the field. The market is changing and the relative ranking of vendors' capacities to satisfy the buyer's needs is subject

TABLE 10–3
Steps in Making the Market Trip

1. Planning the trip
   (a) Preparation of a buying plan. See Figure 10–1.
   (b) Notifying key vendors of visit
   (c) Requisitioning travel expense money*
   (d) Clearing up matters pending at home and instructions of assistants
2. Providing market representatives with a copy of the buying plan.
3. Consulting with market representative upon arrival
4. Examining offerings assembled by the market representative
5. Visiting the retail stores in the market city
6. Attending trade shows and/or fashion clinics that may be billed for buyers
7. Interviewing vendors' sales representatives at the office of the market representative
8. Routing the desired market visits
   Order: (a) Higher price lines first to develop fashion and quality standards
   (b) Lower price lines to determine what may be going out of fashion
   (c) Middle, most popular price lines, where the volume buying will be done
9. Meeting chief executives in firms visited
10. Visiting factory workrooms and stockrooms, if nearby
    (a) Capacity to handle needed output
    (b) Evidence of quality control and good management
11. Keeping the store or central office informed
    (a) Progress of the trip
    (b) Changes that must be made in the buying plan in view of market offerings
12. Making notes on market information to pass on to assistants and to sales and promotional personnel at home

*The federal rules of tax-deductible travel expenses are quite specific even though they may not be audited by the IRS. The taxpayer is expected to keep a record of every outlay for entertainment, travel, and the like including transportation, meals, lodging, and entertainment, indicating what was spent, where it was spent, for what purpose, who was entertained, and what business was transacted.

to change. Buying from samples brought to the store or office allows more careful and accurate buying than can be done in the market. There is more time to look over each line and more opportunity to consult complete sales records and actual stock to determine (1) whether goods are really needed, and (2) the most desirable proportion to round out the stock. Furthermore, the assistant buyer, salespeople, and merchandise manager may be consulted before a decision is made. There is less danger of being swept away by a smart seller's enthusiasm when on home ground than in a strange market; also, the vendor can't enhance the apparent value of goods by display devices and live models available in his or her showrooms.

Calling on store salespeople to express opinions about samples of new

FIGURE 10–1 Buying plan

BUYING PLAN

Stk. & Inv. on Hand Today $ ______
On Order This Month Del. ______
Est. Sales Bal. of Month ______
Planned Stock E. O. M. ______
Open To Buy This Month ______
Planned Sales This Month ______

Trip Buying Limit ______ (month) Delivery $ ______
Planned Initial Mark-up % ______

On Order Next Month Del. ______
Plan Purchases Next Month ______
Est. Sales Next Month ______

Dep't. ______
Store ______
Date ______

ALL ABOVE SPACES ON THIS PLAN MUST BE FILLED OUT BEFORE BEING SIGNED BY BUYER

1	2	3	4	5	6	7	8	9	10	11	12	13
On Hand	On Order	Total	Estimated Sales Till Delivery	Stock Remain-ing	Planned Stock Desired	Open to Buy	Plan to Buy	DESCRIPTION OF MERCHANDISE	Cost	Retail	Total Retail	QUANTITY PURCHASED

Delivery Date ______ Signed ______ Buyer Approved ______ Mdse. Mgr.

merchandise before purchase leads not only to better buying but to better selling. The morale of store salespeople is improved as the buyer takes them into his or her confidence. They feel themselves a vital part of the merchandising organization and are more zealous in selling the goods in the selection of which they had a hand. However, the buyer must be tactful in handling the instances where the advice of counselors is rejected.

See all sales representatives who call

An important rule made by stores and offices is that the buyer must see all sales representatives who call and see them promptly, because their time is valuable too. Sales representatives are constantly bringing merchandise and ideas to the store; although many of these are unsuitable, no buyer can afford the risk of losing a good buy or not getting a good idea by failure to see a caller. Many buyers have seriously curtailed their value by limiting their contacts to a few established sales representatives, to some old cronies who have been allowed to gain a monopoly on the buyer's orders. Refusal to see certain sales representatives not only closes the door to an immediate opportunity but often leads to a sales representative's refraining from further attempts to present merchandise and instead making the attractive offer to the store's competititors.

With the growth of branch stores, vendors' sales representatives sometimes maintain a closer check on the assortment of their merchandise in each branch than the buyer can. Thus they should be doubly welcome—they supplement unit-control records and reports received from department sales managers in the various branches.

Methods for seeing sales representatives

In order to carry out a policy of seeing all callers, large stores and offices set regular calling hours—perhaps from 9:30 A.M. to 11:00 A.M., 5 days a week. Buyers hold themselves in readiness during this time to see sales representatives and do not let any other duties interfere. In localities where most sales representatives come long distances rather than from local offices, it is probably necessary to see them at the time of the day they can come; but the number of visiting sales representatives is not so great as to cause any difficulty. Special appointments often have to be made with out-of-town sales representatives outside of the regular hours, but these sales representatives should be instructed to arrange such meetings in advance. During the regular hours, many buyers find it desirable to give out-of-town sales representatives preference over local ones in the order of interview. The local sales representatives are around frequently, and time at their disposal is not as limited.

Speeding up interviews

To make it physically possible to see all sales representatives who call in a short span of time, buyers should distinguish clearly between those with samples and those without and between those who come frequently and those who do not. The man without samples can be given a greeting and a word as the buyer goes from the inspection of one line to that of another. Often the sales representative can come back, possibly with samples, or the buyer can say that there is no immediate need for such goods. Local sales representatives who are continually coming around with nothing new to show or say can be dismissed with a word and a request to come back when they have something new in merchandise or price. Unknown sales representatives should be given time to explain their propositions thoroughly enough for the buyer to determine their significance in relation to store needs.

Rules for Seeing Visiting Salespeople

1. Set regular hours to see salespeople; give time preference to those from out-of-town.
2. See everyone who calls during the hours set.
3. Work two sample rooms simultaneously.
4. Treat each salesperson as a friend.
5. Don't destructively criticize goods.

Inspection of sample lines

To speed up the inspection of sample lines, it is a good plan for stores located in centers where many sales representatives call each day to arrange two sample rooms for each buyer. While the buyer is looking over a line in one, the succeeding sales representative can be laying out a sample line in the other. Thus merchandise inspection is not held up while sales representatives unpack and repack their goods. It is a good plan for buyers to have a back entrance to sample rooms so that they do not have to pass large numbers of waiting sales representatives who try to make contacts out of turn.

In large resident buying offices, especially in New York City, the number of visiting sales representatives is sometimes so large as to make impractical the rule to see everybody. In these instances, sales representatives obtain cards at a reception desk on which they write their names and business. These are taken to the buyers, who mark on the cards whether or not they will see each sales representative, sometimes indicating that they will call at the sales representative's office or requesting that a definite appointment be made at another time. The sales representatives are notified of the disposition at once and continue to wait in the reception room only if the buyer indicates that they will be seen that day.

Attitude toward sales representatives

Perhaps the most important point in connection with interviewing sales representatives involves the buyer's attitude toward them. They should be treated as associates, there to aid the buyer to increase sales and profits, and not as pests who are wasting time or as confidence men who are trying to trick the buyer into an unwise purchase. Sales representatives are not only the source of merchandise, the lifeblood of the retail business, but also of ideas. A few hours spent in listening to rival sales representatives present their wares is a most valuable educational experience. There is an increasing adoption by vendors of the "service concept" in selling. Those who follow this practice make themselves quite cognitive about retailing problems and are prepared to offer useful guidance and counsel to those who will receive it.

Constructive criticism is respected by sales representatives, if not always welcomed. Sometimes a buyer suggests changes that will take the item out of direct competition. Sometimes suggestions may improve the styling or quality of the merchandise (see the section on specification buying later in this chapter) or lower the manufacturing cost and consequent selling price without lowering sales appeal. In short, constructive criticism may improve the selling speed and/or the profitability of an article for the buyer and for the manufacturer.

Buying Based on Mail or Telephone

Letters and telephone calls are largely depended on for the reorder of merchandise, the style, quality, and price of which are definitely known. Much staple merchandise is procured and fashion runners are kept in stock in this way.

New fashions and new qualities and styles in relatively staple articles are purchased largely after inspection of a sample or of the actual merchandise. Those smaller retailers, however, who are somewhat isolated from the buying centers, frequently depend on descriptions of new goods appearing in vendors' catalogs and in price lists. Here the retailer suffers the same difficulty in selection that a consumer experiences in buying by means of a mail-order catalog rather than at a store. Furthermore, the buyer who orders in this way does not have immediately the vendor's acceptance or firm delivery date.[1]

Where the store retains a resident buyer in the market city, "open" orders may be mailed or phoned to this representative carrying details of type, price range, and quantity. These authorize this person to select the most

[1]See Chapter 13 for further discussion of the legal aspects of the order.

suitable vendor and particular style or lot numbers. Orders may also be made out in the store on a basis of samples that have been submitted by the resident buyer.

In the case of a multiunit operation where a listing system is used, the store managers order by mail or phone from the catalog of listed vendors and items provided by the central buyers, as explained in Chapter 2.

SELECTING NEW ITEMS

In view of the limitations of time, space, and money, with which every buyer is faced, and in view of the multitude of new items continually being offered in the wholesale markets, the buyer must be highly selective. Although some of these items are distinctly new in type or function, most are variations of existing items—in such details as color, design, materials, and features that make the product more attractive or more convenient to use or repair.

Narrowing the Search for the New Item

The sales and buying plans, prepared in advance of market visits and discussed in some detail in Chapters 7 and 8, provide a framework or map that helps to narrow the number of different items that must be compared in the selection process. The plan reflects anticipated customer demand by merchandise classification, type, price, and often other selection factors. But it leaves considerable latitude for final selection.

There is nothing dogmatic about the order of elimination—as long as it is done in any series of successive stages. For example, the buyer may first want to scan the whole range of the vendor's offerings in order to get some ideas or perspectives and then quickly eliminate all clearly unwanted styles, leaving only clearly wanted or questionable patterns.

The buyer is now ready to settle down to the really difficult selection problem: The final choice, if any, from this vendor's line will be complicated by trading as the buyer strives to get the best buy for the store's customers within the limitations of the firm's and the vendor's profit needs.

The buyer cannot always find in the market an item that fits his or her plan. In this dilemma, the buyer may elect to change the plan somewhat. In any event, the plan would not be allowed to act as a strait jacket. But it does help to confine on-the-spot thinking to the more subtle considerations.

Considerations for New Item Selection

Table 10–4 provides a guide for the buyer as he or she analyzes each style or pattern that fits into the framework of the plan. Many of the selection factors that are to be incorporated as features of the product have already been considered in drawing up the buying plan. But the same considerations that have shaped the broad outline of the plan must now be applied to the individual items inspected.

TABLE 10–4
Check List for Selecting a New Item

A. Features of the product:
   1. What is its breadth of appeal?
   2. Does it have a relationship to items of proven acceptance?
   3. Is it in line with current trends?
   4. Does it have significant and observable distinctive features?
   5. Will it provide continuing utility or total satisfaction in use?
   6. Is it packaged to best advantage?
B. Relationship to stock:
   1. Does it fit into the buying plan?
   2. Is it clearly different from items now in stock or on order?
   3. Is it a key item or part of a manufacturer's distinctive line?
   4. Can it be reordered?
   5. Is it already available in competitors' stocks?
   6. Is shelf space available?
C. Reconsideration:
   1. Has the item been considered twice—from different points of view?
   2. Have the opinions of others been obtained?
   3. Can acceptance be tested by a small-quantity purchase?
D. Promotion:
   1. What is the best way to promote this item if purchased?
   2. What selling points should be passed on to the sales force?
   3. Will the seller provide advertising support and/or suitable display fixtures?

Features of the product

1. BREADTH OF APPEAL *Merchandise selection decisions always begin with the question of suitability to the buyer's clientele.*

Examination of the stainless steel plan (Table 8–3, Chapter 8) will reveal that a simple, free-flow design appeals to customers at all price levels. As previously mentioned, simpler lines seem to dominate demand as one goes up the price scale—but the one simple type called the "free-flow" has appeal across the board. On the other hand, this pattern of demand does not hold true for the buyer's sterling silver line. It should also be noted that the "heavy embossed sterling type" flatware was contemplated for a specific group of customers.

Individual Customers. Small-specialty-store buyers can actually buy with particular individuals in mind. They know most of their customers personally—their tastes and the current status of their wardrobes or of their home furnishings. Accordingly, they can come to the market with the needs of actual people in mind. As they look at the different styles, they judge which of their customers, if any, would like the style in question. When they get back to their stores with their purchases, they notify customers of what they have selected especially for them. Even if the styles are not just what customers would have selected had they been in the market themselves, the style may be preferable to anything else in local shops. Also, customers will be strongly moved to buy the style and like it because it was chosen for them—and there are few forces more powerful than the desire to be important in the eyes of someone else, in this case the store buyer who has represented customers personally in the wholesale market. *This ability to buy with individuals in mind is one of the two major advantages of the small store; the other is the personal selling service that can be provided.*

Limited Groups. An item that is suitable to a limited group of customers will obviously have a limited sales potential but may be essential to an assortment. Customers are not fixed in any one group for all their requirements. The grocer who buys a small quantity of York apples is satisfying the taste of a few who like a dry, crunchy apple. But these same few join the profitable many in their preference for best-selling beans, bananas, and barley.

Furthermore, because these limited groups offer a low sales potential, their preferences may be so ignored by other retailers in the trading area as to offer a fine opportunity; satisfying their wants may lead to a steady, profitable patronage. Everyone fights for a share of the big markets: Their volume potential must consequently be diluted among many competitors—with profitability getting somewhat bruised in the fracas. *The big share of a small market may compare favorably with the small share of a big market—at least in sales and profit yield per unit of time, space, and money expended.* Hosiery departments that carefully maintain a small stock of outsizes and other specialty items have discovered this truth.

In forming mental pictures of these groups and their requirements, the buyer may be guided by the theory that for every group there is a leader who sways the opinion of the rest, or a prototype who emobodies the characteristics of the group. Thus, if buyers could form a mental picture of these individuals and their preferences, they could successfully buy for limited groups.

Teen-age customers are a very special problem. They are great faddists. An idea may start quietly in any section of the country and sweep across the land with electrifying speed. But a fad may also be confined to a particular school, society, or community. Within the group, a fad may become the uniform of the day. Outside the group, it may be spurned. Nor are fads always short-lived; it is just that they do not give the warnings associated with a lingering decline. To buy a new item because it strongly resembles a currently successful type may be to buy a variant of something that is about to drop dead, leaving a heritage of costly markdowns.

Occasion or condition of use may limit the appeal of an item. Obviously, there is a greater market for versatile daytime handbags than for evening bags, for birthday cards than for wedding cards, or for toothpaste than for corn removers.

Price line and taste are two focuses of customer grouping that require special comment. Price is a quite obvious distinction, and most buyers are well aware of the relative popularity of various prices in each classification of goods. *But best-selling price lines may reflect a retailer's adherence to traditional practice rather than the actual needs of the community.* An item with features of broad appeal but somewhat high in price may be just the thing to point up the possibilities of up-trading a little. It should be sampled cautiously, as an item of limited appeal, and once again it should be repeated that individual price lines are a flexible element of demand within a price range.

Customers may also be grouped by varying degrees of discrimination in taste. The buyer's own aesthetic sensibilities may be offended by customer groups who insist on crowding bulky furniture and heavy draperies into small rooms, but he or she would be ill-advised to provide them only smaller pieces scaled to the size of their rooms. It is true, nevertheless, that social mobility, new status concepts, and cultural influences are creating a demand for better designed and more appropriate goods, and tastes in a community may change accordingly.

Major Groups. Many products of a utilitarian nature meet the needs of most of us. Basic foods, cleaning preparations, paper goods, toiletries, and household tools are examples. Here the buyer does not have to consider the requirements of limited segments of the population. The major selection features have to do with price, adequacy of quality for the purpose intended, brand preference, and attractive packaging.

2. RELATIONSHIP TO ITEMS OF PROVEN ACCEPTANCE Something "new" that is only a minor variant of something old and successful represents an easy sampling decision. Unless the buyer suspects that the attributes that made the old item successful are losing their vogue, he or she may sample the new in considerable strength. Risk increases as the new product bears less similarity to others of recent experience.

Radical Difference The once simple, staple bed sheet underwent a metamorphosis that illustrates the point. When the idea of color was introduced into this world of whiteness, it represented a radical departure from recent and even long-past experience. The buyer who prized leadership was faced with a dilemma. To forecast public reaction, buyers had to think back to the introduction of color in other consumer goods, such as autos and clothes for older women. How well and how quickly were these innovations accepted by the clientele? What other factors, such as psychological and cultural changes, might augur well for the acceptance of colored bed sheets? How strongly were they being pushed in the advertising media read and viewed by fashion leaders in the community?

These are necessary elements of decision-making for buyers who must be early with innovations in order to maintain leadership status. Other buyers have the advantage of gauging the normal lag in acceptance from the fashion-leader clientele to their own. They can wait for notice of forthcoming heavy promotion in mass media. They can wait for bulletins from their resident buying offices or reporting services.

Minor Difference Once the idea of color had been generally accepted, the move to printed designs on bed linens was a much less radical innovation. Early sampling in depth was now a "must"—even for mass retailers. From that point on, the introduction of stripes and border prints became minor variants of a tested product. In other words, buyers could see *definite trends in the analysis of their own sales.*

3. RELATIONSHIP OF THE ITEM TO CURRENT TRENDS The new item under inspection must be related not only to successful items already in stock but also to observable trends in fashion.

Our silverware buyer was faced with some trying decisions in the early days of the steel flatware vogue. When German and Scandinavian imports showed what could be done with the styling of steel flatware, housewares departments used the new lines to trade-up their kitchen flatware categories. As the vogue grew and the "new" product was featured in increasingly high-price lines, it began to compete with the lower ends of the silver flatware price range. So silverware buyers had to decide whether the newcomer was a suitable product for inclusion in their haughty departments. Like confreres in domestics, the silverware buyer had to think in terms of general trend in consumer preference. Of course there was some jockeying, because many waited to see what the "competition" was doing. But the aggressive, decisive retailers made their own decisions based on their own interpretation of trends.

They recognized the general trend toward sleekness of line and simplicity of trim (although not unbroken by occasional regressions to the tastes of a more florid era). It had already been reflected in the changing designs of silver plated and sterling flatware. They recognized the growing taste for "Functional" design. Particularly, they were able to equate the new flatware with the "less work for Mother" and the "casual living" trends. Here was a line of flatware that did not blacken through oxidizing and therefore did not need frequent polishing. The tendency of steel to rust and stain was being overcome by new metallic compositions and finishes. The new product could withstand the rigors of the dishwashing machines that were becoming increasingly popular.

It should now be quite apparent that trends are available to those who seek and see. They may be waiting right in the departmental cash register or may require more distant perspectives to see the longer, broader causal relationships.

In attempting to determine trends, it is only natural to seek corroboration of one's own opinion. One such source, *sponsorship,* is worthy of special mention. Buyers who can hold back long enough to watch consumer reaction in higher-priced, fashion-leading stores should take advantage of this lag. They should, however, make certain to choose the right stores as bellwethers. Some retailers buy only fashions of proven acceptance.

Certain resources are likely to be in tune with a given buyer's timing. So are certain media. For some buyers, sponsorship in highly sophisticated "class" media may be too far in advance of the clientele's acceptance. It would be better, in this case, to watch closely the more popular media.

4. SIGNIFICANT AND OBSERVABLE DISTINCTIVE FEATURES A great many items are suitable for a particular customer or group of customers and reflect the current trend but lack any feature that sets them apart from dozens of other equally suitable products. A good rule is to pass them temporarily in the search for a more distinguished item.

A case in point occurred in the children's swimwear market. A basic knitted suit of elasticized material was excellently accepted. As so often happens, the garment became a price "football." One manufacturer, determined to differentiate his product and take it out of this price-cutting class, sought ideas from buyers. The result was a decision to incorporate the popular blouse-on effect. This was easily done by knitting a little more material into the suit, drawing it in at the waist, and finishing with a little corded bow. The garment subsequently outsold the original basic—and at profitable prices for both manufacturer and retailers.

In apparel, a good feature to look for is one that "does something" for customer groups; it should enhance a good physical attribute or disguise a poor one. One dress may tend to disguise broad hips; another have lines or patterns that slenderize the stout figure; another a neckline that covers scrawny necks; another a pocket that adds to the utility of the garment. Sometimes a classic simplicity is in itself an important element of appeal. A type of dress that achieved remarkable popularity was a simple basic, which, by the use of different accessories, could be "dressed up" or "dressed down" or just dressed differently. Its versatility was the distinguishing feature.

Sometimes distinction lies in the brand or hallmark; sometimes it is a style; it may be a trim, pattern, color, material, or detail of construction; but always there is the possibility of avoiding the commonplace. When silicon-coated frying pans appeared on the market, there was a rush to copy them in cheaper variations. Many became available, all with accompanying narrow wooden spatulas. One buyer lifted his price-competitive pan out of competition by the simple device of ordering a wider, plastic, and therefore much more practical spatula.

5. CONTINUING UTILITY *The buyer should picture the item after it has*

been in customer use for some time. This requires the development of a practical imagination, triggered by keen observation and grounded in thorough product knowledge. The handsome billfold of fine leather may have a weak inner pocket that will rip out before extended use. The pretty shoe with poor construction that causes it soon to gape at counter and quarter is no longer a pretty shoe. The electrical appliance that wears out too soon or turns out to be a costly repair and maintenance problem may have been a thing of joy at the time of purchase but certainly fails to give lasting satisfaction.

The continuing and total utility of a product cannot be accurately measured until it has served its term of use. But here the buyer faces a dilemma. With people continually hungering for change, it is expected that planned or inspired obsolescence will be fostered in the design and promotion of consumer goods.

Why make a fine serge suit to last for years or a pair of shoes that will wear and hold their shape "forever" when customers grow tired of them so soon? How many now want furniture items of such construction that they may be handed down as heirloom pieces, when they "go out of style" before the destined heirs have reached adolescence? "Purchasing agent" buyers must help to make these decisions for their customers. They must reconcile appearance, need for change, durability, and cost and ease of maintenance, with price. Although the weight of individual considerations shifts with price lines, one conclusion remains constant: *The customer has not gotten good value for the money unless rational and emotional satisfaction is derived from the use of the purchase.* This is to be distinguished from the comparable satisfactions felt at the point of purchase.

One way to assure this satisfaction for the customer is to learn about the construction and materials of goods. When our flatware buyer is working the higher-price ranges, he becomes very conscious about the percentages of nickel and chrome used in the blanks. He wants to know about the number and kind of finishing processes and the techniques of quality control or inspection. In the lower-price ranges, he knows that he must lower his standards—but not yield them completely. He knows that his low-priced promotional set will be subject to harsh treatment, in use and in washing. If it rusts or tarnishes or stains, or if the finish gets dulled or scratchy, his customer will forget what was paid for the set.

The buyer must envision the product *in normal use.* The material and construction of products should be *functional.* The cheaper the price line, the more important it becomes that the legs of a chair withstand heavy weights and rough usage. A heavy lamp shade on too slender a base can constitute a hazard—the product should not be carried—mere warnings will be forgotten. A walking shoe should not sacrifice comfort to style. An active sportswear garment should have roomy sleeves and strong seaming at points of strain.

6. GOOD PACKAGING An increasing proportion of articles are sold in containers. In such cases, the attractiveness and utility of the package is a major factor in customer choice. *Well-designed packages attract favorable attention and act as silent sales representatives for the goods they enclose.* The astute buyer analyzes the package as closely as the contents. If the former can be improved, the buyer makes suggestions to the manufacturer and may refuse to buy if improvements are not forthcoming.

Table 10-5 shows a convenient way to analyze the package.

TABLE 10–5
Check List for a Package

1. Protect the merchandise
   (a) in transit,
   (b) in storage,
   (c) on the counter or other selling fixture.
2. Conserve storage space and stock well in selling fixtures.
3. Avoid unnecessary weight.
4. Reduce danger of pilferage (such as a small product attached firmly to a bulky card that is hard to secrete).
5. Provide "eye" (sales) appeal.
6. Identify the product clearly (especially factors like size, price, color).
7. Allow a reasonable degree of inspection by the customer in advance of purchase, such as a cellophane covering or window or even an exact illustration of content.
8. Provide information on care and use of the product.
9. Be functional—easy to open, close, remove, and put back contents; or conversely—be resistant to breaking or opening. In some cases, the package may have protective features such as grommets in holes punched for hanging the package.
10. Have supplementary uses in addition to containing the product.

Weighing the merchandise features

Although the foregoing have been presented as factors to consider in selecting an item with the right features, there has been little attempt to weigh the factors. This would depend greatly on individual situations. Bernard W. Smith, Professor Emeritus, New York University Institute of Retail Management, uses the following weights as an illustration of fashion selection.

Fashions with Popular Appeal

Becomingness or wearability	30	points
Outgrowth of previously successful fashion	20	
Related to current trend	10	
Good taste (conformity with group mores) (good design)	20	
Sponsorship	10	
Newness and originality of variation	10	

High Fashions
(new and untried)

New and original design	25	points
Sponsorship	15	
Good taste	20	
Becomingness or wearability	20	
Related to current trend	20	

Rating Scale

80 and over—sure fire
60–80—good
40–60—risky
40 and under—don't touch

Each buyer can draw on experience to make up a scale suitable for the store product lines. This is just another example of a formal procedure that may be used to develop better subsequent intuitive thinking.

Stock relationships

The item under consideration should maintain certain stock relationships.

1. FIT THE BUYING PLAN Even if a buyer should fail to select the best style, the fact that an item in the stock breakdown is needed to round out the assortment enhances the chance of that style being accepted by customers. Decisions as to patterns and designs cannot be made until available goods are inspected, but decisions as to types, price lines, sizes, basic colors, and, often, materials should be made in advance and seldom changed on a basis of what is seen in the market. It is true that occasionally the poor styles available at a planned price or in wanted material may make it necessary to revise the buying plan, but this should be a deliberate decision and not merely a result of the careless buying of any style that looks attractive.

One feature of the buying plan is the retail price lines or zones into which purchases should be made, and the plan may indicate, too, the cost ranges into which the items bought for each price line should fall. But the cost quoted by the seller may be above this range and fail to provide the markup required. This may result in passing up the item or negotiating for a lower price.

The best procedure to ensure adherence to plan is to check off each item ordered under its classification and price line as it appears on the plan. Thus, at any time during the buying period, the plan will show what and how much should still be purchased.

2. DISTINCT DIFFERENCE FROM ANY ARTICLE NOW IN STOCK OR ON ORDER Slight variations that cause a virtual duplication should be avoided even if they are desirable from every other point of view. The goal should be to have

every new style add to the assortment in the customer's eyes. Always there is the question of how much business the new item will add to the line as opposed to stealing from or sharing with the sales of the current assortment.

A chinaware buyer has a rack in her office carrying the bread-and-butter plate of every style carried in stock. Whenever a salesperson shows a new style, the first move is to find the pattern in stock closest to the new pattern. The new one must be distinctly different from any already on hand to warrant further consideration.

3. RELATIONSHIP TO VENDOR'S LINE The relationship of the item to the manufacturer's line, of which the item is a part, must be considered. There is some difference of opinion as to whether a buyer should buy simply the "cream" of one manufacturer's line or buy most of the styles presented if reasonably satisfactory. It is no doubt desirable to concentrate as much buying as possible with a few key resources rather than to buy a style or two from many different manufacturers. Some high-grade stores have had great success with the policy of associating themselves with a few manufacturers noted for their designing leadership and of buying and featuring most of the styles created by these houses. The stores build prestige for themselves by reflecting the prestige of the manufacturer's brand as they create a well-defined character for themselves. Nevertheless, more buyers—particularly in the popular-priced fashion field—prefer to buy numbers rather than lines. They have found that even the best lines contain some poor numbers, and they insist that it is their responsibility to present the best merchandise the market affords, regardless of origin. Judicious selection of the types of clothes they wish to feature in any particular price range—whether these be tailored, sophisticated, sports, or youthful—will, these buyers believe, maintain a character to their stocks. The wish to buy the cream of different lines is, nevertheless, compatible with the desire to develop key resources. The buyer can concentrate most buying with houses that have proven their high merchandise and service standards without having to turn down the cream of other lines.

Concentration on best-selling styles also involves selecting only the best-selling items in a set or line. For example, a complete china set has 38 different items, but 50 percent of the volume is done on 5 of these: cup and saucer, 4- and 7-inch plates, fruit saucer, and soup plates. These are treated as "place settings," just as in flatware, and a substantial part of the inventory is invested in them. "Open stock" requirements are thereby sharply reduced. Again, there are thousands of screws in various materials, lengths, head sizes, and threads, but, by judicious planning, the buyer can select 36 that will satisfy every need of the householder and the majority of the needs of the professional builder.

4. REORDERABILITY Because more profits are often made on reorders of

styles rather than on the initial purchase, it is important to determine in advance of purchase whether a reorder can be obtained and how promptly. Some vendors are not equipped to assure that reorders can be filled, and some styles may have such localized acceptance as to make it unlikely that enough reorders will be forthcoming from store buyers to warrant further cutting or production of the style. Although special values or a short season may warrant buying styles that cannot be reordered, the buyer will give preference to those that can.

5. COMPETITION WITH THE STOCK OF COMPETING RETAILERS Whether competitors have already stocked the new item is an important consideration. Buyers are glad to consider the experience with the item by retailers in other communities, but they may wish to be among the first in their community to handle the line, possibly on an exclusive basis.

6. SHELF SPACE The department for which the new item is being considered may have no space available to house and display the new item in the quantities, sizes, and perhaps colors that may be required. If deemed important, the new item may have to be substituted for an established one, and the buyer will have to weigh the relative importance of the two.

Reconsideration

In addition to making sure that each item to be selected incorporates certain desirable features and bears certain relationships to buying plans and previous stock commitments, the buyer must always reconsider before purchasing and not buy solely on the basis of an initial hunch. There are a number of ways to reconsider:

1. MAKE A DOUBLE INSPECTION OF A VENDOR'S LINE In the case of outer apparel, the usual practice is to view the line first on models and later on hangers. At the first inspection, attention is centered on general appearance; at the second, attention is on detail—material, workmanship, special features. Again, having to inspect the entire line gives the buyer time to defer decision until all the various possibilities are in mind.

One way to assure reconsideration is for buyers to write out their own orders rather than to allow salespeople to do it for them. Writing the order gives a final opportunity to think over each item, make changes, and check purchases against buying plans. It reviews prices and terms and makes sure that there is no misunderstanding.

2. GET ANOTHER'S OPINION BEFORE MAKING THE FINAL DECISION "Two minds are better than one." If the opinion of another informed person coincides with the buyer's, the latter can select the item with more assurance.

In the store, the buyer can call on an assistant, key store salespeople, the fashionist, and, when a particularly large deal is involved, the merchandise manager. Because store salespeople are in continuous contact with customers, they frequently recognize what customers will like and not like; they are sometimes good judges of retail value.

In the market, the buyer may be accompanied by an assistant, the resident buyer, the merchandise manager, a buyer from another department or from a noncompeting store, or the fashionist. Even when the resident buyer does not actually visit the market with the buyer, he or she can provide a list of the styles that on earlier inspection were deemed best. One chain organization has a rule that two fashion buyers, or a buyer and a merchandise person, must always go together to market. For example, the better-dress buyer may accompany the popular-dress buyer to the latter's sources of supply. He or she will provide a different viewpoint often leading to more intelligent style selection.

The vendor may be able to provide information that reflects accurately the opinion of the buyers, or even of customers. He or she may be willing to show the buyer orders already placed by stores catering to customers with similar tastes. Better yet, the maker may be able to show reorders from these stores, indicating that customers have actually reacted favorably to the style in question.

Some chains, especially in the grocery field, have buying committees that pass on final selection. The membership represents different divisions that consider the items from the points of view of shelf, warehousing, profitability, servicing, and promotional aspects. They are not concerned with the sales potential per se, being inclined to accept the buyer's screening for this factor. Other firms, especially in fashion apparel, demand that the buyer present a lineup of samples for a new season before a certain percentage of commitments has been made. The presentation forms the basis of review and discussion by a merchandise manager or by a committee.

Although we have stressed the values of reconsideration and suggested getting the opinions of salespeople, merchandisers, and resident buyers, the final decision remains the prerogative and duty of the buyer (except when a committee takes over). Opinions of others are valuable, but they should never be used as a crutch.

3. MAKE INITIAL TEST PURCHASES There is frequently ample opportunity to reorder if a style proves of interest to customers. It is dangerous to base large initial orders on hunches. There are exceptions, of course; if an offer involves the purchase of an entire supply with no opportunity to reorder, the buyer may find it worthwhile to take a chance. No buyer can be successful by avoiding all risk; he or she must be something of a gambler.

During periods of scarcity, when materials are limited and priorities apply, as in a war period, little reorder business can be done. This is also true in apparel lines when Easter is especially early. But normally, a small initial order will be ample to gauge demand. When reorders are possible, it is foolish to order heavily.

Nevertheless, the initial order should be large enough to produce enough sales volume to determine whether there is (1) sufficient demand to warrant a reorder, and (2) enough of an assortment to permit the customer to act on a possible favorable response. Once buyers would try to sample a new style by ordering size 8 in red, size 10 in black, size 12 in red, size 14 in black, etc. Now they seldom miss a size in an important color and will buy at least 8 to 10 pieces in a new style for every store unit for which they are responsible.

Promotional opportunities

A final important consideration in new item selection is to think through a promotional plan for the item before making the actual commitment. A new item worth buying is worth promoting. Failure to plan a promotion in advance is likely to lead to putting the item into stock and forgetting about it. At times, an introductory advertising allowance may be provided by the manufacturer who will then assist in the promotion plan.

When a group of items is to be bought for a special promotion, it is wise to concentrate on new merchandise that can be sold at a single retail price or that exemplifies an important idea rather than to select something that is already in stock and not new to the discerning customer.

The buyer should decide exactly how to advertise or display the goods and what facts about it to present to salespersons and to the advertising department. Promotionally minded buyers are always on the lookout for items that the advertising manager and copywriters are likely to wax enthusastic about. It is important to obtain all the selling information possible about the merchandise selected. The manufacturer or salesperson should be encouraged to tell all about the merchandise, and any folders or leaflets provided by the source should be procured. One ready-to-wear buyer makes it a rule to jot down on her duplicate order copy the selling points she learns in the market. These are later passed on to salespeople and to the copywriters.

Except in self-service operations, every new purchase should be made not only with the customer in mind but also the salesperson. If salespeople are not sold, they will not present the goods effectively. If, by any chance, the salespeople react to new merchandise very much as the store's customers do, the buyer would be well advised to buy with them in mind. If salesperson reaction is not typical of customer reaction, the buyer must be prepared to "sell" the goods to the sales force.

After a new item has been in stock long enough to determine customer response, one of two decisions should normally be made: "Buy more of it promptly" or "Get rid of it promptly by markdowns or extra selling effort."

BUYING JOB LOTS AND IRREGULARS

Job Lots

After buyers select job lots, they still have a few additional considerations. A job lot is an assortment of styles that a vendor has been unable to sell at regular prices and is now offering at a reduced flat price per item. The general rule for the buyer to follow is not to buy a job lot unless it is cheap enough to ensure that the entire lot will be sold promptly to the store's customers at a satisfactory markup. Because a job lot frequently consists of merchandise of different values, it is a good plan to sort the offering into price classes before buying and to determine the total amount at retail that can probably be realized promptly. For example, a buyer may be offered 100 garments at a flat price of $8 each. Inspection and arrangement of the units by probable selling prices may convince the buyer that 20 can be sold in regular stock at $19.95. The rest can be used for a special sale at $12.95, with 60 selling at that price and the rest being closed out at $9.00. The resulting computation shows the probable markup results:

20 @ $19.95	$ 399.00
60 @ 12.95	777.00
20 @ 9.00	180.00
Total estimated selling price	1356.00
Total cost	800.00
Margin	556.00
Margin %	41% (556/1356)

If this is anywhere near the department's planned margin, it may be considered a good buy, because it provides a bargain offering for customers.

Dangers in job lots

A common danger in buying job lots is that a poor assortment may be obtained, especially from the standpoint of colors and sizes. Even though the styles and qualities are excellent, a job lot may be out of balance in end sizes and off colors. In such cases, the total expected revenue would be lessened, and the resultant margin would be too heavy a drag on the plans. The important consideration is to place a realistic valuation on the expected revenue.

Another common error is to buy an unseasonable job lot because it seems like such a great bargain. For example, in January, a manufacturer of winter dresses regularly costing $16.75 and retailing for $32.95 may offer remainders for $8.00 each, a price that allows them to be retailed for about $15.95, less than one-half the regular price. But January is late for the winter season; customers have almost stopped buying heavy dresses; light prints are coming into vogue. It may take a retail price of a great deal less than $15.95 to sell even a substantial portion of the lot.

Effect of job lot on regular prices

The job lot buyer should also consider the effect of the job's retail price on regular merchandise in the department. For example, a buyer with a considerable stock of dresses on hand at $16.50 may be offered a job lot of very similar goods that can be retailed at $10.00. But to introduce them into the stock may force a markdown on the regular goods before it would otherwise be necessary. The better plan is to sell out a large portion of the regular stock before the job lot is introduced, minimizing the markdown. This can be done successfully only by cautious buying earlier in the season, so that when the peak of demand is reached, the stock will be well below its peak. One merchandise manager handles the situation by putting the job lot into stock temporarily at a high price. For example, there may be on hand $59.50 suits at cost that retail for $115.00, and at the middle of the season a job lot of the same quality may be bought at $39.50 each that could be profitably retailed at $75.00 But this would force a heavy markdown on the former purchases still in stock. Accordingly, the manager marks the new purchases at $89.50 and takes a markdown of $25.50 on each unit of the old stock. After some sales at this price, the lot may be reduced to $75 and still provide an adequate markup.

Irregulars and Seconds

A certain proportion of imperfect and damaged goods is a natural result of manufacture. These substandard units are separated from the "perfects" during the inspection, or quality control procedure. Their proportion depends on the manufacturer's standards for "perfection," the efficiency of equipment and workers, and the rigidity of inspection.

Terminology is a little loose, but "irregulars" usually refer to unobtrusive imperfections or repairs; and the terms "seconds" and "thirds" may be applied to more apparent or extensive damage. Very often the performance or durability of the product remains unimpaired.

Many retailers buy these substandard products at prices that enable bargain offerings to customers. Generally the values so achieved are greater than those of cheaper perfect goods manufactured to lower specification standards. It is very common in "white sales," for example, to find "seconds" of high-quality sheets and pillowcases offered at prices equal to or below those prevailing for "perfects" of poorer quality goods.

Nevertheless, some retailers believe that their quality image is damaged by such offerings and therefore forbid buyers to purchase them. Other retailers encourage such purchases up to a controlled amount. Even those retailers whose dominant competitive weapon is low price are cautious about promoting too great a proportion of imperfect goods for fear of creating an impression of carelessness about quality standards in their offerings as a whole. Ads and signs should honestly spell out the exact nature of the offering, such as:

Irregulars $6.99
Made to sell, if perfect, for $10.95

Buyers are cautioned that one way to achieve this undesirable reputation is to be careless about identifying irregulars and seconds in the marking of goods, on display signs, and in other promotion. Another more insidious way of spoiling one's reputation is to buy from manufacturers who have low standards of inspection or who display carelessness about identification of imperfect goods.

Table 10–6 lists suggestions for the new buyer making merchandise selections for both regular and special offerings.

TABLE 10–6
Hints to the New Buyer

DO'S

1. Ask for the opinion of merchandisers, salespeople, and assistants as often as you can.
2. Check with your buying office, and determine the market's best sellers before you buy.
3. Carefully study every piece of merchandise. Consider appearance, quality of materials, and probable performance.
4. Look for items that will become runners and provide a steady reorder business.
5. Base the quantities you order on past sales of similar goods, not solely on hunches.
6. Buy what you consider to be an outstanding number even though your open-to-buy is exhausted. Cut somewhere else if you have to, but depend on the extra sales of the new item to restore your open-to-buy.

DON'TS

1. Don't pretend to be smart; ask the manufacturer to help you make a success of your job.
2. Don't try to redesign the manufacturer's line, but occasionally suggest a change in detail that should make an attractive style even more saleable.
3. Don't try to be a big operator who writes large orders.
4. Don't get pressured into writing orders before you have inspected all the lines you have in mind, but don't put off to tomorrow what should be done today.
5. Don't get excited over a bargain; be sure the merchandise is right.
6. Don't become obligated to any manufacturer by accepting personal favors.

SPECIFICATIONS, PRIVATE LABELING, STANDARDS, AND TESTING

Selecting new items today often goes far beyond selecting from the offerings that make up manufacturers' lines. It involves setting specifications for products and selling them under private brands.[2]

Specification Buying

Specification buying in its simplest form may be a request for minor changes in a product already manufactured; in its most complete form, it provides directions for manufacture all the way from raw materials to final packaging. Some of our largest retailers are today drawing up specifications for packages with as much care as is devoted to the specifications of the merchandise.

Buyers may suggest alterations that enhance the quality of materials, workmanship, or styling, or they may suggest the elimination of selection factors that add to the cost without adding anything significant or observable to the retail value of the article. Again, they may suggest changes that do not enhance the value appreciably but merely differentiate the product from those versions that will be shown by other retailers.

As already indicated, some consumer goods are today manufactured in factories owned by chains. In these instances, the goods are not "bought" by the stores in the usual sense. Rather, a specification committee works with the production manager to create a product that will be distinctive and "packed" with value.

Developing specifications

Buyers who develop extensive specification buying projects may submit their specifications to several manufacturers for competitive bidding or may work out the program with one or two selected, preferred sources. A joint discussion during the planning stages is likely to result in the best compromise among considerations of price, quality, and reliability of manufacturer's performance. However skilled the buyer and his or her associates may be, a competent manufacturer can often make valuable suggestions with respect to the specifications and manufacturing processes involved.

Profitability is usually worked out on an equitable basis. The manufacturer may settle for a small profit per unit, but the large, reliable volume involved lowers total cost ratios and gives an attractive return on investment. Nor is the manufacturer unmindful of the prestige that accrues from being selected by respected retailers to make their privately labeled products.

Some mass retailers attach a specification manager and staff to buying

[2]About 90 percent of Sears Roebucks' offerings are privately branded, and about 85 percent of J. C. Penney's are privately branded.

departments. Those people are thoroughly familiar with government and industry standards for products and therefore are able to counsel with the buyer on what constitutes commercially acceptable size measurements, material, and workmanship. The buyer is responsible for the final, overall balance of these elements, plus styling, in the finished product. When specification buying is done by groups through buying offices or other associative arrangements, the project may be carried out by a committee of buyers from several member stores.

One large retailer provides manufacturers with samples to be reproduced for its private brand. Initial shipments are checked by the retailer's inspectors to make sure that they conform.

These inspection procedures will continue at intervals through the life of the item in this particular chain. Careful buyers make certain that their products do not fall below the standards originally set. Where necessary, the retailer's own testing bureau or a public testing bureau is enlisted to aid in setting of specifications and in the maintenance of quality control. This not only ensures the general excellence of products but their uniformity as well. Customers like to feel secure in the knowledge that their repeat purchases will be just like the first. National brands make a strong point of this virtue.

Sometimes it is hard to measure standards precisely. In such cases, the buyer's informed opinion must prevail. We recall an interesting quarrel between a large-scale grocery buyer and a fruit processor over the texture and mounding qualities of applesauce, which was being supplied under the supermarket's own label. Although objective specifications had been followed, the sauce was "too fine" and "too liquid" in the buyer's judgment.

Volume requirements for specification buying

A prime requirement for specification buying is a volume of sales that can support large enough orders to make economic production runs. Mass producers must cut many layers of fabric at one time or process hundreds of items through a single machine setting in order to produce cheaply. Sometimes costly dies are involved for cutting or stamping material to required size and shape. Even for minor changes, a mass producer cannot alter the flow of operations. He or she must have quantities of sufficient size to make an economical "lot" for individual processing. Buyers should be on the lookout for manufacturers who make use of the developing minicomputers to achieve low-cost changeovers in equipment while the goods are in process. These cut down the size of the economic lot.

But the retailer who can meet the requirements is thus enabled to have an exclusively owned, differentiated product that could be a better "value for the money" than is represented by standard versions of the same article. In any event, the satisfied customer must come back to the original source for repeat purchases.

Private Labeling

It is this question of repeat patronage that is at the heart of the brand controversy. The producer seeks patronage for his or her product, regardless of the retail outlet. The retailer wants repeat patronage for his or her outlets. The buyers may be instructed to forego the initial pulling power of the producer's promotional investment and buy the identical product under the store's own private brand package and/or label. Or, as previously indicated, the buyers may alter specifications sufficiently to give the store's own branded lines truly individual characteristics.

Like specification buying, private labeling presupposes a certain amount of purchasing power, either individually or cooperatively generated. It also requires patience and promotional expenditures to build up customer demand. Slow-turning inventories and excessive markdown losses may have to be borne until demand is established. Quality must be controlled as explained in the section on "specification buying." In some product lines such as major appliances, it is so hard to compete against producer's established brands that only a handful of very large retailers have succeeded.

Besides repeat patronage, the following advantages are claimed for private brands.

1. Freedom is gained from direct price competition. Essentially comparable products must be priced competitively. But any differentiation avoids the need for slavishly following others who may want to sacrifice a given article on the altar of traffic appeal or low-price image.
2. Stores may merchandise as they will—unhampered by purchase requirements, timing, or presentation demands on the part of a brand producer.
3. Retailers enhance their own prestige with every successful promotion of exclusively owned goods and make ever easier the subsequent development of further items under their firm's names or private labels.

Standards and Testing

Although unremitting quality control is essential to successful specification buying and private labeling, other goods should not be bought like the proverbial "pig in a poke." A professional buyer is expected to become familiar with commercial gradations of goods. Rating agencies like Consumers' Union and Consumers' Research are active in disseminating such information to consumers. Powerful advertising campaigns by manufacturers of branded goods are continually spreading information, although there is some variance in the degrees of veracity.

Government agencies and the American Standards Association publish standards for many materials and products. A buyer may specify that a product should conform to these specifications and occasionally may make a sampling to check for conformance. Where more elaborate tests are required, a laboratory must be consulted.

Services of testing bureaus.

Few retailers maintain their own bureau of standards and testing, but outside sources are available for a fee. Those that do maintain such bureaus use them for all or some of the following purposes:

1. To help set standards and specifications.
2. To aid buyers in comparing competitive offerings and checking vendor claims.
3. To test performance of goods under conditions that simulate actual use.
4. To conduct research with a view to developing product innovation or improvement.
5. To check claims made in the retailers' own advertisements and displays.
6. To cooperate with adjustment departments in testing cases of customer complaint.
7. To check values against competitive offerings where value is not apparent on surface inspection.
8. To keep the buyers informed about labeling legislation and to check on compliance.

DISCUSSION QUESTIONS

1. What deviations from a buying plan may well be made in the market when inspecting offerings? What phases of the buying plan should probably not be changed in the light of market offerings?
2. Should most new items be selected because they seem to have a broad (mass) appeal or because they seem to have a distinct appeal to narrow customer groups? How does the answer to this question differ with the type of store?
3. Are there many opportunities to side-step price competition by purchasing items, comparable to those elsewhere, that have distinctive features not available in the competing items? Suggest a few examples.
4. Bring into class or describe an article bought some time ago that has failed to give satisfactory use. There should be a discussion of the question of whether the store buyer could have anticipated the difficulty before buying the goods.
5. Do you believe that able experienced buyers would consider most of the points in Table 10-4, "Checklist for a New Item," even though they do not think of their decision processes as involving a series of separate considerations?

6. Which of the points in the list are of special importance in buying packaged food products, sportswear, and decorative home furnishings?
7. Which items in the list are most likely to be disregarded by many buyers?
8. When a buyer inspects new lines in the wholesale market, what opportunities exist for reconsideration?
9. Under what conditions, if any, would it be wise to assign to a buying committee the decision about each new item to be purchased, with the buyer responsible for culling and defending his or her choice before the committee?
10. Should most decisions to buy new items be accompanied by decisions to weed out items now in stock?
11. What must be the characteristics of a buying organization to make it feasible to buy by specification?
12. Are private brands, incorporating distinctive specifications, likely to increase their proportionate share of the consumer market?
13. Should most large independent stores and chains install testing bureaus?
14. Do you believe that intuition or psychic sense can be relied on to select the new style item with the greatest potential for sales from a number of new styles that would also meet the requirements of the buying plan?
15. Some highly respected stores offer occasional bargains on "irregulars," whereas others make a point of advertising that they sell no irregulars or seconds. For the majority of stores, which is the better policy?

chapter 11

Negotiating the Wholesale Price and Conditions of Purchase

SCOPE AND PRINCIPLES OF NEGOTIATION

The buying decision, which finds expression in the buyer's order, involves three major considerations: (1) the merchandise both qualitatively and quantitatively defined, (2) the wholesale price, and (3) other conditions of purchase such as packaging, marking, delivery, dealer aids, and promotional allowances.

Even though negotiation with sellers has tended to center on price, there are many other matters that must be agreed upon by both parties. These include:

Terms of sale: dating and discounts and passing of title
Quality guarantees
Storage until need by the buyer
Delivery: when and how
Assumption of transportation charges
Packing and packaging for shipment and for resale
Ticketing by the seller
Reorder availability and price guarantees on reorders
Return privileges
Promotional aids and allowances
Possible changes in the product itself or in the standard size and color assortments provided
Long-term business relationship between the parties, including at times financial assistance to the seller

Thus every initial purchase from a vendor may require a negotiation; it is not simply a matter of accepting or rejecting a seller's price and conditions.

Principles of Negotiation

Successful negotiators observe certain rules of which the following are especially important in retail buying:

1. They obtain from management (a) the goals they are expected to achieve, and (b) the priorities assigned to various goals. These have already been discussed in Chapter 9.
2. They prepare for the negotiations carefully by analyzing their own needs, goals, habits, and intellectual and emotional makeup, and how these relate to the store's goals; and, so far as possible, they determine similar data about the seller.
3. They recognize that the trust of the other party in the buyer and in the firm is essential to a mutually satisfactory agreement. Thus, in all dealings, an attempt is made to be scrupulous in carrying out all commitments and to cultivate business friends who will vouch that the buyer can always be trusted.
4. During the negotiation itself, the astute buyer is careful to explain the needs of the firm and the logic of the agreement hopefully to be reached. For example, the buyer points out the probable resale price to the consumer and the markup that the store requires.
5. The buyer gives the seller every opportunity to talk, to express needs and goals, listening carefully to words, gestures, and facial expressions. The buyer is quick to note the matters on which both parties agree and to limit the points of disagreement to as few as possible. Because in the exchange of views both parties reevaluate their own needs and understand more clearly the needs of the other, both reconsider their original demands and try to come to a conclusion that is beneficial to both.

Bargaining: a Negotiation Process

The ability to obtain price concessions from the seller by any means, fair or foul, was once regarded as a requisite of the competent buyer. But today bargaining is recognized as a negotiating process. As indicated just above, this is the exchange of ideas between two or more parties for the purpose of coming to an agreement on a matter of mutual significance. In a negotiation, it is recognized by both (or more) parties that each has legitimate needs that must be respected and taken into consideration. The older concept placed the emphasis primarily on the price to be agreed on and not other arrangements, such as terms of sale, that might be of greater importance in the long run. It should no longer be a game in which one party must lose and the other must win, with the buyer concentrating on his or her own needs and goals and disregarding the needs of the antagonist. The conclusion of a negotiation is not to establish a winner and a loser but rather for both to win.

Although negotiations are conducted on the individual or personal level and also on the institutional level, they are today of vital significance on the international level, and buyers who have mastered the art may have an opportunity to exercise their expertise in the broader arena. But here we are concerned with the negotiations that a buyer of merchandise or service conducts with a supplier. Both parties may be involved on their own accounts or may be acting as agents for their principles.

PRICE NEGOTIATION

Necessity for Price Negotiation

Although for many buyers the vendor's prices and terms are commonly fixed, buyers of large quantities, and even small-scale buyers at times, have an opportunity to negotiate. With the pressure of inflation and sudden changes in the balance of demand and supply, many prices remain fluid. Again, many buyers do not have typical needs; they have special needs at certain times that are not reflected in a single price.

Although alert buyers are always pressing for advantages in price and terms, they distinguish between regular buying and buying of specials. In regular buying to provide and maintain assortments, they recognize that their success is more dependent on the purchase of the right goods, at the right time, and in the right quantities than in obtaining price concessions. On the other hand, when specials are to be purchased, price often plays a more important role. There is a market in many communities for "off-beat" merchandise at bargain prices. In fact, some highly promotional stores do more business on specials than on regular goods and tend to place price considerations above quality. In the case of fashion goods already manufactured and subject to obsolescence, bargaining is necessary. The seller must quickly procure the best price possible, and the buyer must negotiate a price low enough to permit quick resale at a margin of profit. Most retailers have a one-price policy: Goods are offered to all customers at the same price, and no individual bargaining is permitted. But if an article is not readily accepted at the original price, it may be lowered, or it may be lowered to meet competition, to create a special sale, to reflect a falling market, or to clear out odd selection factors. Vendors in the procurement market follow similar courses. A set price has much to recommend it in the case of the typical small retail buyer. But for many buyers, differences growing out of quantity purchases or special methods of sale must usually be allowed for if mass merchandising is to be achieved.

In the purchase of staples also, price concessions may provide a major advantage, but even here quality merchandise and top brands are not often available at bargain prices.

Price negotiation is sometimes the best way to arrive at the price of new products or new versions. The seller's estimate of unit costs depends very largely on quantity expectations, the average size of anticipated orders, and methods of packaging and delivery. Buyers' opinions of the salability of the merchandise at different price points, the size of the orders they are prepared to place, and the conditions of purchase that they require, all have a great deal to do with the setting of the seller's price. To insist that a wholesale seller of fashion goods set a price and stick to it would throw a roadblock into the profitable distribution of merchandise in volume.

In the apparel trades, there are so-called "carbon-copy" manufacturers who agree to duplicate any style at a submarket price. They may do so by skimping on size, using inferior fabrics, linings, and zippers, and performing poor workmanship. With the superficial look, quick volume may be achieved; the customer clientele is often willing to sacrifice quality for fashion at a price and continues to patronize the store that provides these bargains.

Elements in the Price Negotiation

In their attempts to negotiate advantageous prices, buyers utilize the following techniques:[1]

1. Estimate the retail value of the item under consideration

This is accomplished not by building up from the cost but by viewing the item through the customer's eyes and by applying to the estimated retail the markup established as normal for this line. Thus, if a pair of shoes seems to have the combination of quality and style to warrant inclusion in the buyer's $18 price line, and if the customary markup is 37½ percent, a reasonable cost would be $18.00 less 37½ percent, or $11.25. This may then be compared with the price quoted by the seller. If more than $11.25, there will have to

[1]As will be indicated in the following discussion, the application of the techniques presented is limited by the Robinson-Patman Act. The essence of the Act is to make price discrimination unlawful where the effect of such discrimination may be to substantially lessen competition, tend to create a monopoly, and to injure, destroy, or prevent competition (1) with any person who either grants or knowingly receives the benefit of the discriminatory price, or (2) with customers or either of them. The act is designed to prevent "anti-competitive" discriminations before they become unreasonable restraints of trade. There is a belief in some quarters that the Act is too rigid in its attempt to protect smaller buyers and that it tends to keep prices too high.

be special reasons to justify the low markup, such as unusual volume opportunity or special features important to certain customer groups.[2]

The inexperienced buyer should consistently practice guessing at the normal retail prices of every item in the line, not only in the wholesale market but also in other retail stores and wherever there is an opportunity to observe and check with acquaintances. He or she should make it a practice to evaluate the pricing elements and to estimate prices before looking at price tickets or inquiring about actual prices. In time, the buyer will become a fair judge of retail values, which by means of standard markups can be translated into cost equivalents against which to measure quoted prices.

2. *Learn to evaluate a quoted price in terms of the elements that make up the seller's cost*

Manufacturers often base their prices on a "cost plus" buildup. Sometimes their material and labor costs are higher than necessary because of inefficiencies, or they may allot a heavy overhead or profit burden to the price of the unit. The smart buyer attempts to master the costs of the manufacturing process in order to reconstruct how much it should cost the seller to produce particular goods. This is essential in the case of a private brand that the manufacturer is to produce to the buyer's specifications. If the price that the manufacturer quotes is less than the informed estimate, there is a chance that the manufacturer may try to skimp on material or workmanship. If the quoted price is higher, there may be production inefficiency or an attempt at a large margin of profit.

In practice, the buyer of fashion goods, even in some of the large retail chains, is not conversant with manufacturing costs, whereas the "commodity" buyer is an expert in them. The commodity buyer contracts with mills for quantities of yardage or other materials that are to be delivered to a manufacturer who is to produce the finished goods, such as domestics or denim slacks.

Table 11–1, provided by a well-known manufacturer, is probably typical of the cost–price structure for a moderately priced man's suit with the production in a southern-state unionized plant where wages per hour were about 50 cents less than in the New York, Chicago, and Philadelphia areas in 1976.

3. *Compare price quotations*

This may be done by shopping the market thoroughly by means of the personal visit or the visits of a reliable market representative, shopping the lines of visiting salespeople, checking information bulletins, and requesting key vendors to bid.

[2]See chapter 15 for a discussion of the conditions that justify a deviation from a normal markup.

TABLE 11–1

Cost Elements in a Man's Suit

A.	Polyester* piece goods (58 in.)—3¼ yds @	$2.80 =	$ 9.10
B.	Trimmings		
	1. Coat front	.80	
	2. Linings	1.12	
	3. Undercollar, pocketing, buttons, zipper, etc.	2.03 =	3.95
C.	Examine and sponging	=	.17
D.	Cutting and trimming labor	=	1.48
E.	Tailoring		
	1. Coat	11.60	
	2. Trouser	2.95 =	14.55
F.	Fringes @ 34.3% include vacation (3 wks), holidays (9), contributions to Union Funds for retirement and hospitalization (11.9%), state unemployment (4%), child care centers (2%), payroll taxes, etc.	=	4.99
	Total Manufacturing Cost		34.24
G.	Gross contribution toward—warehousing, factory overhead, shipping, selling, advertising, financing, G&A—Profit		20.76
H.	Probable cost (net—30 days)		$ 55.00
I.	Probable retail price (52.1% markon)		$115.00

* Poly Wool blend	@ $4.25 per yd	= $13.81.
100% Wool	@ $7.00 per yd	= 22.75.

Polyester goods need little sponging. Usually they are shipped "examine only." This is why this item has increased very little.

This item varies according to number of piles high in cutting lay. This estimate is based on 50% plain fabric, 25% striped fabric, 25% plaid fabric. Cutting plaids is 2½ times more costly than a similar suit of plain fabric.

The markon in men's clothing averages about 50% today. This is called a *keystone markon*. It is calculated as a percentage of retail price, not wholesale price. On the item above, the store might elect to retail the item at $110.00 instead of $115.00.

The competitive sealed bid technique is standard practice in the purchasing done by public institutions and by so-called "purchasing agents" generally. But it is seldom used by retailers in purchasing goods for resale, because factors such as brand name, fashion design, and proven reliability are important elements in item selection and because the best resources usually prefer direct negotiation to the trouble of submitting formal bids.

Comparison of price quotations does not imply that the buyer will simply select the lowest price quotation. Under the Robinson-Patman Act, one of the major conditions under which a seller may legally reduce the price to a buyer is where the seller is in good faith meeting the lower price of a competitor and thus protecting his or her business. A buyer may prefer to keep buying from Vendor A rather than Vendor B; Vendor A may deliver more quickly, may be more reliable, may maintain quality standards better, and may be more helpful in providing dealer aids. But B may be offering goods of like grade and quality at a lower price. The buyer is on firm legal ground to advise Seller A of the lower price offered by Vendor B and to ask him or her to meet it. Nor is it apparently necessary for Vendor A immediately to reduce the price to all other customers who may not be customers of Vendor B.

4. For fashion merchandise subject to obsolescence and other goods subject to deterioration, evaluate the asking price against the length of time remaining in the normal selling season for these goods.

Fashion goods have a short life, sometimes for a season of only a few months. If goods are offered at regular prices when the season is well advanced with the probability of declining demand when the goods are received into stock, a reduced price should be negotiated.[3]

5. Qualify for a quantity discount

The Robinson-Patman Act of 1936, which outlaws price discrimination in interstate commerce, does permit sellers to sell goods of like grade and quantity at different prices so long as the differences are limited to differences in the seller's cost of manufacture, sale, and delivery, growing out of differences in method of sale and in quantities sold. Such price differences are permissive, not mandatory.

The question of passing on to buyers concessions not in excess of the savings to the seller growing out of quantity purchased has been complicated by a Supreme Court decision in the 1961–62 term in the case of United States v. The Borden Company. The Court held that the lower prices charged by Borden to A&P and the Jewel food chains must be justified not on a basis of the total sales to the chain but virtually on a store-by-store basis. If the manufacturer must calculate cost savings in terms of deliveries to individual stores in the chain, it may prove (very) difficult to substantiate

[3]The Robinson-Patman Act permits price reductions for clearance purposes and because of changes in market conditions. But there is a question whether clearance offerings may legally be restricted to favored buyers, even though this is commonly done. Some appliance manufacturers attempt to make discontinued models available to all their customers in order to avoid the charge of being discriminatory. Where the quantity to be cleared is limited, however, such a general offering would be unworkable. In most instances, bona fide clearances can probably be made available to whomsoever the seller wishes, but to label a model as discontinued simply to make it available to favored buyers at a reduced price would seem to be discriminatory.

material savings in production costs. However, savings in selling costs would continue to exist. And manufacturers continue to argue that large, stable ordering programs aid substantially in reducing raw material, production, and distribution costs, especially when the goods are shipped to chains' distribution points and not directly to the stores. Litigation on this subject is sure to continue.

Even though a buyer may not be able to increase aggregate purchasing power, he or she can increase the quantities bought from certain resources. This end may be achieved by the following means:

a. Selecting a preferred list of key resources for each year or season and deliberately concentrating the bulk of buying with these; scattering only experimental buying. Even where this practice does not lead to a quantity discount, as in the case of goods requiring much manual skill, it does assure better service and, in the case of shopping goods, the obtaining of confined styles; it also gives the buyer preference when the seller is clearing out seasonal inventory at reduced prices.[4]

b. Placing a blanket order.[5] This is a firm contract for a major portion of a season's estimated requirements, with the buyer retaining the right to requisition against the season's order as needed during the season. The buyer is usually granted the privilege to specify size, color, or other detailed requirements on each of the requisitions. With price, style, quality, and total quantity determined in advance, the seller is often able to realize important economies in the purchase of materials, in manufacturing processes, and in selling costs. In the hosiery field, for example, dyeing of colors can be done quickly during the season, after the goods have been knit. Although the blanket order does not reduce shipping costs, it clearly leads to economies that may be reflected in lower prices to those who buy this way.

c. Investigating the possibility of obtaining a cumulative quantity discount. It used to be a common practice to grant the buyer a quantity discount based not on the amount of each of the individual orders but on the total purchases over a specified period, such as a 6-month season. Sellers of products such as carpeting have felt that the practice was justified in that it tended to keep the retail buyer reordering, without continual application of selling effort on the part of the manufacturer.

The Federal Trade Commission, however, has challenged the legality of

[4]Some large sellers refuse to concentrate their clearances of last season's models with large buyers for fear of being charged with price discrimination. This is not a problem in the fashion industries, where there is a relatively narrow market for any one seller's styles.

[5]In the shoe industry, blanket ordering is called "buying space in the plant." The buyer in effect contracts to utilize a certain amount of plant facilities for the stock of shoes to be drawn upon during the season. Chains depending on the listing plan, discussed in Chapter 2, often find it necessary to place blanket orders.

cumulative quantity discount schedules on the grounds that they may exceed any demonstrable saving to the seller in the cost of manufacture, sale, or delivery. When the buyer asks for or accepts such a discount, he or she should understand that the seller must be prepared to prove for a trial examiner that the special method of sale and the total quantities ordered have led to economies at least equal to the concession. It is easier to demonstrate such economies in the case of individual quantity discounts.

d. Point out the volume opportunities and increased profit for both the seller and the buyer if the cost price can be reduced with a corresponding reduction in the retail price.

e. In the case of staples, where the danger of a decline in market price or depreciation of retail value in the near future is small, order a larger supply to last longer than the customary turnover period. In order to keep inventories at a minimum, some buyers reorder small quantities very frequently. Less frequent and larger orders may qualify for established quantity discounts not now obtained and may also reduce transportation and handling costs. Of course, the buyer must compare the advantages of large orders to the extra carrying costs incurred, consisting of storage charges, and the risk of depreciation in value. The buyer must guard against vendor inducements to overbuy, offering deals that require stocking up with an exorbitantly large supply. But where a buyer has been reordering every week, for example, and can qualify for quantity discount and transportation savings by ordering every month, the change should be carefully considered.

Such discounts frequently take the form of "free deals." For example, the price may be $12 a dozen, with an extra dozen "free" if a gross is ordered. This brings the price down to $11.08 a dozen. The "free deal" is sometimes for other goods than those ordered, such as 10 packs of Brand X chewing gum with every purchase of 100 cigars. In all such cases, the goods offered are not "free" or are not a bargain in any sense unless the buyer can dispose of them profitably and create extra sales volume without costly promotional effort. Brand X chewing gum may be in such low demand as to remain, slowly hardening, on the shelf. The extra box of 50 cigars thus purchased at a "bargain" may be a long time selling—also getting dry and stale. The best buy may have been that of one box of 50 cigars at the regular wholesale price.

f. Occasionally, "free deals" are made available to all buyers regardless of quantity purchased. In such instances, they are given in lieu of a reduction in quoted price. When the future of the price trend is uncertain but a reduced price is necessary at the moment, the seller may prefer to offer a "free deal" rather than to cut the list price. "Deals" are also used by some national brands to force the distribution of items in the line that are in large supply or that provide a large margin of profit to the manufacturer. The buyer must weigh these deals in terms of the profit opportunity they provide: The buyer must consider the sales velocity of the total "package" that constitutes the deal and whether the profit opportunity warrants giving preferred space and extra display emphasis to achieve the potential. Also, an unbalanced inventory must be guarded against.

g. Cooperating with other stores in placing joint orders that qualify for lower quantity prices. The buying club is the simplest example of this plan, with each store in the group agreeing to purchase a proportion of the total, whether ordered collectively or by one buyer in the group. In the grocery and drug fields, retailer-owned wholesale establishments may perform the same function. In other fields, resident buyers consolidate orders for member stores by both group and central buying methods. Where the aggregate purchase is broken down and shipped to each store separately, the seller enjoys no economies in delivery but may substantially reduce both production and selling costs. Thus a price reduction may be justified on a quantity basis. Where the group accepts the entire order at a central distribution point, from which it makes delivery to its member stores, the economies to the seller are increased, offset partly by additional costs to the buying group.

6. Qualify for the functional discount of the wholesaler

In many trades, wholesalers are granted special discounts not based on quantity but on the function they perform in widening the manufacturer's retail market at minimum cost. In order to gain the cooperation of wholesalers in distributing their products, manufacturers find it necessary to offer the wholesaler a discount, larger than the retailer's discount, equivalent to the wholesaler's margin requirements. Although the Robinson-Patman Act makes no mention of wholesaler's functional discounts, they have generally been regarded as lawful on the grounds that the wholesaler is not in competition with the retailer and is operating on another level of trade. Thus a price concession to a wholesaler is not regarded as discrimination against a retailer who might purchase in like quantities.

To qualify for the wholesaler's functional discount has long been an objective of chains and resident buying groups. Chains set up their central warehouses that perform the wholesale function, but under current interpretations of the Robinson-Patman Act, chains may not receive the wholesaler's functional discount because they control and operate retail stores. They must justify any price differentials on a basis of quantity buying or special method of purchase resulting in a demonstrable saving to the seller. On the other hand, buying groups, consisting of independent stores or even groups of multiunit operators, have set up subsidiary wholesale buying divisions that often gain recognition in the market as wholesale establishments, particularly *if they make their services available to nonmember stores* that are not in competition with their members. Some of the resident buying offices have wholesale subsidiaries, sometimes financed by their member stores, that buy in their own names and resell to both member stores and noncompeting nonmember stores. The markup added is frequently considerably less than the margin requirements of full-service wholesalers.[6]

The goods are sometimes shipped to the wholesale subsidiary's warehouse and drawn upon by the stores as needed, and sometimes they are drop-shipped; that is, the vendor is instructed to make shipments direct to the member stores but to bill the wholesale organization for the agreed cost.

There is some controversy in legal and governmental law-enforcement circles as to whether retailer-owned and -controlled wholesalers should be entitled to the wholesaler's functional discount, because the stores that set up or associate themselves with such institutions are in competition with other retailers who may not have a similar opportunity. Some feel that such groups are entitled only to quantity discounts. However, the Robinson-Patman Act does expressly recognize that method of sale as well as quantity purchases may provide economies to the seller and justify a correspondingly lower price. Where a buyer-owned or -controlled subsidiary buys in its own name and takes delivery in its own warehouse, it performs an important distribution service for the manufacturer that widens the market at a much lower cost than is incurred if the manufacturer sells to each store outlet separately. However, where a buying group agrees on certain merchandise but asks the seller to bill and ship separately to each store, the group would in all probability not qualify for any functional discount.[7]

7. Set specifications for the product

In the case of fashion goods, chain, department, and specialty store buyers sometimes submit the designs and thus relieve the seller of some designing costs. This often results in a product that sells in great volume. Although the buyer has exclusive rights to the design in the store's trading area, the seller may be at liberty to sell it to noncompeting buyers. Buyers also suggest variations in the vendor's established product and packaging sometimes to

[6]The low markup is possible because the group deals in relatively fast-selling goods that all members have expressed a willingness to carry and because the goods are often drop-shipped.

[7]There is one functional discount or fee often offered by sellers that a buyer-controlled subsidiary may not receive, as the Robinson-Patman Act is interpreted. This is the discount offered to independent brokers who assist growers and grower organizations to find customers. In the past, some chains have set up subsidiary buying units that have demanded and received the brokerage fee. Federal Trade Commission and court rulings now make it clear that a seller may pay a brokerage fee to an independent broker who acts as an agent, but the seller may not grant the fee to an intermediary representing the buyer. The buyer must recompense any broker retained and absorb the cost of any *dummy* brokerage office set up. Thus a buyer has no opportunity to qualify for a broker's fee even though his or her own broker may perform important services for the seller, who does grant brokerage to his or her own agents.

eliminate costly construction details that they may deem unnecessary from the customer's view and sometimes to differentiate the product they are purchasing from the vendor's standard product carried by competitors.

If specifications are set up by the buyer, the seller is relieved of designing and brand promotion costs, and the product may even be simplified in order to reduce the cost of manufacture. Where the quantities purchased this way are substantial, the seller can often afford to sell for less, because his or her costs are less. Also, the new product may no longer be regarded as of "like grade and quality" to the merchandise the seller makes available to competitors; accordingly, there would seem to be no discrimination.

8. Assume unusual obligations

CASH AND CARRY The Robinson-Patman Act permits price differences growing out of savings to the seller, resulting not from quantity buying only but from different methods of sale. Thus buying cash and carry, when the supplier normally sells on credit and delivers, provides a basis for a price reduction.

ORDERING OUT OF SEASON Similarly, placing orders during a seller's seasonal dull production period, in order to level out peaks and valleys, is a service to the manufacturer and warrants an extra seasonal discount if made available to all buyers who buy out of season, forecasting their needs further ahead than is customary. For example, one concern allows a 15 percent discount on advance orders but only a 10 percent discount on fill-ins. The common justification for this discount on advance orders is that it results in the vendor's obtaining business during the slack period. Because overhead continues throughout the year, the vendor is better off selling at a lower price in dull seasons as long as the price allows some contribution to overhead. Even if the early order merely transfers business from a busy season to a dull one, the producer still saves, because a minimum work force can handle the extra business in dull seasons; at the peak, additional personnel and equipment are needed, and it becomes more difficult to maintain standards and avoid the expense of inferior and damaged goods. When the retailer or wholesaler accepts goods in advance of the season, the producer further benefits by eliminating storage charges and risk of change in price during the storage period. The discount may reflect this reduction in costs. If such discounts are granted to all buyers, they would not seem discriminatory, regardless of whether manufacturing costs are proportionately reduced.

PRIVATE BRANDS Perhaps the most important example of cost savings growing out of the assumption of unusual obligations by the buyer has to do with the development of private brands or buying goods with the seller's brand name removed.

If the goods purchased consist of the manufacturer's standard product but with the label removed and with the right to advertise the goods under the national brand denied, there are sound grounds for a lower price: The vendor need not prorate heavy advertising and brand promotion costs to the portion supplied for private branding. Most manufacturers of branded products have excess capacity and can achieve greater volume and profits by selling in two price markets rather than one. Many customers are more price conscious than brand conscious, and many volume retailers prefer to develop their own brands to assure repeat patronage. Some national branders, accordingly, are willing to give a lower price to the retail buyer who buys the goods without the name. They are convinced that the volume so achieved is mostly extra business that could not be achieved by their national brands. However, court rulings do not support the contention that a change in name or its elimination makes a product of different grade and quality and thus subject to a different price. So the buyer is on safer ground if he or she insists on a change in the specifications for the unbranded product.

Retail buyers assume a variety of problems and obligations when buying for private branding. Among others, the entire promotional cost is on them, and stockturn opportunity may be less, because they may have to place larger orders and carry larger reserves. On the other hand, they are assured of repeat business as the brand develops a following.

Another way for the retailer to assume extra selling obligations in promoting manufacturer's brands is through advertising and assignment of preferred shelf space. These are discussed in the next chapter.

9. Check trade discount opportunities

In many relatively staple lines that enjoy wide distribution, manufacturers frequently quote list prices with trade discounts. Although these are generally granted without specific price negotiation, increased discounts may be available to all buyers during periods of oversupply, and they may be reduced during periods of scarcity. The retail buyer should understand just what they are and how they are calculated in determining the true price.

The trade discount is a percentage deduction from a *list* price that *may* be a suggested retail price. This discount is usually equal to the typical markup requirements of the retail trade involved. Thus, if a battery lists at 20¢ (retail), it may be offered to retailers at a 35 percent trade discount, that is, for 13¢. Functional discounts may be tied in, with larger discounts or additional ones for wholesalers, industrial users, etc. Thus their discounts may be listed as "35 and 10," or "35, 10, and 5 off."

List prices are often set considerably above actual retail prices. There are two reasons for this: (1) In some lines, the trade discounts have been larger than the markups many retailers require, and through competition market prices have dropped below list; (2) manufacturers, often at the instigation of unscrupulous dealers, have deliberately set list prices above market prices in order to permit misleading price comparisons to the public. Although it is not illegal to advertise list prices that are simply for identification, it is illegal to use a list price for comparative purposes where it is not the local market price or the retailer's own former price. In practice, this rule may be hard to apply, because there is no accepted regular retail price for many commodities in the same trading area, especially for goods not readily identifiable and comparable. The same apparent quality of cultured pearls, for example, may sell in different stores at the same time over a wide range of retail prices.

The trade discount is used not only as a device to suggest the retail price of the product but also to provide a ready mechanism for changing prices. For example, on a falling market, a manufacturer may find it necessary to reduce all the prices in the catalog. Instead of going to the expense of publishing a new catalog, he or she sends a notice to the trade that an additional trade discount of, perhaps, 5 percent will be allowed. During a long decline, a long list of discounts may develop as a manufacturer makes successive additions. For example, in the paper industry, the discounts at one time were "10 percent 10 times over." This is not equivalent to a net cost of zero, because each additional discount is deducted. For example, if the list price is $1, the normal trade discount is 35 percent, and the additional trade discount is 10 percent, the cost is computed as follows:

List price	$1.00
Less 35 percent	.35
	$ .65
Less 10 percent	.065
Cost	$ .585

On a rising market, additional discounts can be dropped one by one, or a larger discount can be replaced by a smaller.

If the list price is regarded as 100 rather than as $1, as in the illustration, the net cost would be 58.5 of the list price. This is called the "on percentage," in that it can be applied directly to the list price to determine the actual cost. It may be calculated for any series of discounts commonly obtained and then applied to the total of any invoice cost bearing such discounts. For example, if the total list price is $1700 and the "on percentage" 58.5 percent, the net cost is 58.5% of 1700, or $994.50.

10. Check cash discounts arrangements carefully

The savings that can be realized by these devices alone often exceed the store's entire profit margin and usually represent a very high annual rate of return on the extra financial investment required. For example, with terms of 2/10 net 30 on a billed cost of $100, the buyer can "save" $2 by paying the bill 20 days sooner than normally. In the year, figured as 360 days, there are 18 periods of 20 days each. In each of these periods, the buyer can "save" $2. In a year, $36 would be "saved" on an added investment[8] of only $98. Thus the annual interest equivalent is 36/98, or 36.7 percent. Similarly, terms of 3/10 net 90 are equivalent to 13½ divided by 97, or about 14 percent.

A buyer simply cannot afford to lose cash discounts; it is cheaper to borrow at a high rate in order to become established on a cash discount basis.

Although the cash discount structure itself is becoming more standardized than it was once, and although strong vendors enforce their terms, concessions to the buyer still may take the form of extra cash discounts and freedom from having to pay on time to earn discounts. A demanding buyer may obtain an extra cash discount in addition to the standard one; a resident buying office may insist on an extra 1 percent "for the office"[9]; a chain store buyer may buy net,[10] that is, with the regular cash discount or a little more deducted before billing and with no dating that limits this concession to a normal discount period. Again, there is the semantic controversy as to whether large cash discounts such as 8/10 EOM are really trade or cash discounts. If really cash, the discount would be lost if the bill were not paid by the 10th of the month following shipment. If trade, the 8 percent would be taken off regardless of the time of payment. Tough buyers take the second view.

Such variations in practice are not countenanced under the Robinson-Patman Act. But the difficulties in the way of apprehension and prosecution are so great that the act tends to penalize the "gentleman" or "ethical" buyer in competition with the "tough" buyer.

11. Investigate the opportunity to anticipate payments

There is often an additional cost saving in connection with cash discounts, known as anticipation, that is obtainable by paying a bill before the expiration of the cash discount period. The saving here is considerably less than what the cash discount provides and has been often calculated at 6 percent a year. Stores that maintain a substantial working cash balance find this saving well worthwhile. The following is an example of the calculation involved:

[8]The $98 is called an "added investment" because, if the bill were paid in 30 days at net, instead of 10 days, the retailer would have the use of that money during the intervening 20 days. In fact, retailers have to borrow from the bank an amount sufficient to enable them to pay bills on such short terms. The student may compare the interest cost of $98 so borrowed against the savings accruing from cash discounts and anticipation.

[9]Such a brokerage fee is frowned on by the antidiscrimination laws and interpretations.

[10]Goods that are made to the specifications of a retail chain or cooperative group are commonly bought net. Others, too, may prefer this method.

Terms 3/10 EOM on an invoice for $100 dated April 28 is paid May 10. In many of the apparel trades, invoices dated on or after the 25th of the month are regarded as being dated in the following month. The 3 percent discount then is deductible on June 10. If the bill is paid a month early, anticipation is normally deductible at the annual rate of 6 percent [11] or ½ percent for the month. So a total of 3½ is deductible, yielding a net payment of $96.50.[12]

During recession periods, cash-hungry vendors are more ready to grant anticipation, but during better times they express considerable resistance to the practice. The accounts payable departments in some large retail organizations, however, have earned a great deal this way. These stores have fought for the anticipation privilege, taking off anticipation as a matter of course when making payments to a new resource and turning to the buyer to use his or her influence to make the arrangement "stick."

On the other hand, many small buyers never take anticipation. They may be ignorant of the practice; they may have no spare cash; they may be unable to borrow at less than 6 percent. And the calculation on small invoices is laborious.[13]

12. Reduce transportation charges by providing vendors specific shipping instructions

It is the standard practice among retailers to regard transportation and transit insurance on incoming goods as part of the cost of merchandise. Most stores procure most of their merchandise from out-of-town sources; as a result, transportation becomes an important element in cost of merchandise, averaging in department stores about *1.50–2.00 percent to cost purchases.* In some departments, costs are much higher, where bulk and weight relative to price are high, e.g., housewares.

The methods a buyer may use to keep these costs at a minimum include:

a. Prevailing upon vendors to absorb the cost or to bear the risk while in transit: Most goods are bought FOB factory, meaning that title passes as soon as the goods are shipped and all transportation and insurance costs are borne by the buyer. From the buyer's view, ideal shipping terms are FOB store, where title does not pass until the goods arrive and where the seller pays all charges. (See Figure 11–1.) Combination terms appear in the glossary of

[11]When interest rates are high, anticipation may be calculated at more than 6 percent.

[12]Some vendor groups have insisted that anticipation be figured on the balance after the cash discount has been deducted: in the example, on $97.00 rather than $100.00, making the net payment $96.515. Although this practice may have logic in its favor, the customary practice is to deduct both discounts from the billed cost.

[13]Some buyers "anticipate" bills after the cash discount has been lost but before the final due date. Thus a 2/10 net 90 bill might be paid in 30 days and "anticipation" be deducted for the remaining 60 days. This is 1 percent deducted from the bill. Such deductions are not usually regarded as fair, because the period between the discount date and the final due date is regarded as a grace period, with the full amount being due any time during the grace period at which the payment is made.

FIGURE 11–1 Illustration of the effect of selling terms on distribution

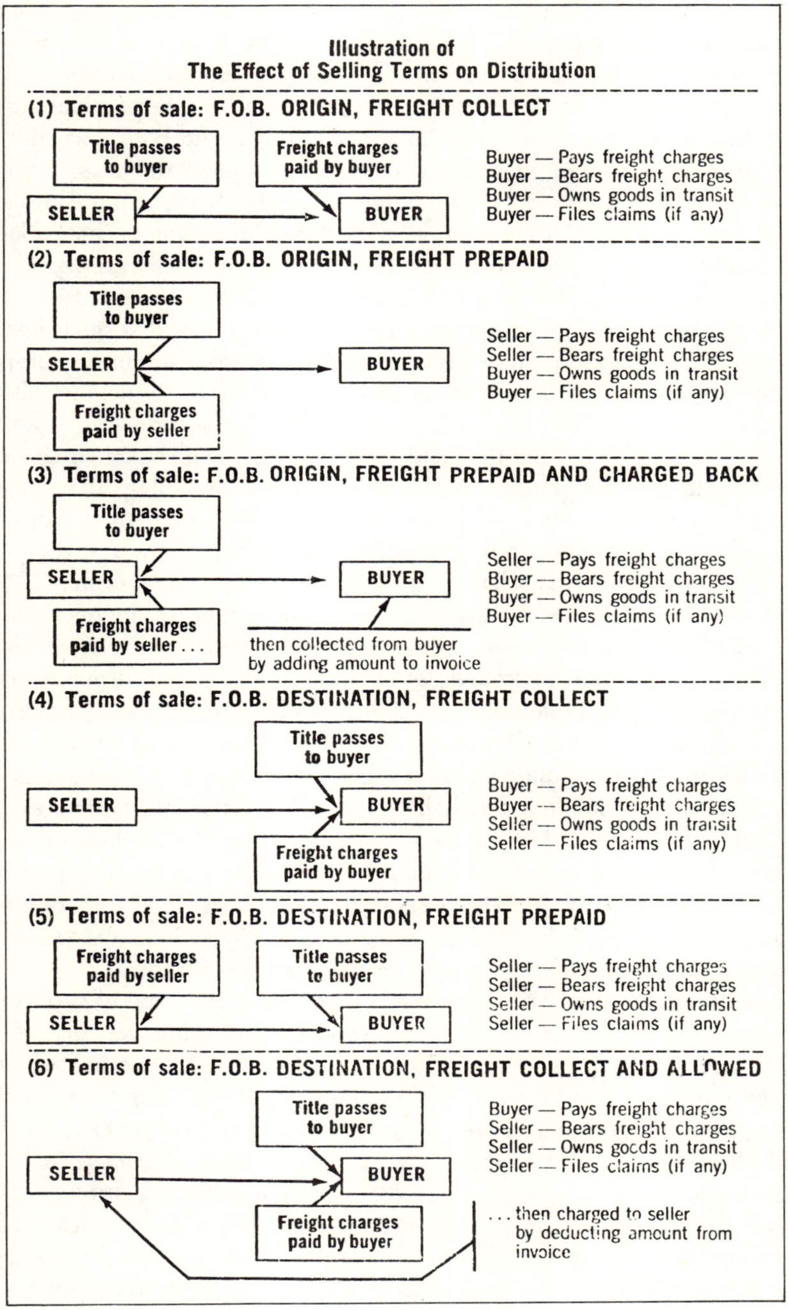

shipping terms in the Technical Appendix at the end of Chapter 14. Federal and state laws prohibiting price discrimination make it difficult to obtain any shipping concessions unless they are made available to all buyers. However, a vendor may legally meet the price competition of another vendor situated nearer the buyer. Thus, if a vendor in New York and another in Chicago are competing for the patronage of a Philadelphia buyer and both normally sell FOB factory, the Chicago seller may legally equalize the transportation charges by absorbing the difference between freight charges from Chicago to Philadelphia and the charges from New York to Philadelphia. The Philadelphia buyer would be on firm legal ground to ask for such a concession on goods of like grade and quality available from either resource.

b. Checking incoming shipments carefully to make sure that the seller has observed the transportation terms agreed upon: If the shipment is prepaid and the buyer is charged as agreed, the charge added to the invoice should not exceed the actual cost incurred by the seller. If the order called for the seller to pay the charges but the goods arrive collect or the charge is added to the bill, the amount should be charged back to the seller. If damaged, substandard, or unordered goods are returned to the seller, they should be sent collect, or the seller should be billed for the cost of the return.

c. Planning shipments in largest quantities of weight practicable: Carload shipments are much cheaper than LCL lots, and freight shipments of under *200–250 pounds* are to be avoided, because minimum freight charge is for *200–250* pounds. Reorder schedules should be planned in order to avoid ordering less than the minimum at a time; suppliers should be charged back when they make partial shipments at extra total cost; and arrangements should be made through a packing company or freight forwarding company to receive and consolidate small shipments from different vendors to take advantage of carload and "piggyback" rates. It is sometimes cheaper to pay for more pounds than actually shipped. For example, one truck shipment of 568 pounds was originally charged at the 100-pound rate of $14.46, or a total of $82.13. But it was determined that the rate on 650 pounds was $12 a 100, or $78—a saving of $4.13 by paying for 82 phantom pounds.

d. Routing the shipment: This involves selecting the type of carrier and the specific carrier that will be the cheapest considering delivery needs. (Small packages may be cheaper by parcel post than by *specialized small package carriers.*) For example, certain lightweight *bulk shipments (if they meet size and weight limitations) will probably cost less via parcel post than small shipment package carriers; special small shipment package carriers rates should be checked against parcel post rates.* Placing orders well in advance of the need may allow shipment by a slower but less expensive route (by water *or rail* rather than by *common over-the-road carriers,* for example.) On bulk merchandise, transportation is a major element in selecting a resource, except where the more distant resource is willing to equalize the charges. See Table 11–2 for an example of comparative rates.

TABLE 11–2
Portion of a Freight Comparison Chart

From NYC To:	*Via*	*Min. Rate*	*10 lbs*	*20 lbs*	*50 lbs*	*100 lbs*	*Rate Per 100 lbs above min*
Chicago, Ill.	Parcel Post	—	$ 1.88	$ 3.08	$ 6.68	$13.36*	
	UPS	—	1.85	3.10	6.85	13.70*	
	Motor Carrier	14.07				14.07	$10.22 under 500 lbs.
	REA	13.65				13.65	9.91
	REA Air**		8.50	12.00	20.61	25.70	
	Air FF**	5.60	5.60	6.80	17.00	17.10	
	Airline**	12.65	12.65	12.65	13.50	19.79	

* Check size and weight limits.
** Rates indicated do not include pick up and delivery.

e. Specifying transit insurance: It is cheaper to instruct shippers to insure goods in transit at minimum valuations and to carry blanket insurance to cover any loss over the minimum than to have the goods valued at full price. On parcel post shipments, it may be less expensive not to have the shipments insured at all but to have the seller simply secure a receipt (certificate of mailing) from the post office to attach to the invoice as evidence of shipment of ordinary mail *(at a minimum charge.)* A saving can also be realized if a shipment containing a number of packages is insured as a lot rather than separately.

f. Developing better packing materials and methods: Weight of shipments can be cut down sharply by working with the seller to develop lighter but even more protective shipping containers. Some of the leading store groups have brought about some amazing results in this area. New packing materials and the application of engineering principles are making containers much lighter and providing better protection.

g. Checking descriptions of merchandise used on shipping documents so that the goods will qualify for the lowest possible rate classification: *All shipments must be properly, accurately, and fully described (in accordance with classifications regulations) in order to assure the lowest possible freight rate.*

h. *Having freight bills audited after payment* to make certain that the amount of charges paid is correct in view of the classification and weight reported: If discrepancies to the disadvantage of the store are found, a claim is filed against the carrier. Usually an outside audit specialist is used for this purpose, and the rebates resulting from successful claims are shared.

The functions of routing, classifying, and otherwise instructing about shipments to get the best compromise between speed and cost is known as "traffic management." Not all retailers are large enough to have a full-time traffic manager, but someone in the controller's or superintendent's office can assume the function as a part-time duty. Buyers should, in any event, become familiar with traffic management at least to the extent to being able to give proper shipping instructions for most of their order.

There is no doubt that retail buyers, as a group, are paying considerably higher transportation charges than necessary. The chief cause is probably the careless practice of instructing the seller to ship the "best way" or the "cheapest way." This is really an invitation to the vendor to ship the most convenient way. Another major cause is careless checking at the store—failure to make sure that the vendor actually follows the instructions given.

13. Check all services to be provided or paid for by the seller, and make sure that they are provided

These are discussed in the following chapter. Note the suggestions in Table 11–3 for buying in an inflated economy.

Strategy in Negotiating for a Special Price

Good negotiators often employ one or more of the following strategies:

a. They keep their limits hidden. They refrain from revealing at the start the most they will pay rather than pass up the deal. They do this by insisting that the sellers quote a price rather than stating how much they are willing to pay. This strategy gives buyers a clue as to the seller's limit and avoids them offering a price higher than what the seller really expects to get. Another way to hide the limit is to show little outward interest in the goods offered or in a particular lot discovered in the seller's stock. Even though the lot may be just what is looked for, any impression that the goods must be had is avoided, because this would permit the seller to push the buyer close to the buying limit. Rather, the buyer appears to want to buy the goods less than the seller wants to sell them. It must be recognized that limits that may at the start be in both buyer's and seller's minds are not fixed. The light thrown on the transactions in the negotiating process is likely to get both parties to change their original limits. The seller may be convinced that it would be wise to close the deal at a price below what he or she had thought was the selling limit, and/or the buyer may decide that the opportunity of a successful promotion, at a higher price than he or she had first conceived of as a limit, is still too good to pass up.

TABLE 11–3

Suggestions for Buying in an Inflated Economy

1. Resist or offset price rises by such devices as pushing for cash discounts, promotional allowances, and extended credit terms as well as prepayment of transportation charges by the seller.
2. Consolidate orders with fewer suppliers in order to obtain quantity and seasonal discounts.
3. Search for substitutes if prices of items in demand are getting too high.
4. Avoid overordering of goods in advance of production, because inflation may not affect goods already on the market.
5. Put the emphasis on fast-moving goods that yield a high return on the merchandise investment.
6. Increase insurance coverage to protect the inflated value of the inventory against loss.
7. Resist manufacturer's price quotations that are subject to upward adjustment in price in case the sellers' wage, rent, and interest expenses increase before the delivery date.

b. The buyer avoids a long drawn out negotiation, so often common in the Orient, by indicating the importance of a prompt deal and the amount of time to give to the discussion. Although respecting the right of the seller to think over a proposition, the buyer sets a time limit for a decision.

c. If the buyer represents a company and is not buying in his or her own right, he or she often welcomes a limitation of authority. If the merchandise manager can be blamed for setting a certain maximum price, the seller may adjust his or her price accordingly.

d. Where, after some degree of negotiation, the amount that the buyer bids is only somewhat less than what the seller asks, the suggestion to split the difference may be successful. If the buyer has offered 85¢ and the seller has asked 95¢, the deal may be made at 90¢, provided that this price is within the limits of both parties. This strategy must be used carefully, however, because if the suggested split is below the seller's limit, the negotiations may be broken off.

e. Where a number of issues are involved in the deal, the buyer negotiates for one issue at a time. This is usually price, after which terms of sale and other arrangements are taken up one by one. However, these matters are often interrelated, and price cannot always be the first issue settled. Time of delivery or the store's plans to promote the goods may be overriding considerations. If it is difficult to get a prompt agreement on price, it may be wise to decide on all other conditions surrounding the sale that are clearly advantageous to both parties. It may then be relatively easy to decide on the price.

Sharp practice

Bargaining at its worst is a chiseling device to obtain concessions not justified by the economics of the situation. Buyers sometimes offer to buy at inflated billed costs (called "loading") provided the cash discount rate is increased proportionately. For example, the billed cost may be $16.75 and the terms 2/10 EOM. The buyer demands an 8 percent discount and suggests that the price be adjusted to $17.84. In either case, the net cost would be $16.415. But once the buyer is established as an 8 percent customer, he or she may attempt to deduct 8 percent on future purchases that have been quoted on a 2 percent basis.

Other examples of sharp practice are to promise big future orders that never materialize, to ridicule the vendor for "pettiness" in holding out for a regular price, and to threaten with a boycott. Such practices are manifestly unfair and tend to injure the buyer even more than the seller. The former gets an unsavory reputation in the market, and smart vendors take great satisfaction in getting the better of the bargain. Again, as already indicated, this kind of buyer may be so intent on getting bargains that he or she fails to select the right goods.

Bargaining, at its best, is tough negotiation. The buyer with a broad knowledge of customer demand, of costs, of competitive offerings, and of the person with whom he or she is to deal negotiates for an agreement that will be profitable in the long run and still keep open the channels of supply. Nor will such a buyer eschew sound techniques for fear of being ridiculed and called a "chiseler."

The ideal bargain brings profit to all: the buyer, the firm, the vendor, and the consumer. The buyer who drives an unreasonable bargain must not be surprised to find the vendor squirming out of the dilemma by sharp practice in the manufacturing process—if only by lowering the standards of quality control. The vendor thus shifts the battle to his or her chosen ground, and the buyer who is not thoroughly familiar with the terrain may find that the initial victory was dearly bought.

DISCOUNT MATHEMATICS

1. What is the annual rate of interest equivalent to terms of 5/10 net 60? Compute the answer in terms of the net cost, that is, on a $100 invoice, only $95 is prepaid.
2. Do the same for 3/10 net 90; 2/10 net 120; 4/30 net 60.
3. A bill for $500 bearing the terms 8/10 EOM is made out on August 6. Compute the amounts of payment that should be made if they are paid on each of the following dates: August 11, September 10, September 30, October 30.
4. A bill of $1000, carrying terms of 3/10 EOM, is dated April 27, received May 1,

and paid on May 10. Is anticipation allowable? How much should be paid on May 10?

5. Is it more advantageous for a store to purchase a lot of goods (a) at a billed cost of $100 and terms of "3/10 net 30," or (b) at a billed cost of $97 with terms of "net 10 days"?
6. A manufacturer of boys' clothing produces a suit on which he wishes to realize $8 net. To accommodate buyers who wish different discounts, he will quote the billed cost at any discount desired from 1 percent to 10 percent. Compute the billed price for each of the 10 discounts.

DISCUSSION QUESTIONS

1. Why is it important for a buyer to engage in self-analysis—basic business and personal needs and emotional and rational makeup—in order to be a good negotiator? Why should similar information be gathered about the vendor with whom the buyer is going to negotiate?
2. A textile yarn producer sells its product to a large weaving mill that sells yard goods to a leading clothing manufacturer who in turn sells to a large retail chain. The retail chain stopped buying draperies from the manufacturer, because he did not meet the chain buyer's specifications adequately. This meant a considerable loss of business for the yarn producer, who made many attempts to patch up the matter and prevail upon the chain buyer to renew his business with the manufacturer but to no avail. The chain buyer simply did not trust either the manufacturer or the mill to keep its promises to the letter. Finally, the producer sent its most experienced consultant, who had an unblemised record in the trade for integrity, to make another attempt. She visited the mill and the manufacturer and assured him that they could and would produce exactly what was required. She then called on the chain's central buyer, with whom she had had many dealings in the past, and assured him that she would be personally responsible for seeing that the manufacturer would deliver just what was needed. With little hesitation, the manufacturer agreed and placed an order for several thousand ready-made drapes. What is the lesson from this incident?
3. Is price negotiation more suitable for goods not yet manufactured or for goods ready for delivery?
4. Which of the six methods described in the text to qualify for a quantity discount are likely to be challenged by the Federal Trade Commission?
5. Do you regard the setting up of a wholesale subsidiary by a group of retailers a legitimate way to obtain the wholesaler's functional discount, or would it be a justification only for quantity discounts?

6. If a manufacturer sells the identical merchandise under both national brand and retailer's private brand, is the private brand of "like grade and quality" to the national brand? If so, how can a lower price for the private brand be legally sustained?
7. Is the cash discount device essentially a reward for prompt payment or a penalty for late payment?
8. If anticipation is calculated at 6 percent a year, is the saving large enough for most buyers to take advantage of it today?
9. If an invoice is paid after the expiration of the cash discount period but 30 days before the final due date, is the buyer entitled to any discount?
10. In the long run, will prevailing upon the seller to assume transportation costs and risks reduce the cost of merchandise?
11. Are there any advantages to the vendor in billing regularly FOB destination rather than FOB shipping point?
12. (a) Because the Robinson-Patman Act permits a seller in good faith to reduce price to a buyer to meet the equally low price of a competitor, would the seller have to determine whether the competitor's price offer to the buyer was legal? (b) Would the seller have to offer the lower price to other buyers who might not be aware of the availability of the lower price from the seller's competitor? (*Note:* Such questions are not readily answered, because they involve a study of Federal Trade Commission rulings, court interpretations, and an estimate of the enforcement "climate" in the future.)
13. Is the ability to bargain successfully one of the most important attributes of a buyer?
14. Is the Robinson-Patman Act tending toward standard prices and reduction of the amount of price negotiation undertaken?
15. A buyer who knowingly receives a discriminatory price may be found guilty of price discrimination, along with the seller. Does this mean that the buyer is well advised (a) not to study the Robinson Act? (b) Not to inquire what prices the seller is charging competitors?

chapter 12

Vendor Services Available to the Buyer

As indicated in the previous chapter, the negotiations of the terms of purchase include other matters than the merchandise and the price. The seller is often willing and able to provide services to the buyer, along with the goods, and to pay the buyer for services the latter may perform in giving extra promotional attention to the seller's product. And at times, the seller is willing to protect the buyer against eventual markdowns on the purchase by means to be discussed.

Under the Robinson-Patman Act, it is legal for a seller to provide services and to pay for services the buyer performs, provided these are made available to all competing customers on proportionally equal terms. Just what "proportionally equal" means in any given case is still a matter of dispute. It is variously interpreted by Federal Trade Commission rulings and by court decisions.

CHECKLIST OF VENDOR SERVICES

The variety of services that may be available appears in the checklist of Table 12–1. In connection with these, the buyer decides whether the service available is in the interests of the firm and its customers. It may be provided wholly in the interests of the seller, and the cost of the service may be reflected in the price of the goods. The buyer should pose such questions as the following:

Will the service or services increase the sales in my store or department or simply transfer demand from one product stocked to another?
Because the cost of the service is absorbed in the price paid for the product, is the saving in the store's expenses greater than the increase in the cost of the merchandise?
Is the seller in a better position than the buyer's firm to develop effective promotional tools?
Does the seller's interest in certain promotional tools, such as premiums, run counter to the best interests of the store?
Is the store's ability to function as a purchasing agent for its customers reduced when it looks to the seller for promotional services that are designed to move specific products over against competing products that the store may also handle?

In specific cases, the answers to these questions are most difficult, especially because the buyer is generally under great pressure to reduce expenses of operation and because a cost hidden in the price of the merchandise may escape criticism by management.

In the case of supermarkets in particular and for all promotional stores, the service the retail store buyer wants most from suppliers is the offer of specials—mainly goods whose quality is readily recognized by the customer and that are offered at reduced prices for a sale period. Along with such merchandise, dealer helps and allowances are welcomed.

Dealer Helps

In the case of convenience and impulse goods sold under manufacturer's brands, many of the aids listed in Table 12–1 are useful in attracting customer attention and are welcomed by the buyer. In the case of fashion and other shopping goods, the aids that educate the salesperson and that provide care and use information for the customer are important. Information on fiber content and care instructions must be provided by law for most textile goods.

Nevertheless, there is considerable waste in the preparation and provision of such materials, because better stores avoid cluttering up their interiors and windows with vendor displays touting particular products. Many small stores do use them, because they substitute for independent planning and execution. A drugstore may devote a whole window to a vendor-prepared display of a certain cigarette simply because it is available and attractive (and may bring "rent revenue") even though the store may reap very little profit by selling more of this particular brand. Except in the case of an exclusive franchise arrangement, where the store has decided to tie its fortunes to a particular brand, the store should promote the goods that are in its customer's interests and that provide a reasonable return for the effort.

Certain of the helps deserve special comment. Manufacturers of food and drug products frequently provide free samples for stores to distribute to their customers. If the samples are small and quickly consumed, they may

TABLE 12–1

Checklist of Vendor Services

The checklist of the variety of services available provides a guide for analysis:

I. *Nonpersonal Promotional Aids*

a. *Dealer helps*

(1) Advertising cuts or mats to make it unnecessary for the retailer to prepare a suitable layout to guide the newspaper or other media.

(2) Radio and TV scripts ready for use by a store commentator.

(3) Blowups of manufacturer's advertisements for store display, direct-mail pieces, bill stuffers, and package inserts.

(4) Samples of merchandise for display and free distribution purposes, including empty packages for display.

(5) Swatches of material, sold by the yard or attached to finished articles, for similar purposes.

(6) Visual displays, such as counter cards, posters, display fixtures, and window display units, ready to be set up.

(7) Specially designed fixtures to contain and display the vendor's products.

(8) Sales instructional booklets (pamphlets to distribute to customers, including "stuffers" to enclose in packages and with charge statements).

(9) Motion picture and sound slide films for showing to salespeople, customers, or both.

(10) Unit packaging, labels, and price tickets to ready the goods for resale.

b. *Provision of supplementary attractions*

(1) Special inducements for customer to buy.

c. *Promotional allowances*

(1) Advertising allowances.

(2) Display allowances

II. *Personal Selling Aids*

a. *Training of store salespeople*

b. *PMs and awards to salespeople for selling the particular product*

c. *Provision of demonstrators*

d. *Servicing the goods sold*

III. *Financing and Risk Taking by the Seller*

a. *Extension of credit*

b. *Guarantee against price decline*

c. *Consignment selling and the return privilege*

d. *Markdown insurance*

e. *Providing warranties*

IV. *Assumption of Inventory Responsibilities*

a. *Controlling the inventory of the merchandise bought while it is in the store*

b. *Warehousing purchases until needed for sale, including drop-shipping*

c. *Stocking the selling fixtures, displaying the goods, and doing associated housekeeping.*

prove effective in launching a product new to the consumer. If samples are larger, they may restrict sales, because the sample is not completely consumed before the initial interest and enthusiasm for the new product are forgotten. In some states, retailers have to be careful in distributing drug samples, because it is illegal there to leave or deposit such samples where they are accessible to children.

Unit packaging

The tenth item in the checklist, under dealer helps, includes readying the goods for sale. One form this takes is to pack the goods in resale quantities. Before World War II, most merchants bought in bulk, and the retailer handled the wrapping and packing of individual items, usually when completing the sale. The trend toward self-service and the advance in the art of packaging have led most buyers to recognize that many items take on more value in a well-designed unit package than in bulk and that they also save selling time to consumers. This is especially true in the case of many foods, cosmetics, and staple utilitarian items of many kinds that have little eye appeal in themselves.[1] The evidence seems conclusive that such unit packaging can best be done in bulk and by mechanical methods at the vendor level rather than at the retail level. Perishable goods may be an exception, with the packaging of meats and fresh vegetables still commonly done in the store but in advance of the time of sale. Even in this area there are experiments in vendor prepackaging.

To obtain goods in unit packages may involve an extra charge by the seller, but in many lines today, the unit pack is standard and demands no extra price. But even as the astute buyer analyzes every element of the merchandise being selected, so every element of the package is also studied and improvements often requested. The buyer may even seek changes in the unit quantities involved. For example, the manufacturer may be packing golf balls three to a package, but the buyer may wish to offer four to a package in the belief that customers will readily accept the larger unit.

Some of the large multiple-store buyers that develop private brands have special packaging departments that design all packages and have them produced under contract and delivered to the sellers who have been commissioned to make the goods.

Labeling

Readying of goods for sale involves not only packaging but also labeling. The package can also perform as a label, but for products not readily unit-packed, such as much clothing, there is need for labels attached directly to

[1] This is less true in the case of fashion merchandise bought on the basis of exact style, color, and fit. However, unit prepackaging does not eliminate the opportunity for customers to inspect the product itself. For such items as hosiery, it is common to provide samples for inspection, with the customer receiving a like prepacked and unopened article.

the merchandise. Vendors of branded products have for years attached labels emphasizing their brand names but providing very little factual information. It used to be a common practice for buyers to remove them, because they attracted attention to the resource rather than to the store itself. Also, they differed greatly in size, shape, and nature of the message proclaimed.

Today there are a number of federal laws that make it mandatory for the seller to label merchandise and for the labels to remain on the goods until after resale to the customer. The Federal Food, Drug, and Cosmetic Act requires that certain information be divulged on labels or packages, including net weight and names of ingredients in decreasing order of prominence, and "warning" labels in some cases.

The Fur Products Labeling Act sets a standard nomenclature in naming and describing furs and requires that the used or reused fur be revealed by label. The Federal Textile Fiber Products Identification Act requires that most textile products be labeled with the generic name of the fiber content, the percentage by weight of different fibers in the case of mixtures and blends, the name or registered number of the sponsor[2] of the product, and the country of origin if made abroad. Brand names used in juxtaposition to generic names are not to appear in larger type. If a buyer removes such mandatory labels, they must be replaced with the same information. The Flammable Fabrics Act requires that fabrics so highly flammable as to be dangerous to consumers be kept off the market or be treated to meet standards of flammability prescribed for various classes of goods. Although not required, the label may indicate the flammability standard met or exceeded.

The Federal Trade Commission has promulgated many trade regulations under the authority of the Federal Trade Commission Act. Examples include:

Permanent care labels for most clothing items are required to be attached and readily available at the time of cleaning by the consumer.

Nutrition information is required for certain packaged foods including vitamin and iron content with percentages of minimum daily requirements and amounts of protein, fat, and carbohydrates in a serving of stated size.

Furniture labels must reveal woods, veneers, nonwood components, and place of origin.

In addition to federal labeling regulations, there are also state and local ones covering the labeling of such articles as bedding. The seal of approval of the Underwriter's Laboratories, Inc., appears on electrical appliances and that of the American Gas Association on gas appliances.

Again, certain localities are now requiring unit pricing (the price per unit of measure in addition to the price per package) and dates that reveal the expiration of the period during which the goods may be sold as "fresh."

[2]The sponsor is the national advertiser of manufacturers' or wholesaler's brands, or the retailer or his or her supplier in the case of retailer's brands or unbranded goods.

Because much labeling, then, is mandatory today, it is in the buyer's interest to negotiate for labels that will best satisfy the customer's needs in such matters as number, size, appearance, and type. In order for labels to be as useful as possible to the consumer, they should provide more than the legally required information, adding facts about performance. Also, arrangements should be worked out to include all information on one label that is attached at a standard point to the merchandise. In the case of clothing, some vendors attach three to five labels of different sorts. Because these are confusing and unsightly, certain trade groups of buyers are demanding consolidation of all desirable information on one or two labels.

Responsibility for labeling

It has become a growing practice for manufacturers to attach price tickets with additional information covering date of purchase, classification, type, style number, size, color, and house (vendor's) number, because these may be required for unit-control purposes. It is argued that the job can be done better and more cheaply at the point of origin than in each of the many selling units. Manufacturers have been asked to absorb all or part of the expense in their current selling prices. If this succeeds, the seller's prices will ultimately have to be adjusted upward to cover the added expense and protect profit margins.

Rather than depending on a price-ticketing service from the vendor, a number of big multiple units have worked out arrangements with ticketing companies. The vendors deliver to the companies, which for a fee attach price tickets as the buyers instruct and distribute to each store unit comprising the group.

The most far reaching development in this area is "Universal Vendor Marking" (UVM), and the Universal Product Code (UPC) already discussed in Chapter 8, pp. 218–220.

Supplementary Attractions for the Consumer, Sponsored by the Vendor

In addition to putting tools into the hands of the retail buyer to help in the reselling of the product, manufacturers (of foods especially) often attempt to provide certain inducements to the customer so that he or she will purchase a certain brand in the store. These are important to the retail buyer, because a certain amount of cooperation of the store is required and because the manufacturer's attempt may disturb the orderly conduct of the business and the volume to be realized from competing brands.

The premium

A common selling device of this sort is the *premium,* an article of value distributed to customers who buy a specific brand. Sometimes the premium is attached to the product or to two or three of the products banded together. Thus the store is forced to warehouse and distribute the premium as well as the goods. Frequently, the retailer has no hand in the promotion; the manufacturer advertises the goods nationally, offering an article to the customers who send in evidence that they have bought the advertised product. A small charge is often made for the premium. There is great variation in the degree to which the customer gets a bargain. Although customers frequently secure premiums well below market price, they often pay as much as they would have to had they shopped around with no need to purchase specific products in advance. From the legal point of view, the Robinson-Patman Act implies that premiums may not be used as a form of price discrimination among competing retailers. And the prohibitions against deceptive advertising are interpreted as making it illegal to call a premium free if its cost is included in the purchase price of another article sold in connection with it.

Some state laws bar premiums if they are used as a device to sell goods below cost or below minimum prices set in resale price agreements.

The coupon

Another device is the coupon that the manufacturer may distribute to consumers through the mail, in packages of the product, or through the cooperation of the retail store.[3] These coupons have values stated in cents and may be used like cash in the purchase of certain branded products. The dealer is expected to accept them in lieu of cash and to turn them in for redemption. The retailer is normally granted a small commission for the bother of handling and waiting for the money, but there is a question as to whether the payment covers the cost. Occasionally, the coupon is a device to force the retailer to carry a product not currently stocked. For example, a 10¢ coupon in a cake-mix package was good only for the purchase of another product not stocked by the store organization and not even made by the same manufacturer.

The consumer contest

Still another device used by some sellers is the contest, usually with enormous prizes and requiring that the customer present evidence of purchase to enter. The contest itself often involves extolling the virtues of the particular product. These do not always require direct dealer involvement,

[3]Discount coupons are commonly supplied by supermarkets in their frequent flyers and advertisements. These are good for relatively short periods.

but often the dealer is expected to distribute entry blanks, and employees may become involved in the contest and give undue sales emphasis to the particular product. Some chains now conduct their own contests, such as the Instant Money scheme of the A.&P.

The deal

Manufacturers sometimes try to force distribution by deals, or temporary special retail price inducements. These take various forms. One is to band two packages together. For example, 59¢ merchandise may be banded to sell "two for 99¢." The separate package costs the store 47¢, providing it a margin of 12¢ a package, or 20 percent. The cost of the deal is 83¢, providing a margin of 16¢, or 16 percent for two banded packages. Such a customer inducement may be a disservice to the store: It must move more tonnage at a lower margin of profit; its stock of unbanded packages is "dead" until the deal is over; and in all probability its total sales of the class of product is not increased (rather one product is sold in lieu of another). Another popular device is to put on a special label reading "2¢" off. The FTC rules that the base for "cents off" must be the lowest price in the past 30 days.

In all such schemes as premiums, coupons, contests, and deals, there is a degree of pressure on the retail buyer to stock the items involved in substantial quantity. In negotiation with sellers, the buyer is well advised to be acquainted with vendor policy regarding such consumer promotions and decide what action, if any, should be taken in the interest of customers.

PROMOTIONAL ALLOWANCES

In order to assure cooperative effort between the seller and retail buyer of branded products, it is a common practice in many lines (1) for the seller to pay the buyer for promotional services that the latter performs (such as advertising and display of the vendor's product),[4] and (2) for the seller to provide the buyer with promotional aids (such as display materials and prizes). Such payments and contributions are recognized as legitimate under the Robinson-Patman Act[5] provided they are made available to all competing buyers in any given trading area on "proportionally equal terms." As mentioned previously, the meaning of this phrase is subject to considerable legal dispute.

[4]The fields in which the allowance practice is especially entrenched include toiletries, hosiery, lingerie and corsets, men's wear, shoes, household appliances and housewares, and radios and TV sets, but they are offered by scattered sellers in most fields.

[5]For a detailed statement of how the Federal Trade Commission interprets the Robinson-Patman Act, see Guides for Advertising Allowances and Other Merchandising Payments and Services, as amended in 1972, Federal Trade Commission, Washington, D.C.

Probably the most common practice in connection with advertising allowances is for the manufacturer to pay an agreed percentage of the amount that the retailer elects to spend to advertise the product, up to a specified limit in dollars or as a percentage of the buyer's purchases. Thus, if an allowance of 50 percent is limited to 5 percent of the buyer's purchases of $10,000, the seller agrees to reimburse the store half of what it spends for advertising, up to $500. There are other permissible arrangements: The buyer may pay a fixed amount per unit of purchases or a fixed amount per line of newspaper space or minute of broadcast time. Or the buyer may agree to pay all of the advertising cost up to a stated percentage of the retailer's purchases.

Practices in Vogue

Allowances are generally limited to manufacturer's branded lines, where the store agrees to feature the brand name in promotion. In some cases, however, stores receive allowances on their private brands or on unbranded goods. From the vendor's point of view, this practice may be questioned on the grounds that it does not build good will for a brand. But branding is not the only means of identifying a product. Inherent attributes of material, workmanship, and design many differentiate it sufficiently so that repeat patronage may be developed. In any event, promotion helps to move goods; and if the vendor can gain more promotional effort by contributing to its cost, he or she may consider the investment to be profitable. A 10¢ price reduction on 1000 $2 items may not accelerate their sale notably. But a $200 advertisement, gained by contributing $100, may have a very sharp effect on sales.

Funds granted for advertising are usually used for the purchase of newspaper space or broadcast time, but a considerable portion is used by the store to publish catalogs or other direct-mail pieces. Buying offices regularly put out seasonal catalogs for their member stores to distribute to their customers. Most of the cost is provided by payments from the vendors whose merchandise is featured. Sometimes vendors also pay for the merchandise flyer and catalogs prepared by the buying office for buyer, not consumer, use.

In the textile trades, a major part of the advertising allowance money is not actually provided by sellers of the completed product but by the large fiber and yarn sellers who provide the yarn under a nationally advertised brand name. Thus a curtain manufacturer may be granted by the yarn maker a specific fund that he or she may allot to retail customers, on proportionately equal terms, provided they advertise the product in such a way as (1) to make the name of the fiber conspicuous, and (2) to conform to correct usage of fiber identification as specified by the Federal Trade Commission. The actual payments to the stores are not made by the seller of the finished product but by the yarn manufacturer, after receiving evidence that the ads were run and that they measured up to the standards set.

There are variations in the time of paying the allowance to the store. The safer plan, from the seller's viewpoint, is to require proof that the agreed advertising has been inserted in the newspaper or other medium before issuing credit. But sellers may allow deduction of the allowance from the face of the invoice. Here there is danger that the store may regard the allowance as a disguised price concession and fail to advertise as agreed. In fact, some stores have permitted buyers (1) to accumulate reserves of allowance money not expended for advertising the products of the vendors providing the allowances, and (2) to use these reserves for advertising at their own discretion.

Vendor control of allowances

Retailers are often granted complete control of the kind of advertising they undertake at vendor expense, but it is more common for the seller to exercise some control. There is often advance agreement as to the featuring of the brand name, the copy treatment, and the size and cost of the space. Sometimes days on which the ads are to be run, plans for repetition, and intervals are also included in the agreement. Sometimes vendors insist on the use of their mats or cuts for illustrations; sometimes they insist on using their own prepared advertisement.

It has been seriously proposed that it would be a good policy for the seller to give retailers complete control, as long as they present evidence of the expenditure. It is argued that retailers would take more interest in promoting the goods if allowed to make their own decisions. Where they have strict orders from vendors, cooperation often stops with what is demanded, and the advertisement is neither adapted to local conditions nor tied into the personality of the store.

Accounting for allowances

From an accounting standpoint, there is a question as to whether an advertising allowance should be treated as a reduction in the cost price of the goods or as a reduction in the store's advertising expenses. From the standpoint of accurate comparison, the former is preferable, but many stores are treating the allowance as a reduction in their advertising expenses[6] on the theory that the vendor is substituting cooperative advertising for his or her own consumer advertising and is not reducing the price of the goods.

This handling tends to distort the true cost of advertising in that the net cost, after allowance money is deducted, is compared with the total sales,

[6]The *Expense Manual of the National Retail Merchants Association* sanctions this handling.

including those of the advertised goods. The device exaggerates the productivity of the store's advertising.

Space brokerage by retailers

There has been a trend for large retailers to contract for radio and television time or for magazine space and then to resell the time or space to manufacturers. For example, one chain sponsoring a television program sold spot commercials to manufacturers. Also, a group of department stores, sponsoring a series of 15-minute telecasts, sold 1-minute commercials to manufacturers. Another ran a multiple-page section in a national magazine, parceled it out to participating manufacturers, and charged them for it. Because the retailers involved bought time or space at bulk or wholesale rates and sold them at retail rates, they reaped a profit quite independent of consumer response to the joint promotional effort. Manufacturers show some resistance to such schemes, in that such retailers are becoming dealers in space. A practice that subjects both the retailer and the advertising agency to prosecution is for the latter to charge the retailer at the low local advertising rate but to make out the bill for the cooperating manufacturer at the higher national rate.

Advantages of Advertising Allowances

The cooperative plan has advantages for both retailer and producer. The store is able to reduce its advertising outlay or to undertake more advertising than it could afford alone. In those instances where the seller does not insist that the allowance be used for advertising, the store reduces the cost of its goods. Again, the small store may obtain better copy and art work from the cooperating advertiser than it could provide itself. Fresher and better expressed ideas increase the retailer's sales. As already indicated, the store may also reap a profit from advertising brokerage although the ethics and wisdom of such practice is questioned.

The allowance plan may also be of advantage to the seller. It is an excellent way to provide added selling pressure for new products or services the seller may be offering and to ensure adequate advertising that the retailer's restricted budget may not permit. When the sellers have control over the advertising, they may tone up sluggish copy and achieve greater returns for themselves and the retailer. Again, local newspapers or broadcast stations may prove the best media for the manufacturer, and a local store, with its low, contractual linage rate, may be able to buy the necessary space more cheaply than the vendor. Furthermore, the store may have great local prestige, and the vendor's sales opportunity may be enhanced by associating the product with the fine store. An equitable plan does seem to cement good relations between the manufacturer and the merchant, keeping the latter sold on the product.

Disadvantages

To the Store

On the other hand, advertising allowances tend to disrupt store advertising programs and make the store more a distributing depot for the manufacturer than a purchasing agent for the consumer. *Instead of promoting the best merchandise at a price, the retailer is tempted to promote lines on which most advertising allowances can be obtained.* Certain items may be given more space than they deserve and tend to dominate store copy. Again, the type of layout and copy upon which the vendor insists may vary from the store's established characteristics and "mess up" advertising. As indicated previously, there is much to be said for giving the retailer greater freedom in the use of his or her allowance.

To the manufacturer

From the manufacturer's viewpoint, a great danger is that the allowance being granted may not be used for advertising, or, at least, not used effectively. Many manufacturers report that allowances are unproductive and do not stimulate sales. Some regard them as simply price-cutting devices.

Another objection is the difficulty in making allowances proportionally equal. Manufacturers are quick to blame store pressure for any discrimination that might be uncovered. Retailers, on the other hand, insist that they are entitled to be tough negotiators and are in no position to determine whether allowances granted them are being made available to their competitors, but this argument may not stand up in court.[7]

The investigation raises the question as to the proper meaning of the clause "proportionally equal." Should its meaning be limited to quantity of purchases or of store expenditures for advertising, or may it also allow for value of the promotion to the manufacturer? For example, a high-class store buying no more than a discount store performs a more valuable service in advertising the manufacturer's product in that the high-class store's sponsorship carries more weight with the public and with the buyers of other stores who are considering the purchase of the manufacturer's line.

The Federal Trade Commission, based on the Fred Myer Case, has insisted that, where a manufacturer sells both to retailers direct and also through wholesalers, allowances may not be limited to those who buy direct. The

[7]It should be noted that a U.S. Circuit Court decision in 1962 let stand a lower court ruling that held that a good-faith meeting of competition is legal justification for the payment of a discriminatory promotional allowance.

manufacturer is expected to make allowances available to the wholesaler's customers on a proportional basis, which is generally interpreted as proportionate to the amount of the product purchased by each retailer.

In practice, even where the allowances are proportionately equal, it is the large retailers who take advantage of them. Either the rules for the allowance are so complex, or the amount available to the small retail store so small, that the store does not bother to apply. A buyer of 5000 pieces may qualify for an allowance of $2500, enough to promote effectively. The small retailer buying 36 pieces might qualify for only $18.00, not enough for an ad. Under such conditions, the Federal Trade Commission insists that the vendor develop an alternate plan that will be suitable and usable by the competing store that is unable to take advantage of the regular plan.

To the consumer

From the point of view of the consumer, there are objections to allowances as they are often applied. They have been used to keep retail prices at a high level, replacing fair trade arrangements that have now been generally eliminated. Rather than reduce price in order to move more goods, the seller may grant a substantial allowance, which the retailer uses to promote the goods more intensively at current prices. Thus the retail price structure may tend toward rigidity, with the consumer paying for the extra promotional effort. But this objection may be made to all advertising of branded products.

Another objection from the consumers' viewpoint is that the allowance may make the retailer less exacting in quality standards. It is reported that some manufacturers have prevailed upon retailers to keep defective and shoddy goods by offering them extra allowances to foist them on the public. Of course, the reputable retail buyer would perceive the injury to good will and avoid such deals, but some retailers succumb.

Conditions Justifying Allowances

Although there is little doubt that advertising allowances have become an industry disease—a bribe to the retailer—the difficulty seems to be in the abuses rather than in the principle of cooperation between manufacturer and retailer in promoting goods.

To be truly cooperative and economically sound, the following conditions should normally be met:

1. The goods are sold under the vendor's brand, and the vendor, as well as the merchant, incurs good will by the cooperative effort.

2. The allowance is paid or credited to the store after the latter has presented evidence that the agreed amount has been spent for the promotional purpose specified, and the store charges the seller at the rate the store itself pays for space or time, plus perhaps a reasonable handling fee.
3. The allowance represents a portion of the vendor's normal advertising budget and not an additional concession.
4. The goods in question meet the quality and fashion standards of the store and would deserve promotion even though the vendor did not share the cost. Normally, the store should back up the cooperative advertising with other promotional devices.
5. The allowance is not being used as a device by the seller to avoid a price reduction indicated by the forces of supply and demand.
6. The store has enough control over the use of the appropriation to avoid a disruption of advertising plans and to maintain the character of the store.
7. Advance agreement has been reached in regard to any control to be exercised by the seller over such matters as media, timing, size, and character of proposed advertising, as well as in regard to charges to be made for preparation of advertisements.
8. The seller is careful to avoid discrimination among competing customers.
9. Especially for broadcast advertising, the store employs an agency to assure careful planning and execution.

It must not be concluded, however, that advertising allowances must be granted by national advertisers if they expect dealers to feature their brands in local advertising. Many case histories prove that excellent dealer cooperation can be obtained without the benefit of advertising allowances, provided manufacturers support their lines with impressive advertising programs and offer newspaper mats that meet retailer requirements. Leading retailers want intelligent help in selling but do not insist that it take the form of an allowance.

Display Allowances

The pros and cons of other forms of vendor allowances are much the same as those that apply to advertising. Some vendors pay for special displays set up by the retailer. For example, one national brand promoter offered a chain 15¢ a case if special 10-case displays were set up for a specified period of time. These deals sometimes take the form of "buying" preferred shelf space. Some chains, for example, allot certain cigarette manufacturers preferred shelves in the store on which other brands of cigarettes and other products are not to be displayed. The manufacturer pays the store "rent" of an agreed amount per store in which such shelf space is to be made available.

In addition to other objections common to advertising allowances, this plan often leads to the use of the best space by marginal sellers and often to the existence of bare places on the reserved shelf. It would perhaps be wise for the chain to refuse such offers and to use the space to greatest advantage to sell merchandise in volume and at a high rate of stockturn—not to favor one brand over another.

VENDORS' PERSONAL SELLING AIDS

Aid from the seller in connection with personal selling is often welcomed by the buyer. For major lines, especially where the store has an exclusive agency arrangement and where technical information is required of the salesperson, it is appropriate for the seller to send sales trainers into the stores to provide salespeople with merchandise facts and selling techniques. Such arrangements should be made when franchise arrangements are worked out and at the time seasonal orders are placed.

PMs

Some vendors offer to pay the store's salespeople extra to move their particular brands. The pay may take the form of a "PM," a fixed amount for every unit sold, or it may take the form of a prize to the salesperson who sells the most of a product during a season. Where the buyer has an agency arrangement and does not carry competing brands, such payments may be countenanced, but the question may be raised as to the wisdom of allowing the vendor to provide part of the remuneration of the sales force. Other items, even though noncompeting, are likely to be neglected, and salespeople may develop more allegiance to the vendor than to the store. Certainly, the policy of allowing such payments is bad if the store does carry competing brands, including perhaps its own private brand. If the store has a policy of acting as the consumers' purchasing agent rather than as the manufacturers' selling agent, it could not in good faith allow the seller to provide part of the salespeople's wages.

Demonstrators

In a few lines, especially toiletries and housewares, vendors commonly provide their store customers with demonstrators. Some of these demonstrate only, turning over any resulting sales to regular salespeople. Others consummate sales. Where the store has a policy of arranging the department according to brands, with a person in charge of each brand classification, and is attempting to build a reputation for being a headquarters for leading brands, the use of demonstrators can be defended. The store's selling cost is reduced, and trained experts handle each classfication. On the other hand, the considerations against allowing salespeople to accept payments from the vendor apply here also. Hidden demonstrators who pose as regular employees deceive the customer who is looking for impartial help. Where they are attached to a certain brand classification, the customer is less likely to be misled, because the very layout indicates to the customer that the salespeople have a definite interest in promoting a particular brand.

If the decision to engage demonstrators is made, it is a wise policy to put them through the regular employment procedure and have it clearly understood that they are employees of the store, subject fully to its policies, procedures, and systems. Otherwise it may be difficult to get them to abide by store regulations.

The provision of demonstrators and other promotional aids is subject to the Robinson-Patman Act. The Federal Trade Commission has taken the view that the cost of demonstrator service must be in proportion to each buyer's purchases, if they are to be proportionally equal. When the value so calculated is insufficent to provide even one demonstrator for an effective period of time, the seller is expected to provide an alternate service, such as display. Many sellers and large buyers feel that this is too stringent a definition of "proportionally equal" and that the value to the sellers of having demonstrators in well-known stores should be considered. At all events, the buyer who accepts demonstrators should be aware of the limitations set by the regulating authorities and that he or she may be found guilty if a discriminatory arrangement is knowingly accepted.

Servicing Goods Sold

Especially important in the field of mechanical contrivances is the vendor's policies about installation, service, warranty, and repair. Few stores are equipped to set up and maintain the necessary repair and installation departments; most stores prefer to purchase lines where the wholesale distributor assumes these functions and has a proven reputation for quality and speed in performing the servicing required.

FINANCING AND RISK TAKING

Financing by the Seller through Credit Arrangements

Most retail buying is on open account, with 30 days commonly allowed from date of the invoice to pay for the shipment, often with a discount if paid for in a shorter period of time, such as 10 days. No credit instrument is involved. The seller is a general creditor, without the right of repossession.

Dating

There are many variations in dating, the length of time in which to pay, and also to earn cash discount for paying earlier. These generally become standardized by trades. The chief variations appear in the glossary at the end of Chapter 14.

COD

If the seller is pressed for cash, is uncertain of the buyer's credit standing, or attempts to keep prices down by eliminating credit, the requirement may be cash on order or cash on delivery. Some small, general merchants often buy most of their grocery requirements on a cash basis. They make frequent trips to nearby wholesalers, select what they need, much as does the consumer in the supermarket, and pay cash at the checkout point. And some daily deliveries are paid for as soon as received.

Drafts

A sight draft may be drawn by the seller demanding payment upon shipment of the goods, or the draft may take the form of a trade acceptance or a banker's acceptance. These are used primarily in foreign trade.

Floor plan

Another credit device is floor planning, common in the appliance field. The seller turns an assortment of merchandise over to the buyer, who signs a *trust receipt*.[8] Title remains with the seller and the buyer agrees to make payment as he makes sales. These payments, if on credit sales, include turning over the customer paper to the seller or his agent. The seller may agree, for a limited period, to replace what has been sold.

As commonly practiced in the TV appliance industry, a dealer may be provided an inventory of 100 units for which he makes a 10 per cent down payment and additional payments as he makes sales. But any merchandise not sold in 90 days is to be paid for then. There is no interest charge during this period.

Should the dealer fail to sell all the floor-planned stock in 90 days and have, let us say, 40 pieces left, he may, in lieu of paying up, make another 10% down payment on the remaining inventory and agree to pay a small

[8]See the Glossary of Credit Terms in the Technical Appendix at the end of Chapter 14 for an explanation of the terms in italics.

carrying charge on the outstanding balance each month. Since the buyer in such a situation is reluctant to pour more money into slow-selling goods, he has two alternatives: (1) to cut prices sharply in order to get his money back with no margin for expenses and profits, or (2) to try to persuade the seller to take the goods back. In either case, the market becomes flooded with distress merchandise.

In their zeal to have their products in as many retail outlets as possible, some manufacturers and their distributors enter into floor-plan arrangements with weak store operators, who soon own virtually none of the inventory they carry. And some of the dealers, under pressure to meet operating expenses, are slow in turning over their sales collections to the seller. Unless floor-plan arrangements are most carefully entered into, there is grave danger of retail failure and loss to the manufacturers' distributors.

With the current emphasis by retailers to keep their inventories as low as possible, the floor planning of an assortment with back-up stock has declined. Instead, many retailers carry samples only and, as they make sales, "pull-in" the items from the manufacturers' local distributors or have the goods "drop-shipped," as explained later in this chapter.

Guarantee Against Price Decline

There is always considerable risk that the market price of a merchandise commitment may drop, and the buyer is under temptation to shift this risk back to the seller. There are three ways this may be done: (1) to obtain a guarantee against a price decline, (2) to take title to the goods but with a return privilege if they fail to sell in a specified time, and (3) to have the seller retain title to the goods until resold, with the return privilege before resale.

In some lines, such as domestics, where seasonal requirements are ordered well in advance, it has sometimes been possible to obtain guarantees against price declines. For example, to induce ordering in December for a season that starts in March, the vendor may agree to credit or refund to the store the difference between the contract price and the market price on delivery date or on a future specified date, if the market price should be lower then. If the contract price in December was $1 a unit and the price on March 1 (when the goods are delivered) is 95¢, the vendor would credit the buyer with 5¢ per unit.

Guarantees sometimes continue while the goods are in the retailer's possession, but they usually expire when the goods are delivered. Under these conditions, astute buyers demand that delivery be withheld until the goods are actually needed for sale. Manufacturers who find it necessary to cut prices sometimes ship out most of their outstanding orders just before announcing a price reduction. As soon as the goods are in transit, the manufacturer is not bound to a price guarantee good until delivery and can hold the buyers to the higher contract price. Accordingly, it is wise for the buyer to specify that goods bought under a guarantee are not to be shipped before a specified date.

Expiration of the guarantee with the delivery of the goods would seem to be justified in the case of some staples that are subject to unforecastable price changes. It is thus an inducement to early ordering and helps to keep the vendor's plant in operation during dull seasons. It also tends to induce the buyer to carry a full line of the manufacturer's products rather than to be limited to the best sellers.

On the other hand, the practice may encourage speculation. Protected against drops in price, buyers may order more than they need in the hope that the market price might go up and thus yield extra profit. The practice also may lead to inflexibility in the manufacturers' prices, leading them to defer necessary downward price adjustments because of the heavy obligations they would have in reimbursing customers on previous transactions.

A guarantee of price to continue after delivery of the goods can probably be justified only when the buyer takes delivery before the start of the selling season in order to accommodate the vendor. Even though no guarantee may exist, vendors occasionally, when they reduce price, grant refunds on unsold goods in retailers' stocks to protect good will.

The economic problem in connection with guarantees is this: *Any profit the retail buyer may hope to achieve is the reward for taking calculated risk. If he or she embraces every opportunity to pass such risk back to the seller, his or her profit opportunities are being passed up*. In the long run, at least, goods bought without a price guarantee will be cheaper than those purchased with one. As a general policy, buyers should make their own estimates of the requirements and buy the goods needed with no strings attached.

CONSIGNMENT SELLING AND THE RETURN PRIVILEGE

Another device to shift risk back to the seller is to get the vendor to agree to take back the goods if they are not sold in a specified period of time. Because the markdown risk is borne by the vendor, the buyer's maintained markup is equal to the initial one. The return privilege may take one of two forms: consignment selling or sale with the privilege of return. *In consignment selling, title does not pass to the store but instead passes directly from the vendor to the store's customers*. Thus the store acts simply as an agent for the vendor.

In the case of a sale with return privilege, title passes to the buyer, ordinarily when the goods are shipped, but the vendor continues to assume a contractual obligation to take back the unsold portion at a specified time.[9]

[9]In determining whether title has actually passed to the buyer or not, the courts are guided by the real nature of the transaction rather than the language used in the contract.

This legal distinction is important for two reasons: First, the vendor has complete control over the retail price charged customers when the goods are sold on consignment, whereas in the case of sale with return privilege, the store can normally sell at any price it may choose; second, if a vendor should refuse to take back consignment goods, the store assumes merely the responsibility of a bailee rather than that of an owner—it is under no obligation to pay for the goods but must merely keep them safe. If bought with a return agreement, however, the store is legally liable to the vendor for the price of the goods but can sue for any loss it may incur through failure of the vendor to take them back.

The phrase *on memorandum* used in connection with a consignment sale or a sale with the right to return has no generally agreed-on meaning. The details of the memorandum itself determine its significance. In the jewelry trade, for example, it is generally understood that title remains with the seller but that the retailer receiving the goods is either to sell them and account for the proceeds or to return them.

In one legal case,[10] a buyer refused to return some textiles that he had bought on memorandum claiming that he had title. The Appellate Term of the Supreme Court ruled that the memorandum bill was entirely consistent with an agreement of bailment rather than with the contract to sell and that the goods belonged to the seller. The buyer had a right to purchase them, however, upon the terms in the memorandum agreement.

Controlling Distribution

Formerly, the vendor could control the resale of a product in two ways: (1) by selling on consignment, and (2) by selling under a legal price-maintenance agreement. Because relatively few vendors were willing to assume the risk of obsolescence and deterioration and possible failure of the retailer to promote the goods, selling on consignment has not been widely used to control resale prices.

Sale under a minimum price-control contract enjoyed wide acceptance for over 30 years but now has been virtually eliminated by the repeal in 1975 of the federal legislation that had recognized such price fixing over state lines as not subject to the antitrust laws.

A form of price concession

Both consignment selling and sale with return privilege are frequently used with no intent to control retail prices but as a price concession to obtain sales that would not be obtained otherwise. For example, a retailer may refuse to pay a price of $12 per dozen outright but may agree to this price if he or she need pay only for the goods sold at a reasonable markup and is then permitted to return the rest. From the vendor's standpoint, the practice may

[10]Oppenheim Co., Inc., v. Warsaw, 199 N.Y.S. 235.

be desirable if limited to new, untried lines or old stock on which he or she may have to take a large markdown unless sold in this way.[11] But if it becomes the general rule, with most buyers obtaining the concession on all purchases, the vendor will bear the retailer's normal risks of loss as well as his or her own. Unless the vendor is in a position to merchandise the stock assortment in the store, to transfer or mark down slow sellers promptly, and to insist on the store's giving adequate promotional emphasis to the goods, returns of unsalable stock may be found excessive.

Advantages and disadvantages to the buyer

From the buyer's standpoint, consignment buying has the advantages of eliminating markdowns and of increasing stock assortment with no increase in invested capital.[12] The disadvantages are so marked that merchandise managers usually oppose the practice except under a few special conditions. These objections are:

1. Goods offered on consignment are generally unsalable outright. Something is wrong with them; they are not likely to sell well or be up to the store's standards of quality or fashion-rightness.
2. Desirable goods can generally be obtained at a lower price if bought outright. With careful buying, the possible saving in price through an outright purchase should more than offset the markdown loss.
3. Lack of obligation on the buyer's part may lead to overbuying. A quantity of unneeded goods not only fills up valuable storage space but may lead to neglect in the promotion of regular goods and compete with them for customer preference.
4. The practice frequently leads to bad feeling between retailer and vendor. Often the latter feels that the retailer has failed to make a real effort to promote goods, knowing that "most of it is going back anyhow." What is returned is generally much the worse for wear and quite out of style and may be an almost complete loss.

Conditions justifying consignment buying

Under the following conditions, however, consignment buying is desirable from the retailer's point of view:

1. In the introduction of a new line by the vendor where the retailer is not in a position to pass judgment on probable customer demand. For example, some toy buying on consignment is defended on this basis.

[11]Under the antiprice discrimination law (Robinson-Patman Act), such concessions are apparently permissible when applied to stock for clearance, but, if offered on new lines, they must be made generally available.

[12]To the extent that they compete with goods owned outright, slowing down their turnovers, consignment goods *do* tend to increase the investment.

2. In stocking items not regularly carried in the store, particularly decorative or prestige items on which little volume is realized but which add "tone" to the store. If the vendor gets a prospect for the article outside the store, it can be withdrawn. Many gift shops and general stores find it advantageous to stock on consignment goods created by local craftspeople in need of widened exposure for their handicrafts.

3. Occasionally, in stocking for a special sale or the Christmas season, especially if it is difficult to anticipate the amount that will be required. A common plan is for a store to purchase outright a quantity equal to the minimum of possible sales. Additional goods are stocked on consignment to take care of customer demand in case the sale is a decided success. Again, when a "key vendor" is anxious to hold an end-of-season sale of merchandise in the store, he or she may offer the goods on consignment, estimating that more will be realized this way than by selling the goods outright in job lots. If the vendor is regarded as a preferred resource, the store may agree to hold a sale as a courtesy in exchange for past favors. Definite and short-time limits should be set for final settlement.

4. In buying merchandise in demand by a special group of customers only and during a short intensive period. For example, a college bookstore needs texts for classes at the beginning of each term. It is difficult to determine the size of classes in advance, so the store orders a substantial supply on consignment, returning any that are not needed. Because the goods are staple, the publisher runs no risk of markdowns and sells more books by having them available when students want them. In fact, return privilege is part of standard practice in much of the book field.

5. When buying is done by an inexperienced buyer who has little knowledge of the kind and quantity of merchandise that will be in demand in different seasons. This buyer may find it wise to buy on consignment even though more than the cash price is paid as an insurance premium against markdowns, should his purchase prove unwise.

Because consignment plans are justified at times, even though frequently subject to abuse, both merchants and vendors should establish definite policies governing the conditions under which these arrangements are to be accepted.

Markdown Insurance

A pernicious form of risk assumption by the seller has occurred in the women's apparel field. Certain buyers asked manufacturers to guarantee them against markdowns, partially at least. The sellers were asked to reimburse the buyers for one-half of the amount of the markdowns the latter found it necessary to take late in the season.

In the long run, should such a practice ever become prevalent, buyers would tend to buy carelessly, with an increase in the cost of distribution.

Warranties

Many manufacturers of branded products provide written warranties whereby they agree to assume responsibility for certain failures of their products. If these are clear-cut and believable, they protect the customer and thus facilitate selling. But they often have been inadequate.

In response to wide consumer complaint that product guarantees are ambiguous and that redress for product failure is difficult to obtain, the Congress in 1974 passed the Magnuson-Moss Warranty Federal Trade Commission Improvement Act, which became effective in 1975. Although Title I of this Act does not require that a seller guarantee a product, it does set stringent regulations where a warranty is provided. Although the law applies to "consumer goods," certain products such as food and drugs covered by other laws are not included. The written warranty must protect both the retail customer (who buys the product) and the user.

The terms and conditions must be presented in clear and simple language. The Federal Trade Commission is authorized to draw up specific regulations in regard to warranty statements for different products, including the name and address of the warrantor, the product or parts covered, the time period for which the warranty applies, procedures for the consumer to follow if the goods fail to perform as warranted, and costs that the consumer must bear; nor may the warranty include any disclaimer of implied warranty (such as the safety, effectiveness and suitability of the goods to the purpose intended). The warranty is not effective if the consumer damages the goods through improper use or handling.

The warranty may be either a *full* warranty for the period stated or a *limited* one. The former, which few sellers are likely to offer, assures that any defect will be remedied without charge, and, if this fails, the buyer will be offered a choice of a refund or replacement without charge. Limited warranties must reveal their exact nature. The warrantor may set up procedures for handling complaints.

In case of disagreement, informal procedures may be provided, and the consumer may seek redress in the courts if the product cost more than $10.00. Class action suits for damages may be brought by groups of 100 or more consumers who have each suffered a loss of $25.00 or more.

Retailer's Responsibility

Although most warranties are made by the manufacturer, the retailer has the responsibility to make available for consumer review before purchase the written warranties of all articles costing more than $15. This may be accomplished by any of the following means: (1) conspicuous display of the text of the warranty in close conjunction with the product, (2) provision of binders that contain copies of the warranties of the products in question, kept in a location readily accessible to customers, (3) where the warranty is on the package, arrangement of the display to make it clearly visible, or (4) provision of a written notice displaying the text of a warranty that applies to an entire line of goods. In the case of catalog sales to be consummated by mail or phone, the warranty must be displayed in close proximity to the description of the product or a notice included that the warranty may be obtained upon written request.

The warrantor must provide the retailer with such copies of warranties and notices required to comply with the rules. Each buyer should follow up to make sure that such materials are provided and applied as required.

If the written warranty is provided by the retailer, it is subject to the same rules. If the goods are privately branded, the store should procure legal aid as to the wording of any warranty the organization decides to make and as to the procedures to be set up to dispose of complaints quickly to the customers' satisfaction. Otherwise, the store may be faced with a suit in court and substantial damages.

Vendor Control of the Stock in the Store

Assumption of inventory responsibilities

In some lines, such as hosiery and domestics, where frequent reorders are necessary to keep up an adequate stock assortment, many vendors offer an additional service to buyers: They undertake to maintain the required unit-control data and to keep the store supplied with an adequate assortment.

Where the vendors who are permitted to control retail inventories are reliable and represent standardized branded products, the system relieves the buyer of the cost and trouble of routine checking and reordering. The vendor or his or her representative may even do the job better than the buyer could, because they are experts in the line. The plan permits the buyer to concentrate on the purchase and promotion of special and seasonal merchandise. The vendor gains as well, being assured that the merchandise is adequately represented and, with immediate knowledge of customer acceptance or rejection.

Warehousing Inventories Until Needed for Resale

When a rise in price is anticipated, it is often wise to make purchase commitments at current prices for larger quantities than are needed for current selling and to make arrangements with the seller to store the goods until needed. If an extra charge is not exacted for this service, the retailer saves on storage costs. Furthermore, the purchase commitment may be broadly written as a blanket order for a class of goods with colors, finishes, and sizes not specified until requisitions are made against the stock. Goods are held in undifferentiated form for a longer period with considerable increase in stockturn.

Drop-Shipping

A similar arrangement is for the vendor to agree to stock inventories ready for shipment and to make deliveries directly to the store's customers when orders are booked in the stores. This plan is especially suited to furniture, major appliances, mattresses, and other bulky goods. Because the stores need stock samples only, stockturn is materially increased. With proper inventory control by the manufacturer, prompt deliveries can be made to the store's customers.

With a sizable group of stores involved, the total inventory maintained by the manufacturer is considerably less than what would be required if each store had to carry a sufficient stock to make its own deliveries.

DISCUSSION QUESTIONS

1. Do most stores make adequate use of services available from vendors?
2. Do enough customers read labels to warrant the elaborate labeling requirements set up by federal and local governments? Is current customer practice a prime issue in setting the requirements?
3. Should food stores resist manufacturer's premiums, coupons, contests, and deals for which their cooperation is expected?
4. Is it ethical for a store to charge a manufacturer more for newspaper space than the store actually pays for the space?
5. In view of the possibility of misuse of advertising allowance money and of undue pressure on sellers to grant allowances, would it be desirable to outlaw the whole system?
6. Is it in the interest of a supermarket chain to reserve a shelf for a certain manufacturer's products in return for a payment to the store of a fixed amount per month?
7. Is it an undue restriction of trade for the federal government, acting through its Federal Trade Commission, to demand that all allowances for promotional purposes be *proportionally equal*? Consider, for example, the manufacturer who sells to large stores direct but gets goods into small competing stores by selling to wholesalers. How are the required proportional allowances to these retail customers of the wholesale ac-

counts to be granted? And how is the vendor to develop an alternate plan for a small store that would be entitled, under the demonstrator plan, to only a fraction of a demonstrator?

8. Is it usually unwise for a buyer to try to have the seller assume the risk of a price drop or of the store's failure to resell after the goods have been ordered and/or delivered?
9. Would buyers be wise to permit more of their key vendors to control the stock assortments of their merchandise in the stores? What are the lines in which this plan is more likely to be successful than in others?
10. Does an arrangement for the vendor to drop-ship to a store's customers save expense or simply shift it?

chapter 13

The Buyer's Order and Vendor Relations

THE ORDER

After the decision to purchase is made, with terms and conditions of sale agreed upon, the next step is to fill out the buyer's order. Formerly the sale contract was fairly simple; conditions were relatively uninvolved. With an increased scale of buying, more and more care was exercised to assure the buyer that ordered goods were delivered according to specification, in proper condition, with agreed service features and, in case of loss or delay, to make clear where to place the responsibility.

Goods are still sometimes ordered orally. Such an agreement is legally binding in most states for amounts under $50, but a witness would be necessary in case of dispute. Because many buyers are agents for others, and because memory is faulty and oral evidence uncertain, it is a practical necessity for all stores to place written orders on printed order blanks.

The Order Form

Small merchants who do their own buying and buyers in small stores frequently use an order blank provided by the manufacturer or the salesperson-representative in each line. Where most orders are small, and where the form is carefully scrutinized, the plan works fairly well. Because each form is different, however, there is danger that some essential notation will be omitted and lead to controversy later. Also, from the buyer's standpoint, the order form may include some unreasonable conditions in fine print that may pass unnoticed at the time.

In the large store, it has been found essential for the store to provide its buyers with an order form or blank that provides all necessary protection to the buyer. Vendors are notified that no agreements are valid unless incorporated on official order blanks. The buyer is familiarized with all details on the order and instructed in how to fill it out properly. Furthermore, the store form may act as a check on every order placed, because the controller may keep a record of the serial or register number of every order form issued. In many stores, each must be accounted for, and no goods are accepted unless there is a corresponding order duplicate on file. Although there has been some attempt by manufacturing groups to prevail upon retailers to use a standard order blank, not much progress has been made. Stores usually draw up their own forms. See Figure 13–1.

Copies

The buyer's order is generally made out with three or even more copies. The original is delivered to the vendor. One copy is sent to the store's central order department to compare with the vendor's bill when received. One copy is kept by the buyer. If order information is needed for unit control data, whether compiled manually or by a computer, a copy is needed for this purpose and/or the fourth copy for the markers who prepare price tickets. Still another may be required for the resident or central buying office to be used in following up the store's orders.

With the growth of multiunit operations, order forms have increased in number and complexity. For example, Brandeis, one of whose forms appears in Figure 13–1, uses five versions of its order form for: (1) shipments limited to a single store (illustrated), (2) multistore shipments for clothing where columns must be provided for sizes, (3) multistore shipments that do not require size information, (4) furniture where special columns are needed for finish, cover, and color, and (5) special orders. These also have extension sheets where all the items ordered from one resource cannot be entered on one sheet.

In many stores, the buyer is required to indicate the retail price on the duplicate order copies. This plan forces the buyer to consider the retail price at the time the goods are ordered rather than when they come in. The plan also makes it possible for goods to be marked promptly on arrival without waiting for the buyer to decide on the retail price. Retails are commonly "extended" (multiplied by quantities ordered) and totaled to determine the total retail value of the order. This is charged against the department's open-to-buy, if that record is kept at retail. There are two objections to the plan: It may result in the buyer's becoming lax in inspecting incoming goods, because the pricing procedure will go on automatically; and the system may

FIGURE 13–1 A store order form. Brandeis, a department store chain, with the parent store in Omaha and branches throughout Nebraska and Iowa, uses this order form for goods that are to be shipped to a single store. Where the purchase is to be shipped to the branches as well, a wider form is used with columns for the quantities to be shipped to each store. On the three duplicate copies of the order form, the space used on the original for billing instructions is used for the unit retail price and extensions. This store will soon convert its order forms into a computer format to be used in connection with a point-of-sale computerized system.

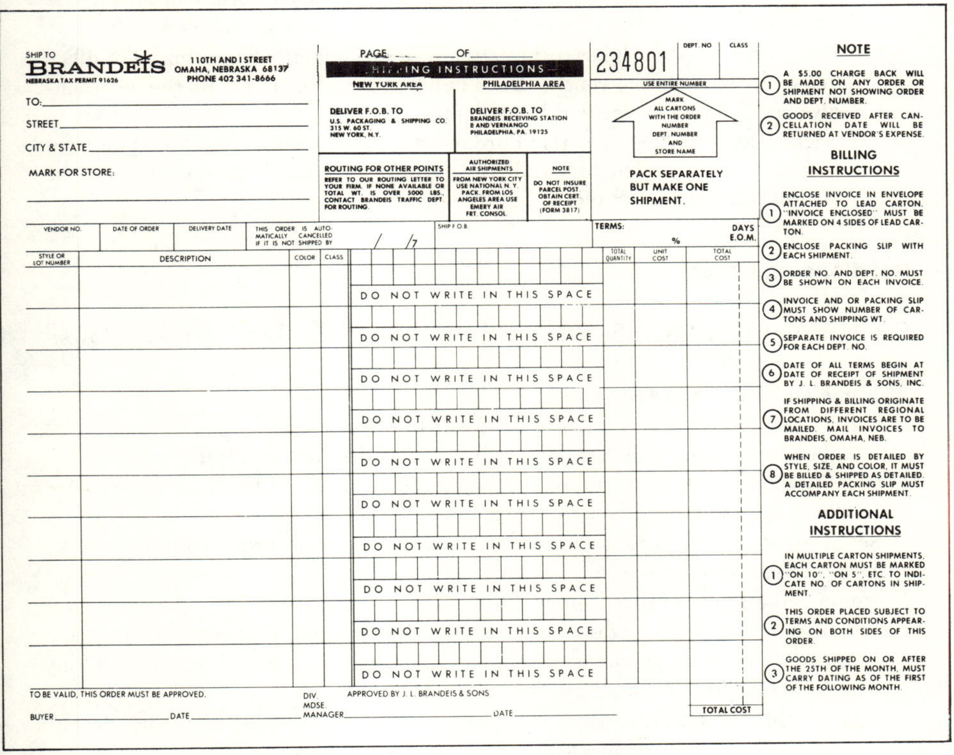

SHIP TO
BRANDEIS
NEBRASKA TAX PERMIT 91626
110TH AND I STREET
OMAHA, NEBRASKA 68137
PHONE 402 341-8666

TO: ____
STREET ____
CITY & STATE ____
MARK FOR STORE: ____

PAGE ____ OF ____

SHIPPING INSTRUCTIONS

NEW YORK AREA
DELIVER F.O.B. TO
U.S. PACKAGING & SHIPPING CO.
315 W. 60 ST.
NEW YORK, N.Y.

PHILADELPHIA AREA
DELIVER F.O.B. TO
BRANDEIS RECEIVING STATION
B AND VERNANGO
PHILADELPHIA, PA. 19125

ROUTING FOR OTHER POINTS
REFER TO OUR ROUTING LETTER TO YOUR FIRM. IF NONE AVAILABLE OR TOTAL WT. IS OVER 5000 LBS., CONTACT BRANDEIS TRAFFIC DEPT. FOR ROUTING.

AUTHORIZED AIR SHIPMENTS
FROM NEW YORK CITY USE NATIONAL N. Y. PACK. FROM LOS ANGELES AREA USE EMERY AIR FRT. CONSOL.

NOTE
DO NOT INSURE PARCEL POST. OBTAIN CERT. OF RECEIPT (FORM 3817)

234801 | DEPT. NO | CLASS
USE ENTIRE NUMBER

MARK ALL CARTONS WITH THE ORDER NUMBER DEPT. NUMBER AND STORE NAME

PACK SEPARATELY BUT MAKE ONE SHIPMENT.

VENDOR NO.	DATE OF ORDER	DELIVERY DATE	THIS ORDER IS AUTOMATICALLY CANCELLED IF IT IS NOT SHIPPED BY / /7	SHIP F.O.B.	TERMS: % DAYS E.O.M.

STYLE OR LOT NUMBER	DESCRIPTION	COLOR	CLASS		TOTAL QUANTITY	UNIT COST	TOTAL COST
				DO NOT WRITE IN THIS SPACE			
				DO NOT WRITE IN THIS SPACE			
				DO NOT WRITE IN THIS SPACE			
				DO NOT WRITE IN THIS SPACE			
				DO NOT WRITE IN THIS SPACE			
				DO NOT WRITE IN THIS SPACE			
				DO NOT WRITE IN THIS SPACE			
				DO NOT WRITE IN THIS SPACE			
				DO NOT WRITE IN THIS SPACE			
				DO NOT WRITE IN THIS SPACE			
							TOTAL COST

TO BE VALID, THIS ORDER MUST BE APPROVED.
BUYER ____ DATE ____
DIV. MDSE. MANAGER ____ APPROVED BY J. L. BRANDEIS & SONS DATE ____

NOTE

1. A $5.00 CHARGE BACK WILL BE MADE ON ANY ORDER OR SHIPMENT NOT SHOWING ORDER AND DEPT. NUMBER.
2. GOODS RECEIVED AFTER CANCELLATION DATE WILL BE RETURNED AT VENDOR'S EXPENSE.

BILLING INSTRUCTIONS

1. ENCLOSE INVOICE IN ENVELOPE ATTACHED TO LEAD CARTON. "INVOICE ENCLOSED" MUST BE MARKED ON 4 SIDES OF LEAD CARTON.
2. ENCLOSE PACKING SLIP WITH EACH SHIPMENT.
3. ORDER NO. AND DEPT. NO. MUST BE SHOWN ON EACH INVOICE.
4. INVOICE AND OR PACKING SLIP MUST SHOW NUMBER OF CARTONS AND SHIPPING WT.
5. SEPARATE INVOICE IS REQUIRED FOR EACH DEPT. NO.
6. DATE OF ALL TERMS BEGIN AT DATE OF RECEIPT OF SHIPMENT BY J. L. BRANDEIS & SONS, INC.
7. IF SHIPPING & BILLING ORIGINATE FROM DIFFERENT REGIONAL LOCATIONS, INVOICES ARE TO BE MAILED. MAIL INVOICES TO BRANDEIS, OMAHA, NEB.
8. WHEN ORDER IS DETAILED BY STYLE, SIZE, AND COLOR, IT MUST BE BILLED & SHIPPED AS DETAILED. A DETAILED PACKING SLIP MUST ACCOMPANY EACH SHIPMENT.

ADDITIONAL INSTRUCTIONS

1. IN MULTIPLE CARTON SHIPMENTS, EACH CARTON MUST BE MARKED "ON 10", "ON 5", ETC. TO INDICATE NO. OF CARTONS IN SHIPMENT.
2. THIS ORDER PLACED SUBJECT TO TERMS AND CONDITIONS APPEARING ON BOTH SIDES OF THIS ORDER.
3. GOODS SHIPPED ON OR AFTER THE 25TH OF THE MONTH, MUST CARRY DATING AS OF THE FIRST OF THE FOLLOWING MONTH.

not provide for changes in market price. Competition may force revision between the time of purchase and receipt. A good plan is to require that the buyer retail orders but to insist that he or she recheck prices when the goods and invoices arrive.

Kinds of Orders

Orders may be classified as follows:

1. Regular or stock orders—those placed by the buyer directly with the vendor for stock requirements and giving full specifications as to the time and amount

of shipment. In buying for a chain or branch store system, the requirements for each store unit may be indicated.
2. Reorders—orders for additional quantities of goods purchased before.
3. Special orders—those placed by the store for single units to satisfy the demands of individual store customers.
4. Advance orders—regular orders placed for delivery some time in the future rather than for quick delivery.
5. Blanket orders—orders covering the store's requirements for all or part of a season but not indicating specific shipping dates or details of size or finish. The store places requisitions against these orders as goods are needed.
6. Open orders—those placed through a resident buying office where the office fills in the name of the vendor that it believes is best suited to fill the merchandise requirements specified by the store.
7. Back orders—orders or parts of orders that the vendor has not filled on time and that are intended to be filled as soon as the goods in question can be manufactured or procured.

Notations on Orders

Essential notations that should appear on every order blank are as follows:

Name and address of the store.
Where the goods are to be delivered if not to the store.
Number of the selling department if the store is departmentalized.
Classification number, a subdivision of the department or store for which purchase and sales records are segregated.
Serial number of the order, to provide a control on every order form.
Date of the order.
Name and address of the shipper.
Credit terms, indicating when payment is to be made and what cash discounts are available for early payment. (See the glossary in the Technical Appendix at the end of Chapter 14 for various terms).
Date of shipment. (Date when shipment is to be completed should be clearly stated along with a cancellation date, and such terms as "at once" and "as ready" should be avoided).[1]
Method of shipment, including carrier to be used and whether the goods are to be delivered to a consolidator or freight forwarder and where title is to pass.
Free delivery point (generally expressed by FOB terms).
Description of the merchandise, including style and lot numbers, colors, sizes, finishes, etc.
Quantity ordered.
Unit cost price of each item.
Functional, trade, quantity, or seasonal discounts, if any.
Total estimate of the order. (Estimate is used here because the buyer is commit-

[1]If the completion date is some months ahead, the order should indicate what portion of the order is to be shipped in each intervening month.

ted to a certain number of units at unit prices and would not be bound by a mistake in arithmetic.

Signature of the buyer and commonly of the merchandise manager and sometimes of the vendor's representative.

Standard and special instructions. In some cases, these may include a statement of warranty and special service that the seller agrees to provide, such as advertising allowances.

Signatures on orders

In many stores, the signature of the buyer is the only one that must appear on the order to make it binding on the store. An order signed by the buyer indicates the store's offer to buy in the quantities and at the price specified. If the vendor gives the buyer in exchange a signed confirmation or acceptance of the order in the form made out, the order becomes binding on both. Sometimes the vendor's representative is authorized to sign the original order along with the buyer. The order might then bind the firm without a confirmation being sent to the buyer. Many manufacturers, however, allow their sales representatives to take orders only on the definite understanding that they are not binding until a confirmation has been mailed from the vendor's office. Frequently, a vendor's acceptance of an order takes the form of actual shipment of the goods without any written acceptance.

The signature of the merchandise manager as well as that of the buyer is required in a large number of stores. By signing orders placed, the merchandise manager keeps a close check on the activities of the buyers. If it is one of the store rules that all orders be countersigned by the merchandise manager, no order for merchandise is valid unless it has been so signed. If a store has such a requirement, however, the vendor should be explicitly notified of the fact; otherwise, he or she is justified in assuming that the store buyer has the authority to contract for merchandise. Because store buyers have had this authority so generally, it may be regarded as one of the authorities of the buyer unless the store clearly indicates to the contrary.

Question of merchandise manager's signature

There is some difference of opinion as to whether the merchandise manager's signature should be required. Those in favor argue that he or she should control every order placed and thus be able to prevent any purchase that may be considered unwise. On the other hand, it may be argued that the merchandise manager cannot have the buyer's intimate knowledge of merchandise and of customers' requirements; therefore, the former should not be in a position to dictate what is and what is not to be bought. Again, to get quick delivery of new goods with a fashion appeal, it is prudent to give the vendor the order while the buyer is still in the market rather than to wait for an order signed by a superior. The dilemma can be handled by having a divisional merchandise manager accompany the buyer to market and countersign orders, even for the buyers in other divisions. In the case of central buying in New York, the merchandise manager's office may be in the market city.

In most stores, signature of a superior is advisable. Yet, paradoxically, it is the largest stores that may find this practice unnecessary, because they often have buyers who are the equal of the merchandise managers of the smaller stores. They are fully competent to do their own buying and need to be controlled only in the amount of money they are allowed to spend for merchandise each week or each month. In many stores, however, the merchandise manager keeps the open-to-buy records and controls order placements against them. In such cases, his or her signature indicates, among other things, that the order has been approved and charged against open-to-buy.

The signed order is sometimes called the "order confirmation." This distinction is made, because buyers often write out, while in the market, a duplicate list of what they want to purchase on a blank provided by the vendor, who keeps the original. Stores with their own order forms regard this not as a bona fide order but rather simply as a memorandum from which, in case of purchase, the order will be copied onto the store's official form. Buyers may be tempted when placing memorandum orders, sometimes by phone, to demand immediate delivery before the official order is received by the vendor. When the buyer has a change of mind or when a required signature by the merchandise manager is not forthcoming, vendor relations deteriorate. Usually, the careful vendor will not ship until the official order or confirmation is received.

Standard conditions of purchase

General conditions are usually printed on the order. They vary with each store and refer for the most part to the store's freedom from obligation if the order is not fulfilled to the letter, and the legal obligations that the vendor assumes in accepting the order, particularly in connection with federal and state laws and regulations. See instructions in Figure 13–1. The major laws having provisions that must be observed in buying contracts are listed at the end of this chapter.

Special conditions

If the seller has agreed to provide a special service, such as labels, samples, informative brochures or demonstrators, or to make an advertising or display allowance, the nature of the agreement should be clearly specified on the order.

Writing the Order

As indicated in Chapter 10, it is sometimes wise to defer the writing of an order for new goods until the buyer is back from a market trip, free from any vendor pressure. Generally, buyers write their own orders and do not let salesrepresentatives do the job. This ensures that the orders are correctly filled out and that there is an opportunity for reconsideration. Many buyers, however, leave this work to assistants. These buyers believe that detailing the order is time-consuming work that can best be done at a lower level. Where goods for different classifications are being ordered from the same vendor, separate order blanks for each may be desirable. Care should be taken to avoid overcrowding the form; descriptions of goods should be complete.[2]

After the order has been made out, and preferably before it is given to the vendor, the items should be checked against the buying plan in order to indicate what the buyer still has to purchase and to avoid overpurchasing in any classification, price line, size, color, or material grouping.

Order Follow-up

Prompt delivery is as important to the store as low price. Sales will be lost if goods do not arrive as planned, and fashion merchandise may depreciate in value between the time the order is placed and the goods are received.

In order to make sure that vendors ship on time, buyers find it necessary to set up an organized follow-up system. Copies of orders are arranged by due date, and on the due date, or shortly before, vendors are communicated with. In the case of fashion merchandise, stores that have resident buying offices may assign this duty to them.

The need for such a practice is particularly apparent during seasonal peaks when buyers are clamoring for goods. Goods come through the factory in lots of different styles and sizes, and these are grouped by orders, an attempt being made to fill early orders first. But buyers on the spot frequently "steal" styles that the manufacturer has laid aside for shipment to another. Because many manufacturers are small and poorly organized, they fail to prevent this practice. Accordingly, to protect their interests, stores may have to provide follow-up representatives to see that the goods they have ordered are not deflected to someone else. Of course, the store could cancel the order if the

[2]In some stores, shipping instructions are not entered on the order by the buyer but by a traffic clerk in the store who processes orders before they are delivered to vendors.

goods failed to arrive in time, but frequently the goods are badly needed. It is more important to get the goods than to exercise the privilege of cancellation. It is not uncommon for vendors to answer queries by stating that goods have been shipped and are on the way when, in fact, they have not been shipped. Tenacious expediters always ask for a bill of lading number or some other registered number that ensures that goods have been shipped and enables the buyer to trace them if need be.

Follow-up sometimes involves communication not with the shipper but with the transportation company. Delayed and lost shipments have to be traced, and sometimes the movement of a whole carload is expedited by bringing pressure to bear on the proper railroad or express authorities. Such work is one of the chief duties of a traffic manager in a large store.

Order Checking

After goods and corresponding invoices have been received by the store, orders must be checked against them to make sure that the vendor shipped exactly what was ordered and that all conditions in the contract were abided by. The usual practice is to compare merchandise with invoice and invoice with order copy rather than to compare the order with the goods.

In small stores, buyers can check their own orders, circling items that have been received so that the order copies always show balances on order. In larger stores, this function is performed by a staff order-checking department, where copies of all orders placed by the different buyers are filed and where the comparison of invoice and order takes place. The reason for this centralization is threefold:

1. Some buyers cannot be depended on to check carefully. They allow too many discrepancies between order and invoice to slip by.
2. The buyer's time is too valuable to be spent performing clerical and routine duties.
3. A centralized order department makes it possible for the store to determine at any time how much merchandise is on order for each department. This information is of primary importance in determining how much each buyer ought to be allowed to spend for merchandise at any time.[3]

Cancellation of "deadwood"

Because the amount a buyer may spend at any time depends partly on the amount on order, it is important that he or she cancel all outstanding balances that in all probability will not be shipped or that have overrun their due

[3]The computation of the open-to-buy is discussed in detail in John W. Wingate, Elmer O. Schaller, and F. Leonard Miller, *Retail Merchandise Management* (Englewood Cliffs, N.J.: Prentice-Hall, Inc., 1972), chap. 17.

dates and are no longer desirable. Unless carefully cleaned out periodically, the order file is certain to accumulate much "deadwood." Unless such "odds and ends" are canceled, they remain in the order file as bona fide commitments and are included in the outstanding orders or total amount on the order register, thus limiting the amount a buyer is entitled to purchase. Take the limit of $5000 with $4800 commitments and $200 open-to-buy. It may be that of that $4800 worth of orders, $500 worth is nothing but "deadwood." If the buyer would clear this out by cancellation, the open-to-buy would be increased to $700. Because the successful buyer always wishes to be open-to-buy, in order to be ready to take advantage of any special opportunities in the market, keeping the order file clear will be of great assistance.

Receipt of Ordered Merchandise

There are a number of distinct responsibilities in connection with the receipt of the merchandise. In addition to making sure that the shipment agrees with the information on the order, the buyer is responsible for the *quality check* to make sure that the goods (1) are the identical items selected in the market, (2) agree with the samples on which this order was based, (3) agree with the description on this order, *or* (4) incorporate all of the specifications drawn up for the merchandise. Some retail organizations employ inspectors to pass on established standards of workmanship, but the buyer must usually be depended on to check style and other subtle factors. In the case of the central buyer, located in the market, he or she can often arrange to inspect the goods on the manufacturer's premises just before they are shipped and thus avoid costly returns. An exception may occur where a sample of the ordered goods is retained at the store or warehouse for inspectors to compare with the shipment. Standardized goods usually do not require inspection for quality.

The *quantity check*, involving the counting of the number of each item, color, and size actually received and the comparing of this with both invoice and order, may also be a buyer's responsibility, but in the larger organizations, specialists in merchandise checking and in order checking perform these functions, relieving the buyer of much routine.

The buyer also has the responsibility of making sure that price tickets have all the information required. And for determining the disposition of the goods, the buyer decides whether the goods should be moved at once to forward stock (or stores in a chain) or to be held in warehouse or reserve.

In case of discrepancies between shipment and invoice and/or invoice and order, it is usually the buyer who must decide what action is to be taken. If goods are to be returned to the vendor, appropriate forms must be filled out and in some instances approval of the merchandise manager obtained. Any returns growing out of the vendor's errors should be sent collect.

Where marking and ticketing is done centrally in a multiunit organization, it is presumed that all units will sell the goods at identical prices, although the buyer usually has the authority to allow regional differences in price, where local conditions warrant.

No-order shipments

Goods often arrive at the store or warehouse with no buyer's order at hand. Sometimes the vendor has shipped unordered goods; sometimes the buyer while in the central wholesale market has failed to get a copy of the order to the store before receipt of goods; or an oral order has not been followed by a written confirmation to avoid expected rejection.

Although a few stores return at once goods for which they have no order on file, the usual practice is to check with the buyer to prepare an immediate written order if the shipment has been authorized. It is considered poor policy to accept unordered goods even if they are desirable, because the practice would encourage vendors to keep sending in unordered merchandise in the hope that the store would keep much of it. Until such goods are actually returned, the buyer should exercise no act of ownership, such as displaying some of the goods to the store's customers. Such an act would constitute an act of acceptance of the seller's offer (in the form of delivery of the goods), and the buyer could be required to keep the entire shipment.

VENDOR RELATIONS

The Buyer's Loyalty

Vendor relations are largely determined by the buyer's sense of loyalty. The loyalty a buyer feels toward the store employer may be contrasted with that felt toward suppliers. Three types of buyers may be recognized: (1) the buyer who feels no obligation to resources, only to him- or herself and the store (the vendor tends to be regarded as an adversary to be overcome); (2) the buyer who feels more comfortable with and more dependent on key suppliers because they treat him as a VIP and because he can turn to them for help if ever in search of a new position elsewhere; and (3) the professional buyer who recognizes obligations both to his or her employer and to suppliers, convinced, as explained in Chapter 11, that both parties must win if negotiations are to be successful in the long run.

Vendor relations characterized more by cooperation than by conflict

Any discussion of buyer-vendor relations tends to focus on differences and antagonisms. Yet vast amounts of goods move routinely through the channels of commerce, bringing profit and psychic satisfactions to many people and many enterprises. This is said not to waive aside the conflicts that do exist but to get a perspective that clearly views them as discordant intrusions rather than as dominant features of the trading scene.

Table 13–1

Some Suggestions for Vendor Relations

The buyer and the vendor are not antagonists; they are cooperators.
Be open with key resources and acquaint them with long-range goals.
Involve the merchandise manager in vendor contacts; he or she, too, should meet with the store's suppliers.
Learn how to say *NO* to sales representatives, rather than to place tentative orders that will be cancelled in whole or in part.
Never accept personal favors from vendors, or you will become beholden to them.

Whenever people have to identify their special personal desires with the conflicting needs of others, there is bound to be some attendant noise. Most of it is an undertone effect commonly known as "griping" and is probably a healthy escape valve for the excess energy involved in running the social machine. See Table 13–1.

The fallacy of the "good" versus the "bad" guys

This is the kind of understanding that comes only from comprehension of the continuum idea. No one is wholly good or scrupulous, and no one is completely bad or unscrupulous. Between these two points are the degrees of goodness that characterize individuals and groups. And rating an "opponent" on this scale is one of the skills that a buyer must cultivate. It is not helpful to view all vendors as alike.

Antagonistic attitudes lead to wasteful efforts by each to gain advantage at the expense of the other—efforts that tend to end in higher distribution costs. They impede entry of the ethical buyer who looks for profit by providing good service to customers rather than by attempting to profit from suppliers' losses.

Although the buyer with high personal standards is well advised to assume that most vendors are grouped around the "good" to "excellent" stretch on the continuum of scrupulousness, he or she should recognize that one way to bring them down the scale is to offer too much temptation. The buyer who is ignorant about the merchandise line does just that. So does the buyer who is timid, complacent, careless, or indiscriminately trusting. A competent buyer generates an ethical seller.[4]

Complaints on both sides

Although many of the complaints made by sellers against buyers and by buyers against sellers have remedies at law, only a small part of the numerous disputes are presented for impartial legal adjudication; the great majority

[4]Refer to the method of vendor analysis presented in Chapter 9.

are settled out of court. Unfortunately, such settlements do not necessarily indicate mutual accord. Rather, the party with the strategic market position is often able to force demands on the other. If a retailer is a potential customer for a large volume of a vendor's product, he or she may be able to force unreasonable concessions from a vendor before the latter will take the matter to court or even to arbitration. A vendor's business depends on the good will of his or her customers, the store buyers. Good will is one of the most important assets in merchandising and is based on confidence. Just as retailers often make adjustments for customers who are in the wrong, so vendors will often undergo considerable injustice in order to avoid losing large accounts. Again, vendors and buyers alike are reluctant to undergo the tedious and expensive process of resorting to the courts to enforce contracts. The money spent in gaining a favorable decision may often far exceed the amount of the judgement won. These considerations have given a kind of immunity to contract breakers, especially those with particularly large accounts.

Sometimes the vendor has the strategic position. In times of heavy demand, retailers are clamoring for goods. Not only are they willing to pay high prices, but also, if necessary, to buy unwanted goods in order to be allotted some they want. At such times, the vendor is likely to break the contract by making late shipments; substituting styles, sizes, and colors; or shipping inferior merchandise. And seldom is the buyer in a position to hold the vendor responsible for loss of sales caused by breach of contract.

Unfair practices are seldom the result of one party's deliberate desire to injure the other. They are rather the outgrowth of conditions of supply and demand. During slack periods, when vendors are in urgent need of orders, buyers see an opportunity to save money by demanding concessions that vendors find it hard to deny. During busy periods, vendors find it almost impossible to ship all goods on time and to avoid making substitutions in style numbers.

Vendor Relations Policies

For the large store, with a group of departmental buyers, a code of conduct takes the form of store policies governing a number of specific activities. The following suggestions as to elements in such a code have been drawn from many sources.

Policies concerning the order contract

Policies related to the ordering of merchandise have been suggested by the NRMA Vendor Relations Committee for the consideration of their member stores. These appear in Figure 13–2.

FIGURE 13–2 NRMA voluntary vendor trade guidelines

NRMA VOLUNTARY VENDOR
TRADE GUIDELINES

ADOPTED BY NRMA VENDOR RELATIONS COMMITTEE
NOVEMBER 8, 1973

THE FOLLOWING VOLUNTARY GUIDELINES ARE OFFERED TO RETAILERS FOR POSSIBLE USE IN WHOLE, IN PART, OR NOT AT ALL, IN THEIR INDIVIDUAL DEALINGS WITH VENDORS. NRMA OFFERS THESE GUIDELINES ON A COMPLETELY VOLUNTARY BASIS, REMINDING ITS MEMBERS THAT THEY ARE FREE TO ALTER OR VARY ANY OF ITS TERMS.

1. SELLER'S ACCEPTANCE OF PURCHASE ORDER

It is mutually agreed and understood that all the terms and conditions set forth in this order are satisfactory and that the seller will make complete shipment of this order unless seller notifies purchaser to the contrary not more than 10 days after receipt of this order. If seller so notifies, buyer must confirm any changes of this purchase order in writing. Seller will not ship before the beginning delivery date or after the completion date specified herein, without prior written approval of the purchaser, unless otherwise specified herein.

2. CANCELLATION OF ORDER BY PURCHASER

Purchaser may not cancel this order before date for completion of delivery, unless seller consents thereto, or unless a cancellation date is specified on the purchase order, in which event this order, or any unshipped portion thereof, is automatically cancelled upon that cancellation date, unless purchaser authorizes further extension in writing.

3. RETURNS OF MERCHANDISE TO SELLER

Merchandise received from seller that is defective, or shipped beyond cancellation date, or not specifically ordered, or otherwise in violation of the terms of the purchase order may be returned to seller, and shall be accepted by the seller, at seller's expense, F.O.B. buyer's store, within a reasonable time after receipt, and without requirement for return authorization. Seller shall bear the risk of loss with regard to such returned merchandise. Merchandise not immediately discovered defective may be returned at time of discovery and will be accepted by the seller.

4. INTERRUPTION OF BUSINESS

In the event of the material interruption of the business of either the Seller or Purchaser by reason of fire, war, Act of God, governmental action, or strikes which materially affect the performance of this contract, the party so affected may cancel the order for such merchandise as has not been delivered, upon notice to the other party, notwithstanding any other provisions herein.

5. PARTIAL SHIPMENTS BY SELLER

In the event that the seller shall not be able to manufacturer or deliver any part of this order, after having shipped part of this order, purchaser must be notified immediately. Seller shall not be liable for non-delivery of such merchandise except that purchaser has right to cancel and/or return any remaining portion of the order whose saleability may be affected because of non-shipment of the remainder of the order.

6. LIMITATION OF CREDIT

Seller shall have the right to limit credit extended the purchaser; however, seller shall inform purchaser in writing of any limitation.

7. SELLER'S INVOICE

Seller's invoice shall:

a) include statement(s) of conformity with all existing State and Federal laws;
b) not be dated prior to actual date of shipment;
c) follow format of NRMA Standard Invoice wherever possible

8. MODIFICATION, WAIVER AND DEFAULT

No modification of the terms of this agreement shall be effective unless stated in writing, and no waiver by either party of any default shall be deemed a waiver of any subsequent default.

Other store policies that affect vendor relations

These include:

1. PRICE CONCESSION POLICY In general, buyers feel that they have a right to demand the lowest price they can get. Many do not know that it is unlawful under the Robinson-Patman Act knowingly to seek or receive discriminatory prices. A policy to cover this responsibility makes it a standard condition of every order that the price granted is not discriminatory under the Robinson-Patman Act. On the other hand, the buyer may insist on equal treatment if he or she believes that competitors have been given advantageous prices.

2. ADVERTISING ALLOWANCE POLICY Allowance practice has been treated in detail in Chapter 12 with a comprehensive store policy, fair to both parties.

3. POLICY OF SEEING SALES REPRESENTATIVES Many stores and their buying offices have a policy of seeing all sales representatives who call at set hours or at least giving such callers firm appointments for a later date.[5]

4. ADVANCING SEASONS A practice that stems from competition is the advancement of seasons, whereby both vendors and retailers cut prices before a season is over and while an active customer demand still exists. This is accompanied by the promotion of next season's line before the time of normal customer demand. Such early markdowns cause unnecessary losses to both vendors and stores. Because an individual vendor or buyer may find it to his or her immediate advantage to act ahead of competitors, there may be a need for a general but flexible recognition as to the proper time to institute seasonal clearance and offer new season's goods.

5. STYLE PIRACY As a rule, this is a matter of relationship among vendors themselves. But many do complain about the practice of some buyers who get hold of a sample or make a sketch with the purpose of getting some other manufacturer to reproduce the article at a lower price. Some stores prohibit such practices.

Protective Measures against Certain Vendor Practices

In view of numerous vendor practices that are found objectionable by retailers, the latter have found it necessary to introduce various protective measures that require discussion.

1. Substitution and failure to follow instructions

Careful analysis of goods bought by sample or inspection and careful checking of shipments against sample and specification details is found imperative in order to avoid misrepresented or substituted merchandise.

[5]See the discussion of this point in Chapter 10.

Buyers occasionally find it necessary to ask manufacturers to provide statements from an independent testing bureau attesting to the facts about the product offered. In some instances, stores maintain their own testing laboratories or make use of independent laboratories. Another device is to insist that sellers make their guarantees in writing.

Substitutions are sometimes a service to the buyer. For example, in the garment trade, a manufacturer is frequently unable to obtain unlimited quantities of certain materials or certain color combinations. When reorders come in, they are filled with the closest substitute.

Likewise, the difficulty in anticipating exactly when orders can be completed leads to the vendor's failure to live up to delivery dates. Buyers can help to improve conditions by ordering early enough, placing reasonable delivery dates on orders, and by dealing with the vendors who have their production schedules so well organized as to be able to live up to their agreements.

As indicated in an earlier chapter, failure on the part of vendors to follow shipping instructions may add greatly to the cost of transportation. This has led store checkers to compare shipments with the shipping instructions of the buyer and to charge back to the vendor the added cost caused by failure to adhere to the instructions provided.

2. *Price and service discrimination*

Small-store buyers frequently complain that their suppliers grant to large-scale buyers low prices, rebates, and large allowances that are not made available to them. These matters are covered by the Robinson-Patman Act and the rulings of the Federal Trade Commission based upon it. If a small buyer has reason to suspect discrimination, he or she may bring the matter to the attention of the Commission for investigation. However, it must be observed that a lower price to a large buyer is not by itself evidence of discrimination, because the law recognizes the validity of certain price differences growing out of quantity purchased or special method of sale.[6]

3. *Indirect price increases*

From time to time, vendors have attempted to increase the net price to themselves not by advancing the billed price but by lowering established discount rates, by charging the buyer an increased portion of the transportation cost, or by reducing advertising allowances. They may consider these to be less objectionable ways of realizing more for their merchandise, particularly in periods of rising cost.

A management complaint is that buyers are not sufficiently concerned about cash discounts. To overcome this, many stores maintain a record of all cash discounts received and check each subsequent order against the record.

[6]See Chapter 11 for a discussion of the Robinson-Patman Act.

Where any lowered discounts are spotted, buyers are urged to seek the restoration of the former terms.

Although buyers who insist that there must never be any reduction in discounts or terms of sale may be taking an untenable position, they have every right to demand to be consulted whenever manufacturers deem price increases necessary, so that the least disruptive method of introducing the increase may be followed.

From the consumer's point of view, there is a much more objectionable type of hidden price increase. This is for the manufacturer to reduce the weight or volume of the product unit without reducing the price and sometimes increasing it. This is to compensate for inflationary cost increases without a corresponding price increases that might discourage consumer buying. Examples are candy bars, household drug products, and paper towels.

4. Refusal to sell to price cutters

Manufacturers who sold in the past under a resale price agreement plan complained that retailers frequently violated their contracts, pricing below the contractual minimum. Even if the seller refused to sell to habitual price cutters, the latter often obtained the goods through devious channels—from a wholesaler or even from another retailer who bought more than his or her own needs demanded.

With "fair trade" now eliminated in interstate commerce, retailers increasingly have the right to price outright purchases as they please. Nevertheless, there is a continuing tendency for some manufacturers of branded lines to set retail prices indirectly by refusing to sell to price cutters. Some quality retailers have even urged manufacturers to cut off the discounters. A 1919 Supreme Court decision, involving Colgate & Co., affirmed the right of a "manufacturer engaged in entirely private business freely to exercise his own independent discretion as to parties with whom he will deal." Such decisions must be unilateral ones and not the result of hidden agreements with dealers not to sell to price cutters. The FTC takes the position that the refusal to sell to a price cutter is often more than a unilateral decision, and it may even challenge the Colgate doctrine. Buyers who pressure manufacturers to refuse to sell to price cutters may be found in violation of the antitrust laws.

5. Manufacturing "to order" only

Some vendors refuse to take an inventory risk, putting nothing into production until firm orders are received. Buyers feel that vendors should share the inventory risk, at least in the case of staples and fashion goods that have the potential of becoming reorder numbers. In the apparel fields, they urge the manufacturers to cut a larger quantity of a style number than they have orders for in order to be able to fill reorders promptly should the style prove a success. The risk of stocking an extra supply is less for the manufacturer than for the retailer, because the manufacturer supplies customer demand all over the country whereas the latter may be limited to customer acceptance in one or a few localities.

Because prompt replenishment of retail inventories is a prerequisite to maximum sales, it would seem to be to the mutual advantage of both buyer and seller to share the risk; and the able buyer will solicit cooperation in the light of the manufacturer's own interest.

6. Vendor agreements

The antitrust laws for many years have prohibited agreements among competing vendors that were "in restraint of trade," and price agreements definitely come in this category. Nevertheless, vendors' trade associations that may legitimately exchange information sometimes may go too far and bring about uniform prices and terms of sale. Flexibility of price seems to be necessary to adjust production to distribution; price-fixing tends to prevent economic balance. Retailers are on sound economic ground in opposing vendor agreements aimed at price fixing.

TERM STANDARDIZATION Vendor agreements frequently take the form not of price-fixing but of standardization of credit terms. Vendors' trade associations often succeed in getting their memberships to agree on terms of sale. The purpose of these efforts is to stabilize the industry by eliminating "chiseling." Although standard terms strengthen each seller's bargaining position, they also tend to decrease price competition and to make price structure rigid in that adjustment cannot be accomplished by the time-honored method of negotiation.

7. Direct selling to consumers

Except for job lots, retail buyers attempt to avoid purchasing from vendors who make it a practice to sell also to the genral public. It is the conviction of responsible merchants that manufacturers and wholesalers should not compete with them by selling to ultimate consumers unless they wish to give up selling through retailers entirely.

8. Selling competitors

Most buyers of convenience and shopping goods recognize the necessity for their suppliers to sell to their competitors as well, but they expect manufacturers of specialty products to designate a limited number of stores as their franchised agents—and in some instances to set up a single exclusive agent in a retail trading area. Also, in the higher-priced shopping lines, they expect certain styles to be confined to them and not to be made generally available.[7] Vendors who start selling with a selective or exclusive distribution policy sometimes decide to seek a wider market by selling to competitors or by making heavy demands on their franchised agents to increase their volume materially. Discount houses provide a shiny lure.

There is no easy solution to this problem from the buyers' viewpoint. They have to be very careful to tie up with vendors whose lines are clearly specialty ones and who will not soon feel that they must have mass distribution. Also, buyers should demand the right to considerable advance notice of any change in policy, so that they may liquidate the inventory, if they wish.

Fear of becoming dependent on a vendor who may change his or her policy of distribution is a major reason why many retailers have introduced their own private brands. These make it possible for them to change resources without losing the good will and assurance of repeat trade associated with the brand.

9. Tie-in sales

A vendor of an article in short supply may refuse to sell it unless the buyer accepts with it some other article in oversupply or provides a large margin of profit to the seller. Such tie-in sales are illegal under the Clayton Act, but the law is not readily enforced, and buyers may go along in order to get much-needed merchandise. Also, it must be recognized that some tie-in sales provide the buyer a form of discount on regular purchases and thus may make the deal worthwhile. Where the tie-in demand is not in the buyer's interest, he or she may be able to "soft-pedal" the brand in question and attempt to develop another brand where similar tie-in demands will not be made.

10. Commercial bribery

Commercial bribery may be defined as the giving of something of value by a vendor to the agent of another in order to induce purchase or special promotional attention. Three types may be recognized: money, gifts, and subsidies.

Gifts may vary from a cigar to an automobile; and subsidies include cash prizes, rewards, and commissions paid by vendors to retail salespeople to induce them to push their products. There is the greatest secrecy and the greatest sense of obligation on the recipient's part in the case of the money bribe, and the least secrecy and obligation in the case of the subsidy. On the other hand, gifts and subsidies are more dangerous than money

[7]Buyers who are favored as selective agents in a trading area must be certain that their selection came about as a general policy of the vendor and not by private agreement between vendor and buyer, which might be interpreted as a conspiracy in restraint of trade under the Sherman or Clayton Acts.

bribes, because they can influence so many. The great majority of agent-buyers would not take a money bribe, because they look upon it as dishonest and as a consideration to buy from the giver; but many take gifts and believe themselves not definitely obligated to buy. Yet there is generally a sufficient sense of obligation to make it virtually impossible solely to consider the best interests of the store when they choose resources.

The subsidy is often defended on the grounds that it does not injure the store in merchandise selection and that it is usually known to the store management. Nevertheless, it has the sinister influence of putting the store that presumes to sell customers what they want in the position of pushing certain products, not on their merits, but in order to benefit some employee personally. Furthermore, the practice is unfair to competing manufacturers who do not give subsidies. Should they do so, there would develop an expensive competition that would add greatly to the selling costs of all manufacturers with little increase in customer demand. Subsidies to retail salespeople in the cosmetic industry, called "manufacturer's PMs," have been very common. The revised Trade Practice Rules for the industry, however, made it an unfair practice for a manufacturer to provide "push money" to a clerk in a store that carries a competing brand or brands if the consuming public might be erroneously led to believe that the clerk is without special interest or influence. Thus, in this field at least, it would seem that a salesperson receiving a PM from the manufacturer would have to be assigned solely to a section handling that manufacturer's product. In effect, such rules may eliminate subsidies, except in the case of a specialty product handled under an exclusive agency agreement. Whether a vendor will grant subsidies to salespeople when the dealer handles no competing products is questionable, however, because the subsidy has been used previously as a competitive device to get one product promoted at the expense of other lines.

11. Providing gifts and favors

One major chain of stores has established the following policies in regard to gifts and favors to their buyers from vendors.

Gifts: No gift of any kind, regardless of its worth or the circumstances in which it is given, should ever be accepted. Any other approach inevitably creates confusion and potential problems.

Luncheons: Luncheons with a resource as part of the regular day's work are an accepted and often valuable part of the buying process. Although such luncheons are not to be solicited, they may be accepted on a restrained and reasonable basis. They should be reciprocated as a token of company attitude by taking the vendor to lunch on occasion. This does not require a "one-for-one" approach but simply a periodic gesture. In the central office, reciprocation is made easy with the luncheon facilities available in the building.

Favors: Favors, such as golf dates, theater tickets, and dinners, should be ac-

> cepted only on a very infrequent basis and only if they are reciprocated *in each instance.* The reciprocation need not be a return of exactly the same favor, but it must be adequate in the buyer's judgment. The social aspect of the buyer-source relationship is in itself not necessarily unhealthy or contrary to the company interest. If handled the wrong way, however, it can be insidious and dangerous, leading to abuses.

Some buying organizations do not have policies as strict as the foregoing. They do not regard a small Christmas remembrance or anniversary remembrance as a "gift," but they do expect the buyer to pay for anything of appreciable value that the vendor may provide in order to avoid any possibility of the buyer feeling an obligation to favor the vendor in some way.[8]

Improving Trade Relations

Better trade relations may be promoted in three ways: education, self-regulation, and government regulation.

Education

Education is the surest but the slowest way. Courses in business ethics and in the private competitive enterprise system are taught in many schools and colleges, and these subjects are touched upon in many commercial courses. Trade associations, too, try to educate their members in principles of sound business conduct (refer to Figure 13–2).

Although such cooperative educational efforts give the greatest promise of effecting results in the long run, there are always those who resist education and whose unfair activities injure either competitors or customers. In consequence, regulatory measures are also deemed necessary. These may be imposed by business interests or by government.

Self-regulation

At various times, groups of both retailers and manufacturers have attempted to regulate the trade practices of their member stores. Retail associations have collected instances of what they deemed to be unfair practices of specific vendors and have brought pressure on them. Manufacturing groups have attempted to stamp out piracy and to exchange price and discount schedules in order to thwart cut-throat price cutting. But such attempts run afoul of the antitrust laws in that the exchange of price information may lead to price fixing.[9]

[8]When a buyer and his or her family have become close friends with a vendor, it is permissible for them to exchange gifts at Christmas time as long as the exchanges are of comparable value.

[9]A number of prominent retail merchants in New York were found guilty and heavily fined when they agreed to sell the apparel from leading manufacturers they all patronized at fixed retail prices.

Government regulations

Much of the improvement in trade practices has been the result of trade and consumer pressure on government bodies to regulate. There is now a long history of federal, state, and even local regulations that affect retail buying practice. The Robinson-Patman Act, perhaps the most important, is discussed in detail in Chapter 11. A brief summary of the federal regulations every retail buyer should know appears in the following section.

FEDERAL REGULATION OF BUSINESS

Every standard work on marketing and on government regulation of business discusses in considerable detail the various laws that have been enacted to foster competition and to protect the consumer from certain selling practices and injurious merchandise. And the student of buying will find it useful to have a list of the legislation involved, because under the authority of these laws, many specific regulations have been promulgated.

A. Major Laws Primarily to Promote Competition

1. *The Sherman Antitrust Act* of 1890, which made contracts and combinations in restraint of trade unlawful. For example, a group of stores may not conspire together to maintain the price of some article they all sell. This act prohibits contracts between sellers and buyers to maintain resale prices, and "horizontal" contracts for this purpose (those among sellers) are also illegal. See 5 and B-16 below.

2. *The Clayton Act* of 1914, which outlawed (a) price discrimination, (b) the sale or lease of merchandise on condition that the buyer would not deal in competing products, (c) acquisition by one corporation of the capital stock of a competitor in the same line, and (d) interlocking directorates in the case of large businesses, provided the device lessens competition.

3. *The Federal Trade Commission Act* of 1914, which established the Federal Trade Commission for the purpose of preventing unfair methods of commerce. What these methods were was not spelled out, but they have been established in regulatory codes. See Part B for the FTC's responsibility for consumer protection.

4. *The Robinson-Patman Act* of 1936, which amended the Clayton Act in order to define price discrimination clearly. The basic provisions have already been presented in Chapter 11.

5. *The Miller-Tydings Act* of 1937, which amended the Sherman Antitrust Act by removing the prohibition against resale price maintenance contracts on a "vertical" level (that is, contracts between buyers and sellers) among those states that had their own fair trade acts. The McGuire Bill of 1952 affirmed that dealers who did not sign resale price contracts were bound

to observe minimum or stipulated prices. These have since been repealed.

6. *The Lannan Act* of 1946 (effective 1947 and replacing the Trademark Act of 1905), which protects trademark owners against encroachment by others for a period of 17 years.[10] Although trademark rights exist independently of registration under the common law, registration under the act and marking the merchandise accordingly provide the trademark owner complete protection against subsequent use by another company in interstate commerce. After it has been registered for 5 years, a trademark cannot be overthrown by those then claiming prior registration.

7. *The Magnuson-Moss Improvement Act* of 1974, which permits the Federal Trade Commission to develop and adopt, after industry hearings, trade regulations that have the force of law and that become binding on an entire industry. The section of the law on warranty provisions is included in Part B.

B. Major Laws Primarily to Protect the Consumer of Products

1. *The Federal Meat Inspection Act* of 1907, which requires the labeling and inspection of meats.

2. *The Federal Trade Commission Act* of 1914, which set up the Federal Trade Commission and restrains unfair methods of competition as defined in codes drawn up by the Trade Practice Conference Procedures. False and misleading advertising and selling methods are defined in detail in these codes. Unfair advertising includes misrepresentations as to (a) place of origin, (b) quality, condition, or composition, (c) value, (d) endorsements and recommendations, (e) curative properties, (f) trade status (distributor claiming to be a producer), and (g) cost (designating goods as free when other goods must be bought or postage paid). A 1975 amendment gives the courts the authority to prescribe relief, particularly public notification by the seller when found guilty of unfair and deceptive acts. See part A for the FTC responsibility to promote competition.

3. *The Federal Food, Drug, and Cosmetic Act* of 1938, which prohibits adulteration, misbranding, and use of deceptive containers and which requires "warning" labels in certain cases. Potentially dangerous food and drug products may be removed from commerce. The act set up the Federal Food and Drug Administration to administer this law and was aimed primarily at consumer protection rather than at better[11] trade relations.

[10]Design patents protect for 3½, 7, or 14 years depending on the fee.

[11]The FDA also administers the food and drug aspect of the Fair Package and Labeling Act as well as a number of acts that have to do with safety of certain products, particularly the Radiation Control for Health and Safety Act (includes radiation in color TV and microwave ovens), the Public Health Service Act (biological drugs and sanitary practices in the production and marketing of certain foods), and the Caustic Poison Act.

The act has been amended a number of times, especially the food additive clause in 1958 that prohibits the use of chemicals in foods if they have been found to cause cancer in either animals or humans, and the 1962 amendment that requires that drugs must be effective for the use intended, not simply safe.

4. *The Wheeler-Lea Act* of 1938, which extended the Federal Trade Commission Act's coverage to deceptive acts and practices, gave the Commission jurisdiction over the advertising of foods, drugs, and cosmetics, with the power to issue temporary injunctions rather than to be powerless to stop misleading advertising of foods, etc., until formal hearings had been held. This act, too, was aimed at consumer protection but also protects the retail store buyer from misleading advertising.

5. *The Wool Products Labeling Act* of 1939, which requires the labeling of fiber content with percentages of wool, reprocessed wool, reused wool, and other fibers. This act was also designed for consumer protection but may be an aid to the inexperienced store buyer.

6. *The Fur Products Labeling Act* of 1951, which requires that if reused fur be used, the garment should be labeled accordingly, and that the English name of the skin should be used on each article and on invoices and in advertising. Furthermore, the name of another animal cannot be used with the skin's actual name. Thus it is illegal to advertise a coat as "mink-dyed muskrat." The purpose of the law is to protect against misnaming, mishandling, and misleading advertising of fur products and articles made in whole or in part of fur.

7. *The Flammable Fabrics Act* of 1953, amended in 1964, which contains prohibitions against the sale in interstate commerce of wearing apparel and other articles so highly flammable as to be dangerous when worn. The Tris controversy stemmed from this act.

8. *The Textile Fiber Products Identification Act* of 1959, which requires that most textile products be labeled with the generic fiber content (in the case of mixed goods with the percentage of each fiber by weight), the country of origin, and the sponsor (either name or registered number). This is also enforced by the FTC.

9. *The Hazardous Substance Act* of 1961, which requires the revealing of possible injurious substances in products used in the home (other than foods, drugs, and cosmetics, already covered by law).

10. *The Cigarette Labeling and Advertising Act* of 1965, which requires warning labels on cigarette packages and in advertising.

11. *The Fair Packaging and Labeling Act* of 1966. For packaged foods, it requires that containers be labeled to readily reveal the weight or volume of contents, weight of a single serving if the number of servings is stated, limited air space, and no misleading designations. Food package labeling is administered by the FDA, and nonfoods by the FTC.

12. *The Consumer Products Safety Act* of 1967, which set up a Consumer

Products Safety Commission to ban the sale of products, other than food or drugs, that are unsafe to use (such as certain toys and sporting equipment) and to implement the Hazardous Substance Act, the Poison Prevention Packaging Act, the Flammable Fabrics Act, and permanent-care labeling regulations for many textiles.

13. *The Consumer Protection Act* of 1969 (Truth-in-Lending), which requires that all relevant credit terms be revealed to customers and that the carrying charges be stated at the annual rate in order to permit a comparison of available credit deals.[12]

14. *The Poison Prevention Packaging Act* of 1970, which requires the use of "child-resistant" packages for substances that might poison children if in their reach.

15. *The Magnusen-Moss Warranty section of the Improvements Act* of 1974, which requires guarantees to be clear and dependable from the consumer point of view.[13]

16. *The Consumer Goods Pricing Act* of 1975, which eliminates "fair trade" in interstate commerce. Manufacturers and wholesaler distributors may no longer dictate the resale prices at which their products may be resold to the consumer.

17. *The Federal Communications Act* of 1936, which gives the Federal Communications Commission power to license broadcasting stations and thus the power to withhold a license from a station that is carrying deceptive commercials declared to be against the public interest.

DISCUSSION QUESTIONS

1. Is it necessary to include on the order a demand that all goods, labels, and prices covered by the order confirm with government regulations?
2. Does central marking lead to undue retail price rigidity in the various units of a chain or cooperative group?
3. Is it a sound practice for a store to refuse shipment for which approved order copies are not on hand?
4. Do the federal laws designed to foster competition lead to undesirable rigidity in the price structure?
5. Do the frequent government attacks on business people's buying and selling practices and the resultant lengthy defense add an undue burden to the cost of distribution? Explain.

[12]Other acts that have to do with the availability of credit and correct information are the Fair Credit Reporting Act, the Fair Credit Billing Act, and the Equal Credit Opportunity Act.

[13]The provisions of this act have been discussed in detail in Chapter 12, p. 000.

6. What recent decisions of the federal enforcement agencies or the courts are changing the meaning of the existing legislation?
7. Is there any justification for store buyers to be more loyal to their suppliers than they are to their merchant employers?
8. As time goes on, do you think that buyers will feel less loyalty toward the stores that employ them and more toward the evolving profession of retail buying? (This would result in more buyers moving about from one store group to another and not tying their personal destinies to one organization).
9. What are the responsibilities of the buyer to keep the seller ethical?
10. What are the responsibilities of the buyer and the retail firm in regard to product safety?
11. Should the buyer be responsible for making sure that allowances received are proportionally equal?
12. Consider each of the eleven vendor practices to which retailers often object (pp. 342–348). For which can the seller probably make an excellent defense?
13. Do you agree with the sentiments expressed in the policy of a leading department store chain regarding the accepting of favors?
14. Can buyers and sellers be expected to improve their trade relations voluntarily, or is government pressure required? Elaborate.
15. In view of the quantity of federal legislation to protect the consumer in the 1960s and mid-1970s, do you believe that additional legislation of this sort is still required?

chapter 14

Foreign Buying Including a Glossary of Credit and Shipping Terms

The availability of foreign-made merchandise in the retailer's stock has been growing and continues to grow. Inflation has caused increases in the retail prices of domestic merchandise while the lower wage costs and increasing production skills abroad have made foreign-made goods more attractive to the American consumer. For example, the men's clothing racks in one store organization carry suits, slacks, and sport jackets imported from Japan, Korea, Taiwan, Poland, Germany, Holland, and Equador.

REASONS FOR BUYING FOREIGN GOODS

The increased emphasis placed on foreign goods by American retailers may be summarized as follows:

INDIVIDUALITY The cultures of foreign lands, such as India and China, provide unique and intriguing design elements. The styles created are often the work of gifted local craftspeople. Their handiwork is hard to copy, and the variations from a fixed mechanical pattern have considerable appeal to many.

FASHION LEADERSHIP Many new designs, destined to become popular, originate abroad. American buyers flock to the markets in Italy including MAIT, the knitwear show, and in France to the *Pret a Porter*, the ready-to-wear showings. Although only samples often are bought for copying in the United States, the new fashions increasingly are imported for sale here. In the Far East also, new items are being developed for the American market, such as ultrasuede from Japan and the PVC (polyvinyl cloride) jackets.

QUALITY There has been a marked increase in the quality of foreign goods. In fact, some of it is reported to be equal or superior to domestic products. In the TV field, for example, Sony and Panasonic are outstanding. But the superior technology abroad may be short-lived. For example, Japan had a strong advantage in calculators and cameras, but the subminiaturization of them brought this market back to the United States. Similarly, Switzerland's leadership in watches has been overcome by the development of the digital watch in this country.

LOW PRICES The low cost of labor in most foreign countries permits the setting of retail price lines below those permitted by domestic costs. In fact, the low prices plus greatly improved quality, are providing severe competition for many U. S. manufacturers. For example, most TV sets are now made in Japan. Taiwan, and Mexico.

FAVORABLE CURRENCY EXCHANGE As the dollar strengthens relative to foreign currencies, the dollar buys more abroad and makes importing more profitable. Of course, this is only a cyclical advantage, because when the value of the dollar is depressed, it becomes more costly to buy foreign goods. On the whole, foreign price advantage has been slowly shrinking as foreign wages push upwards in developing countries and as the value of the dollar weakens, as long as imports (largely oil) exceed American exports.

BUYING FOREIGN GOODS FROM DOMESTIC SOURCES

There are three major types of domestic resources for foreign goods: the *import merchant*, the *resident sales agent*, and the *import commission house*. The import merchant may confine the operation to selling a single class of goods or a number of related classes including both foreign and domestic goods in order to broaden the line. Even some American manufacturers include in their lines some merchandise manufactured abroad.

The resident sales agent represents a group of foreign manufacturers and may or may not carry stocks. If not, the agent is ready to handle the paperwork involved in bringing in the goods. Sometimes the resident sales agent places the goods in a "bonded warehouse," where no duty is paid until the goods are withdrawn for delivery to the buyer.

The import commission house represents one or more foreign manufacturers. It deducts its commission in remitting sales receipts to foreign principals. It may also collect a commission from the buyer.[1] These agents commonly make periodic trips abroad and keep buyers in close touch with market developments.

[1]In this country, intermediaries operating on a commission basis are expected to act as agents for either the buyer or the seller but not for both. Foreign agents often collect from both parties.

Except for chains and affiliated groups, most stores that carry foreign goods depend largely on wholesale importers of the three previously mentioned types rather than going directly to foreign sources. Even though it is possible to get lower prices and a higher than average markup when buying direct, there are many risks involved and problems to overcome.

Advantages

The advantages of depending on American sources are:

1. The importer is usually highly experienced in the merchandise lines carried and has excellent foreign connections. The importer is a skilled negotiator and alert to fashion change.
2. Regular credit terms are made available to the stores, whereas the foreign producer may demand an irrevocable letter of credit or some other payment device that ties up the buyer's capital for a considerable period before the goods are received. It should be observed, however, that major retail chains can establish lines of credit to be drawn upon as needed and accordingly do not have their funds tied up before shipment.
3. The import wholesaler customarily assumes many of the fluctuating risks inherent in importing, such as fluctuations in foreign exchange, changes in duties, export taxes, and foreign regulations. The importer usually offers a firm price that is good for a given period of time even if importing costs change.
4. The importer assumes the liability for an increase in duty as originally calculated. The Customs Service of the Treasury Department reviews the appropriateness and accuracy of the original computation in determining duty, but this may not be done for several years, long after the goods are sold. If any deficiency in payment is found, the importer must then pay up within 30 days.
5. The importer keeps in touch with all government trade regulations both here and abroad, such as the new regulations of the Consumer Products Safety Commission that apply to both domestic and foreign goods imported. This is difficult for all but the large retail chains and affiliated groups.
6. It is much easier to adjust complaints with a domestic seller in regard to quality, quantity, and timing than to deal with a foreign source. To return goods to a foreign seller is often impossible.
7. Large-scale purchases made by the importer often provide price advantages that are shared with store customers.

Disadvantages

Depending on importers, however, does have its disadvantages. They are not the sources for exclusive merchandise made expressly to the order of the retail store or group. The prices they charge to cover costs, expenses, and profit may be more than the "landed" cost of the goods bought directly from the foreign resource. Again, importers may not be able to assure the foreign producer of continuity of reorders, because they have no control over the purchases made by retail customers, whereas chain buyers have considerable control over the lines handled by their retail outlets.

BUYING FOREIGN GOODS FROM FOREIGN SOURCES

The American buyer may purchase goods abroad from (1) the manufacturers themselves, (2) foreign export merchants, wholesalers who confine themselves to exporting and provide faster delivery than is available from manufacturers, (3) export sales representatives, who confine themselves to selling the output of certain manufacturers in their countries but do not maintain an inventory (they may make periodic trips to the United States), (4) export commission houses, which act as export departments of foreign manufacturers and receive a commission from manufacturers on the volume of sales developed. They may do some of the paperwork in connection with shipments to be made abroad.

In making contact with any of these resources, the buyer nearly always requires the assistance of a foreign resident buying office. This may be an office owned and operated by his or her own organization or by the resident buying office in the United States that represents the firm. Often, however, it is a foreign independent buying office. If under native management, it is commonly called a *commissionaire*;[2] if under American management, a *purchasing agent*. It generally charges the buyer a commission of 5 to 7 percent for its services, which are similar to those of the American office that usually charges a monthly fee.

Buying Direct

There are certain *advantages* in buying direct from foreign resources: (1) Prices available are often considerably lower than those that can be quoted by intermediary sources. (2) Specifications can be developed as to quality, style, and fit to meet American standards, and inspection can be arranged to check on the specifications before shipment. (3) The buyer is enabled to procure exclusive merchandise that is not available to any other competitor. This permits a higher markup than usual, commonly well above the 50

[2]The commissionaire is not as important now, because big retailers with their own foreign buying offices have expanded their import operations to include nonaffiliated independent retail firms. Examples are Allied, AMC (Associated Merchandising Corporation), and May Department Stores.

percent of retail (100 percent of cost) obtained on much fashion merchandise bought in the domestic market. (4) Fashion changes that originate abroad can be spotted quickly. (5) Rapport with the manufacturer can be developed, leading to long-range plans to develop the resource as important and continuing. This may involve studying the facilities of the manufacturer for expansion and perhaps providing some assistance in this direction. (6) The long delays after shipment in obtaining delivery by boat have now been overcome for soft goods and small items of considerable value relative to weight by having them shipped by air. This is sometimes even cheaper than by boat, because it shortens the period in which funds are tied up and reduces the danger of damage and deterioration.

There are, of course, *disadvantages* to direct buying: (1) The trips are very costly, and there is danger of overbuying, because the goods tend to look more exciting in their foreign setting than they do when back in the store. This danger has been greatly minimized by the common requirement that buyers must have set buying plans approved before going abroad. And just before departure, they are provided with up-to-date unit sales and stock reports, often in the form of computer printouts. (2) The orders have to be placed far ahead of delivery, with payments made upon shipment, tying up funds, and with the date of receipt uncertain. (3) Reorders and adjustments are often impossible to obtain, and the vendors abroad are loathe to provide "back-up" merchandise should the buyer find that more than the initial order is needed. Thus there is considerable danger of buying too much or too little.[3] (4) Unless Ex Dock[4] (port of importation) terms are negotiated, the buying organization must assume the importing costs that would be borne by the importer or selling agent in the United States were the store to depend on one of these.

Procedure for Direct Buying

Retail-store buying abroad directly from producers is generally limited to the central buyers for chains and branch-store systems and to the resident buyers who travel abroad often accompanied by the buyers of some of their largest accounts. These buyers often make one or more foreign trips a year and are assisted either by their own offices located in foreign cities or by

[3]One large retail chain sometimes solves this problem by arranging with an importer in this country to buy from the foreign manufacturer a quantity of the identical merchandise at least equal to the chain's initial order. Although the price will be 10 percent or more higher, the store is protected against overbuying and is assured of an additional supply if needed. The importer has the opportunity of adding an excellent item to the line, one that he or she can sell to others if the store organization cannot absorb the back-up stock promptly.

[4]See the glossary of terms in the Technical Appendix at the end of this chapter.

commissionaires. These agencies assist in the market visits and check on packing, delivery, and adherence to set standards.

Because commitments for the stores' estimated requirements usually have to be made in advance and because reorders are seldom assured, the determination of the quantities to buy depends on the merchandise plan followed. If a completely central merchandising plan is in operation, the buyer estimates total needs on a basis of the sales and stock information provided by each store. If the stores have control over their purchases, the buyer or buying committee obtains "distributions" from each indicating how much each agrees to spend abroad in the pertinent departments, classifications, and sometimes specific types of goods. The sum of these distributions determines the total to be purchased. The buyer must then distribute this amount according to his judgment regarding the various orders placed during the trip. If shipments are to be warehoused in this country, the distribution to stores may be made after the goods arrive. If the shipments are to be made directly to the stores, each order must indicate what is to go to each. If the resident buyer is accompanied by certain store buyers, the latter indicate their own requirements on the spot.

Although some foreign manufacturers are beginning to permit American buyers to purchase on open account, the almost universal practice in America, most payments are made by means of letters of credit on a foreign bank. When the goods are shipped, the foreign seller presents a draft along with shipping documents to the bank for payment. When the exchange value of the dollar may be rising relative to the foreign currency, the buyer attempts to negotiate the purchase in the foreign currency, at the exchange rate at the time of shipment, because the dollar is expected to buy more units of foreign money at the time of shipment than it did at the time of ordering, perhaps 6 months before. If the price of the dollar is dropping, the buyer prefers to buy at the exchange rate at time of order.

Although prices are usually quoted in foreign currency, buyers may specify on their orders the exchange rate to be used in payment. This is essentially setting the price in American currency.

Some Special Problems in Buying Abroad

Language and practices as well as legal restraints differ in foreign countries. It is not easy for an American buyer to make needs exactly understood and for the manufacturer to make clear just what can be produced and how quickly. Ways of doing business vary. For example, intermediaries who have a hand in consummating a transaction often expect and demand a fee that we regard as a bribe. However, it is usually the sellers rather than the buyers who are pressed to make such questionable payments if they are to assure themselves of markets.

Another problem has to do with foreign practices that upset established relationships. A case in point is Hong Kong, long the prime foreign source of jeans for the American market. The United States sets a quota on the quantity of jeans that may be imported from each country. The Hong Kong quota is allotted by its authorities to established manufacturers and exporters. The newer entries into the field now doing a majority of the business are allotted little or none. To obtain the right to export to the United States, they have to buy quotas from those to whom they have been assigned. Some quota holders have given up manufacturing, finding it more profitable to become quota brokers. The demand is so great that the price of a quota to export a dozen pairs of jeans has risen from 60¢ only a short time ago to $16 and more in 1975. This increased the American price of the jeans about two-thirds.

Other countries, such as Taiwan and South Korea, also are subject to quota for American shipment; however, the problem of obtaining quotas has not become acute. Thus they have a price advantage that the American buyer must consider. Hong Kong is trying to maintain its market position by emphasizing high fashion design and quality, factors that the American buyer must weigh.[5]

SOURCES OF INFORMATION

There are a variety of information sources available to the store buyer who would buy foreign merchandise:

1. Domestic trade directories often contain advertisements and/or listings of wholesale firms that carry imported merchandise.
2. Trade lists published by the Bureau of International Commerce (U.S. Department of Commerce, Commercial Intelligence Division) are available at local offices of the Department of Commerce.
3. The "International Commerce Weekly," published by the U.S. Department of Commerce, contains lists of incoming business visitors with types of merchandise they have for sale.
4. The classified "Yellow Pages" of many telephone directories contain listings of importers who carry a wide range of merchandise. This is especially true of New York City's Manhattan Directory.
5. The "Directory of New York Importers," published by the Commerce and Industry Association of New York Inc., is available in many local libraries.
6. Commercial representatives of foreign governments provide the names of foreign manufacturers interested in exporting to the United States. There are often commercial attachés in foreign consulates, as well as quasipublic organizations such as Japanese trade centers with offices in many cities, who are helpful.
7. For a store associated with a resident buying office, its import division is a major source.

[5]*Business Week* (April 12, 1976), pp. 44, 46.

CUSTOMS REGULATIONS AND LANDED COST

American buyers purchasing abroad must have at their command customs experts in their own organizations or customs house brokers who can guide their foreign purchases through the intricate procedures required for entry. Exporting from foreign countries to the United States is governed by U.S. customs laws and regulations that are administered by the U.S. Customs Service in the Department of the Treasury. This service polices what may be imported and the labeling and invoicing requirements and also determines the duty, if any, that must be assessed.[6]

Certain foreign merchandise is prohibited, such as confectionary that contains any alcohol (except for a minute amount derived from the use of the flavoring extract), counterfeits of coins circulated in the United States, and immoral and seditious matter. Certain other merchandise is restricted, such as fruits and vegetables, meats and meat products, and pesticides. Even textile products are restricted, insofar as they must conform to federal laws governing treatment of the product and labeling. In fact, many of the consumer products imported are subject to one or more of our laws and regultions that govern the labeling and/or material content and construction of the goods.

Most imported goods, when not merely in transit through the country, must be legibly and conspicuously marked with the country of origin. However, there is a list of items exempt from this requirement, notably some small hardware articles and some in the notions category.

Duty

Goods imported are subject to duty unless specifically exempted, such as antiques bought in certain countries. The federal government has developed a Generalized System of Preferences (GSP), which permits the importation without duty of almost 2700 items bought from and produced in 100 developing countries and 37 dependencies. These include most of Central and South America, the Caribbean, Africa, India, and Southeastern Asia plus island territories of developing countries. Indonesia, Hong Kong, Taiwan, Israel, Yugoslavia, Rumania, and Portugal are included, but most of the European countries are not. The list of items that are duty free include various appliances, chinaware, furs, furniture, jewelry, leather goods, perfume, silverware, skis, and wooden carvings. Watches, most footwear, and most

[6]For additional details of customs procedure, see *Exporting to the United States*, Department of the Treasury, U.S. Customs Service, 1975, Washington, D.C. 20229. (For sale by Supt. of Documents, U.S. Government Printing Office, Washington, D.C. 20402.)

textiles are not included on the GSP list. Buyers must obtain certification of origin for all items valued at more than $250.[7]

Before placing an order, the importer should obtain from the customs officer of the expected port of entry a statement as to the applicable rate of duty. The port official will render a decision or will refer the matter to the Commissioner of Customs in Washington, D.C. The information needed for determination of dutiable status includes:

1. Description of the goods and samples, sketches, or other material as may be required to properly classify the goods.
2. Method of manufacture.
3. Specifications and analyses.
4. Quantities and costs of component materials, with percentages if possible.
5. Expected use of the goods in the United States.

Duties, when required, are levied in one of three ways: (1) Ad valorem—a stated percentage of the dutiable value, (2) specific—a specified amount per unit of weight or other measure of quantity, and (3) compound—a combination of ad valorem and specific, such as 10¢ a pound and 35 percent of value.

Dutiable value

The determination of dutiable value required for the foregoing methods (1) and (3) may be a complicated process. If the goods are listed on what the Treasury calls the "final list," the dutiable value is usually either the *foreign value* or the *export value*, whichever is higher. The *foreign value* is the market price at which the goods are freely offered for sale for home consumption in the exporting country. The *export value* is the market price at which the goods are freely offered for sale for exportation to the United States. Goods not on the "final list" are normally valued at export value. Thus goods need not be valued by Customs at the price actually paid.

When neither of these two methods are applicable, the goods may be valued at "cost of production" or at "constructed" value. The two terms mean essentially the same thing, although the methods of constructing the cost vary somewhat. Both include the manufacturing cost plus general expenses and a profit margin, as well as the cost of packing the goods for shipment but not the cost to the port of embarkation or the fee paid to the buyer's foreign agent, such as a commissionaire. The seller's agent's fee or commission would be reflected in the market price for export or in the constructed price.

Most consumer goods bought by retailers for the American market are valued at export value, even if made to private brand specifications, because merchandise of the same type is being bought by other American dealers. In practice, the invoice cost is commonly accepted unless it differs substantially

[7] *Business Week* (November 1, 1976), p. 89. It should be observed that the list of preferences is subject to change.

from the market price of similar goods imported by others about the same time. In principle, the value for duty purposes is the dutiable value at the time of exportation to the United States, not at the time the order was placed. Likewise, the conversion of a price computed in foreign currency is translated into dollars by applying the rate of exchange when the exportation occurs, as certified by the Federal Reserve Bank of New York. Thus it may vary from any rate of exchange agreed upon by buyer and seller in determining payment for the goods.

Entry and payment of duty

When the goods arrive in the United States at one of the ports of entry that are located in most states, the consignee, guided by the invoice, files an entry document. If the goods are to be released at once, an entry for consumption is filed, and the estimated duty is deposited with the district director of customs. If all regulations are met, the goods will be released to the buyer or customshouse broker.[8]

If the goods are to be entered under a warehouse entry and not withdrawn promptly for consumption, they may be stored in a customs bonded warehouse, and the payment of duty is withheld. The goods may remain in the warehouse up to 3 years, with duty paid at the time of withdrawal, or they may be exported without the payment of duty.

Computation of Landed Cost

Landed cost is the cost at the store of goods imported from abroad. Table 14–1 is an example of how it is computed.

Figure 14–1 is a reproduction of the form used by a large group of stores to figure landed cost. In the figure, the rate of exchange used in determining converted cost is 26¢, but the rate used for calculating duty is 30¢. The 26¢ represents the actual rate paid by the store in buying a bank draft to pay for the merchandise.[9] The customs rate is set by the Customs Service and adjusted when the market rate differs considerably.

When there is a mixed duty, the calculation of the duty is slightly more complicated. For example, the foreign cost of an invoice for 50 articles may be 800 pesos, the duty 25 percent and 10¢ specific, and the exchange rate of the peso, 30¢. The converted cost, for duty purposes, is 800 × 30¢, or \$240. Twenty-five percent of this is \$60, the ad valorem duty, and 10¢ × 50 is \$5, the specific duty. Thus, the entire duty would be \$65.

[8]This is a private individual or a firm licenced by the U.S. Customs Service to act as an agent for importers in customs matters.

[9]Some retail organizations figure landed cost by means of an approximate rate of exchange and do not adjust for the exact rate at which they obtain foreign exchange. This rate, however, may vary from the customs rate used in calculating duty.

TABLE 14-1
Example of Figuring Landed Cost for Goods Bought in Swiss Francs[a]

First cost 100 @ 10.00 Swiss francs (5.22)[b]		1,000.00
74 @ 12.50 Swiss francs (6.53)		925.00
50 @ 15.00 Swiss francs (7.83)		750.00
30 @ 17.50 Swiss francs (9.14)		525.00
Total first cost		3,200.00
Less 2 percent discount		64.00
		3,136.00
Packing in Swiss francs		50.00
6 percent commission in Swiss francs		192.00
Shipping in Swiss Francs		172.00
Cost in Swiss francs		3,550.00
37¢ per Swiss francs	U.S.	1,313.50
Duty 25 percent on 3200.00 francs plus 50.00 francs for packing: 812.50 @ 37[c]		300.63
Other expenses in U.S. including inland freight, ocean freight, customs entry, notary fees, cartage, storage, submitting invoice to appraiser		57.50
Total landed cost		$1,671.63
To find landed cost of foreign currency, divide total landed dollar cost by total first cost: $\frac{1,671.63}{3,200.00} =$		0.522

[a] Some buying abroad is done in dollars rather than foreign currency. Thus the seller assumes the risk of fluctuations in the rate of exchange between the date of order and the date of shipment.

[b] Figures in parentheses denote landed dollar cost per unit. They are arrived at by multiplying landed Swiss francs (.522) by first cost of merchandise.

[c] It is assumed here that the Customs Service accepts the first cost plus packing as the dutiable cost. This need not be the case.

When, because of protest or other reasons, there is delay in determining the exact duty, the usual store practice is to include the possible additional duty in figuring landed cost. Later, if the actual duty turns out to be less, the department purchase account is credited for the difference.

Landed cost multipliers

When a buyer is abroad selecting merchandise, he or she is hardly in a position to compute the landed cost of everything bought, and yet some method of estimating it quickly is needed to know whether or not a profit can be made on the goods. At the time of inspection, the buyer should form an idea of the price at which the goods can be sold in America. Therefore, he or she must know the landed cost in America before buying. This may be accomplished by finding the average ratio between each franc, peso, or other monetary unit of foreign cost and the landed cost in the United States. The

FIGURE 14–1 Import cost calculation form

F 22-1M-1-29

PENCIL—ESTIMATED
INK—ACTUAL

IMPORT COST CALCULATION

LIQUIDATION:	DATE:
NO CHANGE	....
INCREASE $........	PAID: ....
REFUND $........	REC'D: ....

INV. DATE SHIPPER: *Argentina*

SHIPPED BY S.S. P.P. ARRIVAL DATE:

CASE No. RATE OF EXCHANGE *.26*

INV. No.:

ENTRY No.:

THRO AGENT:

REMARKS:

FOREIGN CURRENCY: *Peso* CUSTOMS RATE OF EXCH. *30*

	TOTAL	
DUTY RATE:	*17½%*	
MERCHANDISE:	*Allig. Bags*	
MANUFACTURER:		
GROSS INVOICE *pesos*	*500*	*00*
NET INVOICE	*500*	*00*
PACKING	*50*	*00*
TOTAL INV. COST	*550*	*00*
A—CONVERTED COST	*$143*	*00*
1.—FOREIGN CHGS.	*12*	*00*
2.—OCEAN FRGHT.		
3.—BROKERAGE	*4*	*50*
4.—CARTAGE	*2*	*00*
5.—		
6.—INSURANCE	*1*	*40*
7.—FOREIGN COMM.	*8*	*58*
8.—TRAVELING		
9.—		
10.—		
B—EXPENSE 1-10	*28*	*48*
C.—DUTY	*28*	*88*
TOTAL A-C	*200*	*36*
D—LOADED DISC.		
TOTAL LANDED COST	*200*	*36*
CURRENCY COST	*$1.4007*	

total landed cost of purchases of a department made abroad during a period, and falling within a certain duty rate classification, may be divided by the number of francs or other foreign currencies in which purchases were quoted. For example, if the shipment computed in Table 14–1 were typical of the cost of importing some classification of goods, the ratio would be determined by dividing $1671.63 by 3200 francs, the foreign billed cost. This gives 52.2¢. Every franc of foreign cost is equal to 52.2¢ of landed cost.

With this multiplier in mind, the buyer is able to translate quickly any foreign cost quoted for the same class of goods into the approximate landed cost. Of course, there may be differences in transportation and cartage rates and in the value of the goods at the time of transportation, but the estimated landed cost will be close enough to act as a reliable guide in the foreign market.

Every store that imports from abroad should work out such a multiplier for each classification and every country of origin. When the buyer makes the trip, a list of multipliers to use for each type of merchandise he or she intends to purchase should be provided.

The multiplier, called "currency cost" in Figure 14–1, may also be used to determine the landed cost per unit of goods actually purchased. This aids the buyer in pricing. Note this use in Table 14–1 also.

DISCUSSION QUESTIONS

1. Is foreign-goods buying by retailers still on the increase? Are retailers depending primarily on importing wholesalers or on direct purchase?
2. Do any of the objections to buying directly from foreign manufacturers apply to purchasing from importers?
3. From the current tariff regulations, find the variables that determine (and prove) the duty on the following articles: Wedgewood china, Sarouk rug, and pearls.
4. Do tariff duties tend to restrict the assortments available in stores?
5. Assume a foreign cost of 150 units at 10 Australian schillings each, packing and labor charges of 50 schillings, ocean and railroad freight and insurance of 300 schillings, other importing costs of 100 schillings, ad valorem duty of 35 percent, specific duty of 10¢ each, and a rate of exchange of $0.056. Compute the landed cost. Compute the multiplier.
6. The analysis of imports in one classification from England over a current period showed a total foreign cost of £5000 and a total landed cost of $12,000. The buyer is now inspecting similar goods in London that are quoted at £3½ each. What will be the approximate landed cost? If the necessary department markup is 90 percent of cost, at what price must the goods be salable to justify the purchase?
7. When buyers make commitments abroad, how can they avoid gambling on consumer acceptance in America?
8. If the American sale of a foreign purchase proves the existence of continuing consumer demand, how may the buyer improve his or her chances of obtaining reorders?
9. In figuring the landed cost of foreign purchases, should the following be included?
   (a) The cost of the trip abroad.
   (b) The buyer's salary while abroad.
   (There are at least two serious objections to the suggestions.)
10. Should the United States set restrictive quotas and/or higher duties on consumer goods made abroad that are cutting into employment in American factories? Discuss.

Technical Appendix for Part III

GLOSSARY OF CREDIT AND SHIPPING TERMS

A. CREDIT TERMS

Advance dating The time for payment is calculated from a specified future date, not from the date of the invoice or from the date of receipt of goods. Example: A bill is dated July 5 with terms of "2/10 net 30 as of September 1." This means that the bill may be paid on September 11 and the 2 percent discount be deducted, with the entire bill payable October 1. Where advance dating is granted to induce purchasing in advance of the normal buying season, it may be called "season dating."

Anticipation Deduction of an extra discount for paying an invoice in advance of the cash discount date. Many vendors allow such extra deductions for the period of prepayment at the rate of 6 percent a year. Example: terms "2/10–60 extra" means that the buyer has 70 days from the date of the invoice to earn the 2 percent discount. If the buyer elects to pay in 10 days rather than in 70, he or she is prepaying for a 60-day period, or 1/6th of a year. At the 6 percent annual rate, this would be 1 percent extra, or a total of 3 percent deducted in 10 days. (Some deduct the 2 percent first and then the 1 percent from the balance. This results in a slightly higher payment to the seller.) Some stores "anticipate" when they pay an invoice before the final due date but *after* the expiration of the cash discount period. It is questionable whether this deduction will be recognized as permissible by many manufacturers, because the time between the final due date and the discount date is generally regarded as a grace period.

Averaging due dates The determination of a single day on which invoices with different dates may be paid together in order to earn a cash discount on the lot. In the case of 10-day terms, it requires paying some of the bills in less than 10 days and some in more than 10 days. A date is determined that will average 10 days from the dates of the separate bills. This may also be done where the terms provide 30 or more days to earn the discount. This practice is not common today, because in lines where there are usually a number of purchases during the same month, the goods are billed on an EOM basis; that is, they are paid together during the month following purchase, usually on the 10th.

Banker's acceptance Similar to a trade acceptance except that the buyer's bank agrees to "accept" the draft and to collect from the buyer when due. This gives added security to the seller or other buyer of the draft.

Cash discount A reduction in price allowed for prompt payment and expressed as a percentage of the billed price. Example: "2/10," which grants 2 percent discount for paying within 10 days of the date of the invoice, which normally coincides with the shipping date.

COD dating The bill must be paid upon delivery of the goods to the carrier. The initials are variously interpreted as "cash on delivery" and "collect on delivery."

Dating The length of time the seller will extend credit to the buyer. Example: "net 60," signifying that the billed amount is to be paid within 60 days of invoice date.

Draft An order drawn by the seller upon the buyer demanding payment of a bill of sale when certain conditions are met. See Banker's acceptance, Sight draft, Trade Acceptance, and SD/BL (under Shipping Terms below).

EOM dating The time for payment is calculated from the end of the month in which the invoice is dated (and goods shipped) and not from the date of the invoice. Example: "3/10 EOM" means that the discount may be deducted if the bill is paid by the 10th of the month following the one in which the goods were billed and shipped. After the 10th, the full amount becomes due, and a 20-day grace period is normally assumed. Thus the face of the bill would be payable at the end of the month following the date of shipment.

EOM ROG dating The length of time for payment is calculated from the end of the month in which the goods are received and not from the end of the month in which they are shipped. Example: "2/10 EOM ROG" on invoice dated June 20, with the goods not arriving at destination until July 5, would be payable with discount deductible on August 10. Normally the billed amount would be payable 20 days later, or August 30.

Extra dating A variation of regular dating, where the buyer is granted a specified number of additional days both to earn the discount and to pay the billed amount. Example: "2/10–60 extra," indicating that if the bill is paid in 10 days *plus* 60 days, or 70 days, the cash discount may be deducted. The billed amount is due after 70 days, and a grace period of 20 days is normally understood. Thus the bill would be payable in full within 90 days of the date of the invoice.

Floor plan A plan to finance the stocks of expensive merchandise such as major appliances while in the retail store. The merchant signs a trust receipt for the merchandise that passes "legal estate" (title) to him. This document also constitutes his promise to remit to the holder of the receipt the proceeds of every sale to a customer (cash or installment paper). The manufacturer may hold the receipt (that represents his "equitable interest") and collect the payments, or the receipt may be held by a bank or finance company. Should the retailer fail to make payments as agreed, the finance company has recourse to the manufacturer.

Letter of credit A set of instructions issued to an exporter by a bank at the request of an importer who is its customer. When all the instructions are carried out, the bank pays the exporter for the goods sold to the importer. In connection with foreign buying by American importers, the request is made by the American importer, and the letter is delivered to the foreign exporter. When the goods are ready for export, the foreign seller presents the letter of credit to a bank in his or her own country, and if all instructions set by the American importer have been met, the exporter is paid by the bank, who charges the account of the American bank representing the buyer.

Loading (the invoice) The practice of increasing the amount of an invoice in order to permit a larger cash discount than the seller makes available at the standard price. Thus a seller with a billed price of $10.00 may have regular terms of 3/10; and expects to be paid $9.70 at the end of 10 days. The price may be "loaded" to provide an 8 percent discount by diving $9.70 by 92 percent. This yields $10.543 (8 percent from $10.543 gives the expected price of $9.70). Loading may be done either by the manufacturer or in the store's accounting office. It may be done by the manufacturer when the buyer insists on a larger discount if he or she is under pressure by management to show better discounts on purchases. It may be done in the store in order to carry all inventory accounts at values that reflect a standard rate of discount. The device has also been used to "pressure" buyers to fight for bigger discounts in the wholesale markets, without having the billed cost prices increased. With the increased standardization in cash discounts and terms of sale, the loading practice has probably outworn its usefulness.

Proximo dating A synonym for EOM dating.

Regular dating The length of time the seller will extend credit calculated from the date of the invoice. Example: net 30, signifying that the billed amount is due within 30 days of the date of the invoice.

ROG dating The length of time for payment is calculated from the date of receipt of goods, not from the date of the invoice. Example: "2/10 ROG" on invoice dated June 20, with the goods not arriving at destination until July 5, would be payable with discount deductible on July 15. Normally the billed amount would be payable 20 days later, or August 5.

Sight draft Terms indicating that the price is to be paid just before delivery upon presentation of an order drawn upon the buyer by the seller. The manufacturer may have the goods consigned to him- or herself in the town where the retailer is located and draws an order against the buyer demanding the latter to pay the amount of the invoice to a designated third party, usually the buyer's bank. The sight draft, along with the bill of lading covering the shipment, is sent to the buyer's bank. The buyer is notified, pays the bank, and is given the bill of lading, which he or she presents to the common carrier in order to have the shipment released. Thus, instead of settling with the carrier, as in the case of COD, settlement is made with a financial institution.

Spot dating Terms indicating that the payment is to be made upon completion of the buying contract, in advance of delivery.

Trade acceptance A credit instrument in the form of a demand on the buyer to pay for the goods at a specified future date that is "accepted" (signed) by the buyer at the time for delivery of the goods. The seller may hold the acceptance to maturity and then present it for payment, or the seller may discount it to the bank, collecting immediate funds, and the bank collecting the draft from the buyer upon maturity. Although most buying for retail stores is done by means of open account, this device gives the added protection of a written instrument and makes it possible for the seller to obtain reimbursement promptly from a financial institution.

Trust receipt A receipt signed by a receiver of goods who takes legal title to them but who at the same time obligates him- or herself to remit to the seller the proceeds of their resale, less an agreed commission or markup. In technical language, the trust receipt states the obligations of the trustee (the store) toward the beneficiary (the manufacturer). Legal estate (title) passes to the store, but the "equitable interest" is owned by the manufacturer, who is entitled to the proceeds of sales to consumers less the retailer's markup or commission, with remittance normally made as each unit is sold. If the store fails to carry out its responsibilities, the manufacturer can have the trust enforced through a court of equity.

B. SHIPPING TERMS

Air express A very fast but expensive transportation service. It uses space in regularly operated air lines when time is of the essence.

Air freight Transportation by means of cargo planes. Carries freight at lower rates than air express. Used for women's fashion apparel, some for fresh fruits and vegetables, replacement parts, and goods of high value and low bulk.

Bill of lading A transportation document that performs (1) as a receipt issued by the carrier and delivered to the shipper, and (2) as a contract between the shipper and the carrier for the transportation of the goods. If *negotiable* (order), the document also acts as an instrument of title; ownership can be transferred by endorsement, and the holder must present the bill to take possession from the carrier. If *nonnegotiable* (straight), the bill calls for delivery to the consignee and does not have to be presented by him or her to secure delivery. This bill cannot be used to transfer title to another party.

Consolidator An agency that combines shipments of less than 100 pounds each into larger units in order to take advantage of bulk rates. It collects small outgoing shipments from vendors in the market city and assembles and ships them daily in over 100-pound units and sometimes in carload lots, shipping to a store, a town, or a locality. It also classifies goods on the bill of lading to take advantage of the lowest applicable commodity rates. (See Freight Forwarder.)

Containerization The practice of loading packaged goods into large standard sized containers that are sealed and shipped by truck, rail, ship and/or air.

Ex Dock (named port of importation) Under this term, seller quotes a price including the cost of the goods and all additional costs necessary to place the goods on the dock at the named port of importation, duty paid, if any.

F.A.S. (free along side) Shipper agrees to pay the charges to the side of the vessel within reach of its loading tackle; title passes at this point.

Fishy-back service Similar to piggy-back, except that the trailers are loaded on ships for the long haul. This is being combined with piggy-back to make deliveries in unopened trailers to any part of the world. (See Piggy-back Freight.)

FOB shipping point Vendor pays cartage charge to depot, store pays the rest; title passes at shipping point.

FOB city of destination Vendor pays cartage and transportation to common carrier's station in city where store is located; store pays cartage to store; title passes when goods arrive at city of destination.

FOB store Vendor pays all transportation; title passes when goods arrive at store.

FOB vessel (named port) Vendor pays all costs of getting goods on vessel; title passes at vessel.

FOB seaboard Vendor pays all costs to seaboard city but not cartage to dock nor dock and loading fees; title passes when goods arrive at seaboard city.

FOB (point) freight allowed to ——— Vendor pays charges to the point stated, commonly the shipping point; the buyer pays the freight but later deducts the amount of the freight paid from the invoice; title passes at the FOB point.

FOB (point) freight prepaid to ——— Vendor pays freight to a point specified, generally the buyer's city or port, but the buyer is responsible for loss or damage at the FOB point, generally the vendor's city or port; title passes when goods are turned over to the common carrier.

FOB (point) charges reversed Vendor pays all charges to the point specified, generally the buyer's city or port, and takes responsibility to that point, but the buyer later reimburses for transportation charges. This results in the buyer's finally paying freight, the vendor assuming risks in transit until the goods are received.

FOB shipping point (New York) freight equalized with (Philadelphia) A New York shipper, for example, may make such a quotation to a Trenton buyer. If transportation from New York to Trenton is $1 and from Philadelphia to Trenton 30¢, the New York seller agrees, according to these terms, to absorb the 70¢ difference. The buyer pays 30¢ transportation from New York, which is what would have to be paid if he or she bought in the nearer market, Philadelphia. These terms allow the New York seller to extend the market. The buyer, in turn, can choose a resource in either city on a basis of suitability of product and services to his or her needs, not on a basis of transportation costs.

Freight fowarder An agency that assembles goods in less than carload lots and ships in carload lots by rail and also by truck. The agent selects the routes for shipments and sets his or her own tariffs at somewhat less than the railroad's less than carload rates. Piggy-backing has become important in this field. Leading forwarders have truck bodies that can be loaded on flatcars and shipped by rail over long hauls. By a combination of truck, railroad, and even water, goods may be moved long distances with only one loading and unloading operation—at origin and at point of destination. (See Consolidator.)

Landed cost The cost of a foreign purchase including all direct costs of getting it to the store, expressed in U.S. currency.

LCL (freight) Freight shipped in less than carload lots and subject to higher rates than carload lots.

LTL shipments A shipment of less than a full motor truck load, subject to higher rates than full truck loads.

N.O.I.B.M. A shipper's indicator—not otherwise indicated by name—that a mixed shipment is unclassified. It is thus subject to the highest transportation rate.

Parcel Post A transportation system for small shipments operated by the federal government. The maximum size of packages is 72 inches in length and girth and the maximum weight 40 pounds (less in some cases). The cost is frequently less than express, but no pickup service is provided.

Piggy-back freight A coordination of local motor and long-distance freight service whereby loaded truck trailers are placed on specially designed flatcars for the long haul and removed for truck delivery at the receiving end of the journey. (See Fishy-back Service.)

Pool car A freight car containing commodities for two or more receivers. Carload rates apply to the point where the shipment is broken down for separate delivery to each consignee; used by some local retail merchants' associations to save freight costs on shipments from New York and other buying centers. It avoids LCL and LTL rates.

Railway express A premium type of freight service operated by private carriers. It is used primarily for small shipments of valuable and highly perishable merchandise. It covers cities not reached by fast-freight lines.

SD/BL (sight draft on bill of lading) The bill of lading with a sight draft for the amount of the invoice is sent to the bank or agent of the seller located in the consignee's city. To obtain the bill of lading (negotiable), the buyer must first honor the draft. The bill of lading is then released to the buyer so that he or she may take possession.

TL shipment A full motor truck load shipped at lower rates than required for an LTL shipment.

part IV

Pricing and Selling

chapter 15

Pricing and Selling Merchandise Purchased

PRICING OBJECTIVES

Success in moving goods properly bought depends primarily on (1) sound pricing and repricing, and (2) effective promotional techniques. Price has a peculiar, ambivalent relationship in the scale of values that affects customer buying decisions. It is only one selection factor among the many that determine ultimate purchase or rejection—and price is not often the most important factor.

But price is a great common measuring denominator. Furthermore, price is a tactically manipulative selection factor. Occasionally, changes can be made in other factors to suit customer preference at the point of sale; some shoes, for example, may be dyed to order and garment alterations may be made to improve fit. But, in most cases, selection factors other than price are set and immutable by the time a product reaches the point of sale. Price remains as the selection factor of tactical choice, governed only by the need to resolve the conflict between the resulting rate of sale and ultimate profitability of the item.

The Utility-Price Quotient

Although price itself may not be the most important determinant in causing a customer to decide which version of a product to buy, it may have great weight in determining how many to buy or whether to buy that product at all. Price, in a money-valued system, is the measuring device that integrates income, utility, and other factors with the elements of supply and demand into a complicated feedback mechanism.

Theoretically, that product and how much of it a customer will buy depends on a relationship: the customer's estimate (perhaps only subconscious) of (1) the satisfaction to be derived from the last unit of a given item purchased, and (2) the price. Economists describe the satisfaction-giving power of the last unit as its marginal utility to the customer. Theoretically, this value decreases with each succeeding unit considered for purchase.

To illustrate this concept, suppose that a customer senses the need for a tie and feels that it would provide him with $8 worth of utility at the moment, and he finds a tie for $4 that meets his requirements. The tie has a utility/price or "impellence" quotient of 2 (8/4). Were he to consider buying a second tie at $4, its marginal utility could probably be less, perhaps no more than 4, yielding an "impellence" quotient of only 1. Although the second tie might be bought because its utility equals its price, the customer would not feel impelled to buy a third, because he "would not be getting his money's worth."

In fact, if the amount of money available for discretionary spending is limited, the customer may not buy any ties at all at this time. The utility of other items (expressed in dollars) may be felt as much more than $8. So, in theory, consumers order priorities in deciding how to spend their money.

As a practical matter, the buyer who is pricing a product must attempt to set a retail price that he or she believes to be less than the marginal utility for the product as it will be felt by the majority of customers interested in the type of product under consideration. The greater the experienced ratio between utility and price, the greater the impellence on the part of customers to purchase.

The review of economic theory presented in this chapter is, of necessity, oversimplified background material. The serious student of pricing theory is urged to reexamine texts on the subject in the light of knowledge gained since introduction to economic theory.[1] For practical purposes it may be said that:

1. Consumer's disposable incomes are limited.
2. They are, however, substantial, growing, and becoming more widely dispersed.
3. The amount available for discretionary spending (above the demands for subsistence) is increasing.
4. *Discretion implies choice and demands choice.*
5. Choice is made on the basis of overall relative utility (a) of products against each other, (b) of products against a growingly available, attractive, and costly list of services, and (c) of products and services against the motivation to save—or not spend at all.

[1]A good survey of the subject, on as simple a level as its nature will allow, may be found in Paul A. Samuelson, *Economics*, 10th ed. (New York: McGraw-Hill, 1976).

6. Ultimate choice of a given product depends (a) on the built-in selection factors that differentiate the versions of that product, (b) on the retail firm's nature, the character of its services, and its presentation of the product, and (c) on the price charged.

The first four points are designed to sum up the consumer purchasing outlook of an affluent society—the need for differentiation and innovation in products and in ways of retailing them. Satisfying this need leads to costly practices in production and distribution.

The buyer must recognize that there are narrowing limits to the segment of the population that is satisfied with minimal assortments, or reduced services, and similar cost-saving devices that permit low pricing. Like so many of the forces we have discussed, these devices work on a curve of diminishing returns. The retailer must pursue efficient means of retailing but, in the process, must learn to know when the utility-price quotient optimizes appeal to chosen customers in a particular competitive situation.

Number 6, the last item on the list, is an attempt to encapsulate the broad elements of total utility, which is divided by price to give the impellence quotient—the total appeal that motivates the customer to buy.

Unfortunately, the denominator of the fraction, price, is most easily measurable and manipulative and therefore becomes an obvious and deceptively easy competitive device. Lowering the price usually is a sure way of increasing the impellence quotient.[2] But it is also the device most quickly emulated. Enhancing the complex of utility factors in the numerator of the fraction also serves to increase the impellence quotient. This calls for a combination of thoughtful analysis, creative skills, and developed wisdom, which, over the long run, is the most difficult kind of competition to match or beat.

PROFIT MARGIN CONTROLS

Management sets certain limitations on the buyer's freedom of pricing in order to cover expenses and costs in order to assure a margin of profit. These are expressed in departmental merchandise plans as goals for the margin to be secured over cost. As suggested in Chapter 1, these margins may be planned and controlled at various stages or levels as follows:

1. "Initial" or "cumulative" markon.
2. Maintained markup.
3. Gross merchandising margin.
4. Contribution toward overhead.
5. Net operating profit from merchandising operations.

[2]Sometimes the lowering of the price leads to customer questioning of quality and fashion rightness. This may reduce the numerator of the equation and thus fail to increase the quotient.

6. Net profit before taxes.
7. Net profit after taxes.

Initial Markup

The key factor to control the buyer's pricing is "profit" at the first level: "initial" or "cumulative" markon. This is the difference between invoice cost[3] and original marked retail or selling price. It is commonly expressed as a percentage of that original retail. Thus, for an individual item:

> If original retail is \$2.00 and invoice cost is \$1.20, the difference is \$0.80. Initial markon is thus 80¢, or 40 percent of the original retail, \$2.00.[4] The costs and original retail prices for all articles purchased in a department are summed for an entire planning period. To them are added the sum of costs and retails represented by the articles that comprised the inventory at the start of the period. The total of these two sums represents the total merchandise handled during the period (TMH)—and the difference between total cost and total retail is known as the "cumulative markon."

Thus, if the opening inventory was \$207,000 at cost and \$400,000 at retail, and if net purchases during the period were \$117,000 at cost and \$200,000 at retail, the sum of all goods handled would be \$324,000 at cost and \$600,000 at retail. The difference would be a cumulative markon of \$276,000. Dividing by the cumulative retail of \$600,000 would express the markon as 46 percent.[5] Management sets seasonal goals for the markon in each department.

Initial markon and pricing strategy

The initial or cumulative markon has been called the "paymaster," because it is the margin that has to pay for all subsequent costs of operation,[6] including its own reductions—eventually yielding the desired profit.

[3]Invoice cost generally includes inward transportation. There is some difference in the practice of handling "cash discounts"—but the National Retail Merchants Association requires that "invoice cost" should be the cost *before* cash discounts are deducted.

[4]A few retailers still speak of markon as a percentage of invoice cost. In this case, the 80¢ difference would be expressed as 66²/₃ percent markon over the cost of \$1.20. Unless otherwise indicated, all markups used in this text are expressed as percent of retail.

[5]The whole subject of pricing and profit levels is covered in several chapters of the companion volume to this book *Retail Merchandise Management op. cit.* Space permits us only to skeletonize the materials as a background for pricing strategy.

[6]Many items never yield a sales amount equal to their original retail price. Circumstances may cause a lowering of the price through "markdowns." Some items are lost through theft, breakage, or other complete spoilage. Some are sold to employees at special discounts. Sometimes bookkeeping errors cause a shrinkage in the value of the inventory as originally entered in the books of record.

Some retailers follow a rule of thumb in setting their initial markups. They add a fixed ratio or percentage to cost prices. A common rule of this sort, called *keystoning,* sets the retail price as double the cost. This is equivalent to a 50 percent markon at retail and 100 percent at cost. Others increase the cost by one-third, equivalent to a 25 percent markon at retail.

But there is a better way that gives attention to expected expenses and price reductions and also sets a profit goal. These considerations are expressed in the following formula:

$$\text{Planned markon \%} = \frac{\text{Planned expenses} + \text{profit}^{7} + \text{reductions}}{\text{Planned sales} + \text{reductions}}$$

Thus, in a given planning period, if a store anticipated sales of $100,000, expenses of $32,000, reductions of $3000, and aimed at a profit of $5000, the formula would read:

$$\frac{\$32{,}000 + \$5000 + \$3000}{\$100{,}000 + \$3000} = \frac{\$\ 40{,}000}{\$103{,}000} = 38.83 \text{ percent required markon}$$

The same formula may be written in terms of percentages of planned sales:

$$\frac{32\% + 5\% + 3\%}{100\% + 3\%} = \frac{40\%}{103\%} = 38.83 \text{ percent required markon}$$

The required markon for each department of the store cannot be figured in quite this way unless *all* expenses are distributed to departments. But the formula, by including operating expenses for the total store or retail enterprise, does express the store's operating philosophy.[8] And the markon for each department is planned to yield the required total for the firm as a whole.

Not all departments operate on the same markon: Some are higher than the store average, some lower. It is from the "mix" of departments that the average results. This concept prevails within departments: *The mix is paramount.* A buyer may price individual products or categories above or below the planned markon; but the proportion of high and low markons in the mix of goods sold determines the final departmental average.

The required markon determines overall pricing strategy—whether to generally mark goods at prevailing market prices, at "market-plus," or

[7]This is the profit exclusive of cash discounts earned on purchases.

[8]For example, if the store in our formula operated as a "discount" or principally price-competitive retailer, services, presentation, and other non-price-competitive devices would be minimized, and total expenses might appear as $20,000. The formula would then read (if all else remained equal)

$$\frac{\$20{,}000 + \$5000 + \$3000}{\$100{,}000 + \$3000} = \frac{\$\ 28{,}000}{\$103{,}000} = 27.18 \text{ percent required markon}$$

"market-minus." Thus the required markon becomes the frame of reference within which is conducted the pricing of individual items.[9]

Maintained Markup

In the formula for computing required markon, above, there was mention of a $3000 item called "reductions." This means that goods totaling $103,000 in original retail value were consumed in generating $100,000 of recorded sales. It is against this $103,000 that the initial markon of 38.83 percent is applied in order to get the dollar markon of $40,000.

This amount, shrunk by $3000 to $37,000 becomes the "maintained markup." As a percentage, it is quoted in relation to net sales, in this case $100,000; therefore, the maintained markup is expressed as 37 percent.

This computation can also be made in percentage figures by subtracting the "cost" of reductions from initial markon. If original retail is considered as 100 percent, the cost (or complement) would be 100 percent minus the initial markon percentage. In this case, 100% − 38.83% = 61.17%, or 0.6117 as a decimal. Applying 0.6117 to 3 percent would reduce this to 1.83 percent (the cost of reductions). Subtracting this from 38.83 percent would give the maintained markup as 37 percent of sales.

As a pricing gauge, the maintained markup would be more awkward to use than initial markon not only because the former represents one extra step in computation but because it introduces one more element of estimate: the guessed rate of reductions for a specific product or product line. In many cases, the result can be shrewdly estimated but nevertheless remains as one more conjecture in a situation that is imprecise at best. Nevertheless, the maintained markup is a useful device for analyzing results to date.

Gross Margin

Many retailers prefer to keep cash discounts and workroom costs separate from the direct cost of goods sold—a figure that then includes only the invoice cost plus inward transportation. After the maintained markup has been figured, cash discounts are added and workroom costs subtracted to yield the final gross merchandise margin figure. A few retailers, however, do

[9]Some pricing experts feel that it is a mistake to regard the planned markon as an important factor in pricing individual items. They point out that the initial markon concept was conceived originally as an element of the retail method of inventory. It was simply set up as a device to determine cost or market value of an inventory from its current retail price. It is nevertheless the conviction of the authors that an average markon goal, set to meet anticipated overall income and cost considerations, is an important element that should be given due consideration in the pricing decision, as the text explains.

not put cash discounts into the picture until after the net operating profit has been calculated. Some, especially chains, reflect cash discounts in initial markon by subtracting these discounts directly from the billed invoice cost.

Contribution Toward Overhead

This profit level is often referred to as "contribution net" and reflects certain direct, allocable costs as immediate subtractions from departmental gross margin, leaving a contribution toward the overhead expenses and profits of the entire store.

As we go further down the profit levels they become less useful for pricing individual items because of the drawbacks previously expressed: awkward computations and increased conjectures. Nevertheless, the Technical Appendix to this chapter illustrates the unit profitability or "merchandise management accounting" approach to pricing. It is especially useful in research to determine which items and lines to promote and which to suppress.

Net Operating Profit

When all operating expenses have been deducted from gross margin, the result is called "net operating profit," or "net profit from merchandising operations." This is the "profit" figure of $5000 used in our illustration of how a store can estimate its required markon. Net operating profit is the goal figure of most operating executives. "Net other income" (which is added to or subtracted from net operating profit to get "net profit before taxes") is not directly resultant from everyday operation of the mercantile business but rather reflects nontrading or financial earnings and deductions.

PRICING INDIVIDUAL ITEMS

Degree of Pricing Freedom

Retailers who deal only in standard goods, manufactured by many and sold by many competitors, are subject to the laws of pure competition. On the whole, their goods are priced at an established market level where (at least in economic theory) supply and demand are in equilibrium.

If this price is too low to cover the retailer's cost of goods plus operating expenses, the item may be "soft-pedaled" or promotionally depressed to the point of being merely available in "under-the-counter" stock. It may be submerged in a display of substitutable products, and substitutes may be urged on prospective customers. Discontinuance becomes the goal. However, if demand is strong enough, the item may be pushed as a substitute for other promotional devices. If sufficiently identifiable and therefore comparable with the same item in other retail outlets, the "loss" product serves as a "price image" builder.

Loss Leaders

Selling at cost or near-cost for promotional purposes is called "loss-leader" pricing. It is designed to draw traffic by direct appeal and by establishing a reputation for "low" prices. An item priced so low that it cannot make a contribution toward general overhead can be justified only by helping to sell more of those products that *do* make a contribution toward overhead and profit. This illustrates the workings of the "mix" concept. Obviously, if a department is to make its required overall markon, these extremely low markon items must be offset by others priced to yield more than the average markon. This does not imply that the latter are exorbitantly priced. If they are, they will not sell—and their markon will remain as "markup on the shelf," with consequent glutting of stocks and subsequent need for repricing.

Loss-leader pricing has long been under attack as an unfair trade practice, misleading to the public and injurious to that competition whose principal stock in trade happens to be the loss-leader products with no mix in which to make up its losses. Nevertheless, the tactic is deeply ingrained in retailing practice, strengthening and weakening in waves. Supermarket advertising has been a long-time example, followed by general merchandise discount stores. Cigarettes and sugar have been noteworthy products so used. Department stores have sometimes operated whole departments such as books, drugs, toys, and electrical appliances, on a loss-leader basis.

Not every sale below average markon is a loss leader. Later discussion indicates the circumstances under which individual items and lines are priced above or below the required average to optimize total contributions from the items in view of volume opportunities.

Tradition and Differentiation

Much pricing is done by habit, custom, tradition, and implied common competitive consent. In the garment trades, for example, it was long the practice to manufacture toward specific price lines. Dresses sold by their makers at $5.75 and $8.75 were traditionally retailed at $8.95 and $14.95. In the same way, $6.75 goods were retailed at $10.95 and $10.75 goods at $17.95. Manufacturers in most other consumer product lines likewise produced their goods to retail at specific, traditional price lines. This did not prevent the specialty chain stores from selling $5.75 garments for $7.95. But that, too, became a traditional price point among chains. This kind of pricing was one of their principal competitive devices aimed at department stores and other "traditional" retailers. But the latter retaliated by insisting that lines be confined to them or that manufacturers differentiate the products sold to low-price competitors. The result of this maneuvering was that each group of retailers eventually developed its own group of manufacturers.

As described in previous chapters, it is by these devices of exclusiveness, differentiation, innovation, and special services that most retailers compete over the long run. The buyer who has a special version of a product has achieved a quasi monopoly: He or she has gained some freedom of pricing—at least within the limits of required markon for the mix.

Otherwise, the buyer prices at points commonly accepted over the years by competitors of his or her own class. This is not agreement by collusion. Rather, it is an outgrowth of the fact that competitors of the same class have similar expense structures and therefore similar markon requirements and therefore end up pricing by a sort of *implied competitive consent.* It is only when competition of a new class, with a stripped expense structure, seeks entry into the market that new markon standards and new price points appear for the same or similar goods. And the same thing can happen when competitors of the same class enter into a "war" based chiefly on price competition. While these conditions prevail, pricing is shaken loose from its normal patterns. But it tends to return to patterns—even though they be somewhat changed.

Application of Markon Percentage

There are two types of situations that call for the use of the markon percentage as a pricing guide:

1. When figuring the "normal" retail of an article the cost of which is known.
2. When determining the "normal" cost price that can be paid for an article of predetermined retail price.

In both cases, the "costing complement" of the required markon is used. To review, this complement is 100 percent minus the markup percentage.

Thus, if a buyer whose required markon is 38 percent is viewing a slide projector that the vendor prices at $46.50, the calculation will proceed as follows:

$$\frac{\$46.50}{100\% - 38\%} = \frac{\$46.50}{.62} = \$75.00$$

the "normal" retail. However, if stores considered to be in direct competition are selling the projector for $69.50, the buyer is faced with these choices:

1. Searching for a more desirable projector at \$46.50, but different and confined to the store, to sell for \$75.00.
2. Searching for a projector as desirable as those shown by this competitor but that can be sold at \$69.50 or less with a normal markup.
3. Buying the projector and retailing it for \$69.50.

Choice 2 presents the second type of application of initial markon in pricing. Having decided to meet or beat \$69.50, the buyer multiplies this price by the costing complement of 0.62.

$$\$69.50 \times 0.62 = \$43.09$$

To make the normal markon, at retail of \$69.50 or less, the buyer will have to find a projector that costs \$43.09 or less.

Assume, for a moment, that one is found at \$42.50. Normal retail would be \$42.50 ÷ 0.62, or \$68.55. If \$69.50 is a common price line, the buyer might very well retail the projector at that price—taking a markup of slightly over 38.8 percent. To introduce an odd price of \$68.55 might also complicate the merchandising without giving the customer a measurable or observable benefit. Furthermore, if the projector really is as desirable as the one that competition sells for \$69.50, a retail price of \$68.55 might be an invitation to price warring. Such are the considerations of implied competitive consent.

Another illustration of this consent, or "agreement without collusion" could occur if the buyer bought the original project for \$46.50 and marked it at \$69.50. The markon would then be 33.1 percent:

$$\frac{\$69.50 - \$46.50}{69.50} = \frac{\$23.00}{69.50} = 33.1 \text{ percent}$$

Unless competition had a firm "underselling" policy, it would not now reduce its projector to some price below \$69.50. Both stores would sell at that price: probably a customary retail price for stores of that type selling projectors in that cost range.

Rate of Sale a Factor in Pricing

Theoretically, each item should be priced to maximize the dollar profit return. Consider an article costing \$1.98. Priced at \$3.00, it would have a markon of \$1.02, or 34 percent. At a retail of \$3.24, the markon would be 38.9 percent, or \$1.26. But if the \$3.00 price produced a demand of 131 units per week, it would yield 131 × \$1.02, or \$133.62 markup margin per week. If the \$3.24 price reduced the demand to 100 units per week, the markon dollars would be only \$126 (100 × \$1.26). At this point, the advantage would lie with the \$3.00 price, although it shows a much lower markon percentage.

The Technical Appendix at the end of the chapter develops this concept right down to the contribution net level of profit. But, for the moment, the buyer must also keep in mind the budget standards for which he or she is responsible. If the buyer is charged with bringing in a 38 percent markon at a planned total sales volume, he or she will be cautious about following this maximizing policy at a lower markon. It should be attempted only with the consent of management. The procedure may not bring as startling results as surface considerations indicate, and repercussions—especially among competitors—could be complex and far reaching.

Traditional practice can become bad practice. It should be challenged. But the challengers should also give heed to the concept that practices that survive in competently managed businesses are likely to be those that do *tend* toward maximum dollar profits. Improving upon them is a matter for thoughtful analysis rather than unqualified acceptance of new approaches.

Checklist for Pricing Items

Following is a list of considerations that may justify a deviation from a normal or average markon.

I. Cost factors

Unusually high or low relative expenses and costs associated with the item to be priced.

1. *Handling charges:* receiving, marking, stock-keeping, special display and advertising, selling, alterations, packing, delivery, and credit.
2. *Carrying charges:* space occupied, interest on the investment risk of obsolescence and shortage. (The rate of stockturn has a bearing on these costs; the higher the turn, the lower the relative carrying charges.)
3. *The price line level* of the item to be retailed compared with the price of the typical item. Handling and space costs increase as higher-priced merchandise is handled, but they seldom rise in direct proportion to the rise in unit cost. Thus they become a smaller percentage of sales at the higher price levels, making it possible to take a lower markon percentage on much high-priced goods and still adequately cover all costs and expenses incurred on the item.[10]
4. *Degree of danger of obsolescence* as measured by markdown.

[10]A policy of a lower-than-average markup on high-priced goods, offset by a higher-than-average markup on low-priced goods, although sound from a cost point of view, is very difficult to execute in practice. Keen competition on low-priced goods has tended to bring the competitive markup even below the department average, and the freedom from competition on the high-priced goods has led to long markup percentages at these levels. To attempt to reverse the practice is likely to result in pricing low-cost goods at unsalably high prices and in pricing high-cost goods at lower prices than necessary to sell them. The analysis of direct costs relative to the level of cost price, although not necessarily leading to a markon adjustment, does often reveal that goods at retail prices considerably below the departmental average are not bringing in enough dollar margin to cover their direct expenses even though the markon percentage is normal. This may lead to a decision to suppress them, eliminate them, or sell them without certain services that are customarily provided.

II. Contractual limitations

Except for a few states, the right of a vendor to set by contract the minimum retail price at which his or her products may be resold has been abolished. And Congress has rescinded the laws that permitted price maintenance among states that had their own price-maintenance laws. It has been generally concluded that although "fair trade" protects the small merchant, it keeps retail prices above the competitive level. However, it is still possible for a retailer to handle goods on consignment, with the vendor as owner setting the retail price.

III. Demand factors

1. COMPETITORS' PRICES FOR IDENTICAL AND COMPARABLE GOODS Regardless of cost and normal markup considerations, if goods in competition with those of others are to be carried, they must be priced close to the competitive level.

2. DEGREE OF EXCLUSIVENESS OF THE PRODUCT If truly exclusive, it is not subject to direct price competition and may sell readily at a price considerably in excess of what is required to cover costs and a normal contribution to overhead.

3. THE VALUE INHERENT IN THE ITEM, AS SEEN THROUGH THE TYPICAL CUSTOMER'S EYES, NOT THROUGH THOSE OF THE COST ACCOUNTANT Such evaluation may depend partly on the usefulness of the item enhanced by exclusiveness but more on the characteristics making for serviceability, versatility, look-rightness, and fashion rightness. These are the elements that affect the numerator of the impellence quotient—enabling it to remain high even with a higher price in the denominator.

4. ACCEPTANCE BY THE PUBLIC OF CERTAIN PRICE RANGES OR LINES For example, cost considerations may point to a 53¢ price for children's socks, but the price of 49¢ may be well established in the minds of the stores' customers. Conversely, a 46¢ price may cover costs and yield a profit, but the 49¢ price may be quite acceptable and more profitable.

In the pricing of products with an elastic demand curve, demand factors are properly given more weight by the buyer than unusual expense and cost factors.

PRICE LINES

Strategy

One of the most useful devices to simplify the merchandise assortment is to buy to predetermined price lines. Rather than pricing each item solely on a basis of cost, markup, and demand requirements, an advance decision is made to establish specific retail price points at which all regular goods are to be carried.

A cost buying range can then be developed for each price, and anything available in that range automatically is fitted into that price point. Thus handbags may be carried as follows:

Retail Price	*Cost Range*
$ 8.00	$ 4.00– 4.40
10.00	5.00– 5.50
12.00	6.00– 6.60
15.00	7.50– 8.25
18.00	9.00– 9.90
21.00	10.50–11.55

Stores that follow the policy of narrow and deep assortments will use few price lines—some chains, for example, being content with two or three for a given product line. Those who plan wide assortments will have more price lines. The upper and lower limits of a price-line structure must be guided by the economic levels of the customers. Very few stores are large enough to cater to all levels.

Two Costs for One Price Line

The planned markup goal plays a part in making use of the cost range associated with each price line. For a purely arithmetical example, the $10.00 retail price has a cost range of $5.00–5.50, and the buyer may find that these are the only two cost prices within this range at which she can find suitable goods for this price line. If her markup goal is 47 percent, the average cost price she should pay is 53 percent of the retail ($10.00), or $5.30. She can then proceed as follows:

Actual costs	$5.00	5.50
Average cost required	5.30	5.30
Markup *over*	0.30	
Markup *short*		0.20

The over and short markups will just equal one another and provide the desired average if 30 units are bought at $5.50 and 20 units at $5.00 (30 × 20¢ = 20 × 30¢). If the total units required is 50, 30/50 or 60 percent should be bought at $5.50 and 20/50 or 40 percent at $5.00, a ratio of 3 to 2.

Advantages

Following are some of the advantages claimed for a formal price-line structure:

1. It provides the customer with a wide assortment at a single price rather than offering as many different retail prices as there are wholesale prices. Such

simplification speeds up the customer's buying decision, because he or she can concentrate the search at a particular price and not have to weigh the merits of small price differences.

2. It reduces the total inventory required to support a given volume of business. If an assortment of selection factors were carried at each of a great number of prices, stock would mount prohibitively. But some merchants who do not formalize their pricing structure get around this by developing an assortment for each price zone.[11] The theory is that prices within this range are highly substitutable, so that what is not found at one price will be readily accepted at another within the zone.
3. The price-line plan reduces errors in pricing when, through faulty communication, markers of merchandise make a mistake. With preestablished price lines, known to all, these errors are infrequent and easily caught.
4. The cost ranges commonly associated with price lines prevent buyers from deviating widely from the norm and thus becoming guilty of "spotty merchandising," which is the failure to offer uniformly good values to customers.
5. Buyers may use the upper cost limit of a price line as a bargaining tool to persuade the vendor to lower cost so that the item may fit into a popular-price line. The resulting increase in sales may prove beneficial to buyer and seller alike.
6. Price-lining greatly simplifies the assortment planning procedure in that control or budget figures may readily be set for the purchases and inventories at a relatively few price lines. The planning would become hopelessly involved if many price lines had to be planned for. This is particularly true, because accurate predictions cannot be made where the weekly or monthly volume is small. When considerable volume is obtained at relatively few price lines, predictions of future volume become much more accurate.

Limitations of Price Lines

By rigidly predetermining prices, the buyer is denied the opportunity to mark certain pieces somewhat above the established price when he or she senses a good public response at the higher price. Neither can the buyer mark an item a little below if a better sales response is anticipated. This lack of complete flexibility may interfere with the realization of maximum sales and may result in a slightly lower markon percent than might have been achieved.

There is also a great deal of merchandise where sale is not facilitiated by price-lining. In shopping goods, particularly of the apparel variety, customers do respond well to an assortment of styles, colors, and sizes all at one price. But in staples, such as foods, drugs, toiletries, and housewares, it has not been found advantageous to offer an assortment of different brands, styles, and sizes all at the same price.

[11]See next page for a further discussion.

Price Zones

To avoid the rigidity of price lines and to be free to meet all price competition, some buyers set up predetermined price zones rather than price lines. Thus, instead of a $5.00 price line, there may be a retail demand zone of $4.50 to $5.50. For purposes of stock and purchase control the zone may be treated as the planning unit.[12] The buyer uses judgment as to where within the zone to price a particular product.

Although this plan has flexibility to recommend it, it reduces the opportunity to establish a reputation for assortments at a specific popular price, and the slight price differences may confuse the customer in the decision process. On the other hand, where sharp price changes are taking place in the wholesale market, the buyer may have to avoid depending too much on a few established price lines.

Principles of Price-Line Determination

Experience has led to the formulation of certain rules in regard to the setting of price lines. The classical procedure may be summarized as follows:

1. Set the lines at points where past sales reports in the store and information from competitors indicate broad public acceptance. Manufacturers have determined many of these points and produce goods to be sold at suggested prices. For example, if an $8.00 retail shirt for men normally costs $52.75 a dozen, it produces a 45 percent markup. If the store's markup requirement is less than 45 percent, a price line of $7.50 may be established, or even as low as $6.50 in a discount house.
2. Plan three major price lines—a high, a low, and a medium, relative to store's clientele—at which especially complete assortments are carried. At each of these, there should be some merchandise providing outstanding quality at the price even though carried with less than a normal markup. There should also be some merchandise, perhaps bearing a longer markup than average, that has unusual fashion appeal and is distinctive.[13]
3. Plan secondary intermediate price lines: one below the low full-line price, one between the low and the medium full-line prices, one between the medium and the high full-line prices, and one above the high full-line price. Add more only where large volume permits broad and deep assort-

[12]Or specific price points may be used in planning but knowingly treated as flags or markers for a zone.

[13]First developed by E. A. Filene in *The Model Stock Plan* (New York: McGraw-Hill Book Co., 1930) and still influencing price line planning in department and specialty stores.

ments at additional points. Although these have been recommended as ideal assortment plans, many stores have found them too costly in stock requirements. And often the market does not offer goods in sufficient quantity at in-between price points. It may happen that nothing significant and observable can be built into the merchandise for the small price jumps represented. It is often better to subdivide merchandise into a budget department, a regular department, and a deluxe department than to offer many price lines over a wide range, all in the same department. Such a plan facilitates adjusting service costs and markup goals in each department to the requirements of different clientele.

4. Plan the price lines near enough to one another to make it possible for the typical customer who fails to find the article that she wants at one price to feel that she can afford to consider the assortments at the next higher price line. This suggests that the dollar jumps between price lines should increase when moving up the price line scale. For example, the price line above $8.95 might be $10.95, a $2.00 or 22 percent increase, whereas a jump from the $39.50 price in the same department would not be limited to $2.00; it might be $10.00, to $49.50.

5. Establish a pattern of price endings. If the store is a promotional one, price ending in odd cents in the lower ranges and in odd dollars in the higher ones tend to reflect a bargain image. If a store is nonpromotional, *even* prices may have better acceptance than odd ones.

6. Vary the fullness of assortments and the promotional emphasis as the season progresses. Normally, early in the season, the upper full-line price should be heavily stocked, and this price should receive the emphasis in advertising and display. At midseason, the middle full-line should be built up and heavily promoted. Late in the season, the emphasis should be shifted to the lowest full-line price.

REPRICING

The original pricing of merchandise represents only a temporary decision, subject to revision in the light of customer reaction to the initial price. Although markdowns are a corrective tool, they are also a major device for sales promotion and profit building.

There are still those who regard markdowns as an unmitigated evil, causing profit diminution; and it is true that many markdowns can be attributed to the following causes:[14]

[14]One large general merchandise chain classifies markdowns into three groups: (1) Clearance merchandise determined by each selling unit independently, (2) price reductions centrally planned for seasonal promotions, and (3) other company-sanctioned reductions, mostly to meet competition.

1. Buying the wrong item.
2. Buying too much of the right item, often by reordering too late in the season.
3. Buying an inadequate color/size assortment of the right item, leading to the inability of interested customers to find just what they need. The few pieces available fail because of lack of support.
4. Pricing the right goods too high in the first place.
5. Underpricing the goods, so that customers question their quality; they are too cheap. An additional markup, rather than a markdown, might be the best solution, in these infrequent cases.
6. Careless handling and wear and tear that results in shopworn merchandise.

Markdowns as a Promotional Tool

Although careful planning of assortments, judicious item selection, and careful stock handling will minimize markdowns of the kinds classified above, many markdowns are not to be regarded as losses but as promotional tools at the buyer's disposal. They may become a device to increase profits.

For example, a buyer may correctly estimate that he can sell 100 units of a style before Easter, *provided* he carries a complete assortment of colors and sizes right up to Easter. To do this, it may be necessary to stock 125 units, even though 25 pieces will have to be sold at markdown right after Easter. The total dollar margin that can be realized by selling 100 at a full markup and 25 at a substantial price cut may be more than would be achieved in buying 100 and selling only 80 before Easter. Because of depleted sizes and colors, there might still be 20 to mark down after Easter, and a good deal of pre-Easter volume might be sacrificed.

In fashion merchandise, it is commonly a prudent policy to buy considerably more of a good thing than can be sold at original prices. The markdown makes it possible to tap two or three layers of customer demand at different times in the season. To buy just enough to tap only the top layer might greatly curtail the sales and profit opporunity.[15] Even the bargain hunters, buying at cut prices, can be made to contribute to profits as long as the margin finally realized exceeds the direct handling costs associated with the items sold. Even when the margin at final clearance is nonexistent or negative, the item sold may have already made its contribution to profit by supporting the assortment that was earlier required to generate maximum buying by customers.

[15]It should be noted in this connection that lower prices, as the season progresses, need not always be procured by the markdown route. It is frequently possible to place midseason reorders at reduced costs so that the normal markup may be obtained at lower initial prices. Nor does this necessarily mean that the vendor, rather than the buyer, is taking a loss. The former's success with the item early in the season may reduce costs of manufacture, sales, and delivery and justify a lower cost.

Of course, caution must be exercised in executing the strategy outlined above. Deliberately to overprice merchandise early in the season and to mark down most of the stock, after a few pieces have been sold to careless consumer-buyers, establishes a fictitious price comparison and militates against the development of a loyal repeat clientele. Where such a policy exists, careful customers have to be on guard; uniformly good values are not being made available to them.

Taking markdowns to increase profits is not limited to fashion merchandise. This is the explanation of a big cut-price promotion offered for a limited time only. Demand for a food product may be stablized at 100 a week at a unit price of 60¢, a cost of 45¢, a unit margin of 15¢, and a total margin of $15. An occasional special sale at 49¢ may move 400 a week and result in quantity discounts that reduce the cost to 42¢ a unit. The 7¢ margin on 400 pieces yields $28, nearly twice the former margin. Handling expenses may be slightly higher but not enough to absorb the difference between $15 and $28.

The accelerated rate of sale cannot usually be maintained for long. As a concentrated event, it attracts customers who would not continue to respond to the low price. There is always the danger of a decline in sales after the event is over (to below the 100 units in the example). Such a contraction might offset the gains realized during the sale period. In fact, some stores have become disillusioned with "special sales from stock," finding that the extra expenses associated with the promotion and the sharp drop in business afterward have reduced rather than increased the profit opportunity.

Planning the Margin Realizable on a Purchase

It must not be assumed that buyers spend their days in constant arithmetical calculations, but the fact remains that, in the end, *the arithmetic of the situation governs the outcome*—and sometimes buyers do use this as one guide to action. For example, when making a special purchase of 100 sport coats to promote at $49.50, the buyer might roughly calculate as follows.

The coats cost $25 each; therefore the total purchase amounted to $2500. It is hoped to realize a maintained markup (after markdowns and shortages) of 41 percent. Therefore, the total retail sales realized would have to be $4237 ($2500 divided by the maintained markup complement of .59).

If 60 were sold at $49.50, the sales income would be	$2970
If 30 more sold at $35.00, the sales income would be	1050
Total sales income at this point	$4020
Sales income needed	4237
Sales income to be realized from remaining 10 coats	$ 217

Taking out one coat for shortage, the remaining nine could be cleared at about half-price, i.e., $24, yielding $216 and realizing the hoped-for 41 percent maintained markup.

Markdown Principles

In order to use markdowns effectively as a promotional tool and also to reduce losses when clearance is necessary, the following rules have evolved from long experience:

1. Take the markdown while there is still active demand for the goods rather than waiting for the slack season when only a giveaway will attract the bargain hunter. For example, the stock of summer shoes that has been selling well at $12.00 through May may total 200 pairs on June 1. Without a markdown at that time, only 25 pairs may sell in June, leaving 175 to be closed out in July, at $7.00 perhaps. Total realized sales in the two months then would be $1525. But a markdown on June 1 to $8.95 might move 175 pairs in June—a period in which customers are still actively in the market for summer shoes. This would leave only 25 to clear in July at the $7.00 price. Thus the sales realized from the 200 pairs might be $1741, nearly $216 more than with the deferred markdown. Of course, such a happy result is not always assured; the markdown may be taken too early, perhaps when a great deal more of the June 1 stock could have been sold without markdown. The buyer must watch weekly, even daily, sales of each seasonable item and compare with seasonal patterns of previous years. But nevertheless, it is probably better to err in the direction of too early markdowns than too late ones.[16]

At first thought, the seasonal clearance of some high-class stores may seem to be an exception to the rule enunciated. But here the store itself creates an active demand late in the season by holding a store-wide clearance sale and by attracting customers that would not buy in the store at regular prices. Early markdowns in such cases might become an element confusing and upsetting to customers in a store that emphasizes quality, leadership, and exclusiveness.

2. Determine the best time in the season to make appeals to customer groups that bypass offerings at original prices. A time should be sought when

[16]Some stores have an automatic reduction plan for fashion merchandise. An apparel store introduces pantsuits that cost about $20 at $39.95. Any unsold in 10 days are marked down to $32. After another 10 days, any left are reduced to $25. Ten days later a "final" markdown reduces that suit to $19.95. Should this not sell the remainder, a sale to a jobber or to employees will clear out the residue.

the markdown, along with advertising, display, and personal salesmanship will tap a responsive audience. The determination of such times requires a willingness to experiment.

3. The first markdown should be large enough to move the major portion of the goods but not so large as to assure a sellout. Allowance must be made for the accumulation of odd sizes and colors and damaged and soiled merchandise as the goods sell at reduced prices. A total of three markdowns is not too much to dispose of an entire lot. To look for complete clearance at the first markdown would mean taking an unnecessary loss on much of the merchandise sold.

4. The amount of the markdown should be expected to vary with the nature of the goods and whether they are high or low in price. A low-priced staple, such as milk, enjoys a heavy response if reduced in price only 1¢ a quart, but a fashion item usually has to be reduced about 20 percent to appeal to a new level of buyers. There is also a difference by price level: A $4 price may move a $5 slow-seller, but a $400 price is not likely to be equally effective in moving a $500 article. The number of customers at these upper ranges is very small, and price is relatively a minor consideration in their decisions. To tap a new layer of customer demand, the $500 article might have to be offered at half price.

5. There is difference of opinion as to whether to mark goods down to lower regular price lines or to establish special and distinctive markdown prices. A good compromise is to mark down experimental, high-priced goods into full-line regular price lines as soon as they fail to draw a response as originally priced. But clearances from regular full-line price lines should generally be made to special clearance prices. This plan assures the retention of the fresh, immaculate look of the regular assortments and makes it easy for the bargain seekers to find what they are looking for.

BUYER'S RESPONSIBILITY FOR SELLING

A truism of retailing is the expression that "goods well bought are half sold." But nothing about the business has produced more controversy and indecision than "the other half." Pricing falls in both halves. It is unquestionably part of the buying function, but, as we have tried to show, is definitely one of the prime selling tools. In most retail enterprises, it remains the responsibility of the buyer, although some chains do permit individual stores to price correctively for purposes of meeting local competition.

Advertising, display and publicity functions have also been quite uniformly delegated to a special division, although there is still some quarrel about the buyer's rights in making certain decisions. Principally, these involve matters (1) of timing, (2) of actual goods and their selection factors to be promoted, and (3) of emphasis to be placed on individual products and categories. But personal selling has been the subject of greatest contention, especially among the first giants of retailing—the large departmentalized stores.

The greatest obstacle to solution of the problems may be the early attitude that, in these stores, consigned personal selling to a tertiary role. The idea that selling in itself is a teachable, trainable useful skill did not really take hold. The personnel hired for the task was near the bottom of the pay scale and performed accordingly. "Training" was confined almost wholly to teaching systems. And when personal selling became a service as distinguished from self-service, many stores wound up with sales forces that could not deliver the promise.

It is easy to identify the great number of individual functions that make up the business of retailing. It is harder to group them for purposes of managerial organization. Hardest of all is the task of separating the responsibilities for the two major *line* functions, buying and selling, while coordinating their activities in a tightly integrated complex. Intellectually, it is simpler to deal with complete unification or with complete separation (dichotomy) than with ambivalence.

Assigning Responsibility for Both Buying and Selling to One Individual

Large departmentalized stores were especially bewitched by the desire to hold on to the simplicities of their original elementary cellular nature. As long as one person could be held responsible for both the buying and selling of merchandise, that one person could be held accountable for the total profitability of the performance. What more logical, then, than to develop the *merchant-buyer* or *department manager* concept? Except for certain duties directly related to administration of finance and physical facilities, the buyer could then retain the characteristics and responsibilities of the "founding father." People selected for the task were presumed to have the attributes of the idol.

Because all activities were conducted under one roof, the buyer was not confronted by physical impossibilities in the performance of this dual task.[17]

The rationale was completed by assuming that the person responsible for buying the goods would be most knowledgeable about their selling points and most eager to sell whatever had been bought at the optimum margin of profit.

But even in the individual store, difficulties developed as the store grew in size and as the buying duties of the buyer-manager became more complex.

[17]This is true also of the small, *local* chain, and in the beginnings of branch-store expansion. But the far-flung units of large chains made the dual task physically impossible.

Buyers became so engrossed in their procurement responsibility, often involving out-of-town trips, that they were absent from the sales floor much of the time and tended to leave department supervision to subordinates. Also, the emphasis placed by management on the shrewd, critical, and trading qualities of the astute buyer led to developing buyers who were weak as department managers. In spite of the growth of labor unions and of a sense of the rights and privileges of the worker, many old-time buyers continued to depend on autocratic methods to obtain sales results. They clearly lacked the qualities of modern leadership and the art of supervision. They tended to insist that the duty of the salesperson was not to give good service to the customer but to sell whatever the buyers had provided.

Service Superintendent Plan

With the growth of the customer-service concept in large stores, it was felt that salespeople should be in a division of the store dedicated to good personal selling and taken out from under the authority of executives primarily responsible for merchandise selection. This line of thinking led to a setup like that depicted in Figure 15–1. Under a store manager or superintendent, heading a division equal to the merchandise division in importance, was established a service superintendent whose responsibility was to serve the customer. Under him were located floor service superintendents and under them section managers, one for each department or for a number of departments. In large departments, more than one section manager was sometimes required.

Salespeople reported to their section managers and not to their buyers. Although buyers were still expected to provide merchandise information and to decide on stock location, they were expected to issue no orders to sales-

FIGURE 15–1 Service superintendent plan

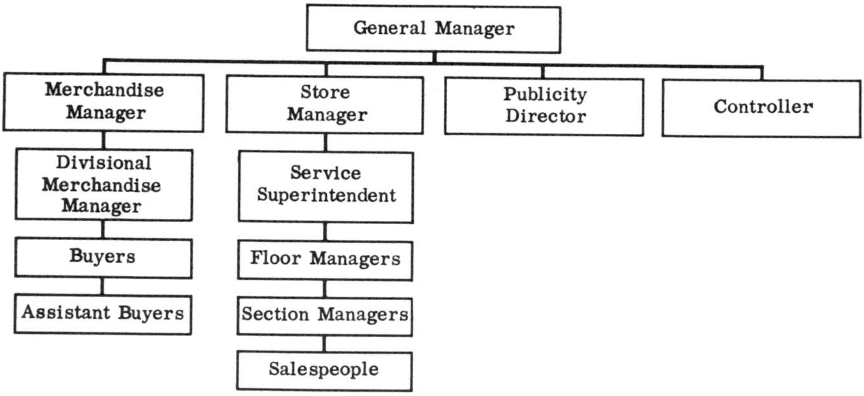

people but rather to consult with the section managers in order to obtain the kind of selling service desired.

This plan achieved only indifferent success, as long as both buyer and section manager were involved in the operation of a single selling unit. Buyers were generally paid far more than section managers and in spite of the organization chart were regarded by salespeople as their real bosses. Section managers were so involved with the carrying out of elaborate sales systems and routines and with the handling of customers' complaints and questions that they had little time to exercise effective leadership. Also, many lacked the qualities of a sales manager. They knew store rules and regulations and how to handle day-by-day routine problems, not how to get effective sales results.

Mazur Plan

These observations led to many experiments in organization. One commonly adopted in the late 1920s and early 1930s was to follow the plan recommended by Paul Mazur[18] to put salespeople back under the buyer but to retain the section manager and service organization. The section manager would handle floor routines and act as a critic of the service that salespeople were rendering customers. By not being personally responsible for this service, it was thought that the section managers would be more objective in observing poor service and that they would report their findings to their superiors—the floor and service superintendents. These would be in a position to bring pressure on the merchandise division to improve its service. Because buyers could not provide the continual floor supervision needed, it was assumed that they would delegate much of their authority to trained assistants.

This plan did not wholly resolve the shortcomings of the old department manager plan. In many instances, neither buyers nor their assistants handled selling supervision as they should. Both were too much involved with merchandising responsibilities.

Divisional Merchant Plan

One solution tried was to leave salespeople in the merchandising division but to have them no longer under the buyer. Under each division merchandise manager there was set up a divisional sales manager, coordinate with the buyers, with the departmental sales managers under him or her. Sales-

[18]Paul Mazur, *Principles of Organization Applied to Modern Retailing* (New York: Harper & Row, Publishers, 1927).

people reported to their departmental sales manager. Buyers were thus to be free of selling supervision, but coordination of the buying and selling activities of each department was assured at the divisional merchandiser level.

The Sales Division Plan

Partly in view of the success of the chains and on logical grounds as well, many organization planners continued to feel that buying and selling should be separated. But they recognized that the service superintendent and section manager approach was inadeqate. It was somewhat passive, lacking the drive to secure volume. It was felt that one of the weaknesses of the typical store organization was that it lacked a division with complete responsibility for *selling*. Under the traditional setup, impersonal selling was under the jurisdiction of publicity, and personal selling was a joint responsibility of service and merchandising divisions. In fact, all divisions, including the controller's, shared in the selling responsibility.

In view of this thinking, some stores set up a major sales division broken down into (1) publicity (advertising, display, and special features), and (2) sales management, with divisional sales managers and departmental sales managers under it. These replaced section managers. Their primary responsibility was to supervise personal selling and to take added responsibility to be sure that their stocks were complete, cooperating closely with the buyers toward this end. In some instances, the entire store was organized in what is called the "two-pyramid plan." Buying and selling divisions comprised the two line organizations in the store. Selling included store operation and maintenance as well as publicity and personal selling. Divisions such as that of the controller and personnel were thought of as staff departments, servicing both buying and selling.

In practice, some practical problems arose. Coordination between the buying and the selling divisions was difficult to achieve. Buyers argued that the two functions were but two sides of a single function. They were not happy to turn over the responsibility for what they had bought to another division over which they could exercise no authority. A special problem had to do with advertising allowances and other special promotional arrangements worked out cooperatively by buyer and manufacturer. Under the new setup, all such plans were subject to the approval of the sales division, and buyers felt they were greatly restricted in entering into arrangements with vendors that involved both buying and selling.

The Branch Plan

The impasse was finally breached for the larger stores by a new development: expansion by means of the branch route rather than increased volume in a single unit. Large independents were being forced to introduce an organization plan similar to that of the chains, where buying and selling are generally separated into twin line functions, joined at the top of the organization chart. Multiple units made it impossible for one man both to buy and sell unless the organization were willing to have a separate buyer-manager in each unit and forgo the advantages of mass buying, thorough market coverage, and sharing of buying costs. The departmental sales managers in the branches are not assistants to the central buyers. They report directly or indirectly to the branch manager and are responsible for the sales results of their departments. As explained in Chapter 2, they do have merchandising responsibilities—keeping up the planned depth of the assortment, reporting local demand, and sometimes reordering merchandise. But they are primarily concerned with selling and the variety of customer contacts that this function entails. With this experience, they are prepared either for a divisonal sales manager position or for that of an assistant or associate central buyer.

Weighing the Pros and Cons of Separating Buying From Selling

In all these attempts to organize and coordinate buying and selling, the nub of the problem is found in the fact that *what should be bought is what will sell most readily; but what has been bought must still be sold, with all due speed and all due profit.* Because no one can perfectly anticipate customer demand, what *has* been bought consists only partly of the goods that *should* have been bought. And what has *not* been bought is the cause of lost sales and customer disappointment. The situation is rife with the elements of conflict.

Separating buying and selling provides an ideal milieu for "buck-passing." If separate executives are charged with the responsibilities one for buying and one for selling, each is likely to blame the other for failures in the functioning of the integrated whole. And who is to prove who is right? In a society of rewards and sanctions, the "rightness" of each executive must be measured, however imperfectly. But it may be even more important to measure *what* is right.[19] Fullest attainment of this objective requires that retailers face up to certain realities.

First is the fact that the functions of buying and selling are dichotomous in the sense that they involve quite separate lines of activity, each of which requires its own body of knowledge and its own set of skills. Can it be said that the requirements of mass distribution depend less on specialized function and specialized skills than do the requirements of mass production? To

[19] The same kind of problem was described in discussing the merchandising function as it is organized in chain stores. These retailers have decided, perforce, that best performance of the detailed function is more important than measuring the accountability of any one functionary.

seek the buyer with the personal attributes and acquired skills for performing both functions often results in finding the person who can perform neither adequately.

Buying and selling exist in a truly symbiotic relationship. Integration and conflict exist side by side. And, as in situations of conflict, one generally does not seek an illusory maximum solution. Conflict must be reconciled in achieving an optimal result: the *best* attainable, if not the *most* possible.

If the buyer is responsible for selling, it is conceivable that the temptations of *short-run interest* will result in forcing on to the consumer the purchases that *have* been made. If someone else is responsible for selling, the tendency will be to sell the goods in "most ready demand," forcing the buyer to alter or reprice the goods in lesser demand in order to equalize their velocity with that of the "easier" sellers. Of the two choices, the latter is oriented more in the direction of the customer, and unavoidable error should be made in this direction—for the *long-run interest* of the business.

It is true that the buyer, who initiates the cycle of activities, is thus put on the defensive *(sic)*, but the choice is of one of "lesser evils." The plan can work only if the selling organization has the status and the personnel to contend on equal terms with the powerful merchandising division. Somewhere, the two must be brought together for coordination. The top of the organization chart is most logical for this purpose. The plan of bringing the buying and personal selling functions together at the "divisional merchant" level is a compromise in this direction.

Minimal Selling Responsibility of the Buyer

Nevertheless, certain selling or promotional duties should remain the prerogatives of the buying organization. These include determination of the selling features of the merchandise to be stressed in promotion and timing of the promotion.

Selling features of the merchandise

No one should know more than the buyer about the selection factors that will appeal most to customers: The buyer is the one who is initially trusted with the responsibility of constant anticipation of customer preferences. It is with these in mind that he or she buys in the first place. It should be the buyer's duty to point out the elements of the "impellence quotient" and which to emphasize in order to reach the value that he or she holds for the quotient.

If price is the dominant element, the buyer should so state and insist that it be emphasized in advertising, display, and personal selling. Similarly, the buyer should stress the style, color, brand, exclusiveness, or any other feature that enhances the numerator of the impellence quotient.

Timing

This is an important element in determining the utility value that customers will place on offered products. Timing may be a matter of featuring something brand new or something in the height of popular acceptance. Either way, the buyer is the specialist who must determine this in his or her purchasing and who should insist on its due emphasis in the promotion of what has been bought.

Stock arrangement

With the trend toward central buying, merchandise presentation to the customer would seem to be a function of sales management rather than of buying. But the buyer is often in the strategic position to develop standardized plans for each of the selling units. Today, with the emphasis on customer self-selection in order to reduce the costs of personal selling, it is imperative that goods be so arranged and displayed that customers can make comparisons and even decisions before they require the attention of salespeople.

Some of the principles that the buyer should incorporate into layout plans are:

1. No merchandise classification should be introduced into stock until it can be presented in adequate depth and breadth.
2. The arrangement must be convenient to customers, with counters and fixtures so arranged that customers can readily locate what they are looking for in both advertised and nonadvertised merchandise.
3. Each fixture, in fact each unit of display and storage space, must be made productive by the proper selection of the items to be housed at each point.
4. The arrangement should dramatize the breadth of the assortment, the fashion rightness of the merchandise, or the high level of taste it incorporates.
5. Color in merchandise and in containers should be utilized for its attraction value. This often requires massing different styles and sizes, all in one color.
6. Goods bought to meet competition should be noticeably presented to the passing customer.
7. National brands of shopping goods, as well as the store's private brands, should be highlighted in the stock arrangement.
8. Fixtures should provide uniformity in design and color and not be introduced simply in consideration of the needs of a single product or brand.

Resolving conflict

The buyer should have the above prerogatives and responsibilities in promotion of his or her own department. But buyers of other departments have also made judgments about the impellence quotients of their merchandise. This produces some conflict in the fight for emphasis in advertising and window displays and lines to be stocked. In this case, decision can best be made by the buyers' superiors. Within a division, responsibility and authority should rest with the divisional merchandise manager. If the contention is between divisions, decision should rest with the general merchandise manager. Authority for this line of reasoning may be found in the very nature of the management concept. The buyer is responsible for anticipating customer demand. But accountability for performance passes straight up the line of authority to the general merchandising manager. Each executive along this line is presumed to have a sound working knowledge about the comparative impellence quotients of the goods bought under his or her jurisdiction.

Technical Appendix
PROFIT MAXIMIZING CONCEPTS OF PRICING

In the chapter just concluded, it was pointed out that at a given moment there is a price point that will maximize profits. This is the point where the sales volume opportunity multiplied by the unit price exceeds merchandise costs and expenses by the largest margin. In economic theory, this is the point where marginal revenue equals marginal cost. The following workouts carry this concept from the sales volume level through several stages of profit computation.

Some warnings from the body of the chapter should, however, be repeated here. As day-to-day pricing guides, these procedures have serious drawbacks.

1. They require awkward computations—even when reduced to charts.
2. They are based on estimates of selling rate that can be seriously imperfect in relation to the fine pricing differences upon which margins are to be calculated.
3. Some of the expense factors in the merchandise management accounting procedure are very hard to allocate to individual products and lines.
4. Much pricing has to be based on competitive situations—which may fluctuate sharply.
5. Optimum pricing is not necessarily a sound goal. Prices less than the optimum increase the customer's utility-price quotient, building good will and growth that may be much more important than immediate profit.

Nevertheless, an understanding of these approaches will serve to sharpen the buyer's pricing judgment. And for those who overcome the hurdle of work involved, there is fruitful material for research into price lining and promotional emphasis. Also, there is much incentive for "trading-up" the price-line structure by paying more attention to utility factors in the numerator of the utility-price or impellence quotient.

Economic Theory of Demand Elasticity

That there is a relationship between price and demand, we all know, but the formula for this relationship in a given set of circumstances is by no means precise. Economic law states that, all else being equal, demand varies in some inverse relationship to price; that is, as the price of a product goes down, demand increases.

Figure 15–2 shows a fairly common kind of demand curve. As price drops 20 percent (from \$5 to \$4), demand increases over 165 percent (from 0.375 units to 1.0). But a 25 percent drop in price (from \$4 to \$3) produces only an 87.5 percent increase in demand (from 1.0 to 1.875 units). Further down the curve, at the \$2 price, it will be noted that a 25 percent drop to \$1.50 produces an increase of somewhat less than 22 percent in demand. These differences *in ratio* between price changes and corresponding demand changes determine the factor known as *elasticity of demand.* At the top of the curve, demand changes much faster than the price change ratio, and demand

FIGURE 15–2 Demand curve showing inverse relationship to price

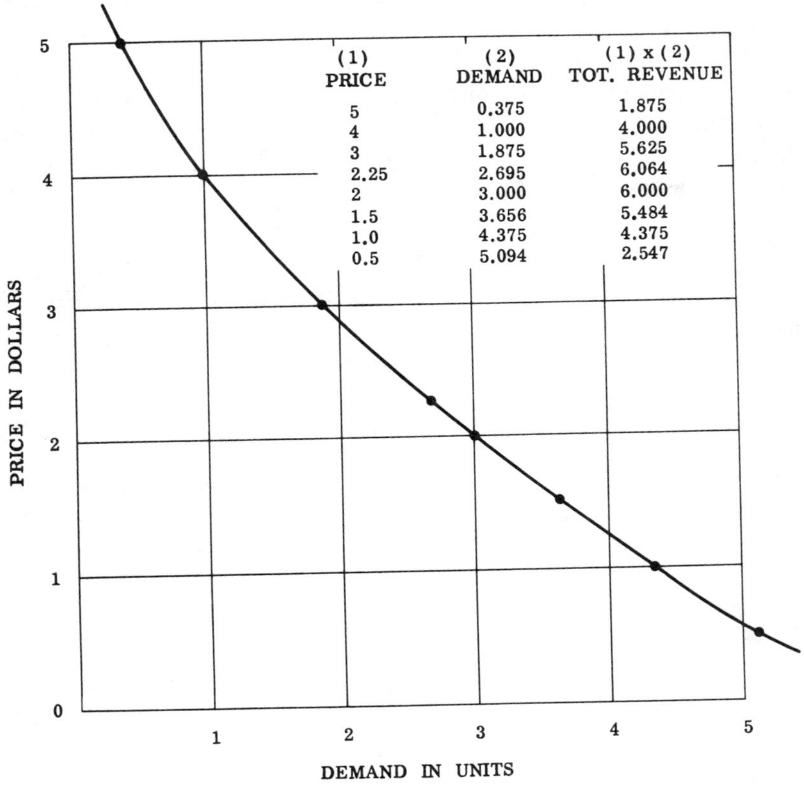

(1) PRICE	(2) DEMAND	(1) x (2) TOT. REVENUE
5	0.375	1.875
4	1.000	4.000
3	1.875	5.625
2.25	2.695	6.064
2	3.000	6.000
1.5	3.656	5.484
1.0	4.375	4.375
0.5	5.094	2.547

is said to be elastic. At the bottom of the curve, demand is said to be inelastic, because its rate of change is smaller than the corresponding rate of change in price.

Around the price of $2.25, the rates are quite even, and demand is said to have "unitary" elasticity. Note that an 11 percent drop in price from $2.25 to $2.00 produces close to an 11 percent increase in demand from 2.695 to 3.0 units.[20]

We said that the curve in Figure 15–2 is a common kind of curve because it illustrates the way elasticity changes at various price levels for most products. When prices are relatively high, a reduction brings sharp increases in sales. But as the price gets lower and lower, equal rates of markdown have a continually smaller effect on the rate of sale. In fact, one reaches the point, somewhere along the road of downward pricing, where the total dollar revenue (price times rate of sale) begins to lessen, though demand is still rising.

The figure shows how sharply increasing demand will produce more total revenue (or dollar sales) even though unit prices are being lowered. This is true at the top of the curve (from $5 to $2.25), where demand is elastic. This increase in total sales reaches its high point at the unitary ratio ($2.25), where sales have climbed to 2.695 units. After this point, the demand response to lowered price becomes more sluggish (less elastic), and total revenue begins to fall off.

Different products under different circumstances have their own elasticities of demand; and although they cannot be put into precise formulas, their general behavior may be understood in the terms we have outlined. The reader may profit by considering demand elasticity for several products under the following conditions:

[20]The coefficient of elasticity (CE) may be expressed as a ratio of the demand rise in percentage (▲ *D%*) over the price drop percentage (▲ *P%*). $CE = \frac{▲ D\%}{▲ P\%}$. When the quotient is around 1, elasticity is said to be unitary; at more than 1, elasticity increases; at less than 1, it decreases. Note these coefficients from Figure 15–2.

Price Change	*% drop (▲ P%)*	*Demand Change*	*% increase (▲ D%)*	$\frac{▲ D\%}{▲ P\%}$
4 to 2	50	1 to 3	200	$\frac{200}{50} = 4$
3 to 1.50	50	1.875 to 3.656	95	$\frac{95}{50} = 1.90$
2 to 1	50	3.0 to 4.375	46	$\frac{46}{50} = .92$
1 to 0.50	50	4.375 to 5.094	16.5	$\frac{16.5}{50} = .33$

1. (a) Meat and fish in warm countries with poor refrigeration facilities. (b) The same commodities in areas where modern freezers are common.
2. Unbranded dresses versus branded dresses or those featuring well-known designer names.
3. Above (in 2) versus branded small electric appliances ("traffic" appliances). (Does this give a clue to the use of highly identifiable goods by price-cutting retailers?)
4. Dresses in season and after the close of a season.
5. Close-outs of odd sizes in shoes versus promotion of items in full size range.

CALCULATING PROFIT FOR THE SALES UNIT

There are many who argue that pricing based on markup is fallacious, that important costs vary considerably from one item to another, and that these variable costs should strongly influence the pricing of each item. At one time this pricing theory, under the title of "Merchandise Management Accounting,"[21] received strong recognition but failed to achieve widespread practicability. This shortcoming may be substantially overcome by the development of computerized analysis, and the theory itself retains importance as an explanation of the workings of the retail merchandise profit machine.

A Model Store

A better understanding of the material may be gained from examining Table 15–1, the operating report of an imaginary store, selling 1 million units at an average price of $6.00 each.

Some expenses (those with *) tend to vary with dollar sales volume. Commissions to salespeople are a perfect example. Interest and insurance

[21]The following are important references on the Merchandise Management Accounting Concept.

GORDON B. CROSS, "A Scientific Approach to Retail Pricing," *Journal of Retailing* (Fall, 1959).

JOSEPH S. FRIEDLANDER, "Perspectives of Merchandise Management Accounting," *New York Retailer* (Dec. 1957).

JOSEPH S. FRIEDLANDER, "Further Perspectives of Merchandise Management Accounting," *New York Retailer* (Feb. 1958).

MALCOLM P. MCNAIR, and ELEANOR G. MAY, "Pricing for Profit," *Harvard Business Review* (May–June, 1957).

Journal of Retailing (Spring, 1958), Special Issue on Merchandise Management Accounting (Vol. 34, #1).

JOHN W. WINGATE, "Is Cost Accounting the Clue to a Better Markup?", *New York Retailer* (April, 1957).

JOHN W. WINGATE, E. O. SCHALLER, and R. BELL, *Problems in Retail Merchandising*, 6th ed. (Englewood Cliffs, N.J.: Prentice-Hall, Inc., 1973), chap. 5.

TABLE 15–1
Analysis of Total Store Operation

	$	% of retail	Operation per average unit of sale
Original retail of goods consumed in selling	6,600,000	100	$6.60
Invoice cost of goods	3,630,000	55	3.63
Initial markon	2,970,000	45	2.97
Actual sales	6,000,000	100	6.00
Reductions (from orig. retail)	600,000	10	0.60
Maintained markup (sales less invoice cost)	2,370,000	39.5	2.37
Merchandise alterations	− 30,000	0.5	0.03
	2,340,000	39.0	2.34
Cash discounts	+ 150,000	2.5	0.15
Gross merchandise margin	2,490,000	41.5	2.49
Dollar variable expenses*	− 420,000	7.0	(Vd) 0.42
	2,070,000	34.5	2.07
Unit variable expenses†	− 630,000	10.5	(Vu) 0.63
Contribution net	1,440,000	24.0	1.44
Fixed expenses‡	−1,140,000	19.0	1.14
Net operating profit	300,000	5.0	0.30

*Expenses that tend to vary with dollar sales volume.

†Expenses that tend to vary with physical volume of goods sold.

‡Fixed expenses, such as fixed rental and depreciation.

charges on inventory also vary with dollar sales. Some costs, such as advertising, tend to vary this way because they are so controlled. In the example, the dollar variables are 7 percent of sales.

Other expenses (†), such as materials handling and sales-check audit, tend to vary with the physical volume of goods sold, with units and transactions. These are usually expressed as a flat cost per unit or transaction on the theory that, within a given category, it costs no more to handle a higher-priced item than one of a lower price. In our store model, the average unit sold is $6. Therefore $6 million in sales are comprised of 1 million units. The total costs for all unit variable expenses are $630,000. Divided by 1 million units, the average flat cost per unit becomes 63¢, as indicated.

Fixed expenses (‡), such as fixed rental charges, bear no fixed percentage relationship to the sales of any one unit. They comprise a total figure that does not vary appreciably with physical or dollar volume of sales (at least over the short run). When rent is based partly on a percentage of sales, that part of rental expense is chargeable as a dollar variable (Vd).

Single expense centers may vary in more than one way. For example, commissions on sales have been stated as a *dollar* variable, but the number of hours of selling time used tends to vary chiefly with the rate of *unit* sales, in which case straight selling expense may be charged as a unit variable (Vu). On the other hand, a certain basic force of salespeople is necessary in even the slowest sales periods. That part of the selling cost should be charged as a fixed expense.

Most expense centers have a fixed core of this sort. Therefore, part of their cost should be chargeable to fixed expense rather than being wholly deployed as unit, transaction, or dollar variables. When handled in such a manner, a larger proportion of retailing expenses are shown as fixed and a smaller proportion as variable with sales activity. In our model, about 52 percent of the total expense is considered fixed, and 48 percent variable.

During the many "slow" periods of the year, expenses are, in essence, even more fixed. These are the times when a great deal more volume could be handled by the basic force already on the premises. That is why items that generate any contribution net at all are valuable at such times: The relatively large overhead can soak up all the contribution dollars it can get. But if too great a proportion of the business is built on these low contributors, a penalty will be exacted in the busy periods, when added facilities are required for relatively small additional amounts of business.

There are expenses that vary with *units* sold and those that vary with *transactions*. In our example, we have used only the unit variable for simplicity, assuming that each transaction represents a single unit of merchandise, and have assigned a 63¢ cost to each unit sold.

Analyses of this kind can become very complicated. Variables do not move in a straight line, and fixed expenses can move in step gradations. But the essence of the Merchandise Management Accounting, or Unit Profitability, approach may be adequately understood from our simplified model, in spite of the fact that it treats the whole store as one homogeneous category.

It indicates, for example, why lower price lines are relatively more expensive to handle than higher price lines and should theoretically be sold at a higher markon percent.

Because few stores have actually succeeded in working on this basis, it is evident that retail management is more concerned with an adequate profit margin from the *mix* rather than from individual items bought and sold.

DISCUSSION QUESTIONS

1. Do buyers generally depend too much on price cutting to increase the *impellence* quotient and not enough on increasing the total utility of the product?
2. The buyer is planning her initial markon goal for the fall season. She

estimates net retail sales of $300,000 for the 6-month period, direct expenses chargeable to her department of $75,000, reduction in prices including shortages of $25,000, and she is expected to make a contribution toward overhead and store operating profit (sometimes called controllable profit) of $30,000.

(a) What initial markon is necessary to meet these objectives?

(b) What other factors should be considered before the actual markon goal is determined?

3. In deciding whether to offer a loss leader, should a buyer consider only the effect on his profits or also the impact on competitors? Explain.
4. Can volume at different price points be forecast with sufficient accuracy to predetermine the optimum pricing point—even roughly?
5. Under what conditions would it be more satisfactory to plan price zones or ranges rather than price lines?
6. A manufacturer reports that he is increasing his price on a popular item from $15 to $17.50 because of increased cost of raw materials and because of higher labor costs. If the retail buyer has 59 of the $15 items, which retail at $28.75, in stock, should she increase the price to about $33.75 or wait until she receives a reorder?
7. If the typical markdown ratio in a merchandise department is 8 percent, and a buyer is operating at 4 percent, what merchandising errors may he be making? (Assume that there has been no manipulation of the figures, such as understating original retail prices to offset unreported markdowns.)
8. Should an automatic markdown plan be generally introduced by retailers?
9. The buyer in a high-class women's specialty store with a national reputation bought an evening dress, size 34, for $100 and retailed it at $210 in August. In early October it was still in stock, and the buyer marked it down to $105. In early November it was further reduced to $85. A month later it was still in stock and was reduced to $58, where it sold promptly to a customer who was delighted with her bargain. Would you revise the timing and amount of the markdowns in order to improve the chances of selling the dress for a higher price than the one realized?
10. A "sleepshop" advertised a clearance sale as follows:
"MAKE US YOUR BEST OFFER. WE RARELY SAY NO! Just make any of our salespeople an offer on any of our Simmons and Sealy mattresses, boxsprings, convertable sofas, hi-risers or famous make headboards, lamps, and recliners. If it is reasonable, they'll accept it! And you'll be sleeping on the best deal in town, because you made it. We're able to do this because everything is one-of-a-kind, floor sample or slightly marred item from our five main stores." Is it wise to invite customers to bargain when a clearance sale is held?

11. The office of aging, New York City, is urging retailers to grant a 10% discount to senior citizens. If you were a retailer who was approached would you comply? Note: discounts to teachers and the clergy, once very common, are now not generally provided. Also, with the great sensitivity to discriminatory practices, the discount might be regarded as discriminatory by younger age groups.
12. Which of the various forms used to organize the buying and the selling functions in retailing are most likely to receive increasing acceptance?
13. Is it of any practical value to determine the point in a demand curve where dollar sales will be at a maximum?
14. How would demand elasticity probably vary in connection with the group of products presented for study on p. 407?
15. Using the data in Table 15–1, discuss the effects of "trading-up" on the net profit. If the average original retail of the average unit of sale could be increased to $7.00 and the total original retail of goods consumed in selling to $7 million, and if all other ratios (except for the unit variable expenses and the fixed expenses that remain the same in dollars) are maintained, reconstruct the table of Total Operations.

SELECTED BIBLIOGRAPHY

BELDEN, DONALD L., *The Role of the Buyer in Mass Merchandising* (New York: Chain Store Publishing Co., 2 Park Avenue, 1971).

BERELSON, BERNARD, and GARY A. STEINER, *Human Behavior* (New York: Burlingame, Harcourt, Brace & World, Inc., 1964).

The Buyer's Manual: A Merchandising Handbook, (New York: National Retail Merchants Association, 1965). (New edition, 1978.)

BUZZELL, ROBERT D., ROBERT E. M. NOURSE, JOHN B. MATTHEWS, JR., and THEODORE LEVITT, *Marketing: A Contemporary Analysis,* 2nd ed. (New York: McGraw-Hill Book Co., 1964).

DALRYMPLE, DOUGLAS J., *Measuring Merchandise Performance in Department Stores* (New York: National Retail Merchants Association, 1964).

DAVIS, KENNETH R., *Marketing Management,* 3rd ed. (New York: The Ronald Press, 1972).

DEAN, DOUGLAS, J. MIHALUSKY, S. OSTRANDER, and L. SCHROEDER, *Executive E.S.P.* (Englewood Cliffs, N.J.: Prentice-Hall, Inc., 1974).

DICKINSON, ROGER A., *Buyer Decision-Making* (Berekeley, Calif.: University of California, 1967).

DUNCAN, DELBERT, and CHARLES F. PHILLIPS, *Retailing Principles and Methods* (Homewood, Ill.: Richard D. Irwin, 1972).

HOWARD, JOHN A., *Marketing Management: Analysis and Planning* (Homewood, Ill.: Richard D. Irwin, 1963).

JOHNSTON, JOHN WALLIS, *The Department Store Buyer,* Studies in Marketing

No. 12. (Austin, Tex.: University of Texas at Austin, 1969).

McNair, Malcolm P., and Mira Berman, *Marketing Through Retailers* (New York: American Management Association, 1967).

Nierenberg, Gerald J., *The Art of Negotiating* (New York: Hawthorne Books, Inc., 1968).

Packard, Sidney, Arthur Winters, and Nathan Axelrod, *Fashion Buying and Merchandising* (New York: Fairchild Publications, 1976).

Rachman, David J., *Retail Strategy and Structure* (Englewood Cliffs, N.J.: Prentice-Hall, Inc., 1969).

Shipp, Ralph D. Jr., *Retail Merchandising: Principles and Applications* (Boston: Houghton Mifflin Co., 1976).

Troxell, Mary D., and Beatrice Judelle, *Fashion Merchandising* (New York: Gregg Div./McGraw-Hill Book Co., 1971).

Wingate, John W., Elmer Schaller, and F. Leonard Miller, *Retail Merchandise Management* (Englewood Cliffs, N.J.: Prentice-Hall, Inc., 1972).

Wingate, John W., Elmer O. Schaller, and Robert Bell, *Problems in Retail Merchandising* (Englewood Cliffs, N.J.: Prentice-Hall, Inc., 1974).

Index